A NEW HISTORY OF EARLY CHRISTIANITY

A NEW HISTORY OF
EARLY
CHRISTIANITY

CHARLES FREEMAN

YALE UNIVERSITY PRESS
NEW HAVEN AND LONDON

For information about this and other Yale University Press publications, please contact:

U.S. Office: sales.press@yale.edu   www.yalebooks.com
Europe Office: sales@yaleup.co.uk   www.yalebooks.co.uk

Set in Minion by IDSUK (DataConnection) Ltd.
Printed in the United States of America by Sheridan Books

Library of Congress Cataloging-in-Publication Data
Freeman, Charles, 1947–
    A new history of early Christianity / Charles Freeman.
       p. cm.
    Includes bibliographical references and index.
    ISBN 978-0-300-12581-8 (ci : alk. paper)
    1. Church history – Primitive and early church, ca. 30-600. I. Title.
    BR162.3.F73 2009
    270.1–dc22   2009012009
A catalogue record for this book is available from the British Library.
10 9 8 7 6 5 4 3 2 1

For Lydia

Contents

Illustrations

1 Selection of papyrus fragments from the Gospel of Matthew, Oxyrhynchus Papyri (P.Oxy LXIV 4401–6). Courtesy of Imaging Papyri Project, University of Oxford and Egypt Exploration Society.

2 Luke 16:9–21, early third-century papyrus (P75).

3 Codices of the Nag Hammadi library. Photo by Jean Doresse/© Institute for Antiquity and Christianity, Claremont, California.

4 Funerary stele of Licinia Amias, late third-century. Museo Nazionale Romano – Terme di Diocleziano, Rome. Photo courtesy of the Ministero per i Beni Culturali Soprintendenza Speciale per i Beni Archeologici di Roma.

5 Fresco of Eucharistic scene from the catacomb of Saint Callistus, late second-century. From Joseph Wilpert, *Die Malereien der Katakomben Roms Freiburg im Breisgau*, 1903. Heidelberg University Library.

6 Christ as a sun god, Vatican, St Peter's Basilica (Necropolis). © 1990. Photo Scala, Florence.

7 The Good Shepherd, Asia Minor, *c.* 270–80. The Cleveland Museum of Art, John L. Severance Fund 1965.241.

8 The Good Shepherd, panel in the mosaic floor at the Basilica of Aquileia. Photo by Mario Zanette.

9 The Good Shepherd, mosaic lunette from above the entrance of the fifth-century Mausoleum of Galla Placidia. Mausoleo di Galla Placidia, Ravenna, Italy/Giraudon/The Bridgeman Art Library.

10 Saints Peter and Paul saying goodbye (two men kissing), ivory buckle, third- or fourth-century. The Art Archive/Antiquarium Castellamare di Stabia Italy/Gianni Dagli Orti.

11 Vault mosaic with the *traditio legis*, Santa Costanza, Rome, *c.* 350. Courtesy of Saskia Ltd., © Dr Ron Wiedenhoeft.

12 Jonah being swallowed by a sea monster, panel in the mosaic floor at the Basilica of Aquileia. Photo by Mario Zanette.

Maps

Preface

IN AD 30, A JEWISH PREACHER FROM GALILEE CALLED JESUS ARRIVED in Jerusalem for the Passover. A crowd of his followers had come with him and the bustle and excitement soon spread to the Jerusalem crowds. Jesus had talked of 'a coming kingdom', a spiritual and political revolution that would renew Israel. The authorities, the Jewish priesthood and their Roman over-lords, felt threatened by the disturbance. They arrested and crucified Jesus, the best way of publicly terrorising his followers. It appeared they had snuffed out the movement.

Somehow, in the bleak hours and days that followed, a core of Jesus' followers began to conceive of him as something more than an ordinary mortal. There was talk that his tomb had been found empty and that favoured disciples had seen him risen from the dead. Then, after forty days at most, the appearances ceased, although some believed he would come again.

As the months and years passed and there was no second coming, his disciples began to speculate on whom Jesus might have been. They had a mass of Jewish titles to draw on – 'Son of God', 'Messiah', 'Son of Man', 'Lord', 'Prophet'. For a Jew none of these implied divinity. 'Son of God' meant only one specially favoured by God; messiahship was associated with the (inevitably violent) liberation of Israel from foreign domination by one of 'the royal house of David'. From the earliest days Christians debated and argued among themselves as to how one could find a coherent understanding of Jesus. In his anguished First Letter to the Corinthians, one of the oldest Christian texts to survive, the apostle Paul complained that his readers had divided into followers of himself, of the apostle Peter, of an intellectual, Apollos, and of Jesus now seen as *Christos*, 'the anointed one' (1 Corinthians 1:12–14).

This picture of Christians in debate may seem startling to some readers. All too often Christian doctrine is presented as fixed and unchallengeable, but even the slightest contact with the history of Christianity shows that this was never so. This book takes it for granted that there were competing traditions within the emerging church and explores the difficulty in ever finding any one 'true' Christianity. In fact, it was only when the Roman emperors of the fourth century used the enormous coercive power and patronage at their command to insist on a uniform set of beliefs that one could talk in such terms.

So while, traditionally, the history of the church has been written as if the doctrines chosen by the emperors, in particular the Nicene formulation of the Trinity, were the only ones possible, I have not made this assumption here. I prefer, for instance, to highlight the impossibility of achieving any form of consensus on the nature of the risen Christ and his relationship to God. I hope this makes for an altogether more absorbing narrative and one that corresponds to the debates as they are recorded.

At the same time, assertions by biblical scholars that there are no other historical explanations of particular events than supernatural ones need to be challenged. The sources which describe the physical resurrection of Jesus are, for instance, so late, fragmentary and contradictory that the question of whether it happened must be left open. 'Surely, no one would seriously argue that the early Christians did not believe that Christ had been raised', writes Alan Segal, author of an excellent study of 'the Afterlife'. 'But just as surely few if any modern historians would argue that any evidence could move us from this historical fact to the supposition that Jesus was actually and physically raised from the dead and that he appeared in his transformed fleshly body.'[1]

This raises a vital point. Historians and theologians are both committed to finding 'truth', yet both work with totally inadequate evidence. For the historian the past recedes quickly and most events are never recorded. Most historical solutions exist as hypotheses, vulnerable to the discovery of new evidence or to be left for ever unproved. The theologian has the challenge of establishing knowledge of a different sort: what might exist for humans after death, whether a creator designed the world and whether Jesus Christ had a human or divine nature, or some form of combination of them. On the whole, theologians appear to find it easier to come to certain conclusions than historians do. It is rare, for instance, to find a work of theology that proposes a range of hypotheses about the supernatural and leaves it open for the reader to decide.

This was certainly not the case in the early church. One of the fascinations of writing about these centuries is to see how highly educated minds grappled with the problems of understanding the supernatural. The range of debate is far greater than anything one finds in discussions on religion today. Was Jesus' God the same as the Creator God of the Old Testament? Can Paul be read so as to deny the physical resurrection of the body? Did the act of creation involve bringing order to what already existed or was it a totally new

beginning? Can one ever come up with a satisfactory definition of the relationship with the Son and the Father and the human and divine (if any)
aspects of Jesus? This was the grist of early Christian theology.

So a historian of early Christianity must tackle diversity, and I think it helps
if one does not feel that there is a correct answer to be found. Intellectual, not
to say spiritual, life lost a great deal when theological debate was suppressed
in the fourth and fifth centuries. I have tried to preserve the breadth of early
Christian thought without making judgement on it.

The world was transformed by the coming of Christianity. The belief that the
Son of God had come to earth, had redeemed the human race from its apparent
sinfulness, and would be represented by the continuing presence of the Holy
Spirit was revolutionary. It was also, of course, very threatening. The rejection of
the ancient gods and the cultures that had sustained them was a powerful challenge to the ethos of Greco-Roman society. In response to opposition, Christians
had to define for themselves what their faith meant for them while they were
living on earth and how their beliefs could be given continuity and coherence.

The 'triumph' of Christianity in the fourth century, when Constantine
offered both toleration and patronage, was seen by its historian Eusebius as
the inevitable and expected outcome of God's plan. Christianity had now
become politically, socially and, not least, economically the dominant culture
of the empire and its successors. Resources were poured into buildings,
bishops became powerful figures in their own right. The state took responsibility for defining orthodoxy. The afterlife, and whether one would find bliss
or misery in it, began to pervade the Christian imagination in a way that
pagans found incomprehensible. No one can begin to understand the history
of the western world without grasping this transformation in consciousness.

There has long been a need for a 'new' history of Christianity. In a review of
yet another set of essays in a handbook to early Christian studies, one biblical
scholar recently bemoaned the fact that there had been no such introduction
since Henry Chadwick's excellent *The Early Church*, first published in the
1960s. Yet I would never have taken on this book if I had not been challenged
to do so by Heather McCallum, my editor at Yale. It was her vision of the book
as a critical but respectful history, and her continued support during the two
years of writing it, that have been fundamental to its completion.

It will be clear from the text and the Further Reading that there are several
scholars whose work I have found indispensable. I suppose what unites them
is that they accept the difficulty, even the impossibility, of establishing the
truth about the early church without denying the importance of understanding this vital moment in religious history. While I could usually come to
a synthesis of scholarly views which seemed to fit with the evidence, it was

vitally important to have my text read by Yale's anonymous readers. I am most grateful for their insights and encouraging comments. The final work is, of course, my own.

I am always embarrassed by my returned copy-edited texts and I realise how many errors of punctuation and grammar were left unnoticed until spotted by a sharp-eyed copy editor. Elizabeth Bourgoin edited in-house, ably assisted by Charlotte Chapman as copy editor and Lucy Isenberg as proof-reader. Rachael Lonsdale carried out the picture research and Chartwell Illustrators the maps. I am most grateful to them all for transforming my text into the high quality result that is the hallmark of Yale University Press.

Many of my Christian friends are probably not aware of how much I have listened to their ideas and valued their insights. I often felt that there are as many different Christianities as individuals I talked to. Although the parameters of debate may be narrower than they were eighteen hundred years ago, they remain broad and I am grateful for the opportunities I have had to reach a deeper understanding of the ways in which different cultures, traditions and personal experiences relate to the continuing history of Christianity.

Above all, I have rejoiced in the support of Lydia who has made a life with me forty years after we first met. As this book was evolving so was our home, a sixteenth-century farmhouse, a converted studio barn and twelve stables, in the depths of rural Suffolk. Restive horses kick on the back of my bookshelves as I write. Lydia would certainly not agree with everything written here but I would never have reached the end without the love and stability she has given me. I am truly grateful.

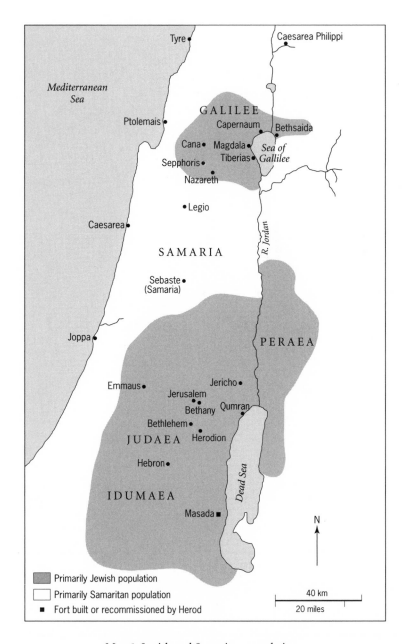

Map 1 Jewish and Samaritan populations.

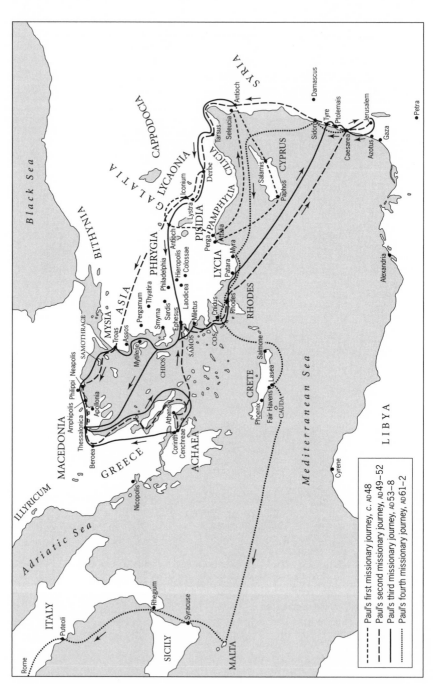

Map 2 Paul's missionary journeys.

Black Sea

ILLYRICUM

Adriatic Sea

ITALY
Rome
Puteoli
Rhegium
SICILY
Syracuse
MALTA

Mediterranean Sea

Nicopolis

MACEDONIA
Amphipolis Philippi Neapolis
Thessalonica
Apollonia
Beroea
GREECE
Athens
Corinth Cenchreae
ACHAEA

SAMOTHRACE
Troas Assos
Mytilene
CHIOS
SAMOS
COS

BITHYNIA

MYSIA
Pergamum
Thyatira
Smyrna
Sardis
Ephesus
Miletus
Cnidus
RHODES
Rhodes

ASIA
PHRYGIA
Philadelphia
Hierapolis
Laodicea Colossae

GALATIA
LYCAONIA
Iconium
Lystra
Derbe

CAPPODOCIA

PISIDIA
Antioch

PAMPHYLIA
Perga Attalia
LYCIA
Patara Myra

CILICIA
Tarsus
Seleucia
Antioch

SYRIA
Damascus

Sidon
Tyre
Ptolemais
Caesarea
Azotus
Gaza
Jerusalem

Petra

CYPRUS
Salamis
Paphos

CRETE
Salmone
Phoenix
Fair Havens Lasea
CAUDA

LIBYA
Cyrene
Alexandria

- - - - - - Paul's first missionary journey, c. AD 48
- - - - - - Paul's second missionary journey, AD 49–52
—————— Paul's third missionary journey, AD 53–8
· · · · · · · · Paul's fourth missionary journey, AD 61–2

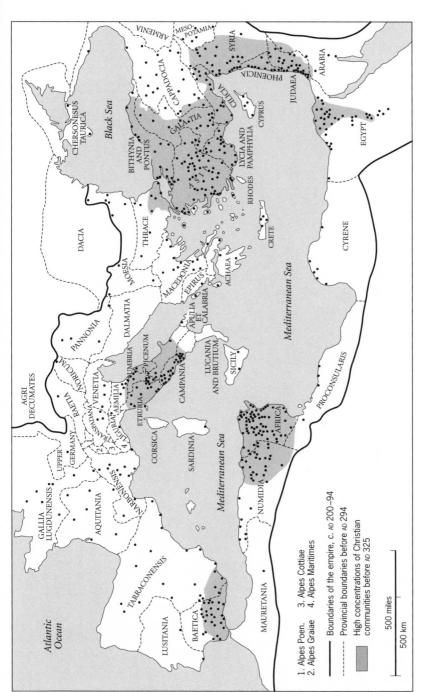

Map 3 Boundaries of the Roman empire.

1. Alpes Poen.
2. Alpes Graiae
3. Alpes Cottiae
4. Alpes Maritimes

Boundaries of the empire, c. AD 200–94

Provincial boundaries before AD 294

High concentrations of Christian
communities before AD 325

500 miles

500 km

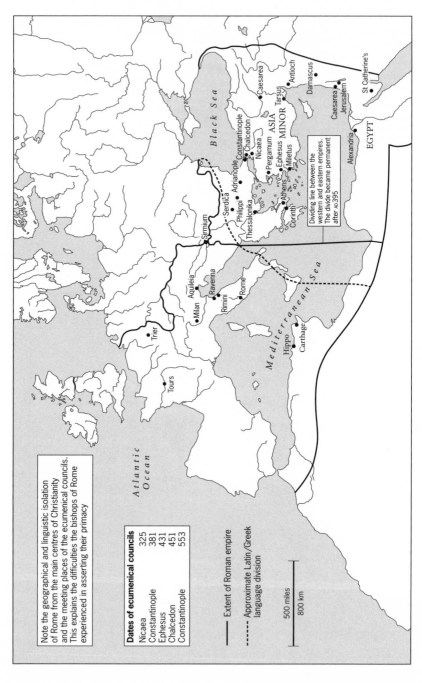

Note the geographical and linguistic isolation
of Rome from the main centres of Christianity
and the meeting places of the ecumenical councils.
This explains the difficulties the bishops of Rome
experienced in asserting their primacy

Dates of ecumenical councils

Nicaea	325
Constantinople	381
Ephesus	431
Chalcedon	451
Constantinople	553

—— Extent of Roman empire

------ Approximate Latin/Greek
language division

500 miles

800 km

Dividing line between the
western and eastern empires.
The divide became permanent
after AD 395

*Atlantic
Ocean*

Mediterranean Sea

Black Sea

Trier

Tours

Milan
Aquileia
Ravenna
Rimini
Rome

Sirmium
Serdica
Philippi
Thessalonika

Hippo
Carthage

Adrianople
Constantinople
Chalcedon
Nicaea
Pergamum ASIA
Ephesus MINOR
Miletus
Athens
Corinth

Caesarea
Tarsus
Antioch
Damascus

St Catherine's

Caesarea
Jerusalem

Alexandria

EGYPT

Map 4 Rome and the main centres of Christianity.

PART ONE: BEGINNINGS

CHAPTER ONE

A Trial

THE PRAEFECTUS, THE ROMAN GOVERNOR OF THE PROVINCE OF
Judaea, can never have looked forward to travelling up to Jerusalem from
his headquarters at Caesarea on the coast. It was his task to supervise the
keeping of good order at the feast of the Passover each year. Some hundreds of
thousands of Jews from throughout the Mediterranean would have gathered for
the feast and there was always the chance of disorder. Pontius Pilate, appointed
the governor of the province in AD 26, certainly had no reason to expect a warm
welcome. On his very first visit to Jerusalem he had entered the city with standards flaunting the image of the emperor Tiberius. This was taken as a provocative display of graven images and ensured his period of office started in tension.
Things got no better. Pilate drew on Temple treasure for funds with which to
build an aqueduct and then caused further offence by placing standards with
the emperor's name on them in his palace. The Jewish philosopher Philo wrote
in a letter of complaint to Tiberius of Pilate's 'briberies, insults, robberies,
outrages, wanton injuries and executions without trial'. He was finally to be
dismissed by the emperor in AD 36 after he had attacked a group of Samaritans
whose gathering he considered seditious.[1]

Whatever Pilate's personal inadequacies, the governorship of Judaea was
never a prestigious posting within the hierarchy of the Roman Empire. The
neighbouring provinces of Egypt and Syria were much wealthier (Egypt)
or more strategically vulnerable (Syria). The latter was always granted to
officials of senatorial rank with a history of successful military command.
The province, which bordered on the expansionist empire of the Parthians,
had recently been allocated a fourth legion, making a total of well over twenty
thousand highly trained and seasoned men always in place. The praefectus –
literally one who is placed in charge – of Judaea came from the equestrian
class, the class below the senatorial, and was not granted even one legion.
The governor's own complement of some four thousand men were auxiliary troops drawn from the local population. Faced with serious unrest, a

praefectus would have to plead with the governor of neighbouring Syria for help.

Judaea had first come under Roman control in 63 BC. A brilliant and energetic Roman general, Pompey, had swept across the eastern Mediterranean, clearing up the pirates who were threatening Roman trade, next overrunning Syria and arriving in Jerusalem, then the capital of the independent Hasmonaean kingdom. Here he outraged the Jews by entering the Holy of Holies in the Temple, still in his battledress. The age of Jewish independence was over. In 40 BC Pompey's conquest was threatened by a Parthian invasion that also reached Jerusalem before it was repulsed. A strong man was needed to represent and protect Rome's interests in the region and the Romans chose Herod, an Idumaean, from south of Judaea, whose abilities had been spotted in the aftermath of the Parthian invasion. As an outsider to the traditional priestly families of Jerusalem, Herod would always be resented by the Jews. He was insensitive to the traditions of Jewish community life, a bully, vindictive even to his own family, but the Romans trusted him. The emperor Augustus confirmed his status as client king in 31 BC and his territories were extended. Despite all his cruelties and intrigues, Herod opened up his kingdom to the bustling commercial and cultural world of the eastern Mediterranean.

It was only on Herod's death in 4 BC that resentments over his cruelty exploded. Brigands roamed the countryside and order began to break down. The Romans were forced to intervene and ruthlessly suppressed the unrest before splitting the kingdom among Herod's three sons, none of whom was given the full status of king that their father had enjoyed. This proved a much less effective arrangement and when complaints reached Augustus about the brutality of one son, Archelaus, the ruler of central Judaea, the emperor decided to impose direct Roman rule on Judaea, which was now declared a province of the empire. Quirinius, the governor of Syria, was sent south in AD 6 to carry out a census for tax purposes (previously taxation had gone direct to Herod) and the first *praefectus* was appointed. It was a messy business. One Judas of Gamala led resistance to the Roman intrusion and his followers were crucified along the roads of the new province.

Herod's legacy still pervaded Judaea. When a governor arrived at his posting he disembarked at the grand harbour that Herod had built at Caesarea and made his headquarters in Herod's palace there. When he made his way up from the coast to Jerusalem, some seventy miles inland, he would have seen the vast Temple built by Herod, for, as Herod himself admitted, the glorification of his own memory, towering over the city. The governor would be stationed in a building, the *praetorium*, which had originally been Herod's palace, some ten minutes' walk from the Temple complex. His troops would have been garrisoned alongside the precinct of the Temple in another Herodian building, the Antonia, so-called because it had been the Roman general Mark Antony who had given Herod his first promotion. However, despite the grandeur of his surroundings, the governor must have felt very isolated. There is no record that Pilate had the group of friends and officials the senatorial governors kept around them and there were virtually no local Romans to keep him company.

Pilate's job was to represent the imperial power of the emperor Tiberius, to keep good order and to ensure that taxation reached Rome. It was not to Romanise the population. The essence of Roman rule lay in delegation and, if a province remained calm, was seldom obtrusive. Among the governor of Judaea's responsibilities was the appointment of the high priest from among the Jewish elders. The high priest would run the affairs of the province on a daily basis and this was why the job was difficult. His traditional role of upholding the rituals and customs of his people did not fit easily with his new role of meeting the needs of his imperial overlords. In practice high priests came and went as they fell out with the governors. Pilate's predecessor, Valerius Gratus, had soon got rid of the high priest Annas on his arrival in AD 15 and then seems to have worked through another three before he appointed Annas' son-in-law, Caiaphas, in AD 18. Against all precedent, this proved to be an extraordinarily successful appointment; Caiaphas saw out Gratus and then lasted the whole of Pilate's term of office, eighteen years in total.

Caiaphas would never have retained Jewish support, especially that of his fellow priests and elders, if he had been obsequious to the Romans. Perhaps the relationship lasted largely because there was so little contact between the governor and the high priest. The skilful management of the few days that the governor was in Jerusalem was crucial. With his known insensitivity towards the Jews, there must have been some apprehension every time Pilate arrived in case he caused new outrages. He would have to be appeased, handled on a daily basis, convinced that Caiaphas was keeping good order and encouraged to return to Caesarea as soon as the crowds had dispersed. For his part Pilate must have been happy to leave Jerusalem for the luxury and calm of his coastal palace.

The high priest presided over the Sanhedrin, the council of elders. It was a powerful body with the right to make laws, judge them in its role as criminal court and oversee the administration of Judaea. It was the sole interpreter of Mosaic law. Traditionally the Sanhedrin, or its leading members, had been able to pronounce a death penalty, stoning for blasphemy, idolatry or murder. Under Roman rule, however, executions had become the prerogative of the governor. The Romans had their own method of execution – crucifixion, the humiliating exposure of a criminal who had been nailed to a cross and left to die in agony. Crucifixions were common when the Romans were dealing with disorder; some two thousand alone were carried out in Judaea in the unrest after the death of Herod.

The Passover of the year AD 30 was probably little different from any other but Pilate appears to have been confused by a prisoner that the Sanhedrin, or at least a group of elders led by the high priest, insisted he deal with. This was a Galilean by the name of Jesus. Galilee was not part of Pilate's jurisdiction – when Archelaus had been deposed in AD 6, it had remained under his brother Herod Antipas who still ruled there – but, by crossing into Judaea and reaching Jerusalem, Jesus was entering territory directly ruled by Rome, through the medium, of course, of the high priest and the Sanhedrin. He had arrived with a band of fellow Galileans, some of them women, and seemed to have received the acclamations of the local crowds when he entered the city. There were stories that he had been teaching in the Temple and had caused a disturbance there, apparently driving out the dealers in animals for sacrifice and overthrowing the tables of the moneychangers.

John's gospel is probably right in placing the trial and crucifixion of Jesus the day before the Passover when the priests would have been free to initiate charges.[2] As soon as the feast began they would have been preoccupied with their duties in the Temple and barred from criminal jurisdiction. In John's account Jesus is arrested in the garden by the Temple police, with Pilate's auxiliary troops in support, and brought in the first instance before Annas, Caiaphas' father-in-law, who seems to have assumed the role of elder statesman after his dismissal as high priest. Jesus is passed on by Annas to Caiaphas himself who in turn sends him on to Pilate. By this time a crowd of Jews has gathered (or been gathered) outside the *praetorium*. The charge is that Jesus claimed to be 'king of the Jews'. Pilate is not convinced and offers to release Jesus according to a custom (which is not recorded anywhere outside the gospels) that a prisoner could be freed at the Passover. The crowd shout instead for the release of Barabbas, a ringleader of unrest in the city, and cry out for Jesus' crucifixion. There is even an attempt to manipulate the situation when the crowd threatens to report Pilate to the emperor if he does not comply (a clear sign of how limited in practice Roman power could be). Pilate capitulates and orders the crucifixion. The sentence is carried out before Passover formally begins at sunset. Two other condemned men, probably bandits, are executed at the same time.

Why were the Jews so insistent on calling for crucifixion, a punishment only the governor could order? There is a plausible explanation rooted in the political scheming of Caiaphas. Caiaphas had been shaken by the arrival in Jerusalem of Jesus and his followers, some of whom acclaimed him as a messiah. The accolade 'messiah' had many connotations, not least an association with the royal lineage of David and the shattering of 'the godless nations' through war. A new messiah would offer a challenge to the status of the priesthood and to the traditional structure of society, possibly through the use of violence.[3] Jesus needed to be dealt with in some public way to show that any claimed messiahship was a sham. The Jews themselves had no right to order an execution. If the Romans crucified him this would serve Caiaphas' purpose: Jesus would have been shown, in the most public and humiliating way possible, not to have been able to establish his own kingdom or threaten priestly authority.

The priests needed to act fast. If Jesus was not dealt with now, Pilate would have returned to Caesarea and the possibility of executing Jesus would have been lost until his next visit. To ensure a crucifixion, the interest of Pilate in the case had to be aroused. So a *political* charge, that Jesus claimed to be 'king of the Jews', and was thus seditious, was concocted. When Pilate still hesitated, every method was used to manipulate the isolated governor into acquiescence and Caiaphas and his supporters eventually succeeded.[4] Jesus was crucified.

The story, of course, does not end there. While Caiaphas might still have had a role to play in defusing any unrest that followed the crucifixion, the memories of Jesus among his followers, the reports that soon circulated that he had risen after three days in his tomb, the belief that he was truly a messiah soon to return to earth in glory, allowed a movement to coalesce in his memory. It grew from within Judaism.

CHAPTER TWO

The Seedbed

JUDAISM IN THE FIRST CENTURY AD

JESUS WAS A JEW. FOR MUCH OF CHRISTIAN HISTORY THIS HAS BEEN denied or avoided. The apostle Paul began the tradition through his own ambivalence about the relationship between Jesus and traditional Judaism. In John's gospel, written some sixty years after the crucifixion by a man steeped in Greek culture, Jesus is portrayed as already distancing himself from his Jewish heritage, above all in Chapter Eight of the gospel where a confrontation leaves a group of Jews ready to stone him. Some sixty years further on (*c.*155), Melito, the bishop of Sardis, presented what had become a conventional narrative: 'O lawless Israel, what is this unprecedented crime you committed, thrusting your Lord among unprecedented sufferings ... For him whom the Gentiles worshipped and uncircumcised men admired and foreigners glorified, over whom even Pilate washed his hands, you killed him at the great feast [i.e. the Passover].' Here Melito creates a Gentile following for Jesus for which there is no historical record, and emphasises the primacy of the Jews' role in the crucifixion. In his celebrated *Life of Jesus*, Ernest Renan (1823–1892) went further still. Renan stated that 'fundamentally there was nothing Jewish about Jesus', and went on, in fact, to describe Jesus as 'a destroyer of Judaism'.[1]

There has never been a consensus over the nature of Jesus. Even today, with much more evidence of the social, economic and religious background available, his biographers have described him variously as a violent revolutionary ready to take up the sword against Roman oppression, an apocalyptic prophet ushering in God's reign on earth, a proto-Marxist social reformer urging an economic and social revolution, a *Hasid*, or Jewish holy man, of whom there were many other examples, an early feminist who elevated women to a higher status than traditional Jewish society allowed, and even a Cynic philosopher who preached the renunciation of all worldly goods. However, despite those who argue that Jesus was a representative of Greek culture and philosophy, there is now general agreement that his Jewishness was central to his identity. At the same time there has been a growing awareness of the vibrant complexity of Judaism in the first century AD.[2]

Like every Jew, Jesus would have been at home with an inheritance that stretched back centuries to the patriarch Abraham, and which gave crucial roles to Moses, leader of the Exodus from Egypt to the 'promised land', and the supreme law giver, King David, the creator of the Jewish nation state and 'the sweet psalmist of Israel'. It had not been an easy history. According to the scriptures, the first kingdom of Israel had been founded by Saul, the father of David, and established its capital at Jerusalem where David's son Solomon constructed the first Temple. All twelve tribes of Israel, each a descendant of one of the twelve children of Jacob, participated in the new state but when, in the tenth century, Israel split into two kingdoms, Judah, which retained its capital at Jerusalem, and Israel to the north, they were divided between the two. Israel became the home of ten of the tribes, Judah of the remaining two. A thousand years after the tribes had been divided, memories of their unity in one state endured. It is probable that the choosing of twelve disciples by Jesus echoes an ancient Jewish yearning for restoration.

The two states existed side by side until the destruction of Israel by the Assyrians in 722 BC. The kingdom of Judah survived but was later destroyed by the Babylonians in 587 BC. This was a traumatic moment for the Jews. Solomon's Temple was sacked and Jewish leaders expelled. Many went into exile in Babylon. 'By the rivers of Babylon, there we sat down, yea, we wept when we remembered Zion . . . How shall we sing the Lord's song in a strange land?' as the haunting Psalm 137 puts it. Yet the upheaval led to a period of great intellectual creativity. The Torah, or Law, was consolidated in the scriptures. It was a people renewed in confidence who set about rebuilding the Temple in Jerusalem when the conquest of Babylon by the Persian King of Kings, Cyrus, allowed them to return to Judaea in the 530s. The prophet Isaiah tells of the return from exile and how the suffering of 'the servant of the Lord' led to the victory of the Jews.

Now began the Second Temple period which was to last six hundred years until the second and complete destruction of the Temple by the Romans in AD 70. The Persians were succeeded by the Greeks after Alexander the Great destroyed the Persian empire in the 330s BC. Alexander's successors, the Seleucid dynasty, tried to impose Greek culture on the Jews but a successful revolt by the Maccabees resulted in the independence of Judaea in 141, an independence which was preserved until the coming of the Romans under Pompey in 63 BC. Etched into Jewish history was the experience of occupation, whether by Greeks with their cultural imperialism or by Romans with their insensitivity to Jewish custom. A sense of defilement by the outsider was pervasive, intensified with each new Roman intrusion. The Maccabees were remembered as martyrs and later provided an inspiration for Christians facing, in their turn, the might of the Roman Empire.

The Jews enjoyed a unique covenant with their God that had been revealed at crucial moments of Jewish history. The relationship was always fraught – if the nation or an individual offended God, his support would be lost and only through repentance would it be regained. Memories of exile or occupation reinforced the fear that the covenant might be permanently broken. Yet so long as there was repentance, God would always renew his trust and bring hope to his people. The chosen people would, in the final order of things, be saved. The idea of a covenant with God was one of the many features of Judaism that was to be absorbed and refashioned by followers of Jesus Christ.

This benevolence of God required a response of gratitude and obedience. Judaism emphasised the importance of the continuous worship of God. 'You shall love the Lord your God with all your heart and with all your soul and with all your mind and with all your strength' (Deuteronomy 5:6–7). This worship was focused on the Temple in Jerusalem, which was the most important symbol of the nation, and God's relationship with it. After Herod's rebuilding of the Temple, a project that went on well into the first century AD, it was a huge and magnificent building, giving Jerusalem the status of one of the great cities of the eastern Mediterranean.

An observant Jew would attend the Temple three times a year: at the Passover, which was linked to the Feast of the Unleavened Bread that immediately followed it, Pentecost, and the feast of the Tabernacles. In coming up to Jerusalem for the Passover, Jesus was confirming his status as an observant Jew. The Passover commemorated the moment when the Jews, in captivity in Egypt, were ordered to kill a lamb and sprinkle its blood on the doorpost, so that their firstborn would be spared from God's slaughter of the firstborn of the Egyptians. The practice of sacrifice, the offering of an animal – cattle, sheep, goats or doves – to God through the priests was universal and all Jews would also pay a Temple tax to be spent on sacrifices on behalf of the community. In between visits to the Temple, Jews would attend their local synagogues for prayer as well as conducting devotions in their own homes. In the synagogues there would be readings of the scriptures so that they would be well-known texts even to the illiterate. The preservation of teachings, prophecies and the Law in writing so that it could be relayed on to each generation was crucial for the cohesion of the community.

In so far as there was a Jewish aristocracy, it was of the ancient priestly families – 'a connection with the priesthood is a hallmark of an illustrious line' as the historian Josephus put it, stressing his own 'aristocratic' ancestry. Powerful among them were the Sadducees, a distinct grouping of priests who paid particular respect to the Temple ritual and who developed their own beliefs, which included a rejection of any belief in the resurrection of the body, apparently on the grounds that it was not to be found in the scriptures. Mark's gospel shows Jesus challenging them on this (12:26). Herod had suppressed the Sadducees but they were supportive of Roman rule and the gospels see them as a privileged elite that was, understandably, antagonistic to Jesus. They probably made up the majority of the members of the Sanhedrin.

The post of high priest had a far higher status than the gospels suggest. Caiaphas was the most powerful person in Judaea, the combination of his status with his own popular support making it almost impossible for a governor to defy him. When the Jews did revolt, in AD 66, it took a massive Roman counteroffensive to bring the uprising to a bloody end. So long as the high priest kept order in his own community and worked at his relationship with the governor he was in a formidable position and Caiaphas' survival for so much longer than any single governor's period of office makes the point. However, there is evidence from archaeological excavations in Jerusalem that the priests were living increasingly luxurious lives and so, in a trend which was probably condoned by Herod, placing themselves apart from the mass of their fellow Jews. This was bound to cause social tension that was probably reflected in unrest in the crowds when they gathered in Jerusalem for the major feasts. This explains the uneasy relationship between high priest and governor at each Passover. The high priest needed the help of the governor's auxiliaries but could hardly afford to be seen as the tool of Roman imperialism.

The Greeks and Romans could never understand the ritual of circumcision, the ancient and obligatory requirement for all male Jewish children. Circumcision was the entry rite to membership of the people of God, one reason why its rejection by the apostle Paul as a requirement for Christians caused such outrage. The Sabbath was sacred and no work could take place on it, even the sharing of meals if this involved 'the work' of taking food to another's house. There is a story relating to a siege of Jerusalem in the second century BC. The Greek historian Plutarch, writing much later, told how, 'because it was the Sabbath day, the Jews sat in their unwashed clothes, while the enemy was planting ladders against the walls and capturing the walls, and they did not get up but remained there, bound there in their superstition as in one great net'. There was continuous debate over exactly what one could and could not do on a Sabbath and it was this lack of resolution that was exploited by Jesus' opponents when they wished to discredit him.

These requirements were enshrined in the Law. The original Hebrew term, Torah, meaning 'teaching' or 'instruction', was contained in the Pentateuch, the first five books of the Tanakh, the Hebrew scriptures (later, for Christians, the Old Testament). It was only when the scriptures were translated into Greek, that Torah was rendered, somewhat misleadingly, as *nomos*, and it was this term which was translated as Law. The teachings of the Torah extended far beyond a list of prohibitions. They underpinned an ethical approach which recognised God's love, not only for his nation, but also for humanity as a whole and even for working animals, which were included within the requirement to rest on the Sabbath. The land too was allowed a 'Sabbath' so that it could lie fallow every seventh year. Piety was always central to Judaism – it was a religion as much of practice as of theological debate. There was a strong emphasis on a commitment to the poor – in one ruling it was said that in a city where there were both Jewish and Gentile poor, the poor Gentiles should also be helped 'for the sake of peace'. Of course, over and above this the Law had a sacred quality that was deeply embedded in the Jewish consciousness. It was little wonder that Paul encountered so much opposition from his fellow Jews when he claimed that Jesus had superseded the Law.

The priests were important in interpreting the Torah, especially as they were responsible for the supervision of the correct rituals in the Temple. There were two other groups who were associated with open discussion of the Law. The first is the scribes who could read and write extracts from the scriptures for themselves. Their reading equipped them with a reservoir of recondite knowledge that was of immense use to those seeking clarification or guidance. In the gospels the scribes are spoken of as if they were ready to pronounce on all kinds of matters. The second group is the Pharisees. The Pharisees appear to have originated as a distinct party in the reaction to the imposition of Greek ways of thinking by the Greek king Antiochus after Judaea had been absorbed into his Seleucid empire in the 190s BC. They stood for the traditional law and supported the Maccabean revolt that led to the independent Hasmonaean kingdom. However, they believed in balancing a study of the written law with oral interpretations of it and so, in practice, they were more flexible than the intrusive and argumentative figures who appear in the gospels might suggest. There also seem to have been far fewer Pharisees than one would think – 1 per cent of the population at most is one estimate. With many of their members coming from lower social classes, they were to be found throughout Judaea and Galilee, especially in the synagogues. Their relatively low social status and their belief that there would be a future resurrection of the body put them in strong opposition to the Sadducees. In contrast to the picture given in the gospels, there was little fundamentally about which they disagreed with Jesus. One disagreement there certainly was: over divorce. The Pharisees accepted that a husband could divorce his wife if the marriage broke down: Jesus would reject divorce entirely, perhaps because it had become a symbol of social disintegration in his native Galilee.

Prophets who claimed that they had direct contact with God could subvert learned disputation over the Law. There were revered prophets, such as

Jeremiah and Isaiah, who had warned the nation of the consequences of their disobedience of God's Law. The eight books of the Nevi'im, the second part of the Hebrew scriptures, are those of 'the prophets' and by the first century AD they appear to have become authoritative in their own right. The gift of prophecy was often linked to the power to cast out demons (exorcism) and to heal and effective miracle working of this kind by *Hasidim*, 'the devout', was seen as confirmation of their prophetic powers. Through his reported miracles, Jesus was affirming his status as a traditional Jewish *Hasid*, one whose piety extends beyond the mere observance of the Torah.

The authorities, both the priestly caste and their Roman overlords, were suspicious of 'prophets'. They tended to bring unrest and often challenged the hierarchical structure of society. In his *Jewish Antiquities*, Josephus tells of several 'deceivers and impostors' who claimed divine inspiration in the tense lead-up to the Jewish revolt of AD 66. Very often they were arrested and dealt with by their co-religionists. Honi, a first-century BC miracle worker, was stoned to death by a mob in Jerusalem. 'Was there ever a prophet you did not persecute?' asks Stephen of his co-religionists in the Acts of the Apostles (7:52) before he too is stoned by the mob. The crucifixion of Jesus was a more formal legal process than this but he falls into the same pattern of the visionary who provides a distinctive but threatening message and who suffers for it.

The rise of holy men with their own public followings was one response to increasing social tension. Another was to withdraw and establish a counter-culture based, in the case of the Essenes, on an idealisation of poverty and asceticism. The Essenes have long been known from references in the Jewish writers Philo and Josephus and the Roman scholar Pliny the Elder. 'The Essenes', Pliny wrote, 'are a unique people and admirable beyond all others in the whole world, without women and renouncing love entirely, without money, and having for company only the palm trees.' Totally unexpected, however, was the discovery in the 1940s and 1950s of a preserved library (the Dead Sea Scrolls) of the so-called Qumran community which must have been part of the Essene movement. Here were almost all the texts of the Hebrew scriptures, some in multiple copies, dating from a thousand years before any other known biblical manuscript. Even this early, there were discrepancies between copies of the same text, showing that there was no strict adherence to any one authorised version of scripture. The copyists felt able to reflect on their texts, paraphrase and even develop them. This was not a religion that was stifled by ritual; it had the means of breaking through convention and Christianity would never have emerged if it had been otherwise.

The Qumran community appears to have split off from mainstream Judaism under its 'Teacher of Righteousness', turned its back on its fellow Jews and insisted on an exact observance of the Law. The Essenes were celibate, strictly regulated their membership and believed in an imminent coming of the Messiah, 'the son of David', who would bring the world to an end. The Scrolls therefore provide evidence of the widespread longing for renewal and the expectation of its immediate fruition which was current in the period. Many of the teachings of Jesus and Paul are similar to those of the community, one reason why the discovery of the Scrolls has proved so important in widening our understanding of the origins of Christianity. The Qumran community also provides a model of a body of believers drawing on their own distinct traditions, notably the works of the prophet Enoch, which may have been rejected by rival Jewish groups.

When early Christians talked of Jesus rising to be with 'the Father', they could only have imagined him within the depiction of heaven they had absorbed through Judaism. It was not believed that God ruled there alone. In early texts, Psalm 82, for instance, he is accompanied by other gods. 'God is a judge among Gods' (Psalm 82:1). Later these divine figures are described as angels and God is referred to as enthroned with the heavenly host. So when the Book of Revelation talks of the angels of the seven churches or the Letter to the Hebrews of Jesus being greater than the angels they are reflecting a Jewish vision of the heavens. Heaven includes exalted angels with distinctive roles: Michael the archangel sees over the people of Israel, Gabriel comes to Mary to announce the conception of Jesus. John the Baptist is described as if he is a herald angel (Matthew 11:10). Not all 'angels' were benign. Angels of darkness, notably Satan, threatened the power of God. This sense of a struggle between forces of light and goodness pervades the Dead Sea Scrolls. It provides a confused picture of God, of one who is supposedly supreme but who can be thwarted by evil spirits. So even if God really did want to protect his people, he might not be able to do so. This more fatalistic message of the possible destruction of the 'light' lives alongside the optimism of eventual victory.

The angels were given a distinct role as the messengers of God and his attendants in heaven. Could God intervene in the world in a more immediate form? The figure of Wisdom, created by God at the beginning of time as Proverbs puts it (8:22), appears to be such an intervention. Then there is the Son of Man, described in Chapter Seven of Daniel: 'one like a human being coming with the clouds of heaven'. The texts are confused but some even suggest that there might be divine figures alongside God. When Jesus says, in John 10:30, 'I and the Father are one', he may not be saying something which was completely alien to Jewish thought, even though his listeners appeared affronted by the claim. Equally God might use human beings as mediators between earth and heaven. So Moses is given the role of revealing the Promised Land to the Jews and is talked of as ascending to heaven. Elijah

(2 Kings 2:11) is another example of one exalted by God – he, too, ascends into heaven, in a chariot. A fragment from the Dead Sea Scrolls suggests that the priest Melchizedek, the priest who blessed Abraham, might also 'have taken his seat in the congregation of Gods'. Perhaps these figures might even have had an existence in heaven before their earthly life. The patriarch Jacob is quoted in one prayer 'as the first born of every living thing to whom God gives life'. One of the challenges facing the first Christians was to find a place for Jesus within the other quasi-human and divine figures that moved between heaven and earth.

A prophet might express himself through apocalyptic visions. The Greek word *apokalypsis* refers to a special and direct revelation from God. The revelation need not relate to the end of the world but in many cases the vision was eschatological, of the last things (the Greek word *eschatos* means 'at the extremes of time or space'), telling, in most cases, of the disorder that was about to break out on earth before the reign of God began. It is difficult to understand the pressures and influences that led to the growth of apocalypticism (which is common in Jewish texts between 200 BC and AD 100). Perhaps the upheavals of the period led to a desperate need to understand the purpose of God or to a particular receptivity towards those who claimed to know it. The most famous of the apocalyptic texts, the Book of Revelation, claims to be a revelation, to John the Divine, from Jesus Christ but Jesus himself was an apocalyptic prophet. The apocalyptic sayings might be rooted in prophecies from earlier scriptures. The Dead Sea Scrolls show that interpretation of these – technically known as *pesher* – was common within the Qumran community. The first (Jewish) Christians were to relate their beliefs about Jesus to precedents within the Hebrew scriptures.

Beliefs in what might happen after an individual's death were varied. It is said that the only definite reference to an afterlife in the Hebrew scriptures is Daniel's assertion that 'many of them that sleep in the dust of the earth shall awake, some to everlasting life, and some to shame and everlasting contempt' (Chapter Twelve in the Book of Daniel). There is the assumption here, and in other texts, that the soul lives on and may be in a temporary resting place until there is a final judgement. In the Book of Revelation the souls of the martyred wait below an altar until the moment that they have been vindicated by God (6:9). The Transfiguration, the appearance of Elijah and Moses alongside Jesus in a vision, shows that prophets who had ascended to heaven could be seen again on earth. The visions of Christ reported by Paul in his First Letter to the Corinthians (Chapter Fifteen) are not unique but suggest his own status as a prophet.

The Jews had, of course, their own scriptural account of God's creation of the world in the Book of Genesis. How the world would end was, on the other hand, the subject of intense debate. Some, the Essenes, for instance, talked of a final battle between the forces of light and darkness, 'good' Jews fighting bad Jews and their allies such as the Philistines, ancient enemies of the state of Israel, others of a general desolation in which the fields would be barren and the storehouses empty, even fountains of water ceasing to flow. 'Then shall the heart of the earth's inhabitants be changed and converted to a different spirit. For evil shall be blotted out, and deceit shall be extinguished; faithfulness shall flourish, and corruption shall be overcome, and truth, which has been so long without fruit, shall be revealed' (4 Ezra (after c.AD 70)). There would then, in similar narratives, be a great gathering in of Jerusalem's children from east and west and even from distant islands. What these narratives have in common is the belief that there will be a 'coming' which will result in a dramatically different society but there is little agreement as to what form this will take – whether there will be a judgement of good and evil, whether all humankind will be welcomed, or only Jews, or some discrimination shown between nations.

Equally there was disagreement over whether a human being, sent by God, perhaps, would usher in this transformed world. The specific figure of the Messiah, as one who is anointed by God, *Christos* in Greek, runs far back in Jewish history. From early times, the Messiah was identified with kingship and a royal investiture marked by anointing with oil. Passages in Isaiah (11:1–5), Jeremiah (33:14–26) and Ezekiel (37:24–8) use royal imagery when talking of the Messiah and the title was even given to a Gentile, Cyrus, the 'King of Kings' of Persia, who freed the Jews from their Babylonian captivity in the mid-sixth century BC. In the first century AD it was common among Jews to talk of a coming messiah who is usually described as associated with 'the house of David'. Some of the Qumran scrolls also talk of two messiahs: one a king and one a priest. Messiahs were expected to bring some form of political and military triumph. The Psalms of Solomon talk of 'the son of David', a king who will shatter unrighteous rulers, destroy the pride of the sinner and then gather together a holy people whom 'he shall lead in righteousness' (Psalms of Solomon 17:55ff.). One tradition talks of the Messiah as suffering for his people but in the scriptures this was not linked to his role of saviour. The latter was a distinct development within Christianity, although the Romans and the Jewish priesthood would always tend to see a self-proclaimed messiah as a disruptive and threatening force.

Ever since the sixth century BC, when the Babylonians had conquered Jerusalem, Jews had migrated from Judaea in a diaspora that had taken them across the eastern Mediterranean. Large Jewish communities had been established in most of the major cities of the east, including Alexandria and Antioch. Others had migrated as far west as Rome. The Jewish ethnarch (the term for a ruler of an ethnic group) in Alexandria, perhaps the largest Jewish community outside Judaea, exercised supervision over religious and commercial activities of his people as well as judging in internal disputes. These arrangements were important so that the food laws could be complied with, the tax for the Temple gathered and the Law upheld. With time the descendants of these exiles no longer spoke Hebrew and the scriptures had been translated into Greek, the Septuagint (so called because of the legend that seventy-two scholars had worked independently on the translation and had come up, miraculously, with the same text). There were Jews, such as the philosopher Philo in Alexandria, who were so at home with Greek learning that they were able to integrate it into Judaism. The works of the great philosopher Plato, said Philo, with supreme confidence in his own faith, are no more than a translation of the wisdom of Moses into Greek.

What is remarkable is the extent to which Jews were accepted within the cities, especially as they had to reject the traditional religious rites, which bound a Greek city community together. The exuberant displays of statues of Greek deities, which were a feature of all classical cities, must have been deeply abhorrent to those who rejected all forms of idolatry. Yet an inscription from Phrygia even refers to a Gentile woman donating a synagogue, much as a patron would build a pagan temple for the glory of his or her city. In some cities synagogues and the *gymnasia*, the meeting places of the Greeks where both sport and cultural life took place, were close together. The evidence from the Acts of the Apostles suggests that when Jews complained to the magistrates about the intrusions of Paul they were listened to. There was also the important group of 'God-fearers', sympathisers with Judaism who may have attended the synagogues without adopting Jewish practices such as circumcision. There is some evidence that they acted as go-betweens in the negotiations between Jews and the city authorities. So, while there are reports of unrest, communal riots in Alexandria and Rome, for instance, one can also envisage Jewish communities that had successfully negotiated a status for themselves within the wider empire. The antiquity of their religion was a major factor in the respect they commanded.

In a period when Greek culture was dominant in the eastern Mediterranean, some 'Hellenisation' of Judaea was inevitable. There was the annual return of many thousands of diaspora Jews for the great festivals and Herod himself had used Greek administrators and erected Greek buildings – a theatre, amphitheatre and stadium – in Jerusalem. Then there were commercial links as the tentacles of the Greek trading networks extended inland. Of the inscriptions found on ossuaries of the period in Jerusalem 40 per cent are in Greek, either on its own or in conjunction with a Jewish text. Acts suggest that the Greek speakers may have had their own synagogues in the city (9:29).

Naturally there were tensions within Jerusalem between the Greek and native Jews and these play an important part in the emergence of Christianity, as the Acts of the Apostles makes clear. It is much more difficult to assess the impact of Greek culture outside Jerusalem, particularly in remote areas such as Galilee. The archaeological evidence has not been supportive of its spread. Excavations in even the larger cities of Galilee, Sepphoris, for example, show that culture remained overwhelmingly Jewish and it would appear that Hellenisation in Galilee was superficial, certainly until AD 70. Jesus and his followers would probably have known of Greek traders passing through Galilee but might never have met them in rural areas or have been able to communicate with them if they had.

As this book continues, we will see how fertile a seedbed Judaism provided for the spread of Christianity. The recent acknowledgement of this has brought a completely different approach to the history of early Christianity, one this book attempts to follow. The development is entirely beneficial, first in the sense that it is more historically accurate and second in that it offers a chance of reconciliation and mutual acceptance where there have otherwise been hostility and rejection. There is probably no other area of the history of early Christianity where so much rethinking has been, and remains to be, done.

CHAPTER THREE

Jesus before the Gospels

WHEN HEROD'S KINGDOM WAS DIVIDED AMONG HIS SONS AFTER his death in 4 BC, one of them, Herod Antipas, was made tetrarch (literally 'ruler of a fourth part', of Herod's original kingdom) of Galilee. He remained in power until AD 39, for the whole of Jesus' life. So, contrary to conventional belief, Jesus was subject to a local ruler rather than directly to the Romans while he taught in Galilee. Herod Antipas' 'kingdom' was a prosperous and well-populated region, its land was fertile and well watered and a wide variety of crops – fruits, vines, olives, grain and flax – are recorded. There was a flourishing fishing industry. The Galileans were Jews who, despite a distinctive accent, appear to have differed little in their beliefs from those in Judaea to the south. However, Galilee was suffering from the impact of Herod and his ruling clique who were involved in a major building programme, including the restoration of the city of Sepphoris and the creation of a new capital Tiberias (named after the emperor Tiberius, on whose support Herod Antipas' survival ultimately depended).

Discontent was not all pervasive: Josephus' description of Galilee, where he commanded Jewish forces, gives no hint of any major unrest during Herod's reign. But the evidence suggests a divided society: a rich landowning elite consolidating their position by driving peasants from the land. There seems to have been a mood of social disorientation, a feeling that the new rich who cared nothing for the ideal of a shared community were destroying traditional Jewish ways of life. This expressed itself in low-level unrest – disruption rather than revolt. Leaders who represented or exploited the discontent, such as John the Baptist, were soon arrested and executed by Herod. This was the world in which Jesus grew up, almost certainly in the small village of Nazareth, a few miles from Sepphoris. Recent excavations of Nazareth suggest that it was a community able to support itself and it was sufficiently close to the road network not to be cut off from the wider world.[1]

Jesus himself never wrote any account of his ministry or his teachings. Most of his followers were illiterate and there is no known document written by an eyewitness to Jesus' life, although eyewitnesses must have contributed material that was retained and later used in the gospels. The only early Jewish source which records Jesus is Josephus who tells us that Jesus was responsible for 'spectacular deeds', that he was handed over by the Jews to be crucified and that his followers, both Jews and Greeks, were still active in Josephus' day, the last decades of the first century. The apostle Paul's own knowledge of Jesus' life appears to have been very limited (and will be discussed further in Chapters Four and Five). So one is left with the four canonical gospels, those attributed to Mark, Matthew, Luke and John, which were written by educated Greeks, themselves outsiders to Judaea, but not to Judaism, between AD 70 and AD 100. The gospels illustrate how four Christian writers envisaged Jesus and his message in the period forty to seventy years after his death and this is why they will be described more fully in a later chapter. They were heavily reliant on oral traditions, some of which may have been written down, which they adapted to provide a coherent narrative for their own audiences. Jesus' death and resurrection are presented as the culminating moment of his life on earth and it is probable that the details of his life are shaped towards this.

The four gospels are the only complete survivors of perhaps twenty gospels that were written. The other gospels were lost or discarded but fragments of some have been recovered and might provide useful historical evidence. A good example is the so-called 'Gospel of Peter', a part of which, relating to the Passion and resurrection of Jesus, was found in Egypt in the nineteenth century. It is dated to the early or mid-second century. It was still being read by Christians at the end of the second century but ideas found within it were then declared heretical by the bishop of Antioch, Serapion, possibly on the grounds that the gospel denied the suffering of Jesus on the cross. It was then discarded.

The Gospel of Peter has material that overlaps with the earlier gospels, and so it may well draw on a common pool of earlier oral tradition. For instance, verses 29 and 30, 'The elders became fearful and went to Pilate and asked him: "Give us some soldiers to guard his crypt for three days to keep his disciples from coming to steal him. Otherwise the people may assume that he has been raised from the dead and then harm us" ', are clearly from the same origin as verses 62 to 64 from Chapter Twenty-seven of Matthew's gospel. Again one finds the story of the figure waiting at the tomb to pass on the information about the rising of Jesus to the visiting disciples which is recorded in all four canonical gospels. Yet the gospel also has narrative detail not known elsewhere. In verses 31 and 38 of Peter it is recorded that, having arranged the guard, the elders went with the soldiers and stayed at the tomb for three days. Crowds come out to visit the tomb on the Sabbath. The difficulty for the historian lies in distinguishing between what might be very early and relevant historical material not recorded elsewhere and material which the writer of Peter might have added himself to make the narrative more dramatic. It is right to treat the gospel, as with any account made many years after the event, with caution but it certainly should not be rejected as an independent historical source.[2]

Again the so-called 'Gospel of Thomas', found in a cache of documents at Nag Hammadi in Egypt in 1945, records further sayings of Jesus alongside the repetition of some already known from the gospels. It has its enthusiasts (some of whom appear to have been excited simply by having a new source to work from) but again it is quite late, probably from the middle of the second century, and it is impossible to know how many of its sayings are genuine. There are simply too many cases in the ancient world of prominent 'teachers' having sayings attributed to them by later admirers for the gospel to be taken at face value. It provides no facts about Jesus' actual ministry.

The predominant question in New Testament studies for the past two hundred years has been whether the gospel sources provide an accurate picture of the life of Jesus. The gospels have important discrepancies and omissions that make them difficult to use as historical texts and their writers provide little critical assessment of their sources, as was commonly done by the more sophisticated Greek historians of the period. There has been a tendency to fill in the omissions with the Jesus we want, the Jesus that suits our needs, to replace the one we believe to be inadequately portrayed in the gospels. A wise nineteenth-century theologian, George Tyrrell, remarked that if one looked down a well in order to find the historical Jesus, the face that peered back at one from the water was usually one's own![3]

In the specific case of Jesus there are further problems to consider. Jesus and his disciples spoke in Aramaic. Aramaic was the lingua franca of a region extending from the Levant coastline of the eastern Mediterranean further eastward into Mesopotamia. We do know that some of Jesus' sayings were transmitted in the original Aramaic: an early second-century writer, Papias, records one Matthew putting down sayings of Jesus in Aramaic in 'an ordered arrangement'. It is tragic that these sayings have not survived as they would have provided the closest we could come to hearing Jesus' original words. (This Matthew should not be confused with the Matthew of Matthew's gospel which was written in Greek.) In all the surviving sources, gospels and others, there are only twenty-six Aramaic words attributed to Jesus which remain.[4] One of these, *marana tha*, 'Come, O Lord', recorded by Paul at the end of his First Letter to Corinthians (16:22), suggests that there were early Christian groups praying in Aramaic. Otherwise native speaking Aramaic followers of Jesus have disappeared from the record.

We do not know quite how the sayings of Jesus were translated from Aramaic into Greek. Greek had spread into the eastern Mediterranean after the conquests of Alexander but was always the language of an educated minority and, in this period, seldom spoken outside cities. Archaeological evidence from the twenty years of digging at what appears to be the site of Bethsaida, where several of the disciples were recruited, confirms the gospel accounts of Bethsaida as a fishing village, the 'lonely place' of Luke (9:13), and thus well beyond Greek influence.[5] Evidence of the Greeks in larger cities also seems limited. Excavations at the city of Sepphoris, an hour's walk from Nazareth, show most houses to have had ritual baths attached to them; in other words it was a Jewish rather than a Greek city, certainly before AD 70.

So, on the present evidence one can hardly argue that the disciples would have learned Greek in their native Galilee although some of them may have picked up the language in Jerusalem in the years after the crucifixion. This reworking of Aramaic into Greek would most likely have been done in Jerusalem when the disciples came into contact with Greek-speaking Jews. One has to assume that there was interplay between Greek- and Aramaic-speaking followers of Jesus that led to the recasting of his teachings into Greek. The difficulty here is that it is impossible to know what was lost, culturally and linguistically, in the process. Few Greek-speaking Jews would have ventured into Galilee and the earliest gospel, Mark, makes elementary mistakes about its geography. Whatever the original sources on which they draw, the gospels were written by outsiders and misinterpretations of the surviving evidence must be expected.

Then there is the problem of timing. The earliest gospel, that of Mark, is dated to perhaps AD 65, the last of the canonical four, John, to 90 or possibly later. The biblical scholar Richard Bauckham has argued for the existence of surviving eyewitnesses as late as the AD 60s and even 80s, over thirty to fifty years after the crucifixion.[6] These, he claims, would have been able to provide accurate material for the gospel writers. It is difficult to measure life expectancy for this period but one estimate is that only four men in every hundred lived beyond fifty. It would certainly be unusual to find living eyewitnesses of Jesus' life after AD 60 and it would be a matter of chance as to whether any of these survivors could provide accurate and valuable informa- tion, especially as their first language would have been Aramaic, not the Greek of the gospel writers. Studies of memory show how recollections of past events can become extraordinarily distorted with time and that eyewitness accounts recorded for the first time many years later are seldom trustworthy.[7]

The assumption must be that the gospel writers relied primarily on earlier oral and written traditions originating from witnesses who had since died. In his prologue, Luke refers to 'traditions handed down to us [i.e. not delivered "to us" in person] by the original eyewitnesses and servants of the gospel'. What cannot be known is how far these had developed over the three or four decades between the crucifixion and the writing of the gospels. Only those records preserved in a fixed, say written, form soon after the events are likely to provide historical accuracy and none are known to survive.

These problems have so taxed scholars that some abandoned the task of finding a 'historical' Jesus from the gospels altogether. As the Lutheran scholar Rudolf Bultmann (1884–1976) put it: 'I do indeed think that we can know now almost nothing concerning the life and personality of Jesus, since the Christian sources show no interest in either, are moreover fragmentary and often legendary; and other sources about Jesus do not exist . . . What has been written in the last hundred and fifty years [i.e. before 1926] on the life of Jesus, his personality and the development of his inner life, is fantastic and romantic.'[8] Bultmann and his contemporary Karl Barth (1886–1968) abandoned the search for historical authenticity altogether, claiming that the scriptures were 'self-authenticating'. For many this represented an opting-out, an uncritical acceptance of scriptural authority that was incompatible with serious scholarship. In the past twenty years, scholars have regained their confidence. In fact, there has been an avalanche of books on 'the historical Jesus'. Some remain cautious, others are imaginative to the point of fantasy, others again burst with insights, which may or may not reflect historical reality but which have helped stimulate further debate. In some accounts, where Jesus seems to have been a 1960s hippy, a Che Guevara or a precursor of 1970s' feminism, George Tyrrell's warning of the face looking back up from the well appears to have been justified.

Any search for a historical 'human' Jesus requires a method of delving through the gospel narratives, those of Matthew, Mark and Luke, the so-called synoptic gospels ('synoptic' from the Greek because they share 'the same eye'), to find the bedrock of the earliest oral traditions about him. Matthew and Luke draw heavily on the earlier gospel of Mark but they also share passages that are not in Mark, so it is possible to deduce that there must have been a document, which is even earlier than Mark, on which they both relied. It has been given the prosaic title 'Q', from the German *Quelle*, 'source' and there are some 220 verses from Matthew and Luke that appear to come from it. It is largely composed of sayings of Jesus. It is assumed that Q was originally written in Greek and contains some of the earliest records of the Greek-speaking Christian-Jewish communities of Jerusalem. Jesus confidently presents himself in Q as the chosen of God, responsible for bringing his message that a transformation is to take place on earth. There is no mention in Q of the Passion or resurrection or to Jesus as saviour so one can hardly call Q an early form of any gospel.

One might uncover the bedrock material in other ways. An event or teaching to be found in each of the traditions recorded by John and the synoptic gospels is more likely to be authentic than one found only in one or the other. The figure found by the women in the empty tomb chamber is a good example. So too is an event which appears to conflict with a positive picture of Jesus and his followers. The betrayal of Jesus by Judas, one of his disciples, or his denial by Peter after his trial are detrimental to the image of early Christians and so it can be assumed that they were so embedded in the original accounts as to prove irreplaceable as later versions were developed. Sayings of Jesus which do not relate to any known Jewish teaching might also be original to him.

Such methods were used in a radical form by the so-called Jesus Seminar, a group of scholars founded in 1985 who took each saying of Jesus, some would say out of its wider context, and then subjected it to a ruthless analysis for its authenticity. Their results were colour coded with the most 'authentic' sayings being given a red marking, those not likely to be authentic a black one, and with pink and grey representing the stages in between. The results tended to be dramatic. The gospel of John ended up with no red sayings at all and only one pink. Mark only had one red saying. As the Jesus Seminar loved publicising its findings, it attracted sensational headlines, among them, 'Bible Scholars Determine Jesus Did Not Teach the Lord's Prayer'. There was more than a suspicion in conservative theological circles that an enjoyment of debunking for debunking's sake had got out of hand. With only 18 per cent of Jesus' recorded sayings and 16 per cent of his recorded deeds being given a red or pink status, he was left as a fragmented figure of whom very little could be said with confidence.

One must, however, start somewhere. E.P. Sanders, one of the most respected authorities on the relationship between Judaism and Jesus and Paul, lists, in *The Historical Figure of Jesus*, what the sources concur in saying about the life of Jesus.[9] It is a limited set of 'facts' and might be a disappointment to those who use the gospels to inform and sustain their beliefs. First, there is sufficient evidence to say that Jesus was born about 4 BC, roughly at the time that Herod the Great died. The earliest gospel account, Mark, refers to him as no more than 'the Son of Mary' and it is clear that there was some uncertainty over his legitimacy. Not everyone accepts his birth in Bethlehem (there are major problems, for instance, with Luke's narrative of events) but there seems sufficient evidence that he was brought up in a family with other children in Nazareth.[10]

The first known public event in Jesus' life is his baptism by John the Baptist after which he selected a number of close disciples and began his own preaching in the smaller towns, villages and the countryside of Galilee. The imminent coming of the 'Kingdom of God' was an important feature of his teaching. In about AD 30, he travelled to Jerusalem for the Passover and he caused some kind of disturbance in the Temple. A 'final' meeting with his disciples over a meal is well attested and he was then arrested by the Jewish authorities, notably the high priest Caiaphas, and handed over for execution by crucifixion at the command of Pontius Pilate, the Roman governor. On the third day after his crucifixion and perhaps afterwards, he was 'seen' by his disciples although what exactly they saw is not clear. It was, however, sufficient for them to believe that he would return shortly to found the promised kingdom and they formed a community to wait for his reappearance.

If these are the apparent historical facts, how can one place Jesus within the fragmenting society of Galilee? The gospel writers do not detach Jesus from his geographical context and the small towns and villages where he preached are often named, as are many of the individuals whom he healed or talked with. The claim, still held by some, that Jesus never existed is never likely to succeed. Clearly Jesus was a charismatic figure able to draw large crowds, even though there was also something of the detached wanderer about him. He had the knack of presenting a complex idea as a parable, easy to remember and to understand, in comparison, perhaps, to the more scholarly analysis of the Law at which the Pharisees and scribes excelled. His healing ministry and his readiness to preach to the poor place him as one who was responding to the social distress of his fellow Galileans. He reached women and tax collectors at a time when both were socially ostracised, yet he remained rooted in the countryside. Even though the city of Sepphoris is only four miles from Nazareth he is never recorded as going there. His people were those of the villages and smaller towns. There is no evidence that he ever married. This was unusual for a Jew. Mark's gospel suggests some friction with his family: as with most prophets there is much of the outsider about him.

Even so, it is difficult to find any teaching of Jesus that would offend Jews. Jesus would hardly have built up such a large following if he had upset traditional believers and he appears committed to the Law. 'Till heaven and earth pass away, not an iota, not a dot, will pass away from the Law' (Matthew 5:18). There is no instance where Jesus permits what the Law clearly forbids and in some instances, his views on divorce, for example, he may be stricter than the Law required. He certainly had his disputes with those who encountered him but, as has been seen, this was in the nature of Judaism where debate was endemic. He was clearly someone out of the ordinary, potentially unsettling to the authorities because of his warning that society was about to be transformed and the broad following his charismatic personality attracted, but in no way outside Jewish tradition.

There is no reason to doubt that Jesus knew the Hebrew scriptures well. He would have heard them read week after week in his local synagogue and he may have been able to read selected texts from the scrolls preserved there. The title of Rabbi, by which some of his disciples addressed him, suggests that he was perceived as a man with some learning. The Jesus Seminar is probably misguided in its rejection of any saying of Jesus that is to be found in scripture – the effective use of scriptures was a traditional means for a Jewish prophet to establish his authority. Like most readers of the scriptures, then and now, he had his favourite texts. Isaiah is the most popular. Jesus quotes or alludes to the prophet some forty times in the synoptic gospels as against fifteen quotations from Deuteronomy and thirteen from the Psalms. Here he is confirming his credentials as an orthodox Jew and his selection seems typical of the time. The most popular text in the Dead Sea Scrolls, in terms of the number of copies preserved there, is Deuteronomy, while there are more than ten copies of Psalms and Isaiah.[11]

The scholar who has done most to confirm Jesus' Jewishness is Geza Vermes. His study, *Jesus the Jew* caused a stir when it first came out in 1973 and he has followed with several books placing Jesus' religious teachings within Judaism.[12] As a result of his intensive study of contemporary Jewish texts, Vermes shone new light on the 'titles' associated with Jesus and showed that while some of these are recognition of his spiritual qualities, none in any way suggested he was seen as divine. For instance, the title 'Son of Man', used so often by Jesus of himself that it must be authentic, was normally meant in a modest 'yours truly' sense. Again, the term 'Lord' (*maryah* (Aramaic) or *adonay* (Hebrew)) was used in different contexts as a designation, variously, of God, a secular dignitary, an authoritative teacher or a person renowned for his supernatural power. The problem for Vermes, then, was to discover which use was relevant for Jesus. He argued (in *Jesus the Jew*) that Matthew and Mark related the title 'Lord' predominantly to Jesus' role as miracle worker while Luke used the term primarily in the sense of a teacher and religious leader. Likewise the titles of 'Son of God' and 'Messiah' had meanings within Judaism which do not accord Jesus any divinity. Vermes suggested that the first Jews who tried to understand Jesus saw him as a *Hasid*, 'a devout man'. There are several of these recorded and their power to heal and to exorcise demons is often seen as proof of their own holiness and acceptance by God.

This was an important step forward even though Vermes has been criticised for using Jewish terminology that came from later texts. It is, however, not enough. Somehow the extraordinary psychological impact of Jesus, an impact that was powerful enough to attract many followers in his lifetime and sustain a continuing movement in his memory, has to be explained.

It seems worth concentrating on what might be called the apocalyptic teachings of Jesus (many, of course, which come from Q).[13] As we have seen, the Greek word *apokalypsis* refers to the revealing of secrets, usually by a privileged person, although in practice these revelations often deal with a transformed society or the end times of the world that follows it. Many of Jesus' sayings tell of the kingdom arriving on earth in the lifetime of his followers. It clearly had not by the time the gospel writers were composing and they would never have included these sayings if they had not been part of an authoritative early tradition which they could not ignore. Hence these sayings are usually assumed to be authentic. So it is likely that the original teachings of Jesus relate to the imminent coming of God's kingdom on earth. By the time one has reached the end of the century beliefs in the imminent arrival on earth of God's kingdom had faded. John's gospel, probably written in the 90s, talks of believers being gathered in the kingdom of God in *heaven*, a good example of how the gospel texts developed to meet the changing needs of the early Christian communities.

The message begins when Jesus encounters John. John empowers Jesus through baptism. The baptism is unlikely to be a later addition by the gospel writers. The story is common to all of them and the implication that John, as the baptiser, is somehow spiritually superior to the one being baptised does not fit well with beliefs about Jesus as they developed after the crucifixion. Surely this reflects some actual event that marks the moment when Jesus starts spreading his message. It also ties in the idea of ritual purification, an integral part of Jewish belief, of course, with the beginning of Jesus' ministry. After a short period of withdrawal and the arrest of John by Herod, Jesus begins at once. 'The time is filled up and the Kingdom of God is almost here; repent and believe in the good news!' (Mark 1:15). The intensity with which Jesus now preaches the coming kingdom is such that he is prepared not only to break his links to his own family but expects others to do the same. 'There is no one who has left a house or brothers or sisters or mother or father or lands for my sake and the sake of the good news, who will not receive them all back a hundred fold in the present time – and in the age that is coming, life that never ends' (Mark 10:39–51). Even the dead must be left unburied (Luke 9:59). What is remarkable about Jesus' teaching is that it is so open and confident. There were other models, such as the Essenes, which would have involved a withdrawal of select followers from society where they would have awaited the coming. Jesus creates no barriers between himself and his listeners and he shows compassion to those for whom the kingdom is intended. No wonder some of Jesus' contemporaries believed that he was 'a prophet like one of the prophets of old' (Mark 6:15).

The kingdom would involve a dramatic reversal of values. Those who are the have-nots, the persecuted and the poor, will have the kingdom, but 'woe to you who are wealthy, for you have your comfort now, woe to you who are full now, for you will go hungry. Woe to you who are rejoicing now, for you will mourn and weep' (Luke 6:24–5). One would have to become like a little child, in other words relinquish adult status, before entry is possible. 'Whoever humbles himself as this small child, this is the one who is great in the kingdom of heaven' (Matthew 18:4). All will be subject to a final judgement. While the epithet 'son of man' appears normally to have been used by Jesus in the 'yours truly' sense, there is also a 'Son of Man' described in the Book of Daniel (Chapter Seven) and other accounts as a judge. A first-century BC (or earlier) text (1 Enoch 69) tells how 'the Son of Man sat on the throne of his glory, and the whole judgement was given [by God] to the Son of Man, and he will cause the sinners to pass away and be destroyed from the face of the earth'. So, in referring to himself as 'the Son of Man', Jesus may be declaring himself as God's appointed judge of sinners.

Likewise accounts of the twelve disciples (this seems a strong tradition even if the gospel writers disagree as to who the twelve are) suggest a return of the original twelve tribes of Israel over whom judgement will be made. 'In the age to come, when the Son of Man is seated upon his glorious throne, you [the disciples] will also sit upon twelve thrones judging the twelve tribes of Israel' (Matthew 19:28, cf. Luke 22:30). Jesus' exorcisms and healings may also be seen as precursors of a kingdom where demons would be conquered and sickness, often interpreted as a sign of sin, at an end. 'The religion revealed by the authentic message of Jesus is straightforward without complex dogmas, "mythical" images or self-centred mystical speculation. It resembles a race consisting only of the final straight, demanding from the runners their last ounce of energy and with a winner's medal prepared for all the Jewish participants who cross the finishing line.'[14] Jesus appears to have taught that only Jews would be subject to judgement or would benefit from the coming kingdom and in this he was firmly within the tradition of Jewish apocalypticism.

Jesus had confidence in his message. In his ministry on earth his authority shines through. Whatever the source of his confidence, it appears to have been absolute. As a result, the opposition he attracted was equally strident. There would always be disputes within Judaism over the boundaries of the Law but it was Jesus' insistence that he had personal access to knowledge of God's intent, that this involved the coming of the kingdom and that he had a prominent role in ushering it in that was bound to cause distrust. 'By whose authority do you teach?' (Mark 11:28) was the question that could not be avoided. One can hardly denigrate the questioners. How, indeed, did one pick and choose between false and true prophets in an age of insecurity where all kinds of self-appointed leaders drew on discontent and the deep-rooted desires for the coming of deliverance? Even those who did believe in him would have cloaked him in their own political or spiritual needs. 'We had been hoping that he was the man to liberate Israel', the men on their way to Emmaus comment to the stranger they meet on the road (Luke 24:21).

If Jesus did believe that the kingdom was about to arrive, then his journey to Jerusalem was to be expected as the culmination of his mission. The Temple was the symbol of Judaism's relationship with God, the medium through which sacrifice could be made. Jesus' entry into the Temple, in the synoptic gospels in the final week of his life, and in John at the beginning of his ministry, is associated with the overthrowing of the tables of the moneylenders and predictions of the destruction of the temple building. As the Romans indeed systematically destroyed the Temple in AD 70 after the Jewish revolt, it is possible that the gospel writers, writing after the event, simply added the story to show how prescient a prophet Jesus was. However, there are earlier Jewish texts, including one from the prophet Jeremiah, which see the destruction of the Temple as a sign of the anger of God against his unfaithful people. The Essenes too had specifically rejected contact with the Temple, as they believed its priests to be unworthy. It is possible that Jesus' physical assault on the Temple workers and his warnings are an expression of this hostility. In that case, it is hardly surprising that the conservative priesthood, increasingly associated as they were with the rich who, he had preached, were destined to suffer, would react against him and order his arrest. Yet, it is important perhaps not to make too much of this. If an attack on the Temple had been a major part of Jesus' message, his followers would not have continued to worship there after his death as the Acts of the Apostles tells us they did.

Did Jesus know that he would die? Did he deliberately move up to Jerusalem so as to offer himself as a sacrificial victim for the sins of mankind? There certainly had been precedents for a death on behalf of the nation, the martyrs in the revolt of the Maccabees, for instance, and Jesus must have known of them. (Their tombs were still respected in his day.) Yet if Jesus had expected the kingdom to arrive on earth in his own lifetime, as has been argued above, his death would have subverted not only his hopes of this but those of all his followers. It is hard to see what purpose it would have served.

It is plausible to argue that Jesus behaved recklessly in Jerusalem on his final visit, innocent perhaps of the implacability of the forces against him, over-confident of God's imminent arrival and then found himself arrested. In short, the crucifixion may have been the result of a serious miscalculation. If so, that most haunting of cries, recorded in Matthew and Mark and in the original Aramaic, 'My God, my God, why hast thou forsaken me', rings out with particular resonance. It was only later, especially through the theology of Paul, that the emphasis shifted towards the crucifixion as the defining moment of Jesus' life. The doctrine of atonement, that the sacrificial death of Christ is the means through which man is reconciled with God, is a later theological, rather than historical, interpretation of the event that cannot be separated from a definition of humankind as deeply sinful and in need of redemption.

Jesus presents himself as favoured by God to the extent that he has been given the role of prophesying the coming of the kingdom. In this he can be related back to the major figures of the past such as Moses and Elijah with whom, after all, he appears in the synoptic gospels at the Transfiguration. It also seems unlikely that (during his lifetime) Jesus spoke of himself as the expected Messiah. There is no mention of Jesus as Messiah in any of the Q sayings, for instance, and the first recorded use of the word Christian, as in followers of *Christos*, the anointed one or Messiah, is from Antioch not Jerusalem (although the title does appear to have been used early on in Jerusalem as well). In so far as the Messiah was normally associated with military or political triumph, then it seems most unlikely (and unrecorded) that Jesus would have seen himself in this role. There would have been no quicker or more certain way of inviting retaliation from both priesthood and Jews. Messiahs needed armed force in their support, as the self-proclaimed messiah Shimon Bar Kokhba understood when he led a revolt against the Romans in AD 132. In short, Jesus probably spoke with confidence of his role as the direct envoy and agent of God, 'the Son of God', a role transmitted to him from God through the Holy Spirit, but as no more than this. John 6:15, where Jesus refuses to let his disciples proclaim him a king, makes sense within this context.

With so few reliable early sources no one can recreate a historical Jesus with any confidence. It is difficult to distinguish the terminology and beliefs that Jesus had adopted from his Jewish background to buttress his authority among his Jewish listeners from those that were unique to him. How original a prophet, if this is the right word to describe him, was he? However, it is certain that if one reads the gospels, particularly the synoptic gospels, with the apocalyptic solution in mind the evidence does have some coherence. There was something in Jesus' presence, the confidence of his teaching, that made his listeners believe that he did enjoy the special favour of God and so had the authority to preach of the coming kingdom. Likewise the very claim would have offended, even outraged, many of his listeners. With the hope of a coming messiah so pervasive, it was understandable that his followers may also have expressed the possibility that he was the Messiah before the cruci-fixion, although there is no clear evidence that he accepted this (and had good reasons for not doing so). The apocalyptic approach explains the emotional intensity of the Jesus movement, the enormous hopes that it raised of an immediate cataclysmic event and the fears among the isolated priesthood that they were losing their authority to the extent that they had to plot a way of having Jesus' pretensions exposed through his death on the cross. If his death had not been recorded, he is likely to have been remembered, if remembered at all, as yet another prophet or holy man in a tradition which was centuries old. In his case, however, his prophecy that he would usher in God's kingdom on earth would never have materialised. The trauma of the crucifixion changed everything.

CHAPTER FOUR

Breaking Away

THE FIRST CHRISTIANITIES

THE DEATH OF JESUS WAS A DEVASTATING BLOW. HOW CAN WE imagine the intense psychological trauma that the disciples must have experienced? They had lived with him for many months, sharing the hardships of the road, the welcoming crowds as well as the mockery of those who despised his mission. Even in Galilee tensions were acute, especially after Herod Antipas' execution of John the Baptist. The message of the coming kingdom grew with the movement and the arrival in Jerusalem must have seemed the culmination of all that had been promised. Where better for the kingdom to be inaugurated? Any followers who believed Jesus was the Messiah may well have dreamed of some form of political or military triumph in which the priestly authorities would be overthrown and Israel liberated. Instead, Jesus had been arrested, subjected to a rudimentary trial and executed as a common criminal by the most humiliating punishment of all, crucifixion.

Christian tradition has dwelled with a somewhat obsessive and prurient fixation on the details of Christ's crucifixion.[1] There is no reason to believe that his agonies and humiliations were any different from the thousands of other similar executions of which we know, but they were ghastly enough. The pain of the nails would have been intensified by the weight of the body that had to be lifted by the arms for breathing to continue. Death was normally by suffocation rather than through loss of blood and it could be hastened by breaking the legs of the victim. Soldiers anxious to get off duty would often have finished off men in this way. If they left the body alive, they risked the possibility of rescue before death had occurred. No one seriously doubts that Jesus died on the cross, probably directly at the hands of the soldiers who nailed him to it.

In many cases the mangled body would have been taken down and left as carrion for burial but Jews were always anxious to fulfil the rituals of a proper burial before sundown on the day of death and the gospel accounts agree that this is what happened to Jesus. It was a bleak moment for his followers. They were adrift in a strange city, recognised as outsiders and totally insecure.

All the promises of the kingdom seemed destroyed. They had every reason to believe that they would be picked up and dealt with as summarily as Jesus had been. As John puts it, the disciples shut themselves behind locked doors 'for fear of the Jews'. Some of the greatest and most moving works of European art record the moment when Jesus' body is lowered into the arms of his distraught family and disciples.

It is hard to say what happened next. All agree that the wealthy Joseph of Arimathea buried the body in the chamber which he had designated as his own tomb. According to Matthew (27: 62–6), the location of the chamber was no secret as guards 'lent' by Pilate to the priests for the purpose had been stationed by it to ensure the body was not taken by his followers. In short, the priests placed themselves in charge of the security of the site. This is hardly surprising as the priests must have feared that Jesus' body would become a focus for dissident worship.

Despite the supervision, three days later the tomb was found open. The accounts are consistent enough for there to be little doubt on this point. In Mark and Matthew, a young man (Mark) or an angel (Matthew), dressed in white, tells the women who have come to the tomb that Jesus has risen and gone before them into Galilee and, in Matthew, Jesus himself appears to the women and says that he will be seen in Galilee. In Luke and John, there are not one but two figures/angels in the tomb chamber. The evidence certainly suggests an empty tomb, (John describes the linen wrappings of the body lying there), but a tomb chamber which is not empty and a demand from a figure or figures within that the disciples return to Galilee. The women are dumbfounded by the opened tomb and, in their confusion, it seems that only when the figures within tell them that Jesus has risen that they consider it a possibility. There is no reason to assume that the men inside were actually angels.

Caiaphas' role in the resurrection must be explored. He was the man who masterminded the crucifixion. He can hardly have abandoned any interest in the Jesus movement and the story in Matthew that the priests took over responsibility for the tomb provides scriptural support for his likely involvement. He had shown the Romans that he was not soft on disorder but he was sensitive to risking his position with his co-religionists by bringing more bloodshed. His survival as a credible authority with both Romans and his fellow Jews depended on a balancing act. It made sense to attempt to thwart any emerging movement in memory of Jesus by sending his disciples back home.

Removing the body, making sure that the tomb was left open and leaving a message with 'a young man' that Jesus would reappear in Galilee would solve the problem without further brutality. The traumatised disciples would, if the plan worked, simply move out of his sphere of authority back into that of

Herod Antipas. Once they were there it can hardly have mattered to Caiaphas what they believed about Jesus. They could not cause the unrest in Jerusalem and jeopardise his status with the Romans. What actually happened to Jesus' body would have been of no interest to anyone so long as the disciples believed it would reappear in some form in Galilee. It would have been important, of course, for the priests to emphasise that Jesus was no longer physically there, but 'risen'. Otherwise rumours might have persisted that his body was still be to be found elsewhere in Jerusalem. Elijah provides a precedent.

This is, of course, pure speculation, but it is a plausible account that does not conflict with the events as they are known and explains the figures in the tomb chamber. If Caiaphas had arranged the moving of the body, then one would have expected them to be priests and the description of their clothes as 'white' or 'dazzling' corresponds to the white linen robes worn by the junior priesthood. As further circumstantial evidence, there is the strange story recounted in Matthew (28:11–15) of the chief priests offering the soldiers who were, as Matthew had recorded a few verses earlier, guarding the tomb on their behalf, a bribe to say that the disciples had moved the body. The priests go on to promise that they will ensure the guards do not suffer for having let the body be stolen. If Caiaphas had removed the body and his men had been seen doing so, it would make sense for the priests to bribe the guards to tell a different story and protect them from Pilate's anger if he heard that the body was gone. This seems the most plausible explanation for this story.

The Gospel of Peter, a fragment of which covering the Passion, crucifixion and its aftermath was discovered in the tomb of a Christian monk in Egypt at the end of the nineteenth century provides further support for this hypothesis. The level of detail recorded suggests a careful writer rather than one who is concerned with creating a version original to himself.[2] There are two sections that are particularly relevant. The first (verse 34) shows that crowds were indeed gathering around the tomb. 'Early in the morning, as the Sabbath dawned, a crowd came from Jerusalem and the surrounding area to see the sealed crypt.' This presents a very different picture from the isolated tomb suggested in the gospels but there is no reason why it should be a fabrication – it is, in fact, just what one would expect after Jesus' tumultuous welcome into Jerusalem only the week before. One can understand why Caiaphas feared continuing disorder.

The second (verses 37–9) describes how the soldiers see two men enter an opened tomb, and then emerge supporting a third man. While the story is presented as an intervention from heaven (the two supporters are recorded as having heads which reach up to the sky and a speaking cross follows them), it may well, by the second century, have grown in the telling, and have been based on an actual story of two men removing the body while the guards were awake.

It is perhaps significant that Jesus is not reported as emerging alone from the tomb. This is what one would have expected from a 'resurrection', in the sense of a spontaneous happening that did not need the support of others. (An image that would have been in most Jews' minds would have been that of Elijah ascending to heaven alone in his chariot (2 Kings 2:1–18).) The writer of Peter would hardly have had any incentive for introducing the story at a later date. Arguably, the story derives, with other verses of this gospel, from the earliest layer of eyewitness accounts. Again the figure in the tomb, that most persistent of interlopers, reappears. At verse 44 he is even described entering the tomb before the disciples arrive and at verse 55 there is an echo of the earlier gospel accounts when he tells the women that Jesus has risen. For whatever reason, this story of one or two figures in the chamber had a profound impact on all reporters of the empty tomb.

All one can conclude from this is that there is circumstantial evidence (and no more than this can be argued from these very fragmentary and late sources) to suggest that Caiaphas put in place a plan which would defuse the Jesus movement, or at least transfer it to Galilee, without further bloodshed. For the disciples an empty tomb was a surprise. The women went expecting to carry out further care of the body and were astonished when they found the tomb empty. The idea that a dead body could be restored to life was not inconceivable as the story of Lazarus shows. There are similar accounts of the prophets Elijah and Elisha bringing two dead boys to life. The synoptic gospels mention in passing that there was a story circulating at the court of Herod Antipas that John the Baptist had been reincarnated after his death – as Jesus. As Herod puts it, 'This is John, whom I beheaded, raised from the dead' (Mark 6:14–16, Matthew 14:1–2, Luke 9:7–9). Again Matthew (27:51–3) tells the story that many 'saints' appeared from their tombs in the earthquake that followed Jesus' death and were seen by inhabitants of Jerusalem. There is, in short, a mass of stories in the gospels of the apparently dead being later seen alive. The resurrection of Jesus cannot, therefore, be isolated as an event. Bearing in mind that John the Baptist was believed to have risen from the dead and been seen as a physical body, one might even argue that it would have been strange if there had been no stories of a risen Jesus.

The gospel writers may also have shaped their accounts to fit Jesus into Jewish tradition. John notes that the disciples did not grasp the scriptural precedents that Jesus would rise from the dead. Yet scriptures there certainly were, of Jonah resting within the whale for three days before his restoration to dry land, for instance, while Hosea describes how 'On the third day He will raise us up and we shall be made whole by His favour.' (In the early creeds, following Paul, 1 Corinthians 15:40, the resurrection takes place on the third day 'according to the scriptures'.)[3] Judging from the number of times that

Jonah is represented in early Christian art, he may have been the most powerful precedent.

Nor was the idea of rising into heaven unknown in the scriptures, as Elijah's ascent shows. Again, a vision of a departed prophet to the faithful on earth is recorded in the Transfiguration accounts of the New Testament in which Elijah and Moses appear alongside Jesus. So the possibility that a dead body can be raised to life on earth, that a prophet could ascend into heaven and subsequently be seen in a vision on earth is not unique to the story of Jesus. Nor was the idea unknown in the pagan world. Writing seventy years later than the gospel accounts, Justin Martyr notes that 'when we say also that the Word, who is the first-birth of God, was produced without sexual union, and that He, Jesus Christ, our Teacher, was crucified and died, and rose again, and ascended into heaven, we propound nothing different from what you believe regarding those whom you esteem sons of Jupiter'.[4] Jewish prophecy and pagan myth both provided a context within which Jesus' story made sense to both Jewish and Gentile Christians. It was not seen as an unique event.

The earliest New Testament sources make no mention of a physical appearance by Jesus on earth between his apparent resurrection to life and the ascension to heaven. Paul, and a number of other New Testament texts (Acts 5:30–1 is a good example), imply that Jesus was simply raised from the dead by God, as other prophets favoured of God had been. For those who knew the scriptural precedents, this would have been an understandable interpretation of the empty tomb. The first reference comes from Paul's First Letter to the Corinthians, written about AD 55, but even this is twenty years after the events Paul describes. By now Jesus is referred to as 'the anointed one', *Christos* in Greek. Paul does not mention the tradition of the empty tomb at all. He has heard of four appearances or visions of Christ, none involving women and none related to any particular place, although an appearance to James, the brother of Jesus, was presumably in Jerusalem. One of these, to five hundred brethren, some of whom were no longer alive, is recorded nowhere else. Paul ends by adding his own vision of Christ, 'on the road to Damascus', as a conversion experience. None of these six accounts, three in Paul's letters and three in Acts, suggests a physical, in the sense of a touchable, dimension to Jesus. In Acts he is simply a light with the power of speech, a clear contrast with Luke's earlier gospel account of a Jesus of 'flesh and bones' (Luke 24:39). Paul appears determined to give himself the same status as the other audiences and it is significant that those travelling with him did not see Jesus (Acts 9:1–9). The implication is that Jesus can appear in a vision at will but only to those he favours, just as Moses and Elijah did at the Transfiguration. This is not a physical person available to all.

Paul had never known Jesus and his letters suggest that he knew very little about the message he preached, that the kingdom would come in his lifetime on earth. Instead he envisages a kingdom, soon to come, on a higher spiritual plane. Those entering it will also be transformed into spiritual bodies and the risen Christ is in a form, therefore, which reflects this. When Paul writes 'It is sown a physical body; it is raised a spiritual body' (1 Corinthians 15:44), he appears to be building on earlier Jewish tradition that the physical body becomes transformed into a spiritual body after death. So the visions described by Paul were not of the physical body of Jesus revived in a material form but of a Jesus already transformed into a spiritual being, 'the first fruits of those who have fallen asleep' (1 Corinthians 15:20). His words at 1 Corinthians 15:50, 'Flesh and blood can never possess the kingdom of God, and the perishable cannot possess immortality', make it quite clear that Paul is not talking of a physical resurrection.

For Paul the risen Christ represents the hope of the future. It is through baptism into Christ that all have the opportunity at the resurrection of the dead to share in the kingdom in heaven. It will be a dramatic moment. 'We shall not all die, but we shall all be changed in a flash, in the twinkling of an eye, at the last trumpet-call. For the trumpet shall sound, and the dead will be raised, immortal, and we shall be changed. This perishable being must be clothed with the imperishable, and what is mortal must be clothed with immortality' (1 Corinthians 15:51–2). The resurrection is the link between the old and the new heavenly kingdom. Christ 'will change our lowly body into the likeness of his glorious body, by the power which enables him even to subject all things to himself' (Philippians 3:2). Paul appears to see the heavenly bodies of those Christians who die as 'the ordinary body subsumed and transformed by the spirit'.[5]

If the resurrection appearances in Mark were, as many scholars believe, not added until the second century[6] one has to wait for a further thirty years, over fifty years after the crucifixion, for any accounts of the risen Jesus appearing *as a physical being on earth* before he rises into heaven. These are to be found in the gospels of Luke and Matthew. They draw on the accounts of the disciples and their womenfolk and so it is important to detail that context in which the appearances took place. Here again the Gospel of Peter may be of use. It records (verse 26) that Peter and his companions went into hiding after the crucifixion, as they believed they were being searched for and that they remained mourning and weeping day and night. This is no more than one would have expected. It would have been impossible to witness the mutilation on a cross of an intimate friend, to deal with the crushed body and not to be overwhelmed by the trauma. The lives of the disciples had already been disrupted by their upheaval from family ties and their hometowns. With the added fear that they might suffer the same fate as Jesus they would hardly have been able to sleep soundly. Here a text and common sense correlate well.

In short, anyone trying to assess the state of mind of the disciples on the third day must imagine for themselves what they would feel like after experiencing the crucifixion of a close friend, perhaps the closest any of them had known, and fearing that they might themselves be picked up next. The most likely outcome would be complete emotional exhaustion. Studies of trauma and sleep deprivation suggest that the expected response is to lose touch with reality, even to hallucinate. Whether this happened can only be surmised (and here it is not being insisted on as an explanation) but it cannot be ignored as a possible factor in what happened next, the record of a number of appearances by Jesus a short time after the crucifixion and their cessation after, according to Luke in the Acts of the Apostles, forty days.[7]

The appearances of Jesus reported in the gospels are to a variety of witnesses, both in Galilee and near Jerusalem, from as early as the third day after the crucifixion. These first appearances were to women and they seem convincing enough to suggest that the belief in a resurrected Jesus grew from initial reports by a group of women visiting the empty tomb where they had been told by the figures within that Jesus had risen. Matthew, Mark (in the verses which appear to have been added later to the original gospel) and John, who is normally seen as working from independent sources, all agree on this, although Luke, like Paul, makes no mention of any appearances to women.

Luke's cited appearances are as follows: two disciples are walking with a stranger near Emmaus. When they sit down with him at the table, they recognise him as Jesus but he promptly vanishes (in other words, he is, in some way, supernatural). Later the same day Jesus appears to the disciples and 'the rest of the company' and walks with them as far as Bethany where he leaves them. In contrast to the ethereal figure described by Paul, Luke is careful to record that Jesus was able to eat and was made of flesh and bone. The problem is that Luke provides a different story in Acts, which was probably written only a few years after his gospel. Here there are forty days of teaching during which the disciples are told not to leave Jerusalem. It is not clear why Luke felt the need to provide contrasting stories: the discrepancy between the one day of his gospel and the continuous presence of forty days of Acts is a significant one.

As soon as one reads the other gospel writers the problems multiply, although perhaps no more than would be expected from a variety of accounts collated by different authors so many years later. The stranger/angel in Matthew and Mark tells the disciples that Jesus will go before them into Galilee and indeed this is reinforced, in Matthew, by the women, Mary of Magdelene and 'the other Mary', when they report a meeting with Jesus in the garden. In Matthew the disciples then make their way to Galilee where Jesus appears to them. John also provides an account which includes the famous recognition by Mary of Magdelene of Jesus in the garden, a meeting with the disciples that same evening and another a week later. This is when Thomas touches Jesus' wounds, certainly the most vivid of the resurrection appearances. Then seven disciples meet him in Galilee.

The problems are twofold: one cannot reconcile Luke with the alternative version of John and Matthew – either the disciples remained in Jerusalem, as Jesus specifically tells them to in Luke, or they did not. If Jesus was fully alive for forty days, with his first appearance by the tomb and his last near Jerusalem, appearing to the disciples in both places, the journey between the two would have taken up a substantial part of the forty days, but there is no mention of such a major undertaking. If, as most scholars believe, Mark ends at 16:8, then his gospel contained no resurrection appearance at all. It simply ended with the empty tomb.

With so much confusion within the gospel accounts, whether women saw Jesus or not, and whether in Galilee or Jerusalem or both, whether he was a spiritual being (Paul) or a human one, able to eat and display his wounds but also with the ability to vanish at will (Luke's Emmaus appearance) and go through closed doors (John), it is impossible to provide a coherent narrative account of what was seen.

If Jesus appeared as a touchable body, it was not at the expense of a super-natural ability to appear or disappear at will or ascend into heaven when the time came. There is no hint in any account that he remained consistently with the disciples unless one takes Luke's second narrative, in Acts, to imply this. Nor can one know whether the story put forward in the gospels was shaped by the need to fit with earlier prophecy, that of Hosea, for instance, of a resur-rection taking place after three days. If the primary aim of the gospel writers was to give Jesus sufficient status alongside other Jewish prophets this is what one might expect. As always one must remember that all these accounts are translations into Greek from the original Aramaic. The highlighting of different lead figures, Peter, 'the beloved disciple', or Mary Magdalene, in the accounts may be seen as the later competition between their followers for supremacy in the emerging Christianities of the later first century. There would have been every incentive for the male apostles to claim 'I saw him too' to maintain their status alongside the women. In fact, it appears that Paul was told only the 'male' version of the story when he met the disciples in Jerusalem.

Most historians would differ from those biblical scholars and theologians who claim that the gaps and discrepancies in the story can only be filled by a supernatural explanation. Tom Wright, for instance, author of a monumental work, *The Resurrection of the Son of God*, asks 'what alternative account can be offered which will explain the data for all the evidence and so challenge the right [*sic*] of the bodily resurrection to be regarded as the necessary [*sic*] one'.[8] So far as one can see from his massive study, Wright does not consider the possible involvement of Caiaphas or the priests in the removal of the body and makes no assessment of the nature and role of the man or men encountered by the women inside the tomb. They perform such a pivotal role in the narrative that a full historical investigation must discuss them. To ignore them, or assume that they were angels, as many conventional accounts do, is impossible to justify.

It is probable that no 'alternative account which will explain the data for all the evidence' can ever be offered. Enough is known about trauma and its effects on memory to know that very distorted accounts of events can occur and that beliefs can quickly become consolidated independently of the historical reality. Such beliefs are often held with unshakable conviction and sincerity. Most historians are naturally sceptical about seeing any intervention of the supernatural in historical events and are content to leave stories such as this as unexplained due to the lack of full and coherent evidence. Whatever events did actually take place in those early days after the crucifixion, it was the developing *belief* of what happened – that there had been a resurrection of Jesus from the dead 'on the third day according to the scriptures' followed by a short period, forty days at most, in which he made appearances to a favoured few (possibly according to Paul in Acts (13:31), only Galileans) – that now took precedence. Here Paul does not link his vision to these.

This involved, of course, a major reinterpretation of Jesus' teachings. Tom Wright puts it well when he writes that the early Christians 'reconstructed [and this seems to be the crucial word in view of the probability that Jesus himself had taught of the coming of the kingdom *on earth*] their worldview, their aims and agendas, around this belief so that it became, not merely an extra oddity, bolted on to the outside of the worldview they already had, but the transforming principle, the string that had pulled back the curtain, revealing God's future as having already arrived in the present'.[9] While memories of what Jesus had actually taught could not be erased from the minds of those who had heard him, what appears to have been the central theme, that he would inaugurate the immediate coming of the kingdom on earth, now receded. Jesus had disappeared, apparently, it was now believed, to heaven. His followers were left with the hope of a Second Coming of Jesus or the inauguration of the kingdom, perhaps on earth, perhaps this time on a heavenly plane.

Today belief in the physical resurrection of Jesus is seen as the core of Christian belief. There has been a tendency to take it out of the context of the times in which it is said to have happened and make it a unique historical experience. However, it is possible to argue that Paul and the gospel writers were placing Jesus within Jewish tradition rather than alienating him from it. Again one can assume all too easily that the resurrection was the most important 'fact' about Jesus within the early church. It is interesting to read the New Testament texts in this regard. Paul mentions visions of the risen Jesus in his letters to the Thessalonians, the Corinthians and Romans but in all the other letters of, or attributed to, Paul there are only ten references to the terms 'resurrection' or 'to rise'. In the remaining New Testament texts, there is a single reference to 'a general resurrection' in the Book of Revelation and a fuller reference to Jesus being raised in the First Letter of Peter but that is all. Jesus had certainly 'risen', but 'rising' was not unique to him, and the stress on the transformation from a physical to a spiritual body (Paul) may have been a means of emphasising his status as a prophet, 'like one of the prophets of old', as Mark puts it (6:15). Perhaps the most controversial claim was that he was believed to have risen as high as 'the right hand of the Father', a major theme of, for instance, the Letter to the Hebrews. It was this belief which led to the martyrdom of Stephen (Acts 7:55–6). It was how to offer him appropriate worship in his new elevated, but contested, status that became the primary concern of the Christian communities.[10]

The earliest 'Jesus movement' is described in the Acts of the Apostles, written in Greek by Luke, probably in the AD 80s. Historians have found Acts difficult to evaluate. There is consensus that it is a second volume of Luke's history, his gospel being the first, but the kind of narrative it represents and the purpose of its writer is hotly disputed. So much of the abundant Greek literature of the period has been lost that it has been hard to relate Acts to any specific genre. Above all it is not clear to what degree Acts can be trusted as an accurate historical record, especially when it reaches its main theme, the missionary journeys of Paul. There are many scholars who reject its historical value altogether.

However, it can be said with relative confidence that a self-defined community of men and women, many from Galilee, who preserved the memory of Jesus, emerged in Jerusalem. Peter took the leading role at first and the community retained the innermost group of twelve, electing one Matthias to fill the place of Judas on the grounds that he had been a witness of Jesus' teaching since his baptism by John. At the subsequent Jewish feast of Pentecost, when they were meeting in a private house, they received a strong sense that 'the Holy Spirit' was with them and this gave them the confidence to proclaim their beliefs to the myriad Jews, from the diaspora communities, who were thronging Jerusalem during the festival. While Acts describes this community as a stable group, apparently at home in Jerusalem, the immediate followers of Jesus were, of course, Galileans, uprooted from friends and family and still coming to terms with the traumas they had suffered. Were they really able to proselytise as freely and confidently as Acts suggests?

All, however, were Jews and the preaching of the fledgling movement, as reported in Acts, remained deeply rooted in Judaism. The traditional Jewish demands – obedience to the Law, insistence on correct diet and circumcision – were retained. Whatever Jesus may have done in the Temple precincts before his arrest, it was not sufficient to break the ritual of worship for them. Its members attended the Temple and gathered in the Portico of Solomon alongside it. The model of synagogue worship, centred on the reading and discussion of the scriptures, probably guided their first meetings. When the apostles were arraigned before the Sanhedrin, Peter stressed that Jesus had come for the Jews. 'He is it whom God has exalted with his own right hand as leader and saviour, to grant Israel repentance and forgiveness of sins' (Acts 5:31). Jesus is still perceived as confined to Judaism.

The group's persistent commemoration of Jesus was likely to have caused continuing concern. Caiaphas remained high priest until AD 37 and the conservative priesthood would have remembered Jesus as a troublemaker. If Caiaphas had hoped that all Jesus' followers would walk back home to Galilee he was mistaken. While many must have returned to assume their family responsibilities and their livelihoods, the inner circle remained in Jerusalem. There would have been other grounds for Jewish suspicion. The power of Jesus' teachings, his agonised death, and beliefs that he had risen from the dead impelled his disciples to find ways of expressing their devotion to his memory. The problem lay in making any form of coherence out of confused and raw feelings that must have gripped them in the months following the crucifixion. It was probably very soon after the crucifixion that the disciples began to envisage Jesus as someone of different order from any other Jewish prophet of whom they had heard. Yet the only terminology available to them, as observant Jews, was that of the scriptures. Figures such as Moses and Elijah, for instance, had been honoured as the chosen of God; yet never at the expense of the status of God as the only true divine force. Somehow an elevated role had to be conceived which would give Jesus some kind of recognition without compromising Jewish monotheism.[11]

Paul's Letter to the Philippians provides an early attempt at definition. The letter probably dates from as late as 61 but Paul appears to have incorporated an early Christian hymn into his narrative (Philippians 2:6–11). The 'hymn' suggests that Jesus had *always* enjoyed some form of divine nature but never approached equality with God. This is an important point because it assumes that he was believed to have been pre-existent with God, instead of being, for instance, a human being adopted by God only after his birth. (The question, which was to become crucial in later centuries, was when this pre-existence began – from eternity or at a moment of later creation.) In his human life, the 'hymn' goes on, he made himself like a slave and after his death on the cross he was raised by God and given a 'name above all names' so that everyone should revere and confess that he is Lord. The term *kyrios*, 'Lord', the Greek equivalent of the Hebrew *adonay* and the Aramaic *maryah*, is used in different senses but the most likely here is as one that associates him with God. So already there has emerged a definition of Jesus in which, unlike that of any other figure in Jewish theology, he has a quasi-divine status. This transformation so early makes good sense – its radical nature is more likely to have been born in the emotional turmoil of the post-crucifixion crisis than later when the trauma had eased. There is no mention here of his resurrection as a physical body – rather Paul describes him as 'bearing the human likeness, revealed in human shape' as if his humanity was always subservient to his divinity.

There is also the development of the concept of the Messiah, *Christos*, 'the anointed one', in Greek. Although the word 'Christian' is first attested in Antioch rather than Jerusalem, Acts suggests that 'Messiah' may have been used in Jerusalem from early on. Whether it was universal remains unclear. The sayings that make up the hypothetical Q do not contain the title at all. However, by the time of Paul, who uses the word 'Christ' no less than 270 times in his core letters, the title can be used alongside Jesus' name (Jesus Christ) or even substituted for it. The Messiah was traditionally a royal figure associated with political and military triumph but this could not be said of Jesus. It appears that the early church came to believe instead that it was the death of Jesus and, above all, his rising from the dead 'according to the scriptures' that gave him messianic status.[12]

Created as they were out of a matrix of memories of Jesus' life and teaching, emotional reactions to his death and scriptural sources, one can hardly expect these formulations to have any theological coherence. It is almost as if all the traditional Jewish titles given to those favoured by God – 'Son of God', 'Lord', 'Son of Man', 'Messiah' – were appropriated and applied to Jesus even though they came from different sources and traditions. The theological complexity, some would say confusion, of Christian belief was established early! This is understandable. The emotional impact of the events was such that the early Christians were struggling to fit their experience of Jesus Christ as some kind of elevated being with Jewish terminology that appeared increasingly inadequate. Even if the titles did not fit easily with each other, they overlapped sufficiently to create a being who had no equivalent in earlier Jewish history.

These tentative formulations underpinned the foundation of the early church. While these first 'Christians' attended the Temple and celebrated festivals such as Pentecost, they also developed their own ritual ceremonies. In Acts (2:38–41), it is recorded that converts were baptised. The concept of purification was intrinsic to Jewish ritual and was required on many occasions, after handling a corpse or preparing for sacrifice, for instance. Christian baptism differed from Jewish purification in that the ritual of baptism provided a once and for all initiation into the community. The baptism of Jesus by John the Baptist provided the model, although it is probable that the baptism is given such prominence by the gospel writers because it reinforced the practice as they saw it around them in the early church. Just as Jesus' own ministry was inaugurated with baptism by John, so initiates were welcomed into the community through water, probably, again, following Jewish precedents, with total immersion. The earliest records suggest that baptism also became associated with the rising of Jesus from the dead. Paul was to talk, for instance, of Christians being baptised into Christ Jesus and into his death (Romans 6:3).

The second important ritual was a commemorative meal, the Eucharist, from the Greek for 'thanksgiving'. The ritual of eating together in a religious context is to be found throughout the ancient world and certainly the miracle of the loaves and the fishes may have been seen in this context (as its frequent representation in early Christian art suggests).[13] The Last Supper, as recorded in the gospels, would have been instantly recognisable to any Greek reader in terms of a teacher surrounded by his loyal male students (and some early catacomb art reflects this). Funeral meals held in commemoration of the dead are also found in both Greek and Jewish culture. The text known as the Messianic Rule from Qumran talks of 'the Priest . . . who shall bless the first-fruits of bread and wine and shall be the first to extend his hand over the bread . . .'.[14] Just as these meals were important, so too was the humiliation for anyone deliberately excluded from one. As Paul recognised when dealing with the recalcitrant Corinthians, the threat of exclusion was a weapon which could be used to reinforce the cohesion of the group (1 Corinthians 5).

Paul confirms in his First Letter to the Corinthians that the Eucharist meal is well established by the 50s as a ritual centred on memories of Jesus. The commemoration is held in the homes of those well off enough to provide the space for a shared meal. From the earliest times it appears that Christ was seen to be present as a living force. Paul tells the Corinthians that they are 'participating' in the body and blood of Christ (1 Corinthians 10:16). This suggests that the congregation may even have believed in some form of transformation into a spiritual body through the common meal of bread and wine. It is likely that it was in discussion after the Eucharist that the participants shared their memories of Jesus and attempted some evaluation of his mission and death; just as the Passover meal traditionally included accounts of the events involved in the flight from Egypt. Even if the participants were illiterate, there would have been opportunities for scribes to write these memories down although no texts survive from this period. This may well have been the genesis of the gospel accounts and one reason why such a significant part of the gospels was devoted to the Passion. The death of Jesus is a deliverance that echoes that deliverance (from slavery in Egypt) which the Passover commemorates. These ceremonies existed alongside prayers, hymns and invocations of Christ, hints of which are to be found in the letters of Paul.

Early in the history of the church there was a major crisis, which Luke felt deserved to be reported in full. The Jesus movement appears to have drawn supporters from both the native Aramaic-speaking Jews and the many Greek-speaking Jews, the Hellenists, some of whom would also have been permanent inhabitants of Jerusalem, their numbers swelled at the great feasts by Greek speakers of the diaspora. Within one of the synagogues of the Greek speakers, which appears to have catered specifically for freedmen (those who had been released from slavery), a dispute blew up over allegations that one of its members, an impressive speaker by the name of Stephen, had been preaching that Jesus would destroy the Temple and alter the Law. Such was the outcry that Stephen was hauled before the Sanhedrin.

In his speech, which Luke recorded in full, Stephen defends himself with a long survey of Jewish history in which he compares his audience to those who had persecuted prophets in the past. Now they have betrayed and murdered Jesus. The crucial moment comes when he claims to have a vision of Jesus standing at God's right hand. This elevation of Jesus was simply too much for those Jews outside the Jesus movement. Stephen was set upon and stoned to death. Luke reports that Paul (then known as Saul) was a participant in that he looked after the clothes of the assailants. It is possible that Paul, if he himself were the son of a freedman (see p. 49), would have attended this same synagogue and his zeal for persecution could have been aroused by his personal abhorrence of Stephen's views.

Stephen's death appears to have been the catalyst for an outbreak of persecution. Although the original apostles stayed in Jerusalem, many of their followers were scattered into the countryside. So began the missions outside Jerusalem. At first they were confined to Judaea and Samaria but then spread north, along the Phoenician coast to Antioch and across the water to Cyprus. Luke records that they preached only to Jews although he also records the story of a centurion called Cornelius, a Gentile but a friend of the Jews, who was converted by Peter in Caesarea (Acts 10). It is one of two instances; the other takes place in Antioch, where Peter appears to have crossed the traditional boundaries by consorting with Gentiles.

If one is searching for authority in the church in the 40s and 50s it remained with the original apostles and thus in Jerusalem. They had been chosen by Jesus in person and had an awareness of what he had taught that no outsider to the movement could ever acquire. They had experienced the agony of the crucifixion at first hand and maintained the movement for many years in an increasingly hostile environment. Their stance on circumcision and other traditional Jewish requirements was also understandable. They had only known Jesus as a practising Jew; there had been nothing in his teaching to suggest that the Law and its requirements should be abrogated or that Gentiles who converted to Christianity should be excused from them. The story of Cornelius suggests, however, that those Gentiles close to the Jews were now becoming interested in Jesus and so the issue of whether they could be excused ritual requirements was to become a live one.

In the 40s James, the brother of Jesus, emerged as the leader of the Jewish Christians. James has been overshadowed partly because in the Catholic tradition his mother is believed to have been perpetually virgin and thus a brother of Jesus was impossible. It is hard for a historian to sustain this view, although Mark suggests that James, along with his mother and siblings, was rejected by Jesus during his lifetime (at 3:31). James would have had the advantage of his family connection and knowledge of Jesus' life before his baptism by John and his status would have risen alongside that of his brother. Doubtless his own personality was important in keeping the movement intact. Peter may simply have been unable to cope with the pressures imposed on him, his own status diminishing as the earliest disciples began to die off or disperse. His ambivalence towards the Gentiles may also have lost him support. By the time Paul reaches Jerusalem for the last time, in about AD 59, Peter is no longer mentioned as a Jerusalem leader. Tradition has it, of course, that by this time he had migrated to Rome where he was to be martyred.

However, there is another report of Peter's presence – in Antioch. Antioch, the capital of the Roman province of Syria, was one of the finest cities of the eastern Mediterranean. On its coins it referred to itself as 'the capital of the east' and its Roman overlords had embellished it. It had always had a large Jewish population and some form of church, presumably based within the Jewish community, like that in Jerusalem, had become established there. In fact, Luke tells us that Antioch was the very first city where the term Christian was used.

It was here that there were outsiders drawn to the movement. Luke specifically notes natives of Cyprus and Cyrene. It was they who began spreading 'the good news of the Lord Jesus' to Gentiles (a reminder that Paul was not the only one doing this). So, perhaps for the first time on a significant scale, the movement had to confront the problem of the treatment of Gentiles. When Peter arrived in the city from Jerusalem, he found himself dealing face to face with the Gentile Christians. He began eating with them, once again crossing the boundaries of acceptable Jewish behaviour. Then a Jerusalem delegation arrived from James and they were furious at what they saw. Peter gave way under the pressure, much as he had done after Jesus' arrest, and broke off his relationship with the Gentiles.

One man who was watching the scene was outraged in his turn. He had met Peter before in Jerusalem and he saw his apparent rejection of the Gentile converts as an affront to them. 'Peter was clearly in the wrong', he recorded.

This was none other than the Paul whom we have already encountered in Jerusalem. He was now no longer a persecutor but a committed Christian who had dedicated himself to the mission to the Gentiles. Peter threatened everything he stood for. No wonder Paul, who was never one to keep his emotions to himself, 'opposed him to his face'.

CHAPTER FIVE

What Did Paul Achieve?

PAUL DOMINATES ANY HISTORY OF EARLY CHRISTIANITY. HE IS THE loner who made Christianity universal, the authoritarian who wrote in terms of the equality of all before God. He transformed the spiritual teacher of Galilee into the crucified and risen Christ. Yet it is impossible to write more than a fragmentary account of his life. The sources that survive, perhaps six or seven letters of the many he must have written, and the narrative of his activities in the Acts of the Apostles, are not full enough even to provide an accurate chronology. The context in which his letters were composed can only be guessed at and it is difficult to find a consistent theology in them. Even though there is a tradition which portrays Paul as if he were a detached scholar, his theology is deeply rooted in his frustrations. His personality was complicated and his relationships with others were often tempestuous. All this makes it challenging to provide a fair assessment of his achievement.[1]

As for many 'teachers' in the Greek world, Paul's fame meant that a variety of texts were later ascribed to him. Only seven of the so-called Pauline letters of the New Testament are now fully accepted as genuine: Romans, 1 and 2 Corinthians, Galatians, 1 Thessalonians, Philippians and the short Letter to Philemon. The earliest surviving letter, that to the Galatians, was probably written in AD 49; the most mature and influential statement of Paul's theology, the Letter to the Romans, in about 57 and his last surviving letter, to the Philippians in 61 or 62.[2] These letters provide direct evidence of Paul's responses to the Christian communities with whom he had contact. They are the primary sources for Paul's life and beliefs even if one can never know how representative they are of his total output. Although the personality of Paul keeps breaking through (in all its rawness in Chapter Four of 1 Corinthians or the Letter to the Galatians, for instance) and at times his eloquence reaches an intensity which places the letters among the finer literary achievements of the ancient world, they are steeped in the rhetorical conventions of his time. Historical accuracy may have been sacrificed to the self-dramatisation that was necessary to make an impact on his readers. As a documentary account of events they must be treated with caution.

The Acts of the Apostles, the second half of which features some account of Paul's travels and his encounters with the emerging Christian communities, was probably written some thirty years after the events it describes. Its author, Luke, may even have been a companion of Paul, or close to those who were, and he covers events in relative detail from between AD 50 and 60 when Paul arrives, under armed escort, in Rome. It is not known how many letters of Paul, if any, Luke himself had seen or whether he had seen others which are now lost to us. (There is not a single mention of Paul's letter writing in Acts.) Many scholars discount Acts as accurate history. It is certainly true that Acts is selective, many events are not clearly described and Luke may have created a much more harmonised life of Paul than the letters suggest. One estimate is that while Chapters One to Eight cover the events of three years, Chapters Nine to Twenty-eight stretch over twenty-five and concentrate on relatively few events within that time span. The tensions with the Corinthians, which play a major part in Paul's letters, are not mentioned in Acts at all. In short Luke never set out to provide a biography of Paul: rather his aim, if one takes the text as a whole, is to describe the progress of the gospel, highlighting the events which he believed contributed to this. Yet, there is a narrative that does outline journeys of Paul that can be traced on the map. Above all Acts provides a vivid picture of the struggle that Paul had with the communities he visited and the turbulence of his experiences fits well with the passion of the letters.

Even Paul's birth date can only be guessed at. Acts refers to Paul as 'young' at the time he began persecuting Christians in the AD 30s and his gruelling missionary journeys of the 50s suggest a man no older than his forties so the first decade of the century seems most plausible.[3] His background and education reflect the melting pot that the east had become. He was born, as a Jew, in Tarsus, a lively trading city that was capital of the Roman province of Cilicia. He may have absorbed, in his childhood or later, an education in rhetoric, including the effective writing of letters, and a smattering of Greek philosophy, above all Stoicism and, perhaps, Platonism. He was sent to study in Jerusalem at the school of the well-known teacher Gamaliel. He must have picked up Aramaic while he was living in Jerusalem but he later refers to himself as a Pharisee and this suggests that he had made a rigorous study of the Torah in the original Hebrew. Nevertheless his own use of scriptures in his letters always draws on the Greek version, the Septuagint.

It is hard to imagine a greater contrast in Jewish backgrounds than that between Paul and Jesus. Paul was a Roman citizen, brought up in a Greek-speaking city and at ease with urban life. He was well educated and aware of two competing cultures, Greek and Jewish. Jesus had no education other than what he had absorbed from the synagogue, his background was rural and remote from city life, and his region appears to have been untouched by the Greeks. Paul was never tolerant of others and was unlikely to have been able to grasp, or even be sympathetic to, the very different context of rural Galilean Judaism. Jesus' life and teachings simply do not figure in his letters and speeches.

Perhaps the most intriguing feature of Paul's background is his Roman citizenship. By this time the whole of the free population of Italy had been granted Roman citizenship and many Italians had migrated to the Greek east either as colonists (Philippi was an established colony of citizens, for instance), merchants or administrators. Roman citizenship among the native populations of the east, on the other hand, was still very rare. Citizenship could be granted to distinguished individuals, as it was for Josephus, the Jewish historian favoured by the Romans, but Paul would never have qualified on his own merits. However, it was a remarkable feature of Roman law that once a master freed his slaves their descendants acquired full citizenship. In all likelihood Paul was the son of a freedman, one released from slavery by a Roman master. When he was in Jerusalem he may even have attended the 'Synagogue of the Freedman' mentioned in Acts 6:7 – Jews from Cilicia are specifically mentioned as members of its congregation. His references to slavery, the coming of Christ for all, 'slave and free', and his support for Onesimus, the escaped slave on behalf of whom he writes to his owner Philemon, need to be read in light of this probability. To have an elevated position as a Roman citizen but only because one's father had been a slave left one in an ambiguous social position. Perhaps this explains why Paul so often felt himself an outsider.

Paul first appears in Acts as Saul. His name probably derives from Saul, the first king of Israel, the most prominent member of his tribe, that of Benjamin. It is under this name that he holds the coats of those stoning Stephen. His zeal for his Jewish faith has turned him into a vigilante ready to exploit the growing unease with the emerging Christian communities. He comes across as an outspoken and violent protagonist, something of a loner (there is no evidence that he ever married and he is puritanical about sex) and probably obsessive about the mastering of texts. It is a type one can recognise but no one could have predicted the way in which his life was to be transformed by Christ.

The dramatic moment of his conversion comes, perhaps in 34, on the road to Damascus, where Paul was planning to extend his campaign against Christians. Christ appears as if in a vision, berating Paul for his persecutions. All the accounts, in the letters and in Acts, date from more than twenty years later but they retain the abruptness of the event. 'I was apprehended by Christ Jesus,' as Paul puts it in Philemon. It is impossible to retrieve the psychological

50	BEGINNINGS

underpinnings of the conversion but a powerful and influential element of the experience as Paul reflects on it was that he, an undoubted sinner, perhaps already wracked with guilt, had been picked out for salvation. He equates his own vision of Christ with that of the apostles. Paul's seems a far-fetched, even contrived, interpretation but it was his confidence in his personal mission that was to drive his activities in the years to come. He believed that he was the agent through whom the divine plan would unfold.

The conversion of Paul did not involve a change from one religion to another. If Paul had not considered himself still a Jew he would never, as a Roman citizen, have submitted himself to Jewish floggings as he did, nor refer, in Galatians (3:28–9), to all believers in Christ as 'Abraham's offspring'. Although Paul's relationship with Judaism, and certainly with Jews, was to be tortuous, he remained a Jew who attempted to portray Christ as some kind of fulfilment of Jewish history, one which would extend beyond the Law and the requirements of circumcision and Jewish diet into the Gentile world. He believed passionately that the Second Coming was imminent and that it was possible to find a place for Gentiles in salvation. 'There is no longer Jew or Greek, there is no longer slave or free, there is no longer male or female; for all of you are one in Jesus Christ', as the famous passage in Galatians (3:28) puts it. In this he was venturing beyond the margins of conventional Judaism. He was in a theological no-man's-land and the boundaries between traditional Judaism, Jewish Christianity as it was emerging in Jerusalem and his own teachings remained without clear definition. It was an extraordinary position to be in, one which exposed Paul to ostracism from Jews and hardly ensured a welcome from more than a tiny minority of Gentiles.

Three years after his conversion Paul made a visit to Jerusalem to meet Peter and James. It must have been an uneasy occasion. Peter and James had unchallengeable status as the chosen companions of Jesus and founders of the movement in his memory. There was little role for an outsider in their circle, especially one who had persecuted Christians, other than as repentant disciple. Were they even able to communicate with each other in a shared language, let alone understand each other's perspectives? The Jerusalem apostles had known Jesus intimately as a human being; Paul could only contribute an apparent vision of Jesus as the Christ. Even if Paul did learn something of Jesus' life it made little impact on him. There is scarcely a reference in any of the letters to any of Jesus' teachings, other than, perhaps significantly, to his prohibition of divorce.

At some point Paul must have shifted his focus to the symbolic importance of Christ's death and resurrection. His psychological make-up may have been of crucial importance here. Paul identifies strongly with Jesus alone in agony on the cross, a reflection perhaps of his own isolation. Yet here was a theological impasse. Like other Christians Paul had to confront the problem of a messiah who had broken with conventional expectations of messiahship by dying. By the time he writes Galatians, Paul has transformed Jesus into a form of messiah who is radically different from the one expected. Rather than triumphing on earth through his majesty he had chosen to die because humankind was sinful (see Galatians 1:4, 2:20). He had risen to his Father in heaven, his humanity transformed in the process (see later Romans 1:3–4), but his return to earth was imminent.

This personal and deeply felt response by Paul did not gain him any standing with the Jerusalem Christians. He left after a fortnight. There is now a long gap in the record, from, say, AD 37, when he met the disciples in Jerusalem, to 48. It remains uncharted. Paul may have mastered his trade as tent maker, made incipient 'missionary' journeys or returned to Tarsus to further his education. He must have had some reputation by the end of the period as it was in his home city that he was tracked down by a fellow Christian, Barnabas, described in Acts as a Hellenised Jew from Cyprus, and taken to Antioch where he preached for a year. From Antioch Barnabas took Paul back to Jerusalem. Here an agreement was made with the apostles that he should preach to the Gentiles while they would continue to work only with the Jews. In return Paul agreed that he would collect offerings for the Jerusalem church. The desire to collect offerings is hard to explain but it can perhaps be seen as evidence of Paul's wish to keep some form of communication between the two worlds of Christianity, as they were in the process of becoming. Maintaining some form of relationship with the Jerusalem Christians was, after all, one of the few ways he could preserve some credibility as an apostle.

Now began Paul's missionary journeys. They were extraordinary in terms of the physical demands made on him. It is possible to reconstruct the day-to-day walks that the overland routes described in Acts (if these are accurate) would have required.[4] A single day's walk of over twenty, or even up to thirty, miles between cities was often unavoidable and this pace was kept up for days at a time. This was on unmade roads, some of them mountainous and beset with the dangers of brigands and wild animals. Paul must often have sought out caravans of traders for protection. Even when a city had been safely reached, Paul was often greeted at best with distrust and often hostility. There is little wonder that he has achieved a heroic status among his admirers. Yet, as the analysis of his journeys below will suggest, his strategy may have been misguided.

The problem lay in the task he set himself. Paul would always face opposition from a variety of groups. First there were traditional Jews – the Jews of the diaspora who were to be found in virtually every city of the east. They were deeply suspicious of the semi-divine status that Christians appeared to give to Jesus. For them he was not the Messiah and, in so far as Jesus himself may never have claimed to be, their stance was understandable. With his message to Gentiles, Paul also threatened to undermine the relationship between Jews and God-fearers (see p. 17) which was so crucial to the political and social survival of the Jewish communities. Then there were the Jewish Christians. Some had been scattered after the stoning of Stephen, others appeared to be undertaking missionary journeys of their own. Whatever agreement Paul thought he had made in Jerusalem it was hardly likely to be recognised elsewhere. He would often be in competition with the Jewish Christians for converts but their direct links to the original disciples would have given them an immense advantage.

Paul did not help himself. He boasts in an emotional outburst to the Corinthians (1 Corinthians 9:19–23) that he tries to be all things to all men, a recipe for confusion that can hardly have earned him any respect. He appears to have had a penchant for being provocative, stirring up unrest and this would often attract the attention of the city magistrates. It is no wonder that Paul describes how his travels were filled with imprisonments and beatings at the hands of Jews. As a result his stays in cities were often curtailed. In the Galatian cities he may have stayed no more than a few days.

This was hardly a strategy that could succeed. Paul claimed to be a Jew but he was extending Judaism into a new context in which the dominant force was now Christ and his imminent coming. What this meant for those who gave his movement their allegiance was not clear, perhaps even to Paul himself. When Paul said that Christ had transcended the Law, he left it unclear how 'his' Christians should behave without its restraining force. Paul craved acceptance as leader of an admiring community but, in practice, there were too many obstacles, the fluidity of his own beliefs and his own inability to establish effective leadership among them. In one of the most revealing passages in his Second Letter to the Corinthians (2 Corinthians 10:10) he records the criticism that has been made of him that he has no presence and is beneath contempt as a speaker.

Possibly in around AD 48, Paul is recorded as leaving Antioch in the company of Barnabas. Their initial stop as they travelled west from the Syrian coast was Cyprus, the home of Barnabas. He, rather than Paul, was taking the lead in this enterprise. Here they were summoned to the local Roman governor, the proconsul Sergius Paullus. Acts tells us that Sergius became a believer (after Paul struck a member of his retinue, a 'sorcerer', blind – a reminder that not all reported Christian miracles are benign) and it is just at this point that Luke replaces the name Saul by Paul in his narrative. The success of this meeting was crucial as it won Sergius' patronage for Paul's activities, a patronage that Saul, as he then was, repaid by adopting Sergius' *cognomen* (family name) as his own. It also explains why Paul and Barnabas ventured into Galatia when they landed from Cyprus. It would have made more sense to launch their mission in the cities of Pamphylia along the coast of Asia Minor. Instead, they headed to Pisidian Antioch, the hometown of Sergius' family, doubtless because they carried introductions from Sergius.[5]

The Galatians were Celts who had migrated to Anatolia in the third century BC and who had thrown in their lot with the expanding Roman Empire. The vast Roman province of Galatia had been established in 25 BC. Acts makes it quite clear that Barnabas and Paul only visited cities in the south – Pisidian Antioch, Iconium, Lystra and Derbe, where there were Roman, Jewish and Greek populations. They concentrated their teaching in the synagogues and on the Gentiles associated with them. Acts records intense Jewish opposition to their visits and, although it appears that Paul and Barnabas were able to set up small congregations under elders and visit each city twice, they may soon have been on their way back to Antioch.

It was in Antioch that the issue festering within the Christian communities broke into an open sore. It was quite natural for the early Christian leaders (of whom James, the brother of Jesus, was now dominant), to insist on circumcision for converts but it is likely that, faced with the knife and the isolation from fellow Gentiles that would follow if they practised Jewish dietary laws, most Gentiles baulked at conversion. Could the movement expand if it was not prepared to compromise on its principles? Even Acts, which plays down the conflicts within early Christianity, talks of 'much controversy' on the matter. Paul and Barnabas set off, as part of a delegation, to Jerusalem and it was here that James masterminded a plan that allowed Gentiles to convert so long as they refrained from meat offered in sacrifice and from fornication. The Jerusalem leaders appointed two of their own representatives, Silas and Judas, to pass the decision on to the community in Antioch. Paul and Barnabas accompanied them back to Syria.

It may have been soon after this that the visit of Peter to Antioch, which caused so much distress to Paul, took place. Barnabas joined Peter in submitting to the demands of the Jewish Christians that they withdraw from eating with Gentiles. We do not know how dependent Paul had become on his companion but it must have been a major blow. Worse was to come. News now reached Paul that the Galatian Christians he believed to be his own had been swayed by 'another gospel', none other than that of the Jewish Christians. One can hardly criticise them for this. Paul may have convinced some Galatians but they were probably still uncertain of what they were supposed to be convinced of, so when missionaries arrived also preaching Christ, but in the different context of Judaism, they must have been bewildered.

It was a personal crisis that shook Paul to the core. He was incandescent with rage at what had happened. Whether he wrote his Letter to the Galatians then or later, it is a fitting example of how his personal emotions, here an intense sense of rejection, drove his theology. There is a single commandment, Paul tells his recipients: 'Love your neighbour as yourself', yet his own letter was certainly not one that showed any love for 'you stupid Galatians'. It begins with a long-winded justification of his role as apostle, culminating in an extraordinary identification with Christ himself: 'I have been crucified with Christ: the life I live now is not my life, but the life which Christ lives in me' (2:20). This was a desperate, perhaps even blasphemous, claim and would have been deeply offensive to those Christians who had actually known Jesus while he was still alive. Imagine the shock to real-life witnesses to the crucifixion if they had read or heard this.

Paul was now forced to develop a theological justification for his conviction that Christ had brought a new era. He goes back to a promise from God that in Abraham 'all nations shall find blessing'. This, he argues, includes all Gentiles who have faith in Jesus Christ. They are now no longer subject to the Law, which was a temporary measure until the coming of Christ. He goes further: if the Galatians continue to observe the Law they will have cut their relationship with Christ; 'you will have fallen out of the domain of God's grace'. He goes on to outline the fruits of faith in Christ. Those who have faith have reached a higher level as a result of having 'crucified' their lower nature with its base passions, fornication, impurity, idolatry, selfish ambitions, drinking bouts and orgies. Now (Galatians 6:11) Paul grabs the pen from his scribe and finishes the letter himself. The reason why the Galatians are required to be circumcised, he claims, is only so that they have some outward sign of the numbers who have been converted! He ends with emotional black-mail: 'In future let no one make trouble for me, for I bear the marks of Jesus branded on my body.' How the Galatians received this letter is unknown. Were they cowed by it, did they ignore it as an emotional rant or did it simply deepen their confusion over what they were supposed to believe?

When Paul proposed that he should visit the Galatians again, he quarrelled with Barnabas over their choice of travelling companion and the friendship was finally broken. Instead Silas agreed to go with Paul. It was a sensible choice: Silas, an appointed representative of the Jerusalem church, enjoyed an authority Paul did not have and he would have been able to expound the agree-ment that had been made over Gentile conversion. So Paul set out again. In Lystra they came across a convert called Timothy, of mixed Jewish Christian and Gentile parentage whom Paul actually circumcised 'out of consideration of the Jews who lived in those parts'. It seems a direct contradiction of all he had told the Galatians but he could perhaps claim that Timothy was Jewish, rather than Gentile, by blood. It also made sense to enter synagogues, his initial port of call in most cities, only in the company of other circumcised Jews. Timothy now joined them and was to prove Paul's most loyal follower.

Clearly things were not easy in Galatia. Paul did not linger and Luke explains that 'the Spirit' forbade him to go into new areas such as Bithynia. Perhaps Silas, with his contacts with Jerusalem, felt that this was now Jewish Christian territory into which Paul should not intrude. They proceeded instead westwards through Asia Minor to reach the coast at Troas from where they took a boat across to Macedonia. Although Acts reports later visits by Paul to Galatia, there is no archaeological record of an early Christian community there. It is not until the third century that Christian activity in this area is attested and even then there is no evidence to link it to the activities of Paul.[6]

There was always the hope that new journeys would bring success. Silas, Paul and Timothy now arrived in Philippi, a Roman colony settled in the late first century BC by veterans of the Roman civil wars. Unlike in most cities of the east, Latin was the dominant language and the city was also distinct in having no Jewish community. Paul attracted a wealthy dye merchant by the name of Lydia who was baptised along with other women. Women were certainly easier to convert as the tricky question of circumcision could be avoided. Lydia welcomed the travellers into her household but the hospitality did not last long. Paul and Silas were hauled before the magistrates after complaints by the owners of a slave girl whose lucrative fortune-telling business had been quelled by Paul. They were beaten and imprisoned for a night before being released when the authorities discovered that they were Roman citizens. Paul may have found it difficult to advertise his status.

Philippi was on the Via Egnatia, the great Roman road built in 130 BC that ran across northern Greece. The next major city on the road was Thessalonica, capital of the Roman province of Macedonia, a thriving port whose position on the main road with access to the Danube basin to the north had made it the most prosperous city of the region. There was a mixed population of Romans and Greeks and also a large Jewish community. Once the travellers had arrived Luke records that Paul spent three successive Sabbaths preaching in the synagogue but here again resentment from the Jews was Paul's undoing. The Jews simply could not grasp how the risen Christ could be assimilated into Judaism. Although Luke records that Paul did make some conversions, the Jews hounded the trio out and then followed them to the neighbouring city of Beroea to interrupt their preaching there. For some reason the three now became separated and Paul is recorded as having taken a boat southwards to Athens on his own.

Anyone who had had even rudimentary contact with Greek culture would have known of the aura of Athens. Plato and Aristotle and a host of other great philosophers, playwrights, historians and others had debated here. If Paul's own acquaintance with Greek philosophy had been through the Stoics he would have known that the movement had been founded there and Stoicism was still strong in the city. Even though the powerhouse of Greek learning, in science and mathematics, was now Alexandria, Athens retained great prestige and still had influential patrons prepared to shower money on it.

Yet it was hardly fertile territory for Paul. The sophistication of its philosophers mingled with their arrogance towards outsiders. Luke records how Paul was exasperated by the mass of statues of gods he saw – idols, of course, to anyone raised as a Jew. Nevertheless, he was treated with some grudging respect and given a hearing before the Court of the Areopagus. One of the duties of this ancient court was to oversee new cults being brought into the city and Paul's individual teaching must have appeared to fall into this category. While in the city he had seen an altar inscribed 'To the Unknown God'. Ingeniously he argued that this was perhaps the same god that he preached – implying that he was not introducing anything new. Even though his speech as Luke records it is relatively sophisticated rhetoric, Paul's talk of a man being raised by God from the dead was hardly likely to convince trained intellectuals and he was widely scoffed at. When Paul denigrates the 'wisdom of the wise' in his letters, it may have been this humiliating experience that haunted him. He remained an outsider to the world of the Greek philosophers.

He was far better off in a city where there were marginal groups ready to give allegiance to new religious movements and he did not have to travel on far to find one. The ancient trading city of Corinth had long exploited its position on an isthmus as a crossing place for goods and boats wishing to avoid the tortuous voyage around the Peloponnese. The city had been sacked by the Romans in 146 BC before being reconstituted by Julius Caesar as a Roman colony. It had quickly regained its former prosperity and its port was one of the busiest in the empire. As a mixing bowl of nationalities and cultures, it provided Paul with the opportunity for a fresh initiative to make up for the disappointments he had suffered.

He was lucky to find a husband-and-wife team, Aquila and Prisca, who were, like him, tent makers. (This is the first mention of Paul as a tent maker. Even though it seems a rather low status job for one of such education, it must have provided him with a means of keeping his independence.) Aquila and Prisca were among those Jews who had been expelled from Rome by Claudius and there is circumstantial evidence that they might also have been freedmen. It is possible that another Corinthian Christian, Erastus, who rose to city treasurer, was a freedman.[7] In short, their relationship may have been cemented as much by a shared background as by shared skills. Certainly this was not a Christian community of high status. 'Few of you are men of wisdom, by any human standard; few are powerful or highly born,' was Paul's own assessment.

Corinth may have been the first city where Paul had an opportunity to preach over an extended period. (Acts suggests that he was there for eighteen months.) Timothy and Silas joined him. Again Paul encountered opposition from the Jews although when members of the community attempted to arraign him before the proconsul of the province, Gallio, the latter refused to respond. To him the arguments over Christ were a matter for Jews alone and he was reluctant to get drawn into the dispute. The down-to-earth Roman governors were well known for being exasperated by the intricate discussions so loved in the Greek east. Soon after this incident, Acts tells us that Paul, accompanied by Aquila and Prisca, left Corinth. As is so often the case in this story, one does not know the background; that the three left together may suggest some kind of division within the Corinthian community and their expulsion from it.

When Timothy had rejoined Paul in Corinth, he had reported on a visit he had made on his own to the Thessalonians. Earlier in Acts, Luke suggests that Paul had preached, unsuccessfully, in the synagogue there, but the converts whom Timothy had encountered do not seem to have been Jews at all. They are recorded as having turned from the worship of idols; in other words they had been pagans. They were also artisans and this suggests that Paul was seeking out marginal groups independent of the synagogues. Not having to worry about offending the Jews, Paul was able to express his frustrations in his First Letter to the Thessalonians. He tells them that the Jews have killed Christ and they have obstructed him in his contacts with the Gentiles. Now, he goes on, retribution has overtaken them. It is possible that Paul is referring to the expulsion of Jews from Rome by the emperor Claudius of which he will have learned from Aquila and Prisca, but there is also the record of a massacre of Jews by the Roman authorities in Jerusalem at this time. Paul's 'being all things to all people' is on display here in his condemnation of his fellow Jews. His hold on his communities was so fragile that it was an understandable, if distasteful, tactic for one seeking to strengthen his position against his Jewish adversaries.

Paul, soothed by Timothy's message that the Thessalonians had valued his teaching and respected him, mentions that he has been worried that they too would be seduced from allegiance to him by 'the tempter'. Reassured by Timothy of their loyalty, his letter is altogether more relaxed in tone than his impassioned outburst to the Galatians and perhaps reflects that for the first time, in Corinth, he enjoyed some form of psychological security. There was one major issue to address. The Thessalonians had taken on board Paul's preaching that the Second Coming of Christ was imminent, so imminent, in fact, that all would be alive to see it, yet some of the community had already died and the rest needed reassurance that all would be saved. The Second Coming, Paul tells them, will come to the unwary like a thief in the night and there will be no escape for those without faith. For believers such as themselves, on the other hand, night will not fall at all. They will always live in the light as they are destined by their faith for salvation. Their duty is to keep sober for the occasion. As elsewhere in Paul's writings, soberness is associated with sexual continence – lust is linked to paganism.

In the letter Paul explains that 'Satan' had thwarted him in his hopes of returning to Thessalonica. After leaving Corinth, he made passage back to Asia Minor. He landed briefly at Ephesus, left Aquila and Prisca there, and appears to have gone on to Jerusalem. He may have had money from his collection to deliver there. He eventually made his way back to Ephesus. This was another of the empire's most successful trading cities. Bequeathed to Rome by King Attalus III of Pergamum in 133 BC, it had become a major provincial centre, a focus for sea routes and the hub of important roads inland through Asia Minor. It was also the home of the great temple to Artemis to which pilgrims flocked from throughout the Mediterranean. Again the mix of nationalities and cultures offered opportunities for conversion. Paul seems to have used his customary tactic of preaching in the synagogue but again he aroused the opposition of the Jews. This time, however, he withdrew his own converts to a separate lecture hall and Acts records that he was able to preach safely for two years. Even now his success offended local interests and a local employer of silversmiths, Demetrius, stirred up the population against a man who threatened the lucrative trade in votive offerings. 'Great is Diana [the Roman equivalent of Artemis] of the Ephesians' became the rallying cry of the rioters. This time the authorities confronted the troublemakers and the city was calmed. However, Paul seems to have left Ephesus soon afterwards.

The short and attractive Letter to Philemon may have been written while Paul was in Ephesus, apparently in some form of custody. Philemon was a Christian, living probably in Colossae. His slave, Onesimus, had escaped and was, for some reason, in the same prison as Paul where Paul became dependent on him. In the letter Paul tells how he is sending back the slave but he pleads for Philemon to be compassionate to him. On one level this letter can be seen as evidence of Paul's desired church in which slave and free will live together as equal. However, Paul's sympathy may also reflect his own awareness of slavery, freedom from which had given him his status as a Roman citizen.

It was probably while Paul was at Ephesus that disturbing news arrived from Corinth. The community with which he had formed his closest links was that of Corinth and Paul felt sensitive about its loyalty. The fundamental weakness of his strategy had been cruelly exposed. It was one thing to talk of the passing of the Law and its replacement by faith in Christ but this provided no guidance in how to confront the everyday challenges of living together until Christ returned. A number of problems were reported to him. First the community had been fragmented by rival allegiances. Some had remained loyal to Paul, but others saw Peter as their mentor. There was now a third leader, one Apollos, an Alexandrian Jew.

Apollos had turned up in Ephesus before Paul had arrived there and Prisca and Aquila had heard him speak in the synagogue. He was a Christian who knew something of Jesus but Prisca and Aquila felt that they needed to give him further instruction. They then sent him on to Corinth. They had failed to foresee the impact he would have. He was clearly learned – it has been suggested, in fact, that he may have been a disciple of the Jewish philosopher Philo. His education would have included training in rhetoric so, whatever form his Christianity took, he would have been able to expound it with greater eloquence than Paul (who was to tell the Corinthians that he was himself no speaker). It is not surprising that Apollos created his own following in the fluid world of the early converts, especially among those who needed a more intellectually satisfying religion. He may, in fact, have been the first Christian preacher to bring Platonism into Christianity. Plato had argued for an intellectual elite who through years of dedicated study were able to transcend the material world with its desires and ambitions and it seems that it was just this approach that was at the core of Apollos' teaching.

Alongside intellectual divisions there were also reports of social fragmentation. It is not known how large the Christian community (if one could talk of such a clearly defined group) in Corinth was. Some reports suggest about forty, others perhaps a hundred. The group would have depended on wealthier householders to let them meet for their Eucharistic meals. The allocation of rooms within a Roman house reflected the status of those who entered there, where they would be received and eat, with more intimate friends welcomed further inside to the more private rooms. The Corinthian Christians were allocated places at table according to status with some being forced to eat outside the main dining room. As if this were not enough, Paul's injunction to love one another was reported to have degenerated into sexual immorality. A man had married his stepmother; another leader appeared to dress as a woman. It was exactly the kind of behaviour that most disturbed Paul.

Paul had communicated with them before but his 'First' Letter to the Corinthians is the earliest of these letters to survive. While Paul is upset about what he has heard of their behaviour, he has learned to be less denigrating of his recipients and more modest. He addresses the Corinthians as a community who can be brought back into harmony and avoids the bullying tone he had used for the Galatians. Their disputes should, for example, be resolved within the congregation and they should shun recourse to the pagan courts. He talks of the importance of the Eucharist as a memorial of Christ in which all must share equally. In Chapter Twelve, he tells how every kind of skill – healing, prophecy and teaching – can be brought together in the service of Christ just as the limbs and organs contribute to a single body. He was developing a vision of a church as a stable and self-governing community. It is also in this letter that he tells of his beliefs in the resurrection, the earliest Christian text to mention it in this context as the spiritual transformation of Jesus after the crucifixion.

There now follows one of his finest bursts of rhetoric: the hymn to charity, charity that transcends all other gifts. There is perhaps no other passage in his writings that has proved a more enduring inspiration than this and it has resonated through the centuries. Paul goes on to provide a blueprint for worship at which hymns, instruction, revelation and even ecstatic outbursts will be welcomed. However, it is only men who can contribute. Women have no licence to speak and must direct their concerns to their husbands at home. This stricture may, of course, have been aimed only at the Corinthian community but Paul's ambivalence towards women is obvious. While the logic of his theology requires that all male and female, slave and free, Jew and Gentile are welcome in the church if they purify themselves (1 Corinthians 6:11 (cf. Galatians 3:28)), he also appears fearful of a breakdown in social distinctions. Here is one of the most ambiguous of his legacies. Within fifty years male supremacy appears to have reasserted itself in the Christian communities but there remained an independent tradition in the third century church that Paul had taught that women had the right to teach and baptise.

At some point after this remarkable letter, Paul visited Corinth again. In his Second Letter to the Corinthians he describes this as a painful visit. His first letter had failed to produce the community living in loving harmony that he had hoped for. One individual in particular seems to have led the opposition to him. Another (lost) letter he wrote to the community had caused great offence. The first chapters of the Second Letter are deeply troubled and rambling, clearly the work of an individual in emotional turmoil. Paul seems overwhelmed with the burdens he is carrying and it is only the promises of Christ that sustain him. The anger with which he condemned the Galatians is replaced by a pleading tone in which he ask the Corinthians for acceptance of his weakness. This chastened Paul is understandably more attractive. Normally he was not a man who understood compromise but he now appears to understand that he must respond to the concerns of the Corinthians rather than impose his views on them.

However, in a separate letter, which was added later to Chapters One to Nine, Paul's emotional state is such that he appears close to breakdown. In a tone reminiscent of Galatians, he is back to a hectoring stance, full of self justification and the denigration of 'his' Christians for being led astray by others, just, he says, as Eve was seduced by the serpent. His rivals appear to have been Hellenistic Jews whose charisma depended on rhetoric and miracle working and Paul clearly feels outclassed by them. He threatens that when he returns to them he will show no mercy and that, somehow, they will see that he, and not other preachers, speaks through Christ. The air of desperation suggests that Paul knows he has lost his flock.

When he was on one of his visits to Corinth, Paul wrote his Letter to the Romans. (It is recorded as having been written at Cenchreae, the port of Corinth.) It is the only one he sent to a community of which he had no direct experience and, free of the tensions that characterised his letters to communities whom he knew, it allowed for a more systematic exposition of his theology. Perhaps he was trying to bring some coherence to his thoughts before he returned to Jerusalem with his collection and had to justify his views to the Jewish Christian community there. Not surprisingly in view of the bruises he had suffered at the hands of his opponents and recalcitrant followers, this letter is preoccupied with the weight of human sin. Everyone is subject to its stifling effect, even Jews who have observed the Law. God's proof of his own love for us is shown no longer through the Law but in the sacrifice of Christ on the cross. 'God did not withhold his own Son but gave him over for us' (Romans 8:32). Baptism is in the death of Christ and the possibilities of eternal life lie with his resurrection. The Law is now transcended and history has moved into a new phase in which all – including the Gentiles, of course – who show faith may be 'justified'.

No issue in Paul's theology has proved more intractable than understanding what Paul meant by 'righteousness' and 'justification through faith'. What did it actually mean to 'set right' as the Greek word Paul used implied? Had the death of Christ, and the freeing of the human race from sin, made those with faith 'justified' in the sense of being released into spiritual freedom? Did one actually have to do anything, good works, for instance, to stay in a state of 'justification' or was it a once and for all gift through the grace of God?

At Romans 6:15–19, Paul brings slavery to the core of the argument. Those who have been slaves to sin can now be redeemed by God through Christ and become slaves of righteousness instead. The word 'redeem' in Greek is the same term used when a slave's freedom was bought – and it is used in the Old Testament to describe the process by which God freed the Israelites from slavery in Egypt. The intensity with which Paul makes his argument is perhaps one instance where he writes from the heart. The personal experience of his family's freedom from slavery is expressed in his theology. When, at Romans 8:15, Paul writes, 'The Spirit [of God] you have received is not a spirit of slavery leading you back into a life of fear, but a Spirit that makes us sons, enabling us to cry "Abba! Father!" '; a personal sense of liberation is patent.

The Letter to the Romans was later to be taken up by Augustine and become one of the most influential documents in western history. Luther went so far as to suggest that 'this epistle is really the chief part of the New Testament, and truly the purest gospel', an astonishingly narrow approach to the totality of the scriptures. However, its impact at the time it was written is completely unknown.

After a stay of perhaps three months in Corinth, Paul returned to Asia Minor. He avoided Ephesus and headed instead for another major port of the region, Miletus, and it was here that he received a delegation from the Ephesian Christians. By now he was in a mood of deep foreboding. There is no evidence that he had ever convinced the Jews of his mission and he must have known that he would hardly have been welcome in Jerusalem where he probably had a collection to deliver. He did not expect to return alive from the city and he was pessimistic about the future of his missions. 'I know that when I am gone, savage wolves will come in among you and will not spare the flock.' His depression proved infectious. The Ephesians were in tears when they escorted him to his boat.

Paul had already talked to the Thessalonians of the retaliation being inflicted on Jews. This may well have referred to the increasing tension in Judaea. When Paul arrived in Jerusalem (c.58) the city was unsettled. The clumsy tactics of Felix, the procurator,† had exacerbated unrest. There had been massacres and these had fuelled the growing sense of Jewish nationalism which was to erupt in the disastrous rebellion of 66. The Jewish Christian community, still under the leadership of James, felt acutely vulnerable and they insisted that Paul went through the ritual of purification to allay the suspicion that his mission to the Gentiles involved a rejection of his Jewish identity.

This may have satisfied James and his followers but Paul was too well known for him to be left in peace. Even before the seven days of purification were over Jews from Asia had attacked him in the synagogue. A rumour that he had offended by bringing a Gentile into the Temple spread round Jerusalem and caused such turmoil that the centurion in charge of the city garrison intervened to rescue Paul. Further unrest followed when Paul spoke to the crowds. He was eventually brought before the Sanhedrin but here again there was confusion when he preached the resurrection of the dead. The Pharisees in the council supported him, the Sadducees opposed him. Sensibly the centurion, who now knew Paul was a Roman citizen, arranged for him to be taken down to Caesarea to be judged by Felix.

Luke provides a series of speeches in which Paul justifies his beliefs before Felix, Felix's successor, Festus, and Agrippa, a descendant of Herod whom the Romans had installed in a small kingdom to the north of Judaea. Paul became passionate and overheated but he said nothing that justified a charge against

† This title for the Roman governor had replaced the earlier one of praefector.

him. Festus, however, was forced to acquiesce to Paul's demand that he should be able to appeal direct to the emperor in Rome. In what is one of the best descriptions of a voyage in the ancient world, Luke describes the tortuous journey across the Mediterranean that followed. Paul was imprisoned in Rome and may have suffered martyrdom there although some traditions (a hint in the First Letter of Clement, for instance) suggest that he was released and able to travel as far west as Spain before returning to Rome to his death, possibly in the persecutions of Nero. Luke's abrupt conclusion to Acts leaves the question open.

In custody in Rome, Paul seems to have found some kind of emotional peace. It may have been the support of Christians in the city that calmed him. Perhaps his imprisonment for his beliefs gave him the respect among them that he craved. He may simply have felt relieved to be away from the tensions of the Greek east which had done so much to distress him. It was probably now that he wrote the Letter to the Philippians, the most irenic of his writings.

The community in the Roman colony of Philippi does not seem to have been disturbed by conflict with traditional Jews. Paul feels confident about its prospects. He assures them that Christ can be preached in many ways, a much more mature attitude than he had expressed in earlier letters. 'You must work out your own [sic] salvation in fear and trembling; for it is God who works in you, inspiring both the will and deed, for his own chosen purpose' ([Letter to the] Philippians 2:12–13). Christ is now the example of good living. For those who believe in Christ circumcision is spiritual, not a physical mutilation. He talks too of his own spiritual journey that is not yet complete. Again, as with the First Letter to the Corinthians, one can warm to Paul in a way which is difficult with his more intemperate letters. The second part of the letter is somewhat darker in tone: Paul warns of 'the dogs' who insist on circumcision, for instance, but one is relieved that he ended his life with a sense of achievement.

Paul's immediate legacy is difficult to assess. It is not known how many of his communities survived and whether any of them had access to a coherent statement of his theology. Did anyone, except possibly a few Roman Christians, read the Letter to the Romans, for instance? Only those able to read Greek would have been able to read them in any case. (Astonishingly, no Latin speaker is known to have read them in the original until the fifteenth century.) All the major centres of the early church – Jerusalem, Antioch, Alexandria and Rome – were established independently of him. In the fourth century when churches developed histories of their foundation by an apostle or evangelist (Rome and Antioch by Peter, Alexandria by Mark), none claimed Paul as their founder. Yet some memory of Paul's missions persisted. When Clement, bishop of Rome, wrote to the Corinthians in the 90s, it was to a community that was still squabbling. Clement urged them to reread the letter (only one is mentioned) sent to them by Paul. Polycarp, the bishop of Smyrna, writing in about 117 to the Philippians reminds them that he himself did not have the wisdom of Paul, the man who had taught them the word of truth and had written them letters (*sic*) which strengthened their faith.

The Acts of the Apostles must have consolidated Paul's memory. It is not known how and where copies circulated but it has been argued that it acted as the catalyst for the collection of Paul's letters.[8] By this time, others were writing in his name. The letters to the Ephesians, Colossians, Hebrews, a second letter to the Thessalonians and letters to Timothy and Titus, which are part of the New Testament, were all attributed to Paul, a sign that his status was recognised by some followers. Yet his legacy remained an ambiguous one. What is remarkable is the number of early Christian writers, the gospel writers and the early church fathers, who do not appear to have been influenced by Paul's writings at all. They were clearly contentious. In the Second Letter of Peter, written in about 140, the author notes that there are obscure passages in Paul 'which the ignorant and unstable misinterpret to their own ruin' (2 Peter 3:16). When, very much at the same time, Marcion, the first great enthusiast for Paul, attempted to create a canon of texts, an early New Testament as it were, of a single gospel and Paul's letters, the attempt failed. The declaration that Marcion was a heretic (see p. 136) did nothing to boost Paul's position nor did Marcions links to the gnostics whose teachings the church condemned. It was not until the late fourth century, as a result of the adulation of John Chrysostom in the Greek-speaking world and Augustine in the Latin, that Paul became fully integrated into the Christian tradition. Even so, he has inspired radically different Christian responses. Is he the conservative champion of an austere moral absolutism or the man who urged the breakdown of all conventional hierarchies? Did he ever resolve the conflict between the revolutionary nature of his message and his personal abhorrence of social disorder? How far, in practice, did his teachings create a Gentile Christianity which would never have evolved without them?

Paul shifted the focus from Jesus' teachings, of which he said virtually nothing, to the drama of his crucifixion and resurrection. He demanded an emotional commitment to Christ that required a rejection of worldly interests, the temptations of the flesh and even 'the wisdom of the wise'. In the contexts of his belief that the Second Coming was at hand this was understandable. But the Second Coming did not come and Paul became something completely different. His letters, which had been received piecemeal by their recipients, were brought together as if they were to define Christian living for all time. The results were not always healthy. The rejection of 'the wisdom of the wise' easily led to an assault on reasoned thought. His concerns over sexuality fed into paranoia about the lures of women and the 'evils' of homosexuality. The stress on sin might be developed into a denigration of human nature. Paul's own ambivalence towards his Jewish background fuelled anti-Semitism.

Paul cannot be blamed, of course, for the ways in which his letters were separated from their original context and used by Christians for other purposes. Tortured as they often are, they stand on their own as fine literature and impressive examples of ancient rhetoric. At its most passionate, their eloquence is remarkable. So one can never wish Paul had never happened. The greatest regret must be that his letters are such isolated survivals. Christianity would have been dramatically different if we had, for instance, fuller records of Jewish Christianity. There might never have been the antagonisms between Jew and Christian that were already in place by the second century. We would have benefited immensely from the survival of some of Apollos' speeches (although the Letter to the Hebrews may reflect some of his ideas.) Apollos may have preached only to an intellectual elite, in the tradition of Plato, but a more reasoned theology would have provided a useful contrast to the impassioned and highly emotional rhetoric of Paul.

Paul will always remain controversial and enigmatic. He was heroic in his endeavours but hardly attractive as a personality. Puritans seldom are. In a comparatively rare moment of insight (2 Corinthians 12:20), he recognised the bitterness and confusion he could bring to those he visited. Even the loyal Timothy seems to have been rejected for failing to live up to his mentor's expectations. The arrival of his letters must have been dreaded. No one could be quite sure what he would demand next or what idiosyncratic interpretations he might make of scripture or the message of Christ. They were, after all, personal to him and not part of an established tradition. For those who were attuned to the apostles who had actually known Jesus, his authority must have been suspect and his apparent vision of Christ hardly comparable to their eyewitness testimony. Yet, there have always been Christians – Augustine and Luther are good examples – who remain intrigued by Paul even to the extent of appearing to give his letters precedence over the gospels. They are the theologians who have given Paul the prominent place in Christian tradition which he occupies today.

CHAPTER SIX

The Letter to the Hebrews

THE LETTER TO THE HEBREWS IS ONE OF THE MOST FASCINATING documents of the New Testament. The story of its eventual inclusion in the canon is absorbing in itself. It was known to Clement, bishop of Rome in the mid 90s and by later Romans such as Justin Martyr in the mid-second century. By 200 it was being used in Egypt and North Africa under its present title, 'Letter to the Hebrews' (and this is the title attached to the oldest surviving manuscript). The author was unknown and in the mid-third century the theologian Origen suggested that only God knew who wrote it. Despite its widespread use, Hebrews is not to be found in the Muratorian Canon, the earliest surviving list of 'canonical' texts, of c.200. It only came to renewed prominence in the fourth century when its theology of an elevated Christ proved useful to those defending the Nicene cause. It was then given added status by Jerome and Augustine by being attributed to Paul and so eventually it became an accepted part of the New Testament.[1]

For a thousand years after Augustine the weight of his 'scholarly' approval and the natural conservatism of the church were such that Paul's authorship went unquestioned, but any independent reader could see that the attribution was false. The author says clearly that his message was 'attested to us by those who heard' while Paul always claimed direct communication from Christ ('Christ lives in me', Galatians 2:20). The resurrection, a key feature of Paul's theology, is mentioned only once in passing (Hebrews 13:20). Its major theme of Christ as high priest occurs nowhere in Paul. The Greek itself is much more sophisticated and polished than Paul's. Martin Luther attributed the letter instead to the intellectual Apollos and there have been modern scholars who have supported him. Others have suggested Barnabas or Silas although none of these attributions can be conclusive. Even if Paul was not the author, the letter's concentration on the symbolic importance of Jesus' suffering rather than on any details of his life suggests someone following in Paul's footsteps.

Whatever its source, Hebrews is perhaps the most elegant and coherent exposition of theology in the New Testament. Only the gospel of John rivals it in sophistication. It may also be quite early. One of its themes is the way in which Jesus Christ has superseded the traditional priesthood and sacrificial worship at the Temple. It would be expected that the author would have hammered home the point by referring to the destruction of the Temple by the Romans in AD 70 if he was writing after then. There are no more than a few hints that the writer knew of any gospel material or the events of Jesus' life beyond his suffering (there may be two allusions, 6:6 and 13:12, to the cruci- fixion) so it is plausible to conclude that Hebrews was a text written later than Paul but earlier than the gospels, which is why it is discussed here.

The audience of the letter is also unknown but its early presence in Rome and a reference to 'greetings to you from our Italian friends' (13:24) suggest the city as one possible destination. It might even have been a follow-up to the same community that had received Paul's Letter to the Romans. Jerusalem too has been suggested, perhaps to a community of Hellenist Jews who shared the views of the martyred Stephen. There is the same emphasis on setting the coming of Christ against the Jewish past that one finds in Stephen's speech to the Sanhedrin.

Those who attribute the letter to Apollos assume that Apollos was a pupil of Philo, the most distinguished Jewish philosopher of his day, in Alexandria and that evidence of Philo's thought can be found in the letter. Philo had been born into a wealthy family in Alexandria in about 20 BC and probably died in the late 40s AD.[2] He was brought up on the Septuagint in the local synagogues but he was also able to immerse himself in the Greek philosophy of the day. No other Jew of his time was so learned in the many currents of intellectual thought which derived from Plato, the Stoics and even the writings of Pythagoras (who was seen as more of a mystic than a mathematician). Philo was remarkable in that he absorbed this learning without compromising the basic tenets of his faith, the belief in one supreme creator god, the importance of the Law and the traditional Jewish requirements of diet and circumcision. In his *Commentaries* on the Jewish scriptures, Philo applied sophisticated Greek exegetical methods to the Pentateuch. He knew when to interpret a passage literally and when to recognise it as an allegory for some deeper spiritual truth. This allowed him to maintain a living and flexible faith.

The most profound influence on Philo was the fourth century BC Athenian philosopher Plato. Plato taught that the material world here below is a pale imitation of the more 'real' immaterial one above. There is a hierarchy of exis- tence surmounted by an overriding divine force, 'the One'. Philo equated 'the One', the transcendent entity which stood at the hierarchy of all things mate- rial and immaterial, with the God of Judaism. The prophets, he believed, had already understood this and Plato had picked up their beliefs and transformed then into his own philosophy. 'Who is Plato but Moses speaking Greek?' as Philo put it. So, for Philo, Greek philosophy was derived from a Judaism that contained the true ancient wisdom. Philo developed an elevated concept of God. 'He is better than virtue, better than knowledge, better than the Good itself and the Beautiful itself.' In fact, he is so far removed from all earthly existence that there is little a mere human mind can say about him. Philo is the earliest-known source of the so-called apophatic approach that was to become popular in later Christian mysticism – God is unknowable, unnameable and totally incomprehensible. Even Moses, said Philo, had grasped little more of God than that he existed. Philo was to prove essential to those Christian theologians who were faced with the challenge of reconciling the emotional and volatile conception of God of the Old Testament with the 'One' of Plato.

For Philo, as with Plato, the world of the flesh and the world of the spirit were totally distinct but God had to find a means of communicating with the material world. Plato had argued that there were a number of different levels of being between 'the One' and the material world, eternal Forms or Ideas that existed on an immaterial plane, 'above' the world of material things. One of these Forms was *logos*, which Philo considered occupied a vital intermediate position between God and the material world. *Logos* is a complex term and the English translation 'the Word' gives little of the breadth or philosophical depth of the Greek original, which includes the idea of rational thought itself. However, new meanings of *logos* were continually being developed. By the time of Philo, Platonists were using the term to suggest the image or shadow of God while the Stoics saw *logos* as a force that acts on the material world. Philo takes this up in his *Commentaries*: 'The *Logos* is an ambassador and suppliant, neither unbegotten nor begotten as are sensible things.' Philo goes on to describe *logos* as a commander or pilot but he uses the term so extensively that it often seems to be a creative force in its own right, akin even to a second form of divinity. In some passages, he refers to *logos* as if it were an entity through which human beings could communicate with God.

Although he never knew Jesus, Philo opened the way for the transmission of Jewish and Greek thought into Christian theology, for which he was revered by later Christians. 'Magnificent in his language and broad in his thoughts, lofty and reaching the heavens in his views of the divine scriptures' was the accolade bestowed on him by Eusebius in his *History of the Church* (2:18). He is often credited with the ideas behind the opening verses of John's gospel but there are hints of Philo in Hebrews that are earlier. So at Hebrews 4:12–13, we read: 'The word [*logos*] of God is living, active, and sharper than any two-edged sword. It can penetrate to divide even soul and spirit, bone and marrow, and it can discern the thoughts and intents of the heart. The creation is not hidden to it; everything is naked and exposed to its eyes.' This is close to

Philo's conception of the *logos*. Again, in Hebrews there is a sharp distinction between heaven and earth, body and spirit, much in the way described by Philo. There are moments when we find a material entity, the sanctuary with the Ark of the Covenant in it (at 8:5) or the Law, for instance, described as a shadow of what is above, again an echo of Philo's Platonism. However, Philo never contemplated a spiritual force so dynamic and universal in its impact as the Christ of Hebrews so that Apollos, if he was indeed the writer, has ranged far beyond his mentor. If, however, one assumes a writer who had read Philo, or even studied with him, perhaps at a superficial level, as Apollos may well have done, then the similarities make sense.[3]

Something of the history of the community for which Hebrews was written can be gleaned from the text. At first it appears to have been made up of Jewish Christians whose beliefs were containable within Judaism. However, they then ran into trouble. There is talk of their property being confiscated and their members being thrown into prison, some kind of official reaction to their beliefs (echoes of a persecution by Nero in Rome?). Now they enjoy a more stable phase but threats remain – they are still abused by their opponents and commitment has fallen off as so often happens in communities that have reached a second generation. The aim of the writer of Hebrews is to pull the community back together by reminding them just how radical a change Christ has brought to the world and how dire the consequences might be if they slid back. Without denigrating their Jewish heritage, the writer emphasises that Christ has wholly superseded it. The rhetorical style of Hebrews suggests its origins as a sermon that was later modified into a letter.

Hebrews is a carefully argued text, certainly very different from those more disordered letters of Paul where emotion often gets the better of the writer. It starts with the assertion that, while in former times God spoke to humanity in fragments and with a variable message (an interesting perception in itself), he now speaks though the Son 'whom He has made heir to the whole universe, and through whom He created all orders of existence'. There are echoes here of the creation of Wisdom in Proverbs (8:22–31) where Wisdom is given an elevated status as the creation of God. The letter continues with the argument that 'the Son', having suffered on earth, is now in heaven and higher than the angels. The message is well put at 2:9: 'In Jesus we do see one who for a short while was made lower than the angels, crowned now with glory and honour [i.e. now above the angels] because he suffered death, so that, by God's gracious will, in tasting death he should stand for us all.' Jesus has come to earth, been tempted and suffered on behalf of humanity and then, as a result of this suffering, been elevated to the right hand of God. He provides the focus for the hopes of all his followers. The letter appears to accept that the kingdom will not come on earth but one will have to enter 'through a veil' (6:20) to reach Christ in heaven. (This distinction between the two worlds, here separated by a veil, is typical of Philo's terminology.) Hebrews is interesting on the humanity of Jesus. He is equal to us in all except sin and it is his humanity that allows him to be merciful and compassionate. His weakness allows him to bear with the ignorant and those who err (5:1–2). There is no mention of a Jesus born without sin; the implication is rather that the sinlessness was as a result of his resisting temptation and of his own suffering.

At 2:17 the idea of Jesus as a high priest is introduced, one which will be developed throughout the letter. In every way, however, Jesus had superseded the early Jewish leaders, Moses and the high priest Melchizadek. Melchizadek was a priest who blessed Abraham on his way back from battle and has been found, in a Qumran text, among 'the congregation of Gods'. He had apparently no father or mother or ancestry and he was perceived in some way as 'a priest for all time'. Here the author of Hebrews seems to be drawing directly on Psalm 110 where Melchizadek is referred to in a similar way. Jesus is the heir to the tradition of Melchizadek. The contrast is made with those priests of the tribe of Levi who are descended from the first high priest, Aaron. While the latter need to make continuous sacrifice in the Temple, 'the Son' as the successor of a different line, the eternal Melchizadek, has made the one sacrifice, his death on earth, which is sufficient to last for ever. Unlike the earthly high priest, Jesus is in heaven itself and is able to intercede continuously with God for his people.

The letter then discusses the traditional covenant between God and the Jews. It has proved faulty (8:7) and, moreover, it is based in an earthly sanctuary, the Temple. A new covenant has come with Christ and this is beyond the material world. While the sacrifices of bulls and goats, the traditional offerings at the Temple, can never remove sins, the once-and-for-all sacrifice of Christ can and has achieved it for those who believe. 'The blood of Jesus makes us free to enter boldly into the sanctuary by the new, living way which he has opened for us through the curtain, the way of his flesh' (10:19–20). All in the community must join in its meetings and encourage each other in love and active goodness, all the more so because the Day of Judgement is near. Here the writer becomes less irenic. Those 'who wilfully persist in sin after receiving the knowledge of the truth' will be consumed by the fire waiting for all God's enemies (10:26). At the end of Chapter Ten, the writer reminds the community of their endurance in days of persecution and urges them to maintain their confidence.

Now comes a meditation on faith. 'Faith', we are told in a highly influential verse, 'gives substance to our hopes, and makes us certain of realities we do not see' (11:1). A list follows of the occasions when faith has been shown by the Jews of old: Abraham's faith that he would find the land promised him and his heirs; Noah's faith that he would be saved by building the Ark; Sarah's faith that she would conceive. If these witnesses could show faith even before Jesus had come to earth, then surely the followers of Jesus, who have experienced his presence among them, should show their own faith in him.

There follows an exhortation to the community to live lives of moral worth. The community no longer stands before the fire of Sinai, with the darkness, gloom and whirlwind, but before Mount Zion and the city of the living God, heavenly Jerusalem. A few precepts for everyday living are spelled out, the loving of one's fellow Christians, the giving of hospitality, the honouring of marriage, the remembrance of those imprisoned, the disregard of material wealth, and obedience to leaders. The community must accept, however, that it is without a permanent home while on earth. It is outside the gates, just as Jesus was when he suffered (this may be a hint of the crucifixion but the sacrifices at the Temple also took place 'outside the gates' so this may be the allusion).

The Letter to the Hebrews is important because it shows how worship of Jesus was developing, some thirty to forty years after his crucifixion, in communities that appear never to have read any of the gospels. The letter originates somewhere between the Jewish and Hellenistic worlds; concepts from the philosophical ideas of each are included. Yet it is one of the earliest documents to provide a theological justification for the replacement of the Old Covenant by the New. There were many priests who were mortals and who represent the Old Covenant; Christ, in contrast, is the one high priest who lives for ever. The mortal priests made their offerings, the sacrifice of animals, on a daily basis; Christ has made one sacrifice – himself. They lived in the material world; he dwells continually with God in heaven as the representative of the New Covenant. The letter has a theological sophistication and coherence which is greater than anything to be found in the genuine letters of Paul. It is a vivid reminder of how mature the Christian communities had become in their worship even before the writing of any known gospel.

CHAPTER SEVEN

Fifty Years On

THE GOSPEL WRITERS REFLECT ON JESUS

THE YEARS 66 TO 70 WERE TRAUMATIC ONES FOR THE ROMAN Empire. The emperor Nero had become increasingly unbalanced and when a revolt broke out against him in Gaul in 68 he panicked and committed suicide. In the power struggle that followed, three emperors came and went before an experienced but relatively unknown army officer, Vespasian, commander of the troops in Judaea, now in revolt against Roman rule, declared himself emperor with the support of the governor of Egypt and the Balkan legions. In 70 Vespasian set off for Rome, leaving his son Titus in charge of Judaea and it was Titus who brought the revolt there to a bloody end with a major sack of Jerusalem. The desperate defenders, some still clinging to the hope that God would intervene to save them, fought back and the slaughter was immense. Josephus tells of bodies piled around the altar, many consumed in the flames and others sliding down the steps in rivers of blood. Whatever his original intention, Titus had no alternative but to describe the sack as the planned culmination of a victorious campaign. His triumphal arch, the booty from the Temple depicted on its reliefs, still stands in Rome.

The shock waves must have reverberated among the Jewish communities of the empire. In the splintering of Judaism that followed, the Jewish Christian movement was scapegoated. This was the moment when the original Jewish core of the Jesus movement began to disintegrate and in this sense the sack of Jerusalem provides a watershed in the history of Christianity. The community's position in Jerusalem had been vulnerable before the revolt – its leader James had been stoned to death in 62. There is a record that in the last years of the 80s Rabbi Gamaliel II introduced the Test Benediction that excluded 'Nazarenes' and other heretics from the Jewish synagogues. (This may be the expulsion referred to in John 9:22 but the impact of the Benediction, how far it extended and even its actual date, is not clear.) While the traditional view that Christians and Jews began to form distinct, even antagonistic, communities from this period onwards has been challenged, Christians were consolidating their own memories of Jesus in a form, the gospel, which was to prove so popular that at least twenty were eventually written.

Forty years on from the crucifixion, the needs of the Christian communities, as they had now become, were very different. Forty years was a long time in the ancient world because life expectancy for most was so much shorter. Any preserved evidence of Jesus' teachings would have passed on through more than one generation in this time. The imminence of a Second Coming appeared to be receding and a more reflective study of the role and status of Jesus was possible.

It is difficult to place the gospels within the literature of the period. In the wider Greek world there was a well-established tradition of writing history and biography that can be traced back to Herodotus in the fifth century BC. The Greek historians were preoccupied with the problems of discussing their sources and providing a narrative whose events were backed by reasoned thought. It was the historian's duty to present an accurate record and show where distortions were likely. The gospel writers made no such commitment. There is only the odd occasion, the prologue to Luke's gospel and John 19:35, where the writer speaks of the trustworthiness of an eyewitness, that the writer comments on his sources. In short, the gospel writers appear to have worked outside the literary culture of the Greek elite. In his *Antiquities* (20:263–4), Josephus mentions that the training in Greek poetry and prose, which he put himself through before he began writing his histories, was virtually unknown in the Jewish culture of his day. This may be to our advantage because a conscious attempt to follow a literary model is likely to lead to the shaping of the evidence to fit the model. One only has to note how far later martyrdom accounts and hagiographical lives of saints actually distorted historical events to make the point. It is perhaps better that the gospel writers worked outside Greek examples.

The gospels were designed to be read aloud. While it has been estimated that 10 per cent of the population of the Roman Empire had some literacy, it would probably have been much lower among the first Christian communities. Transmission of the texts would have been through the readings in the synagogues, a model which one can assume Christian communities followed. The constant repetition over years of the Hebrew scriptures would have embedded them in the minds of the listeners so that Matthew, for instance, would have known that his own audience of Christian Jews would recognise his references to Isaiah and other texts. It is possible, and the case has certainly been made for Mark, that the gospel was composed to maximise its dramatic effect.[1] The evidence suggests that in the early church each congregation would have had its own gospel – exposure to all four might not have been typical until at least the end of the second century.

None of the gospel writers felt it necessary to name themselves. The earliest unequivocal linking of name to gospel is that by Irenaeus in about 185. Irenaeus was anxious to consolidate a single Christian tradition around a limited number of written texts, among which he selected four of the surviving gospels. Each of the four was given an author alongside a line from its beginning so that we know for sure that the gospel Irenaeus attributed to Mark is the same as the gospel we call Mark. Irenaeus' concern was to link the authoritative texts as closely as possible to the apostles themselves so it is likely that his choice of authors – two apostles, Matthew and John, and the companions or secretaries to two more, Mark (Peter) and Luke (supposedly the companion of Paul) – reflect this. There is no other evidence that securely links any of the gospels to their named writers.

Mark

One can, indeed, take the case of Mark as an example of the problems this leaves. Mark was a common name in the ancient world and there are Marks referred to in the Acts of the Apostles. One, John Mark, appears as the son of a Jewish Christian by the name of Mary who was a member of the Jerusalem community. He travelled to Galatia with Paul and Barnabas but fell out with them and returned home to Jerusalem. Later Paul refused to have anything more to do with him but a Mark, the cousin of Barnabas, is mentioned favourably in Colossians (4:10), a letter attributed to Paul but probably not by him, as a Jewish Christian. Then there is 'my son Mark' referred to in 1 Peter 5:13. One could make a composite Mark from these references. He was a cousin of Barnabas, a Jewish Christian who lived in Jerusalem, travelled briefly with Paul, broke with him and then became closely associated with Paul's rival, Peter. To add to these sources, the second-century writer Papias (c.120–30) recorded a Mark who was secretary to Peter (and so who may have been the same Mark talked of in 1 Peter 5:13). Papias had heard from an elderly Christian informant that Mark had taken down Peter's sayings but not in order. Peter 'used to adapt his instructions to the needs of the moment but not with a view of making an orderly account of the Lord's sayings'. Papias goes on to suggest that Mark's account is rather lengthy – 'he made it his aim to omit nothing he had heard'. This is just what one might expect from Peter, a man of little education but brimming, of course, with powerful memories, contributing his reminiscences to a devoted scribe.

However, is the gospel that Irenaeus attributed to Mark the same text as the one Papias refers to? There are good reasons to think not. Irenaeus' Mark wrote in Greek and, as suggested earlier, it is unlikely that Peter would have spoken Greek well enough to contribute coherent material in the language.

Mark's gospel is a tightly organised narrative with an overall theme and important sections of it list miracles, deeds rather than sayings (in contrast to Q and the Gospel of Thomas, for instance) – an important distinction. Mark does not give precedence to Peter and, in fact, speaks negatively of him. Would Peter really have passed on the information that Jesus called him 'Satan'? (8:33) And if Mark had really been so close to Peter would he have repeated the rebuke in his own narrative? There appears to be nothing other than the name Mark to bring the two documents together. The tragedy is that Papias' document was lost; how much our knowledge of the historical Jesus would have been enlarged if Peter's own reminiscences had survived.

If one turns to the gospel Irenaeus attributed to Mark, presumably in the mistaken belief that he was linking the gospel directly to Peter, what can one say about its author? He was a Greek speaker but not a polished writer in the language. There is not a hint that he knows anything about the culture of the Greek pagan elite. His world seems close to that of the Jewish diaspora where Greek would have been learned naturally but without the influence of the sophisticated world of the philosophers. His Jewish heritage is confirmed by his knowledge of the Old Testament but his muddled knowledge of the geography of Palestine suggests a background outside the area and thus some- where in the diaspora. The date of the gospel is usually placed between AD 65 and 75 but there are indications that the writer knows of the fall of Jerusalem (13:2 where Jesus predicts the Temple's destruction) and so a date soon after 70 seems more likely.

So where might Mark be writing? His audience knows Jewish religious terminology but needs Aramaic words and Jewish customs explained to them (7:2). They would appear to be a Greek-speaking community associated with Judaism but not full members of it. Mark also uses some Latin terms, *praeto-rium* (which can mean either the governor's palace or the command centre of a legionary fort), and Latin words for flogging, measures and coins. Bearing in mind that Mark's text circulated and was used by Luke and Matthew, who were probably both based in the east, one might suggest Syria. The Latinisms support this. There were no legions in Asia Minor or Greece but between two and four, at different periods, in Syria. The practice was for legions to buy their provisions from the local community so that Roman coins and measures would have become known among the native population, as would the word legion, its headquarters, the *praetorium*, and doubtless the Latin word for flogging which Mark uses.[2]

While for centuries Mark has been the most neglected of the gospels, there is now greater appreciation of its underlying sophistication which, of course, further undermines the argument that it is a disorganised series of eyewitness memories from Peter. While Mark may not have been highly educated, he deserves credit for bringing together what he had heard about Jesus – baptism by John, a narrative of a period of teaching and healing followed by the journey to Jerusalem and his Passion and death – into a distinctive form. The highlighting of Jesus' baptism and the Passion probably reflects the importance of baptismal and Eucharistic ceremonies in the Christian communities; their origins needed to be given special focus. His message is shaped towards his community who appear to be suffering for their faith and in desperate need of reassurance. Mark presents Jesus as the supreme example of one who has gone through suffering but who ultimately triumphs. Although the gospel remains rooted in the very real concerns of first-century Galilee, Mark provides the first, not always very confident, steps towards defining a universal role for Jesus based on the events of his life.

For Mark, Jesus signifies a new phase in world history. From the start Mark treats him as an exalted figure, no less than the Son of God. This title, as used by Jews, does not suggest divinity, but rather that he is one uniquely favoured by God. Later Peter recognises Jesus as the Messiah (8:30). Again, at this stage this does not imply divinity. In fact, Jesus himself distances himself from God. ' "Why do you call me good? None is good save one, that is God" ' (10:18). Jesus also refers to himself as Son of Man. Here in Mark is a man who has acquired high status through his close relationship with God but who is not himself divine. Mark has a conception of Jesus which, while it exists on the fringes of traditional Judaism, is still acceptable within that world.

In Mark's gospel, Jesus is centre stage, a vigorous figure continually on the move. Although Mark includes passages of Jesus' teachings, these are not as prominent as they will be in Matthew's gospel. The emphasis is rather on activity and emotional involvement. Jesus is more human in his responses than he will be in Matthew and Luke. His status is reinforced by his ability to carry out miraculous deeds. In the first century, the term 'miracle' meant a wondrous happening, something that would draw attention to the person who did it. Peter sums it up well in the Acts of the Apostles (2:22): 'Jesus of Nazareth, a man attested to you by God with mighty works and wonders and signs which God did through him in your midst.' (Note how here Peter does not see Jesus as divine but as a man (*sic*) through whom God works.) As the New Testament shows, this included healing, of course, and the exorcism of demons, but also miraculous feedings of the hungry and the conquest of natural laws as when Jesus walks on water. These are all manifestations of the same power and reflect the high status that God has given him. However, in many cases, a miracle is linked to the recipient showing faith, as with the healing of the blind man (10:52), and Mark is doubtless reminding his community of the rewards arising from trust in Jesus. Again exorcisms represent a direct attack on the devil and they may be symbolic of a process of purification before the arrival of the kingdom.

Alongside his miraculous deeds is Jesus' ability to foretell the future. Again Mark makes a distinction between Jesus and God. Jesus is indeed able to predict something about his own fate: 'The Son of Man will be given up to the chief priests ... he will be mocked and spat upon, flogged and killed; and three days afterwards, he will rise again' (10:33–4). In Chapter Thirteen he predicts how the end of the world will be. However, he then goes on to say that only God actually knows the time this will take place. Mark carefully positions Jesus as close to God but of a distinctly lower status.

Jesus preaches that one must reject the world in order to follow him but equally one will experience rejection by one's own native community and relatives. Mark uses the Pharisees and scribes to swell the opposition to Jesus. The most devastating rejections, Jesus tells his followers, will be those of 'the last times' when the world begins to disintegrate into warfare and famine and people will turn on Jesus' followers. Families will betray each other, even the father his own child. The believers must keep faith to the very end.

An important theme of Mark's gospel is the distinction between those to whom the secret of the kingdom of God has been given and those who are distanced from it. Jesus tells his disciples that everyone can hear his parables but few can understand their meaning. So there have to be explanations and these are given as, for instance, with the parable of the sower and the seed. Yet Jesus is continually frustrated by those of his followers who do not understand. When the disciples complain that there is no bread, he has to remind them of the feeding of the five thousand (8:14–21). Have they not understood that they will be fed if they have faith? They are obtuse in their failure to recognise the message he is bringing. It is through suffering that one will achieve the kingdom but if the disciples do not understand this, then Jesus himself must take on the role of the one who suffers. So 8:31, when he begins to teach them that the Son of Man has to undergo great sufferings, might be seen as a moment of transition within the gospel. The disciples have shown their inadequacy to take on the role Jesus had planned for them.

The paradigm now becomes Jesus' own rejection, which is presented by Mark in graphic detail. Having arrived in Jerusalem fully aware of the suffering that awaits him, Jesus begs to be relieved of the agony. Judas carries out the act of betrayal and there is the abject humiliation of crucifixion, an experience so profound that Jesus feels that even God has abandoned him. The reader is left haunted by the mystery of how God can allow his only son to suffer in this way. In the original version of Mark there seem to be no resurrection appearances; one is simply told that Jesus is risen and has gone to Galilee. There is not the triumphant ending one will find in Matthew. The survival of Jesus and his reappearance at the Second Coming are suggested but the reader is left with no clear message. Perhaps Mark himself, brought up as a traditional Jew, could not conceive of a role for a messiah who had been so humiliated, 'the incredible incongruity of a murdered miracle worker', as one scholar has termed it. At some later date, perhaps only in the second century, another writer added the experiences of a physical resurrection, possibly to bring Mark's gospel into line with the others.

Matthew

Mark's gospel was of sufficient importance for it to be circulated. Within fifteen years two other gospel writers, Matthew and Luke, had drawn heavily on it. Matthew used 80 per cent of Mark but he felt that he needed to revise and build on the text. Anyone reading the original gospel would never have known of the virgin birth or the physical resurrection of Jesus and Matthew must have felt that Jesus deserved a higher status. He had no inhibitions about imposing his own interpretations on the text he borrowed. By the time his own gospel was complete it was some 50 per cent longer than Mark's. So who was Matthew? A Matthew appears in the gospels and Acts as a tax collector or a publican and so his recruitment as an apostle (brilliantly captured in Caravaggio's *Calling of Matthew* in the church of San Luigi dei Francesi in Rome) gives him the status required to be attached by Irenaeus to a specific gospel, even though this gospel was written between AD 80 and 90, long after Matthew would have died. In any case, it contains no evidence of direct experience of Jesus. Papias also refers to a gospel by a Matthew but this again is not the gospel we know as Matthew – Papias tells us that his Matthew 'arranged in order the sayings in the Aramaic language and each one interpreted [or "translated"] them as he was able'. Irenaeus' Matthew, on the other hand, writes in Greek and his gospel is much more than a list of sayings. The name of the true writer remains unknown.

Matthew's community is much closer to Judaism than Mark's. While Mark has to explain Jewish customs to his congregation, Matthew does not. As will be seen, Matthew works hard to place Jesus' roots in Jewish tradition, yet he expresses bitter resentment of the synagogues, the Pharisees and 'the teachers of the law'. So his community's roots are still Jewish but its faith in Christ is powerful enough to break with synagogue Judaism and experience its opposition. Matthew accords a high status to Peter and shows continuing respect for the Law. In effect he distances itself from the theology of Paul. Yet there are Gentiles among the community – a call by Jesus to preach to all nations at the end of the gospel would hardly have been included if there had not been some experience of involvement in a wider non-Jewish world. Throughout his gospel Matthew hints at conflict – conflict with Jews, other Gentile groups and within the community itself. This suggests a mixed congregation, ensconced in a niche between the Jewish and Gentile worlds, but very threatened. The gospel is an attempt by Matthew to use the person and teaching of Jesus to inspire a new focus for the community. It may have been written in Antioch. The Antioch Christians valued Peter and James and appeared to have rejected Paul, who had left the city for ever after his confrontation with Peter over eating with the Gentiles.

Matthew shows a more profound learning of the scriptures than Mark and is altogether more sophisticated in his language, often polishing up Mark's Greek as he rewrites it. He may well have trained as a scribe. He presents Jesus as of much higher status than Mark does – the genealogy he provides is in itself a symbol of status. He is also much more confident of Jesus' role as Messiah. The word Christ appears twice as frequently in Matthew as it does in Mark. Matthew uses the Greek word *proskynein* ('to give reverence to') in association with Jesus in contrast to Mark (and Luke) who hardly ever use it. Matthew deletes any sayings that suggest criticism of Jesus, such as his rejection of his family or the anger the disciples show when the storm blows up and Jesus appears not to care. The disciples are also treated with greater respect. In Mark, as we have seen, they often fail to grasp what Jesus offers. So when Jesus walks on water and quells the storm (Mark 6:52) they are dumbfounded by the event. In Matthew, on the other hand, they are quick to respond to the same event with the proclamation: 'Truly you are the Son of God' (14:33). They grasp Jesus' status. One of the most significant changes from Mark is that Matthew portrays Peter as the first of the apostles, no less than the rock on which the church will be built (16:17–18). This verse was to have extraordinary significance – emblazoned in Latin around the inside of Michelangelo's great dome of St Peter's in Rome it is the text on which the supremacy of the popes within the Catholic church is founded. While Mark's gospel is dominated by the imminence of the Second Coming, Matthew, writing some years later when there is still no sign of the Coming, acknowledges that the church must look to its own survival on earth.

One of the most important concerns of Matthew is to root Jesus more fully within the history of Israel. Every major facet of Jesus' life is therefore placed as the fulfilment of a prophecy from scripture, in eight cases from the prophet Isaiah. The use of scripture is especially marked in the infancy narrative (Chapters One and Two) when five different texts are used to support the account of Jesus' birth and childhood. Mark had begun his gospel with Jesus' baptism by John but Matthew feels that something more is required. Mark had asserted no more than that Jesus was 'the son of Mary' (Mark 6:3). This may reflect a tradition that Jesus was illegitimate, which Matthew felt the need to refute.

Matthew fills what is a significant void by telling how Mary is with child by the Holy Spirit. This, Matthew tells us, is to fulfil the prophecy that 'a virgin

will conceive and bring forth a child, Emmanuel'. Matthew is writing in Greek
and understandably uses the Septuagint (Greek) version of Isaiah's verse.
While the Hebrew original is *almah*, simply a young girl, the Greek translation, *parthenos*, specifically refers to a virgin. So the Hebrew scriptures provide
no support for the idea of a birth to a virgin; it is found only in the ambiguous
Greek translation of them. Matthew's main concern here is probably to establish a link with prophecy rather than to suggest an actual virgin birth as
historical fact. It is impossible to imagine how this unlikely event could ever
have been known to an outsider writing over eighty years after the event.

When Christianity was firmly rooted in the Gentile world Matthew's story
gained new resonances. The concept of a god fathering a human mortal was
well known and great men were routinely declared to be the son of a god.
Zeus, the father of the gods, impregnated Alexander the Great's mother
Olympia in the guise of a penetrative snake while the philosopher Plato was
the reputed son of Apollo. So Gentile Christians would not have found the
concept of a divine paternity strange. It may well be that Matthew was trying
to reassure his Gentile readers that Jesus could hold his own among the other
spiritual figures fighting for their allegiance.

While in Mark the teachings of Jesus tend to be overshadowed by his
miracles, Matthew is keen to highlight his role as an authoritative teacher.
Often Jesus refers to other teachings the disciples may have heard but then
distinguishes his own from them. The teachings take up about a third of the
gospel and many are drawn from Q. They are arranged in five separate
sessions. Matthew, attuned as ever to the Hebrew scriptures, may be deliberately echoing the five books of Moses. The first session (Matthew 5:1–7:29) is
the celebrated Sermon on the Mount that begins with the Beatitudes, offering
blessings for those who are compassionate to others. The Lord's Prayer is also
part of this episode and suggests that the Christian community was developing its own prayers to supplant those of the synagogue. Matthew goes on to
emphasise the continuing importance of the Torah. He stresses that Jesus has
not come to abolish the Law but to complete it. Again, and here the contrast
with the teachings of Paul is obvious, Matthew sees Jesus as the fulfilment of
the Jewish past, not as ushering in a complete break with it, although whether
Jesus is bringing the Law to an end or simply enhancing its status by 'completion' is not clear. In the second session of teaching (10:1–11:1), Jesus concentrates on the disciples, setting out their own mission. He does not offer them
an easy time – he himself has not come to bring peace to the earth, but a
sword, and in the upheaval his followers will be betrayed even by their own
families and flogged in the synagogues. They must desert their own parents to
follow Jesus. Matthew is probably preaching to his own community and these
passages suggest their isolation and experience of persecution. The image of

Jesus, however, is an unsettling one. In the first set of teachings, he is preaching gentleness and compassion, in this he brings the sword.

In the third session (13:1–53) Jesus is again preaching openly and in parables. Much here comes from Mark but this time the disciples are able to understand and share the message of his teachings. In the fourth session (18:1–19:1) Matthew returns to the concerns of his own congregation. Jesus stresses compassion for children and 'the lost sheep'. He also requires those who have disputes with each other to settle them within the community. The distinction is made between the pagan secular courts and the congregation that acts in judgement on its own affairs. So Matthew does seem to be referring to an established community which is taking responsibility for its own business. As in the other sessions, it is the authority of Jesus as teacher that makes the impact and his authority is given status here by accounts of his miracles that closely follow those in Mark.

Finally, as the Passion nears, Jesus turns his attention to the Last Judgement. He lambasts the hypocrisy of the lawyers and Pharisees 'with their fine robes' who mislead those who seek the kingdom of heaven. Here again Jesus highlights the authenticity of his teaching over those who have betrayed their religion, largely by failing to honour new teachers and prophets when they appear. Those who are true followers will recognise the signs, elaborated by Matthew with the help of parables, that will foretell the coming judgement. The decision of final judgement, eternal life or eternal death, will be made according to the ethical behaviour of the judged, the feeding of the hungry or the clothing of the naked. In the fourth century this important passage was eclipsed by an insistence on faith or correct belief as the only means to salvation.

Jesus can do nothing, however, to prevent the Passion and crucifixion, which Matthew, like Mark, recounts in detail. The Passion narrative is rooted in the hostility of the Jewish leaders who believe that they are doing the will of God by ridding themselves of Jesus. Yet Matthew presents Jesus as the one who triumphs. After his account of the resurrection experiences Matthew ends his gospel with the euphoric message of the risen Christ in Galilee. It makes a fine literary flourish with which to conclude and Matthew is clearly aiming to provide a clarion call for Christians everywhere. The very last verse of the gospel, 'I am with you always until the end of time', suggests that one has now moved on from the immediacy of a Second Coming. Instead Jesus tells the disciples to go forth to all nations and to baptise them in the name of the Father and the Son and the Holy Spirit. This is one of the rare moments in early Christian literature where a Trinity is referred to, although there is no hint here that the three figures are of equal divinity as would be taught in later centuries.

Luke

The gospel of Luke and its sequel, the Acts of the Apostles, were probably written in the 80s. Irenaeus made the attribution of his gospel to Luke on the basis that Luke is the 'we' companion of Paul in Acts and had thus established a direct link to an apostle but there is no firm evidence to sustain this. The best case that can be made for Luke is that no one of that name is mentioned otherwise in the New Testament and there is no obvious reason for Irenaeus to have attached the name to the gospel unless there had been some tradition which supported it. This does not get us far. Equally, as with the other gospel writers, there is no consensus as to where or when the gospel was written. Luke draws heavily on Mark so he is unlikely to have been writing earlier than 75. References to Jerusalem surrounded by siege works confirm a date after the destruction of the Temple. Despite his vivid portrayal of Paul in Acts, Luke shows no knowledge of Paul's letters which were probably first collected in the 90s. So a date in the 80s seems probable. It remains a mystery why Luke ends his story in Acts as early as c.62 with Paul still alive in Rome. Perhaps he felt that Paul's arrival in Rome (there is nothing said of any similar arrival by Peter) symbolises the spread of the gospel throughout the empire and it was an appropriate moment to stop. The ambition of the narrative had been achieved.

Luke knows his scriptures well but he is also conversant with Hellenistic culture to a far greater extent than Mark or Matthew. His values have been seen as 'middle-class', in that he seems at home with financial issues, and to understand the humiliation of the professional (the steward at 16:30) who is dismissed. His 'middlebrow' Greek style is probably typical of that found among the professional scribes, often slaves or freedmen, who served wealthier households. His dedicatee, Theophilus, who may have been the leading member of a Christian community, is Greek and the community itself also seems distant from Judaism. In Acts, as we have seen, Luke makes so much of Paul's ministry that it is possible that, twenty years after Paul's death, he is writing for a surviving Pauline congregation. However, Luke reiterates Jesus' words that he has not come to supplant the Law (16:17) so even if he had known Paul he had not absorbed his theology. In short, virtually every-thing about the background to this gospel remains shrouded in mystery – it is not impossible that it was written for Theophilus alone, even from within his own household.

Luke's is the longest of the gospels; together with Acts it makes up a quarter of the New Testament. Some 35 per cent of the gospel draws directly on Mark and another 20 per cent on Q. Perhaps 40 per cent of the gospel is 'new' material. In his prologue Luke says he knows of other eyewitness sources and one assumes that he drew on these. However, he was such a self-consciously literary author that he may well have developed parts of the story himself. He suggests, for instance, in his opening verses that he is attempting to create an ordered narrative and he certainly did not have inhibitions about recasting the order of Mark for effect, notably when he places the rejection of Jesus in Nazareth at the beginning of Jesus' ministry (Chapter Four), rather than later. Jesus also chooses his twelve disciples after his ministry has begun rather than at the start of it as in Mark. Altogether there are seven occasions when Luke reorders Mark's material. Luke follows Matthew rather than Mark in giving higher status to the disciples, perhaps reflecting a similar rise in status among Christian leaders of his day, but differs from him in shortening the teaching sessions. The Sermon on the Mount becomes the Sermon on the Plain. His additions include much of the infancy narrative that is itself enriched by hymns such as the Magnificat, where Mary glorifies God in gratitude for being chosen to bear Jesus, and parables such as that of the Good Samaritan and healing miracles not recorded elsewhere. There is an extended treatment of the Last Supper, possibly because Luke is more aware of the Hellenistic custom of using a meal as a teaching occasion and this is the model he followed for his account.

Luke's gospel must be set in its context as the first part of the story of the spread of Christianity. In fact, it might be said to be the first two parts as Luke begins his narrative with the infancy stories of Jesus that are placed wholly in a Jewish context. The birth of Jesus is linked to the redemption of Israel. 'I have seen with my own eyes the deliverance which thou hast made ready in full view of all the nations; a light that will be a revelation to the heathen and glory to the people Israel', Simeon rejoices when Jesus is presented in the Temple (Luke 2:29–32). Luke suggests that it is part of the glory of Israel to provide a saviour whose message will spread to all nations and this theme is, of course, followed up in the narrative in Acts.

Here we see one of Luke's great strengths, his ability to create a powerful visual impact. No other gospel writer has had his portrayals, above all the annunciation, the nativity in the stable, with the visits of the shepherds and the presentation in the Temple, so often and vividly portrayed in art. So throughout the gospel in stories such as the tax collector Zacchaeus scrambling up a tree in order to see Jesus (Luke 19:3) or the appearance of Jesus to two travellers on the road to Emmaus, the scene is memorably set. In the resurrection appearance to the disciples, Luke stresses that Jesus is very much flesh and bone (contrast Paul's assertion in 1 Corinthians that Jesus is a spiritual body) and able to eat fish. Jesus is also more firmly rooted in history in Luke's gospel than he is in the other three. Note for instance the attempt to provide an exact chronological framework in Chapter Three for the start of Jesus' ministry. This does not mean that Luke is historically accurate. His account of why Jesus was born in Bethlehem is hopelessly muddled and it may have been adapted from an alternative account he was unable or unwilling to check.[3]

Luke's gospel is a gospel shaped by movement. After a sojourn in the desert, Jesus returns to his native Nazareth but is rejected after preaching in the synagogue there. He then initiates his ministry in the small towns and villages of Galilee. Next (9:51 onwards) he orientates his mission towards Jerusalem and there follows an account of a measured journey there during which he confirms and inspires his disciples as bearers of his message. It is the disciples, rather than the local population, who welcome him to Jerusalem as if he was a king. Luke continually tells his readers how Jesus is known throughout the region, even at the royal court of Herod Antipas (9:9). Unlike the other gospel writers, Luke tells of an extended period of teaching by Jesus in the Temple, suggesting that hostility to his mission was not immediate but took time to gather within Jerusalem. (In fact, the priests, having determined that Jesus must be removed, may have had to wait until Pontius Pilate, with his power to order executions, arrived for the Passover before Jesus was arrested.) After the Passion and crucifixion, which Luke, like Mark and Matthew, places within the Passover feast, Jesus' resurrection appearances are restricted to the city and its immediate environs. It is typical of Luke's own focus on the city which relates to his belief that Jesus' ministry is linked to the redemption of Israel.

Luke always presents Jesus as someone who is subordinate to God the Father. Jesus himself tells how he has been sent to spread the good news of the kingdom of God (4:43). The same titles that Matthew and Mark have used for Jesus reappear although Elizabeth, the mother of John the Baptist, who is here presented as a kinswoman of Mary, talks of Jesus as 'my Lord' even before he is born. Luke also brings in a strong role for the Holy Spirit who is 'with Mary' at Jesus' conception, descends on him at his baptism and who, of course, plays a major part in Acts, especially at Pentecost. The Spirit is therefore associated with the continuity of Jesus' presence from his earliest moment to beyond the ascension. At his conception Jesus is referred to as 'the Son of the Most High' and a descendant of David. None of this implies divinity and many of the subsequent examples of use of the title 'Lord' are as a term of respect, as with the leper seeking healing (5:12) or the amazement of the disciples at the calming of the storm (10:17). Peter recognises Jesus as the Messiah and, in 24:26, Jesus tells his disciples that he, the Messiah, was destined to suffer before entering into his glory. In other words, the concept of the suffering messiah is already integrated into Luke's narrative. In comparison to Mark, Luke presents Jesus as altogether more confident of his role as the redeemer of Israel. He appears to be in command of the events leading to his death. Even in the agony of the crucifixion there is a sense of fulfilment rather than the abandonment one finds in Mark.

Where Luke differs from Matthew is in placing more emphasis on the human side of Jesus. As we have seen, Matthew presents a genealogy of Jesus that goes back to Abraham. Luke provides an alternative genealogy that stretches right back to Adam (3:23–38).[4] Luke suggests that the link is to Adam as an individual human being and so roots Jesus within the human race. The infancy narrative has a warmth to it that is totally lacking in Matthew. This is reiterated by the way that Luke presents Jesus as a child growing in wisdom (2:52). His compassion is down to earth and extends to those on the fringes of respectable society. Women play a significant part in the gospel and Luke is the only gospel to give a positive role to Samaritans, normally regarded as outsiders by orthodox Jews. Jesus is often shown at prayer, another way in which a more human side, his submission to his Father, is presented as an example to his disciples, an example that they are to carry on after his death.

The central part of Luke's gospel often becomes little more than a sequence of miracles, parables and individual teachings to which it is difficult to give any kind of coherence. How does one reconcile the teaching, in the parable of the servant who does not use his money to accumulate more and has it confiscated so that 'the man who has will always be given more' (19:22), a godsend text for Christian capitalists, with, only a few verses before, ' "Sell everything you have and distribute to the poor and you will have riches in heaven" '? In Luke 11:5–10, the door will always be open to those who knock on it; in 13:25–30, the door will be locked by the master even against those who have sat at table with him. The Good Samaritan is presented as the ideal, the true neighbour, at one moment (10:30–37), at another (14:25) the crowds are told, ' "If anyone comes to me and does not hate his father and mother, wife and children, brothers and sisters, even his own life, he cannot be a disciple of mine." ' One can make convoluted attempts at reconciliation, as some Christian apologists do, but one is still left with a confused picture of Jesus' ethical requirements. It may be that Luke used a number of sources of varying reliability but respects them to such an extent that he is not prepared to rewrite them even when they are clearly contradictory.

Nevertheless one can still discern an apocalyptic message. Jesus positions himself as a prophet who, like Elijah and Elisha, desires Israel's redemption but who is not recognised in his own country. Those who are not blinded by wealth, an over-confident righteousness, or narrow mindedness will inherit the kingdom of heaven in the not too distant future. Even though the Jewish leaders reject Jesus, the Jewish people themselves are not above salvation. In the famous lament over Jerusalem (Luke 13:34–5) Jesus tells how he has longed to gather her children under his wings, as a hen gathers her brood. His longings bear fruit. In the aftermath of the crucifixion, the Jewish crowd refuses to join in the denigration of Jesus and returns to their homes 'beating their breasts' (23:48). In contrast Matthew has the Jews taking on the responsibility for the crucifixion: 'Let his blood be on us and our children' (27:25). It is an important difference of emphasis and it was tragic that Matthew's record was later to be privileged over Luke's in the Christian tradition.

There are enough similarities between these three gospels to deserve the title of 'synoptic' ('with one eye'). Mark had established (or had himself followed) a model that, with additions and developments, his two immediate successors were prepared to follow. Yet it is also extraordinarily difficult to draw any kind of coherent theology from these gospels. Jesus hovers somewhere in between heaven and earth, sometimes closer to one than to the other, but always in some form of special relationship with God. None of the titles conferred on him assumes divinity – this would have been impossible within the Jewish context in which he is presented. It is not always clear whether the kingdom has already arrived or is yet to come. There remains a tension between his mission as a universal saviour and as leader of a small specific sect that had distinguished itself by an absolute commitment to him and the rejection of others. His relationship with the Jews remains ambiguous.

In the AD 80s the gospel writers were still searching to give Jesus' mission meaning from the varied sources and models of those exalted by God which had come down to them. Inevitably their own beliefs and the needs of their congregations shaped the way they portrayed Jesus and no historians would expect otherwise in 'biographies' written so long after the death of their subject. Later this made the gospels very unstable sources for theology – there were too many contradictions that could be drawn on by rival factions in the major debates of the fourth and fifth centuries. The challenge to use the gospels as sources was made even greater when a fourth gospel that took a very different form and approach was composed at the end of the first century.

CHAPTER EIGHT

John and the Jerusalem Christians

THERE IS A POWER AND SOPHISTICATION TO JOHN'S GOSPEL THAT immediately place it apart from the synoptics. While it is undoubtedly a gospel, with the baptism of Jesus by John the Baptist, miracles, a passion, crucifixion and resurrection appearances, it draws on very different historical traditions. It was probably impelled by the history of the community for which it was written and the focus on Jesus and his mission is intense.[1]

The origins of John appear to lie close to Jerusalem and in distinctive eyewitness accounts, passed on perhaps from an early Christian community. The gospel is centred in the city to a much greater extent than it is in the synoptic gospels – in particular, Jesus seems to attend the great Jewish festivals on a regular basis and to teach in the Temple. John seldom refers to the disciples as Galileans and Jesus' exorcisms, which the synoptic gospels recount as having taken place in Galilee, are not recorded at all. The existence of some of the villages John mentions in the vicinity of Jerusalem has been confirmed by archaeological research. The Jerusalem focus is one reason for preferring John's narrative of the Passion, as taking place before the Passover proper, to that of the synoptic gospels. Tradition attributes the gospel to the apostle John, the son of Zebedee, but the majority of scholars can find no evidence to support this.

However, this early source underwent transmission. It appears that the Christian community that preserved it was expelled from Jerusalem (John 7:35). John specifically rejects Jerusalem. ' "The time is coming when you will worship the Father neither on this mountain nor in Jerusalem ... the true worshippers will worship the Father in spirit and truth" ' (4:21, 23). There seems to be a strong possibility that the community broke with the Jewish belief that no human could be divine by suggesting that Jesus was equal to God. If so this was one of the most crucial moments in history, unrecorded by the synoptic gospels, as it brought a totally different conception of Jesus, as one fully divine, into the Christian arena. The split between Judaism and Christianity would be an inevitable result. The community must have been expelled from Jerusalem. It was able to meet the challenge. Tradition suggests it moved to Ephesus where one of its preachers transformed the earlier versions of the gospel into a coherent and reflective narrative. Chapter Twenty-one is usually seen as a final addition to the gospel. In verses 15 to 17 of this chapter Jesus asks Peter to 'feed his lambs' and this may reflect the importance of a new pastoral carer in the community. More than any other gospel, John stresses the relationships of mutual support within the rejected community.

The writing of the final version of John is usually placed between AD 90 and 110, far too late for an eyewitness to have been directly involved. Overall the gospel has a theological depth that shows that the new writer was working within an intellectual tradition that is much more sophisticated than that of the synoptic gospels. The literary tone is also very different, with themes such as 'light and darkness' and 'eternal life' prominent in a way not found in the others. There is a much greater emphasis on Jesus as the distinctive and unique Son of the Father, a theme virtually unknown in the synoptic gospels. John also appears more at home with Greek literary culture than the synoptics. It has been argued, for instance, that the moving scene where Mary Magdalene recognises Jesus in the garden draws on Greek literary precedents.

One of the unsolved mysteries of the gospel is the identity of 'the Beloved Disciple' who appears towards the end of the gospel (13:23). He enjoys a status above that of Peter. At the Last Supper the disciple is given the closest position to Jesus, and Peter has to approach Jesus through him. It is to this disciple that Jesus entrusts his mother and he outruns Peter towards the empty tomb, although Peter enters the tomb first. Traditionally the disciple was believed to be the apostle John himself and medieval rood screens depicted John and Mary on either side of the cross, John ready to take care of Mary as Jesus dies. The mystery remains as to why he was not named, although it has been argued that this anonymity was deliberate in that the disciple symbolised the intimacy that any follower of Jesus can have with him, one which is even above that enjoyed by Peter. These episodes may also have been a subtle way of suggesting that Peter's primacy in the church was not justified. In addition they initiate the idea that Jesus had privileged relationships with individual members of the twelve.

John's gospel begins with the famous prologue that 'the Word [*logos*] was made flesh and dwelt among us'. The opening verses establish the heightened tone of the gospel. The writer assumes that *logos*/Jesus is pre-existent alongside God – Jesus, in his symbolic form as *logos*, has already been created and is now sent among human beings. This pre-existence is an important theological development in itself. Later, Christians were to identify the *logos* with 'Wisdom' as in the Old Testament Proverbs 8:22 where God created Wisdom, which they believed referred to Christ, at the beginning of time.

Much of John's theology appears to come from Jewish sources and the discovery of the Dead Sea Scrolls has strengthened this belief. There are no discernible direct quotations from the Scrolls but themes such as 'light and darkness' are to be found there and there are similarities in the tone of the texts. However, John may have found the specific concept of the *logos* entering the world as an intermediary in the works of Philo. The idea that the *logos* is God but also distinct from God is to be found in both writers. Philo's conception of the *logos* as 'an ambassador' certainly fits with the way Jesus describes himself in John as 'one sent'.

So Jesus arrives on earth fully formed, as it were. There is no process of maturing into an adult that one finds in Luke. At 3:13, Jesus talks of his home as being in heaven. The next verses, 3:16–17, are especially significant as a statement of his mission: 'God so loved the world that he gave his only Son, that everyone who has faith in him may not die but have eternal life. It was not to judge the world that God sent his Son into the world, but that through him the world might be saved.' As Jesus reiterates at 6:38, 'I have come down from heaven, not to do my own will, but the will of him who sent me.' An emphasis on saving rather than judging marks a different, more gentle, approach than that of the more apocalyptic statements of the synoptic gospels. There is no sword here dividing up families, although there are still hints in the gospel of 'those who have done wrong rising' at the Last Judgement 'to hear their doom' (5:29). Not all will be saved.

John also makes clear in these verses that Jesus is subordinate to his Father. He has been sent to earth to do the will of his Father as distinct from his own. Jesus continually talks of his Father as being greater than he, knowing more, having 'works' of his own which he then reveals to his Son, and enjoying a higher status as the one who sends. However, later in the gospel (10:30) Jesus is to proclaim that 'I and the Father are One', and 5:18 shows the Jews furious with Jesus to the point of wanting to kill him because he was claiming equality with God – blasphemy as far as orthodox Jews were concerned. These contradictions were to cause great controversy in the theological debates of the fourth century. The gospel left it unclear whether Jesus was equal to God the Father or subordinate to him – each side could quote verses from the gospel in support of their case. What is certain is that John gives a far higher degree of divinity to Jesus than the synoptic gospels do and this may reflect not only the specific beliefs of John's community but the process by which Jesus was being redefined and elevated in his divinity by Christians as time passed and the break with traditional Judaism solidified. Jesus' messiahship is also much more closely linked to his divinity than it is in the synoptics where the title is used with hesitation.

The core of John's text is organised into a sequence of six signs that portray the status of Jesus. They are prefaced by Jesus entering the Temple, getting rid of the moneylenders and driving out the sellers of sacrificial animals. In the synoptic gospels this event (narrated in a different form) takes place just before the Passion and it is usually argued that John placed it this early for narrative effect. It also brings the concept of purification to the forefront of the gospel; the Temple must be cleansed before Jesus' teaching can begin. Origen, the great third-century interpreter of the scriptures, meditated on the reordering and proclaimed the story to be 'a spiritual truth in an historical falsehood' and this emphasises that the gospel is as much a theological statement as a biography of Jesus.

The six 'signs' of John's gospel are miracles presented as drama. Here again is a very different focus from the synoptic gospels. While for Mark there was an endless sequence of miracles as if Jesus' predominant role was as healer, here each miracle is highlighted as an event with a specific deeper meaning. The first is the famous turning of the water into wine at Cana, the only miracle where Jesus is shown alongside his mother. Through this miracle Jesus 'revealed his glory and led his disciples to believe in him'. Soon after the miracle at Cana, in an exchange with a Pharisee named Nicodemus, Jesus tells how entry to the kingdom of heaven is through water and the spirit. He makes a powerful distinction between flesh and spirit: 'Flesh can only give birth to flesh, it is spirit which gives birth to spirit.' This dualism, the separation of a spirit world from the material world of the flesh, as with light from darkness, is an important feature of the gospel. It may well originate in the same traditions as the Dead Sea Scrolls. Next Jesus meets a Samaritan woman at a well and contrasts the water from the well with that which he can give believers. As so often happens in this gospel, one element, water, becomes symbolic of something more, eternal life. Other Samaritans are attracted to Jesus and their recognition of him as 'the saviour of the world' may reflect the expansion of John's own community beyond its Jewish origins.

The second sign is the healing of the son of 'an officer in the royal service', again in Cana. The third sign follows soon afterwards in the narrative but Jesus is now in Jerusalem where he heals a sick man who has been lame for thirty-eight years. It is this event that arouses the opposition of the Jews, who believe that Jesus is claiming equality with God. Jesus responds with a discourse on his relationship with his Father. The Father loves the Son and shows him his works. However, he cannot be seen on earth. Jesus can be and the Father expects that he be given equal honour. Yet all is not well. Jesus complains of the readiness of his Jewish audience to give their allegiance to other leaders (5:44). There are echoes of Paul's difficulties here, which probably reflect the experiences of every early Christian group as different leaders struggled for prominence.

The fourth sign is the feeding of the five thousand (Chapter Six). Again Jesus later points to the symbolic importance of the event. 'You must work, not for this perishable food, but for the food that lasts, the food of eternal life ... my Father gives you the real bread from heaven.' Then come the famous words, 'I am the bread of life ... whoever comes to me shall never be hungry.' John says very little about the sacrament of the Eucharist as an institution but he seems to be aware of the symbolic importance of such a sacrament. 'Whoever eats my flesh and drinks my blood dwells continually in me and I dwell in him', confirms the symbolism.

Some kind of crisis was lurking behind these developments as John tells us that 'from that time on many of his disciples withdrew and no longer went about with him' (6:66 onwards). By now opposition from the Jews was becoming intense and some were looking for a chance to kill Jesus. John records the confusion when Jesus returns to Jerusalem and begins preaching in the Temple. No one can decide whether Jesus is the Messiah, simply a prophet or a troublemaker who has to be dealt with. This is one of the most revealing parts of the gospel as it reflects what must have been a genuine debate among the crowds as to who Jesus was. It leads on to the famous confrontation with the Jews in Chapter Eight. Here the conflict is between traditional authorities as the Jews perceived them, 'their' God and Abraham as 'their' father, and the very different conception of God as Jesus' own father which Jesus preaches.

The remarkable thing about this confrontation is that if read without Christian preconceptions (in other words not from the perspective that Jesus must be right), it shows up the dilemmas that anyone listening to him must have faced. One feels that if one had been there one might have been convinced by the arguments on either side and it is interesting that John allows this perspective to survive. The drama is heightened by Jesus' use of the words 'I am', as in 'In very truth I tell you before Abraham was born, I am' (8:58). 'I am' is similar to expressions that God uses to refer to himself in the Hebrew scriptures. Its use (and there are two other examples in the confrontation scene, at 8:24 and 8:28) associates Jesus closely with God and the immediate response to the third use of the phrase (at 8:58), when the Jews pick up stones to throw at him, shows how offensive it must have been to them. Later we are told that anyone who acknowledges Jesus as Messiah has been banned from the synagogue (9:22). This truly was the fault line between Christian and Jew, the beginnings of distinct, and often antagonistic, communities.

The narrative continues (Chapter Nine) with the fifth sign, the healing of a man who has been blind since birth. Jesus' disciples, brought up in the Jewish tradition that suffering is decreed by God as a punishment for sin, ask whether it was the man himself or his parents who were the sinners. Jesus' reply is remarkable, even somewhat discomfiting: 'He was born blind so that God's power might be displayed in curing him.' In other words, the world is set up so that Jesus can show his powers. Another fascinating discussion follows among the Jews as to whether this is a genuine healing at all and where Jesus' power comes from. The healed man's persistence in his faith in Jesus leads to his own exclusion from the synagogue and Jesus himself uses the healing to make another symbolic point – that he has come to give (spiritual) sight to the sightless.

Then comes the teaching on 'the good shepherd', one of the most enduring images of Jesus and one that has persisted at the core of Christian pastoral care (and appears as an important theme in early Christian art). The 'good shepherd' is contrasted with the hireling who flees from trouble when the wolf comes. The shepherd Jesus is prepared to stay with the sheep and even lay down his life for them. He will bring in other sheep so that there will be one flock and one shepherd. When the Jews then begin forcing him to declare whether he is the Messiah or not, Jesus fails to give a clear answer but reiterates that if they were members of his flock he would give them eternal life. He goes on to proclaim (10:30) that he and the Father are one, another statement which leads to the Jews preparing to stone him. 'You, a mere man, claim to be a God', they shout. Jesus is forced to retreat across the Jordan. It is here that he receives news from Mary and Martha, whom he has already encountered in their village, Bethany, near Jerusalem, that their brother Lazarus is ill, near death. Despite the fears of his disciples, Jesus decides to return to Judaea but he arrives too late, finding that Lazarus has already been buried for four days.

The raising of Lazarus from the dead is the sixth of John's signs. It is prefaced by the famous words that Jesus speaks to Martha: 'I am the resurrection and the life. If a man has faith in me, even though he die, he shall come to life; and no one who is alive and has faith will ever die' (11:24–5). With the reappearance of Lazarus from the tomb, still swathed in his funerary linen and his face covered by a cloth, the number of those following Jesus grows further but so does the opposition to him. Reports of the disorder reach the Sanhedrin and there is increasing concern that the unrest will bring Roman retaliation. In the debate that follows Caiaphas puts forward the idea that it is better to kill one man, Jesus, in the hope of calming the tension, than risk the destruction of the whole nation by the Romans. This approach fits well with the possibility, discussed on p.32, that Caiaphas may have quietly removed the body of Jesus from the tomb and attempted to send the disciples back to Galilee without further bloodshed.

The story moves on to the Last Supper, although this is not linked to the Passover feast and there is no mention of the Eucharist. When Judas leaves the room, no one other than Jesus realises that he is about to betray him. These little touches of drama are common in John and illustrate the sophistication of the writing. Jesus preaches his final address to his disciples (from 13:31), presenting them with a new commandment, that they should love one another as he has loved them. He talks of his return to his Father, saying that, through knowing him, the disciples already know his Father: 'I am in the Father and the Father in me.' After he has gone the Father will send another 'advocate' or 'comforter' (the translation of the Greek *parakletos*, the original of Paraclete, used only in John), the 'Spirit of truth', who will 'call to mind all that I have told you'. John is distinctive in portraying the Spirit as somehow within Jesus but continuing as a permanent presence when Jesus has returned to the Father. John's depiction of the Spirit as so closely linked to Jesus, and Jesus as so closely linked to the Father was to prove important when the doctrine of the Trinity was defined in the fourth century.

Now Jesus moves on to explore his own relationship with his disciples. His Father is the gardener and Jesus is the vine which the Father cultivates. The disciples are branches of the vine. The branches cannot bear fruit without the vine itself giving them life and this is what Jesus is doing. If a branch breaks off, becomes separated from the vine, it withers and is burned. In this new relationship between Jesus and his disciples, the disciples are no longer servants but friends who know the mind of Jesus. In another expression of dualism, Jesus tells them that they are no longer of this world, because they have been chosen out of this world. After his going, the Spirit of Truth will sustain them.

The end of this moving address comes with a direct prayer to the Father (beginning at Chapter Seventeen). Jesus has fulfilled his mission on earth and delivered his word to his disciples, thus transforming them into strangers in the world. Nevertheless he prays that God will not take them from the world but preserve them from 'the Evil one'. He goes on to petition that all who have faith in him might be one, just as he and the Father are one. This hope of a unity between God and man is one of the most powerful messages of the address.

The Passion now begins, Jesus accepts the unfolding of events in a much more serene way here than, for instance, in Mark. The crucifixion is the medium through which Jesus can return to his Father, his mission accomplished. The suffering leads on to triumphal glory. His death and the mutilation of his body by a soldier's lance are both said to be in fulfilment of scripture, a reminder that John, however much he had broken with traditional Judaism, knew his scriptures. The resurrection scenes, above all the recognition of Jesus by Mary Magdalene in the garden and the faith of Thomas when he feels the wounds, are particularly moving. Thomas' exclamation, 'My Lord and My God', is the only time in all four gospels that the title 'Lord' is directly linked to that of God.

There follows what is probably a later addition to the gospel (Chapter Twenty-one). Jesus appears on the beach of the Sea of Tiberias where the disciples have returned to their old jobs as fishermen (in contrast to the story in Luke's gospel and Acts, for instance, where they stay in Jerusalem). At first they do not recognise him and it is the 'beloved disciple' who eventually grasps that it is Jesus and tells Peter that it is the Lord. One might think that once again the disciple is being given prominence over Peter but later Jesus specifically asks Peter to 'feed my sheep' and appears to predict his martyrdom as an old man. Peter asks what the fate of 'the beloved disciple' will be. No clear answer is given but the writer (who may have contributed no more than this last chapter) states that he presents true testimony from the beloved disciple himself.

John's gospel is surely the most absorbing of the four. It not only creates a theologically complex portrayal of Jesus as someone much more intimately related to his Father than he is in the synoptic gospels; it is also a drama. The writer sustains a real sense of doubt among Jesus' audience as to who he is. For those hearing the gospel read aloud for the first time, there must have been much anticipation as to what would happen next. Even though Jesus all too conveniently disappears or moves away when the tensions with the Jews become acute, the sense of growing opposition is handled with skill. Jesus talks in a completely different way than in the synoptic gospels and references to any form of apocalypse are few. There is no longer the terrible vision of a complete breakdown of earthly order before the arrival of his kingdom. Believing in him lifts the believer above flesh into the world of spirit. What happens in the world seems of relatively little concern. In this gospel more than any other, Jesus' authority rests on his distinctiveness from other emissaries of God in that he alone has actually seen the Father and come down to earth to reveal something of him. Yet important questions about Jesus remain unresolved. Was he equal to God or subordinate to him? In what sense did he share in humanity or did he only appear to be human (a view known as docetism from the Greek *dokeo*, 'I appear to be')? How does one explain the discrepancy between the human and the divine Jesus? Once educated Greek minds set to work on the gospel, it provided immense scope for debate.

Afterword: Crisis in John's Community

The history of Christianity is full of those who claim a correct interpretation of Christian texts or a special relationship with God or Christ which others have been denied. In many such cases the more apocalyptic verses of the scriptures, those promising destruction on those who are not 'real' Christians, are used to threaten those whose interpretations of the scriptures differ. Such disagreement has been endemic in Christianity from its earliest days. Paul is a prime example of a leading Christian who is violent in his outbursts against fellow Christians who wish to retain a core of Jewish traditions such as circumcision, or who teach 'another Jesus'. Perhaps the earliest example of an actual schism is to be found in the three letters attributed to John which were probably written at much the same time as the gospel or, as some have argued, between the original version of the gospel ending at Chapter Twenty and its later completion with Chapter Twenty-one.

The writer of First John begins by calling his congregation back to the first of command of Christ: to discipline themselves to live as Christ lived. Yet there has been a development in that the community has passed from darkness into light. It walks in the light as Christ himself is in the light (1 John 1:7). (This 'light' versus 'darkness' echoes themes in John's gospel, of course.) This means nothing, the writer tells us, unless the community lives in love with one another and distances itself from the godless world and everything in it. Yet now, and here the letter moves on to its main concern, the Antichrists have appeared, evidence that the last hour is at hand. These 'Antichrists' were originally members of the community itself who have now left it but they can be recognised by their denial of Jesus as the Christ. In contrast 'the true believers' are recognised by their union with God and Christ. There is a powerful sense in the letter of the loyalists becoming transformed through belief in Christ so that they are already living on a different plane, above the materialism of the world.

In Chapter Four the writer shifts his focus to God. We cannot see God but if we love one another, God's love will be brought to perfection in us. 'God is love; he who dwells in love is dwelling in God, and God in him' (1 John 4:16). Jesus must be acknowledged as his Son. Those who recognise Christ 'in the flesh' are the true believers; those who do not recognise him in this way are the Antichrists even though they claim to speak through the Spirit. Jesus is to be known through his coming through water and blood. (This relates to the water and blood flowing from Jesus' side on the cross (John 19:34) and thus provides a reference to his suffering 'in the flesh'.) 'The Spirit' is witness to this. Belief leads to transcendence: 'God has given us eternal life and this life is to be lived in his Son' (1 John 5:11). In the short Second Letter of John, the addressee, 'a Lady chosen by God', in a community some distance from the writer, is urged in a similar way to obey the commandment of love. Here again there is a warning against Antichrists 'who do not acknowledge Jesus Christ as coming in the flesh' who may be heading her way and who must not be allowed into the community's households. Instead the community must live according to established traditions. In another short letter, the Third of John, one Gaius is thanked for offering hospitality to members of 'John's' community, presumably while they were on missions. A congregation, led by one Diotrephes, which refuses to have anything to do with John, is mentioned. John warns Gaius of the baseless charges that Diotrephes lays against him, John, and complains that he will not receive his friends into his community.

While these letters are difficult to date, there are enough similar themes between them and John's gospel to suggest the continuity of the same congregation, but as one that has now found itself in trouble. Clearly the writer of these letters was at home with the terminology of the gospel and its ideas. Yet the focus is somewhat different. It is no longer the Jews who are the threat but those who have offered an alternative vision of Christ. The writer is clearly deeply hurt by what he perceives as a betrayal. The emphasis in the letters on love, loving one's brothers and sisters, for instance, may be a direct reflection of his belief that those who have seceded have broken this commandment.

The letters fail to make it clear what the differences are between the 'loyalists' and the 'secessionists'. The varied ways in which Christ was being perceived in these decades always meant that any development of thought, especially if urged by an influential leader, could lead to division within a community. There was as yet no one way of defining 'true' and 'false' Christianity, however much the writer of First John would claim that there was. There is, however, the suggestion that the secessionists do not recognise Christ 'in the flesh'. They may have been docetists, believing that Jesus only 'appeared' to be a man, but was, in fact, a spiritual being throughout. This was not the only issue. The secessionists claimed to have received their beliefs directly through the Spirit. In John's gospel, Jesus had told his disciples that 'When he comes who is the Spirit of truth, he will guide you into all the truth' (16:13). So it would be within the tradition of the community to expect direct revelations of 'the truth' through the Spirit. However, the writer of First John clearly believes that the revelations received by the secessionists are not those of God! He argues instead for beliefs rooted in traditional authority, the teachings held 'from the beginning' (First John 1:1).

There is no reason to take a 'for' and 'against' stance on the conflicts described in John's letters. Their importance lies in their depiction of the disputes over authority that were to arise throughout the history of Christianity. Some individuals claim that they have a special revelation from God, Christ or the Holy Spirit. They have been given an insight which others, perhaps because of their own sinfulness, are unable to share. Unable to convince their fellow believers, they set themselves up as a distinct church – as this group seems to have done. The primary community is deeply upset, not only because its own teachings and authority have been challenged but because it is deemed unworthy. It can plead for respect for its own faith and for a return to the commandment of love but ultimately it has no way of controlling the secessionists. Bad feeling remains. All this was inevitable in the fluid world of early Christianity and the same issues re-emerge in Christian communities today. However deep the study, however perfect the lifestyle, however sincere the reflection, it remained impossible to say exactly who Jesus was and how he should be worshipped.

CHAPTER NINE

Creating a New Testament

IN HIS EASTER LETTER OF 367, THE EBULLIENT BISHOP OF ALEXANDRIA, Athanasius, referred to a set of Christian writings that he regarded as authoritative. He described them as 'canonised' in the sense of being texts that held the core of Christian belief. There were twenty-seven of them. This was the earliest reference to the complete New Testament, as we know it today, although less complete lists are known from the end of the second century onwards, notably in the Muratorian fragment of about 200. In 393, at a provincial council of bishops meeting in Carthage, further approval of this 'canon' was given. A New Testament was never consolidated in the first decades of the Christian church, it was a process that took centuries to complete. In fact the very idea that one should close off a selection of 'New Testament' texts and declare it a canon was a very late one.[1]

By AD 100 a wide variety of texts was circulating in the Christian communities, some of which would make it into the New Testament, some of which would not. Copies, on papyrus rolls, or the parchment *codices* that were becoming more common, were difficult to come by and would have been valued by those who owned them. Many communities were isolated so that some texts may never have travelled beyond their source. No Christians at this time would have had access to all the texts which were finally included (and some, the Second Letter of Peter, for instance, had not been written by this date). As we have seen, John, writing in the 90s or even later, shows no knowledge of any of Paul's letters. Ignatius, bishop of Antioch in the early second century, does not seem to have read the gospels of either Mark or John. Even at the end of the second century, one commentator, Irenaeus, noted that congregations relied on only one gospel: Matthew was chosen by the Ebionites, a group of Jewish Christians, Luke by followers of Marcion, Mark by the docetists and John by the gnostics. In the early third century the theologian Origen records the large number of gospels available to him in an important cultural centre like Alexandria, all of which he had read 'lest we should in any way be considered ignorant', as he engagingly puts it. While he recognises that the four New Testament gospels are the only acceptable ones to follow, he remains open-minded and refuses to censor other texts. The idea of a closed canon is still not recognised.

A hundred years after Origen, Eusebius, writing his *History of the Church* in the 330s, is in touch with discussions still going on in his day, three hundred years after the crucifixion, over which texts can be counted as authoritative. Among the writings attributed to Peter, for instance, Eusebius acknowledges only the First Letter as genuine. He accepts that the Second Letter of Peter is not by the apostle but is considered valuable enough to be read. Eusebius rejects an 'Acts' of Peter, the Gospel of Peter, Peter's 'Preaching' and a 'Revelation'. He does not include the Letter of Clement in his selection, even though he describes it as 'long and wonderful' and read aloud in many churches 'in early days, as it is in our own'. He also rejects the Epistle of Barnabas and a document of 'Teachings of the Apostles'. He would prefer also to reject the 'Revelation of John' although he acknowledges some would like to see it as authoritative, as it eventually became (the Book of Revelation). He refers to a host of heretical works purporting to come from apostles, 'gospels' by Thomas, Matthias and 'several others' and 'Acts' of Andrew, John and other apostles. It is in Eusebius that we find the references to Papias' gospels of Mark and Matthew although these do not appear to be the same as those gospels Irenaeus later attributed to the same authors. So Athanasius' list marks the culmination of a long period of debate.

Athanasius' final list was not universally accepted. The Ethiopian church acknowledged all his twenty-seven texts but their New Testament contained thirty-five books, including the Letter of Clement from Rome, some apparent writings of Peter delivered to the same Clement, an address by Christ to the apostles after the resurrection and another text from Rome, 'The Shepherd of Hermas'. In versions of the New Testament circulating in Syriac, a written form of Aramaic into which many early Christian texts were translated, the Book of Revelation as well as the letters of James, Peter, Jude and two of John's are missing. The letter of Philemon was also not considered canonical by the Syriac Church but there was a third letter of Paul to the Corinthians which was accepted.[2]

The remaining New Testament texts all have the name of an apostle or a member of Jesus' family attached to them. This may have been primarily to give them status. It was common in the ancient world to add texts to great names, so that Pythagoras' theorem is unlikely to be by Pythagoras and many of Hippocrates' medical texts are much later than his lifetime. In the New Testament there is a further cluster of letters attributed to Paul, the Second Letter to the Thessalonians, the Letter to the Colossians and the Letter to the

Ephesians. These were first attributed to Paul by his follower Marcion in the 130s, but they appear to date from after Paul's death in the 60s.

In Ephesians, for instance, the imminence of the Second Coming has receded and the church is seen as a widespread congregation of (almost certainly Gentile) believers rather than the merely local community of Corinthians, Thessalonians, or Philippians of Paul's letters. The congregation appears to be a stable one in which traditional social structures have reasserted themselves as against the more radical egalitarian message found in some of Paul's pronouncements. Women must be subject to their husbands although it is stressed that men must be loving towards their wives. Children must be obedient to their parents as slaves must obey their earthly master 'with fear and trembling' although, here again, the master is urged to treat slaves with respect as both slave and free have the same master in heaven. (There is nothing in the New Testament to challenge the institution of slavery itself – the first known Christian critique of slavery, by Gregory of Nyssa, dates only from the later fourth century. As the debate over slavery in the nineteenth-century United States showed, the Old Testament was, in fact, used to defend the practice of slavery.) It has been suggested that the writer is adapting Pauline concepts – notably the importance of unity (one body, one Spirit, one Lord, one faith, one baptism, one God and Father of all (Ephesians 4:4–6)), the need for the grace, a grace which has to be given, not achieved through hard work, of God for salvation (2:8), the forgiveness of sins through the shedding of Christ's blood (1:7) – into the new context of a settled church. Particularly important here is a passage which stresses how the barriers between Jew and Gentile have now been broken down (2:14–15) and Jesus has brought an enlarged 'household of God'. The church must be sustained not only by apostles, prophets and evangelists but by teachers and pastoral leaders as well. This is an institution preparing for long-term survival. There is a tone of encouragement for its members which contrasts with the hectoring tone of Paul's more emotional outbursts. A date in the 90s seems likely.

The writer of Ephesians may have drawn on the ideas of the Qumran community for the theology behind his letter. Although his audience is warned of the shallowness of pagans who have abandoned themselves to vice (shades of the Letter to the Romans here), he is more concerned with the fight against 'cosmic powers, the authorities and potentates of this dark world . . . the superhuman forces of evil in the heavens' (6:12). This is the fight between light and darkness which is also to be found in John's gospel (also probably from the 90s) and may come from the same sources. Ephesians introduces a world of devils, demons and dark forces and these were to haunt the later Christian imagination.

The Letter to the Colossians shows a similar concern with 'cosmic forces'. The letter is addressed to a single community, the apparently Gentile Christians of the small town of Colossae in Phrygia. The language is much closer to Paul's than that of Ephesians and a large minority of scholars accept it as genuine. However, here again the community appears more settled than any known in Paul's day. There is a very similar exhortation to respect traditional social structures – women submitting to their husbands, slaves giving entire obedience to their masters – that one finds in Ephesians. Again there is little reference to the struggle against the Jews or Jewish Christians that was such a preoccupation for Paul. Not that references to Judaism have vanished; there is talk of a new circumcision, which is not physical as traditional Judaism required, but spiritual in the form of a rejection of one's lower nature: 'fornication, indecency, lust, foul cravings and ruthless greed' (Colossians 3:5).

The threats to the Colossian community no longer come from the Jews but from 'false teachers'. It is not clear who these are – they appear to be believers in mystical cults or ascetics who go in for 'self-mortification and angel worship and try to enter into some vision of their own' (2:18). The 'angel worship' suggests a cult dealing with cosmic powers. There are hints here too of gnosticism, notably the belief that a spiritual leader could offer a lifeline from a wicked world in which humans are trapped. 'Did you not die with Christ and pass beyond the elemental spirits of the universe?' asks the author of Colossians (2:20). These ideas, despite their echoes in the Qumran writings, are more typical of the pagan world in which Christianity was now spreading and again suggest a date some twenty years later than Paul, and so the 80s.

In what might be an earlier hymn incorporated into the text, Colossians presents an exalted Christ: 'the image of the invisible God, the first born of all creation . . . who exists before everything and all things are held together in him . . . the head of the body, the church'. In baptism the convert becomes 'buried' in Christ and also 'raised with him through faith in the power of God who raised him from the dead' (2:12). In an echo of Paul's belief in Galatians that he lives in Christ, the dead are 'hidden with Christ in God' (3:3). So this, like Hebrews, is another exhortation to surrender all to Christ and it shows how, even before the gospels were known, Christian communities were developing their own patterns of worship, focused on Christ.

In the short Second Letter to the Thessalonians, there is a much more clearly defined threat to the Christians than merely 'false teachers'. The writer talks of an enemy, 'a man doomed to perdition' who even takes his seat in the temple of God, claiming to be a god himself' (2 Thessalonians 2:4). At the present time his wicked purpose is held by 'a Restrainer', a figure whose identity is never revealed by the writer. When 'the Restrainer' withdraws then the full wickedness of the 'enemy' will be revealed and Christ will return to annihilate him. Anyone who chooses sinfulness will be similarly destroyed. So the community must stand firm in its traditions, maintain its commitments and work hard for a living. There are a few echoes here of the concerns of the Thessalonians in the First (undoubtedly authentic) Letter of Paul to them and it may have been written by someone close to Paul who knew the letter and who addressed a new situation in which there was 'an enemy'. The emperor Domitian (81–96) declared himself 'Lord and God' and was associated with persecutions of Christians. However, any persecution at local level would have to be initiated by the local governor who would often exercise restraint to avoid unrest he could not control. Governors often tried to find a way of avoiding persecution of Christians and it may be that the provincial governor of Macedonia (of which Thessalonica was capital) was 'the Restrainer'.

There are three Pastoral letters that claim to be written by Paul to churches in Ephesus (the two to Timothy) and Crete (the Letter to Titus). Their concerns are very similar, the problems of leadership, the ethical values governing the everyday behaviour of Christians and the threats from 'false teachers'. These again suggest a date much later than Paul, probably in the late first or early second century. There are many indications that they are not by the apostle: the theology of Christ is not Pauline and Paul would hardly have had to justify his status to his close companion Timothy as he does in the two Timothy Letters. They may be even later than 100. When Marcion, who will be treated in full later (p. 134), drew up his list of Paul's writings in about 140, he did not include any of the three. This has led some scholars to suggest that they were written in about 150, after Marcion's own canon had been rejected by the church in Rome, to boost the confidence of those clinging to Paul's teachings.[3] The use of the apostle's name and those of two of his prominent companions was a deliberate strategy to give them status. This is an attractive theory but perhaps not strong enough to overthrow the scholarly consensus of a date fifty years earlier.

In comparison to his elevated status in Hebrews, Colossians and Ephesians, Jesus Christ is given a relatively modest role in these letters. The First Letter of Timothy, for instance, opens with God described as 'our Saviour' and Jesus Christ as no more than 'our hope'. The Letter to Titus asserts that 'God has openly declared himself in the proclamation which was entrusted to me [the writer claiming to be Paul] by ordinance of God our Saviour'. Later in First Timothy we are told: 'There is one God, and also one mediator between God and men, Christ Jesus, himself man, who sacrificed himself to win freedom for all mankind' (1 Timothy 2:5). Jesus appears as no more than a man who has acted as mediator, a status that is hardly higher than that of the Old Testament prophets. Later in the same letter it is stressed that God 'alone' holds sway 'in eternal felicity'. 'He is King of Kings, and Lord of Lords, he alone [sic] possesses immortality, dwelling in unapproachable light' (6:15–16). In the Second Letter to Timothy 'the grace of God is ours through Jesus Christ' who is described later as 'risen from the dead, born of David's line'; in other words not of divine conception but 'adopted', perhaps at the resurrection. At 2 Timothy 4:1 Jesus is given the specific role of judge of mankind when the Final Judgement occurs. It may be that the description of Jesus as Saviour and judge is a deliberate attempt to give him equal status with the Roman emperors who also carried the title of Saviour and who acted, of course, as supreme judge in the empire.[4] In short, this is a Jesus who is very much subordinate to the supremacy of God, perhaps even fully human. While First Timothy (1:15) tells us that Jesus came into the world to save sinners, there is no mention of his pre-existence as one finds in John or the Letter to the Hebrews.

Nor would a conventional Jew have found anything to complain about in the precepts for Christian living that are spelled out in these three letters. Bishops and deacons must be of good character. The community must live soberly; family life is respected – the first duty of a widow is to her children and grandchildren. The love of money for its own sake is to be condemned. 'If we have food and covering we rest content.' However, extreme asceticism is also discouraged: in First Timothy those who forbid marriage and demand abstinence from certain foods should be rejected, 'For everything God created is good.' This suggests a community more at ease with the world around it than Paul, for instance, would have expected. Titus is even asked to remind his congregation to be submissive to the government and the authorities, which in this case would be the governor of the Roman province which linked Crete to the North African mainland. So whenever the letter was written, it was at a time when a Christian community could expect to survive within the empire. The imminent Second Coming was no longer its major preoccupation and the community was even proclaiming its loyalty to the empire.

The greatest threat to these communities remains the lure of false teachings. In First Timothy (6:4), it appears that wrangling over words is particularly divisive. Perhaps there were struggles between rival preachers or nitpicking over the interpretation of texts. Again in Titus the congregation is warned to steer clear of foolish speculations, quarrels and controversies over the Law. This implies that the Law's status was still uncertain in this community. In Second Timothy two individuals, Hymenaeus and Philetus, are targeted for upsetting people's faith by teaching that 'our resurrection had already taken place', in other words that the community had through its belief in Christ already moved to a more spiritual plane. In this same letter there is the warning of a 'final age' where money will come first, there will be no respect for parents from their children and men will put pleasure in the place of God. (Virtually every generation since the second century appears to believe that this age has arrived in their own!) These reprobates appear to be succeeding and every Christian will have to face persecution in the ensuing breakdown of order. In First Timothy Christians are required to build up the spiritual resources within themselves in order to reject the threats; in Second Timothy they are urged to rely on the scriptures as these have the power to bring wisdom.

If these three letters had not been attributed to Paul, they would have been unlikely to have been added to the canon. There is very little of theological sophistication in them and they offer a very different picture of Christ from the other Pauline texts. Yet they were added to the canon and thus achieved an elevated status within the Christian tradition (and are frequently used as guides for living in fundamentalist Christian communities). What is new about them is their stress on the importance of scripture, an indication in itself that Christians had moved from the first generation of teachers to an age where authoritative texts were becoming more important. First Timothy sets it out well: 'Every inspired scripture has its use for teaching the truth and refuting error, or for reformation of manners and discipline in right living, so that the man who belongs to God may be efficient and equipped for good work of every kind' (3:16–17). In the early second century, if this was the date of the letters, 'inspired scripture' would be the Hebrew scriptures, but with the gathering of texts for a New Testament important questions arose. Which of the many scriptures in circulation are the 'inspired' ones and who decides? When a full body of scriptures has been assembled, are they all of equal status with each other? If so, how are contradictions between texts to be resolved? Who decides which interpretation of a particular verse is correct? With time, the texts themselves became corrupted with both copying errors and deliberate 'improvements' to suit the concerns of the copyist.[5] As will be seen in later chapters, there is a mass of early Christian texts attributed to the apostles and those close to Jesus. Most of these never reached the New Testament, of course, and it is not always clear why some were selected and some not.

There are, for instance, two letters in the New Testament attributed to the apostle Peter. As Eusebius acknowledged, the Second was not believed to be genuine even in the early church. The First has more supporters as an authentic text by the apostle but there are strong arguments against Peter's authorship, notably the relatively sophisticated Greek of the writer and, as with the letters discussed in the last chapter, a congregation which was more institutionalised than would have been expected in Peter's day. It also shows the influence of Paul, which one could hardly expect in a letter by an apostle who so clearly belonged to the Jewish Christian tradition that Paul had rejected. Again could Peter have possibly written a letter without some reference to the human Jesus he had spent so much time alongside – not even a mention of seeing him after the resurrection?

However, there could well be a link to Peter. In the first verse of the letter, the audience is described as 'exiles of the Diaspora in Pontus, Galatia, Cappadocia, Asia and Bithynia' – in other words, much of Asia Minor. In Acts 2:9, Jews from three of these regions, Cappadocia, Pontus and Asia, are mentioned as being addressed by Peter in Jerusalem. Bearing in mind that Acts also tells us that 'the Spirit' prevented Paul from entering Bithynia and that his message encountered strong opposition in Galatia from Jewish Christians (16:7), one can envisage a distinct church with allegiance to Peter and Jewish Christianity in these areas. So even if Peter himself did not write the letter, someone close to him in Rome (where tradition suggests that he was martyred) may have done so to those communities in Asia Minor who still remembered Peter as their inspiration. The letter's requirement that honour be given to the sovereign and submission to authority suggests a time when the church was not being persecuted by the state, possibly the period between the persecutions of Nero and Domitian and so between AD 70 and 90. Even so, the community is clearly under pressure from outsiders and a major aim of the letter is to boost their confidence and proclaim their distinct identity as, in the famous words of the letter, 'a royal priesthood'.

The term 'royal priesthood' has Old Testament precedents and such precedents pervade First Peter. Here is a writer whose Christianity is rooted in the Hebrew scriptures. Jesus is the cornerstone, as scripture foretold. He even reaches back to release, through his suffering, those who were lost in the Great Flood. He was predestined before the world began and now appears in the 'last period of time'. On earth he suffered and he carried the sins of mankind to the cross so that 'we might cease to live for sin and begin to live for righteousness'. As already suggested, there is no hint of a physical resurrection on earth – in fact, the opposite. 'In the body he was put to death; in the spirit he was brought to life' (1 Peter 3:18). This is close to the Pauline idea of the resurrection as essentially a spiritual event.

A major theme of the letter is the need to endure the present but also to expect the last days. In the second part of the letter (starting at 4:12) 'Peter' talks of the coming judgement, the 'fiery ordeal' that has already begun in 'God's own household'. The community itself will suffer but their suffering will be rewarded by a life of eternal glory with Christ. The behaviour expected of the audience while they wait is conventional: women must accept the authority of husbands, slaves that of their masters. The community must live in love with one another: 'love cancels innumerable sins'. Above all the example of Christ's suffering must provide an inspiration for enduring their own.

With the Letter of James, the next to be considered, we are back in the world of traditional Jewish piety. While some see it as an authentic work of James, the brother of Jesus and leader of the Jewish Christians, written perhaps as early as the 40s, the Greek, as with First Peter, seems too sophisticated for a Galilean villager. The writer describes himself as no more than 'a servant of God' while James would surely have made mention of his relationship to his brother, perhaps even referred to his life. The preference of scholars is for a writer who is aware of the authority and teachings of James but who is writing much later, perhaps in the 80s and 90s. As will be remembered James was a devout Jew and the letter is so steeped in Judaism that it may originally have been a Jewish text adapted for Christian use. There are only two mentions of Christ in the entire letter (would Jesus' own brother really have been so restrained?) – at the beginnings of Chapters One and Two, although the writer clearly knows of sayings of Jesus similar to those found in Q. The letter did not easily find its way into the New Testament. There is no mention of it at all in the Muratorian canon and both Origen in the third century and Eusebius in the fourth list it as a disputed text. It was only when leading authorities such as Athanasius in the east and Augustine in the west championed it in the later fourth century that it became accepted. The letter was known in Rome from the early second century so the original audience may have been there, with the writer possibly a follower of James from one of the scattered Jewish Christian communities of Palestine.

The letter is primarily one of exhortations. Sources for these include the Old Testament, above all the Book of Wisdom, which contains similar encouragement to live piously and trust in God and, as suggested, a collection of Jesus' sayings similar to those in Q that can be gleaned by comparing the text to verses from Matthew. There is no suggestion, however, that James knew the gospel itself. He was living in an age when enduring oral traditions about Jesus were circulating alongside the texts. The tone suggests a man who has integrated his reflections on these sayings into a coherent narrative but whose predominant concern is how to transform them into ethical living.

The community that 'James' addresses is not suffering persecution, but it is facing discrimination for its beliefs, particularly, we are told, from wealthy oppressors. It desperately needs to renew its commitment to God. The response urged by James is to reject the values of the world, avoid any kind of snobbery and boasting and concentrate on good works among the poor. Something more than action is required; it has to be rooted in deeper spiritual values, especially the 'wisdom' of God, 'peace-loving, considerate and open to reason' (James 3:17). The renunciation of wealth is valuable in itself in that those who are poor in material goods are rich in faith. There are specific exhortations for teachers and James embarks on a meditation on how the human tongue can be an instrument for good or bad. It can be used to praise God or curse one's fellows. The teacher must use it only for pure ends.

In this James is urging no more than the recovery of traditional Jewish practice but the famous verses (2:14 onwards) which proclaim that it is of no use for a man to claim he has faith if this has not be shown in action, have led many to believe that he was directly challenging Paul's belief that the grace of God could be earned only though faith. Again at 1:25 James urges his listeners to 'look closely into the perfect law, the law that makes us free' if they wish to find true happiness. Is James deliberately targeting followers of Paul over the Law and 'good works'? James' intention can probably never be recovered but, as we have seen, Paul's teachings aroused considerable opposition among Jewish Christians and James may be echoing this. These were issues over which conflict was inevitable. Martin Luther, a champion of Paul, was so insistent that good works should not form part of salvation that he argued that the letter should be excluded from the New Testament altogether.

Two short letters in the New Testament, Second Peter and Jude can be dealt with briefly. Jude is the earlier of the two, perhaps about 90. The writer claims to be Jude, the brother of James, but there is no link established to Jesus' family and certainly nothing to suggest any independent reminiscences of Jesus. To modern readers the letter comes across as a rant against intruders who threaten 'those whom God has called'. Verse after verse lambasts those who have infiltrated the community, threatened the authority of God and indulged in loose living. They have even invaded the 'love-feasts', presumably the Eucharistic celebrations. No one has been able to argue convincingly who these licentious intruders are or whether they are as destructive as the writer contends or simply the figment of his heated imagination. Some of the same polemic reappears in the Second Letter of Peter, the reason why it is dated later than Jude. Second Peter portrays a defensive, institutionalised church in which faith depends on believed truths, the authority of the apostles and traditions that have become embedded. It reflects the tensions of the second century as the church struggled to find its own identity.

Finally we come to the last of the books of the New Testament and the one which had to struggle the hardest to be accepted, the Book of Revelation. Its very nature has excited controversy from earliest times. While western Christians were more sympathetic to Revelation, it was widely rejected as authoritative in the Greek-speaking world. 'Not a revelation at all, since it is heavily veiled by its thick curtain of incomprehensibility' was the view of the third-century writer Dionysius of Alexandria. It was only Athanasius' championship of the book in the fourth century that earned it its place in the canon. At the Reformation, many of the Protestant leaders rejected it or gave it low status. Thomas Jefferson was even harsher: 'Merely the ravings of a maniac, no more worthy nor capable of explanation than the incoherencies of our own nightly dreams' was his opinion.[6] The modern view is more accepting and the biblical scholar Richard Bauckham reminds us that Revelation's legacy is substantial: 'It is a book that in all centuries has inspired the martyrs, nourished the imagination of visionaries, artists and hymn writers, resourced prophetic critiques of oppression and corruption in state and church, sustained hope and resistance in the most hopeless situations.'[7] Not least, its images of Jerusalem as a city of gold, its walls studded with precious stones, provided a rationale for opulent church building in the fourth century, the gold-encrusted marble basilicas being a pale imitation of the heavenly Jerusalem which would one day descend to earth (Chapter Twenty-one).

While the Book of Revelation sits bizarrely alongside the other New Testament texts, there are precedents within Jewish literature for 'The Apocalypse' as the book is also called, notably the Book of Daniel. An 'apocalypse' involves a disclosure of some heavenly truth to 'a seer'. In such visions the world is invariably seen as evil but God will establish his reign, usually in an extraordinary 'apocalyptic' visitation. The whole experience is described in extravagant imagery of beasts, dragons and harlots, with numbers such as seven taking on a quasi-mystical significance (seven acts as a symbol of wholeness). Much of this can be traced back to Old Testament sources and at one level the book can be seen as a widening of the scriptures to incorporate the advent of Christ as the instrument of God in his judgement of an evil world. Serious study of the text of Revelation has always risked being subverted by the mass of fantasists who relate every event of the contemporary world to one or other of its predictions and then retire discomfited (or to revise their calculations) when the world continues on its normal course. It makes more sense to relate its prophecies solely to the age in which it was written, as undoubtedly the author intended.

The receiver of this vision from Jesus Christ calls himself John and in earliest times it was assumed that this was none other than John the apostle and evangelist. Some of the symbolisms used in the Book – water providing life, the fertility of the natural world as a symbol of divine life – echo John's terminology. However, even in the third century, Christian scholars were noting that the styles were so different that they could not come from the same author. The Greek is not nearly as sophisticated as that of John's gospel. The clinching argument is that John of the gospel always writes of human beings *ascending into heaven* from a world which is left untouched by cosmic drama while the John of Revelation talks of Jerusalem *coming down to earth* as the culmination of terrible destruction and punishment of evil-doers.

An alternative John, John the Elder, a disciple of Jesus described by Papias, was proposed and championed by Eusebius but scholars today prefer to attribute the text to an unknown John. He claimed to be living on the island of Patmos, not far from Ephesus, apparently banished there for his faith (Revelation 1:9). (It is known to have been an island to which the emperors would send exiles.) The letter is addressed to seven churches in cities in western Asia Minor including Ephesus itself and its prosperous neighbour Smyrna (the modern Izmir). Each is given a message about the coming judgement and encouragement or warnings about how they will fare. Some cities such as Philadelphia and Smyrna are praised, others, notably Sardis and Laodicea, castigated for their spiritual barrenness. They are assailed by false prophets and prophetesses, slandered by Jews and prone to street violence. The retribution of Jesus is at hand; some will be saved and others will be smashed to pieces as if they are earthenware. The Book is essentially a warning of the dramatic events that will befall those who compromise with the evils of the world, idolise false gods or offer worship to the emperor. This was the time when cult worship of Roman emperors was spreading in the Greek cities of the empire and it must have been a concern of the writer. (Perhaps he was in exile in Patmos because of his resistance to the imperial cult.)

A door into heaven opens and the Spirit takes John through it. God sits in authority on the throne with elders around him. On his right hand is a scroll which at first, apparently, no one has the right to open. It is then announced that 'a lion of the tribe of Judah' is allowed to do so. Next 'a Lamb' with the marks of slaughter on him appears and is declared by the elders to be worthy of breaking its seal. The number seven reappears: seven seals are to be broken, seven trumpets are to sound and the contents of seven bowls to be poured out. Destruction is unleashed upon the earth in the shape of plague, earthquakes and other disasters while those to be saved will be bathed in the blood of the Lamb and clothed in white garments. Next a pregnant woman 'robed with the sun' appears with a dragon waiting to devour her child when it is born. (Here there seem to be classical allusions. Greek myth told the story of the birth of the sun god Apollo to Leto being attended by a threatening monster, the Python, which Apollo later slew.) The child (Jesus) is born and sucked up into heaven where a great battle between Michael and the dragon, who is no less than Satan, breaks out. The forces of heaven are victorious. The woman too escapes but back on earth Satan wreaks his revenge on those who remain faithful to Jesus. Satan also delegates his powers to beasts – one of which carries the mystical number 666. The beasts are normally assumed to be Roman emperors. (If one transliterates the Greek form of Nero Caesar into Hebrew consonants and then replaces each consonant by its numerical equivalent and adds them together, the total comes to 666.) Then there are dire warnings of the fall of their capital, Babylon, or Rome. The writer describes how seafarers saw Rome disintegrating in a great fire. (It is not impossible that this involved memories of the fire of AD 65 that destroyed a large part of

Rome. According to the historian Tacitus, it was as a response to the fire that Nero launched a persecution of Christians.)

Now the heavens open and a rider on a white horse (Jesus) appears, robed in a garment drenched in blood. Those who have been martyred or are not compromised by worship of 'the beast' come to life and reign with Christ for a thousand years until the final judgement. After the thousand years Satan will reorganise his forces but the old heaven and earth will vanish and a new heaven and earth are to emerge, the holy city of Jerusalem itself coming down from heaven 'like a bride adorned for her husband'. John is lucky enough to be shown the city descending. It is built of gold, with each of its gates made of a single pearl and the foundations of its wall precious stones. This Jerusalem has no need of a temple because the sovereign Lord and the Lamb have taken its place. Down the middle of the main street runs the water of the river of life. A tree of life is to be found on either side of the river, each producing a new crop every month.

This description hardly does justice to the vitality of the language of Revelation. Even though the text is often incoherent, it benefits from being read through as a whole so as to grasp an overview of the author's vision. The narrative makes its way through the chaos of the breakdown of order towards a new society at the end of time. Cosmic forces sway to and fro as the new heaven and earth are achieved and there is dire punishment for those who offend. The references in the gospels to Jesus bringing a sword are here acted out as he comes down to 'smite the nations'. It is perhaps this image that allowed Jesus to be incorporated so easily into the imperial iconography of fourth-century Christianity where he becomes no less than the 'leader of the legions' (see p. 253). In short, Revelation has infiltrated itself into the Christian tradition in many different contexts and reinforces the image of the Old Testament God as essentially punitive to those who offend him but as the champion of those who do not.

Whatever the forces that brought the final canonical texts of the New Testament together in the fourth century, they did not achieve a coherent body of teachings that could be used easily by believers. They were not selected for their compatibility on major issues, such as the nature of Christ. They show rather the *different* ways in which Christ was being worshipped in an age when communities were still trying to find meaning for their beliefs. When the demand for theological certainty grew in the fourth century onwards, different factions in the debates were drawn to different texts, some to the synoptic gospels as against the gospel of John, some to Paul as against the gospels. This was understandable and inevitable. It would prove particularly difficult to define the relationship between Jesus and God and the degree to which Jesus was divine while on earth and, if so, how this related to his humanity. Did he swap over from divinity to humanity at will or was he some kind of composite spiritual/human being at all times? The New Testament certainly provides no unambiguous answers to any of these questions. What it does provide is evidence of vitality and diversity within the early Christian world, an important legacy for those trying to understand how the history of Christianity developed.

CHAPTER TEN

No Second Coming

THE SEARCH FOR STABILITY

THE EARLY CHRISTIAN COMMUNITIES PRESENT A MAJOR CHALLENGE
for the historian: the sources are so limited. However, we may gain insights
from modern examples of small independent churches. In James Ault's account
of Baptist fundamentalism in the United States, *Spirit and Flesh*, for instance,
he explores the setting up of a small Baptist community in Worcester,
Massachusetts in the 1980s. The average size of a congregation was about a
hundred. The personality of the preacher proved important, as did the atmosphere of welcome that the community provided, especially as there were so
many rival Christian groups in the town for believers and searchers to choose
from. What was interesting was how the church relied heavily on existing
kinship or family groups and Ault suggests that rather than communities being
new expressions of religious commitment, they were reinforcing traditional
social networks. Even though the community claimed to be relying heavily on
a literal interpretation of the Bible, all of whose texts were assumed to be mutu-
ally consistent, often specific texts appear to have been isolated and used in
support of traditional values, while others were ignored.[1]

These communities tended to develop their own interpretation of
Christianity. There was a contrast between those congregations that relied
heavily on the written word of the Bible, avoiding any form of spontaneous
and charismatic involvement, and those for which it was central. Each relied
on a different set of texts of which the other seemed unaware. Some congregations imposed restrictions on the way women should dress in church, others
became fixated on homosexuality as the major sin, citing the Letter to the
Romans as their main source, even though Paul gives a long list of other sins
in the same text. Ault perceptively notes that many communities split when
they became of a size where members felt that they had lost their personal
contact with their pastor. Ault's study reminds us how many issues Christians
can disagree on, especially when situations arise when a very small disagreement reflects deeper personal tensions within the group. So when one reads

in the New Testament of 'false teachers' and those who deny Christ in the flesh, there is little to be surprised about. The so called *Didache*, 'The Lord's Teaching Through the Twelve Apostles to the Nations' of about AD 100 speaks of the problems of recognising genuine prophets in a way that would have been instantly familiar to Ault's fundamentalists.

The New Testament texts suggest a variety of communities struggling to define Jesus in a way that does not conflict with the ultimate authority of God. The definitions vary considerably just as one would expect when the congregations giving primary focus to the worship of Jesus as the Christ were so scattered and culturally diverse. They could draw on a layer of memories of Jesus as a historical figure preaching first in Galilee and then in Jerusalem. By the time he arrived there on his final journey, expectations of some kind of transformation of society – perhaps the coming of God's kingdom, perhaps a social revolution that would overthrow the power of the traditional priesthood – were high. The trauma of the crucifixion involved not only the destruction of the hopes of the disciples but also the gruelling torture of Jesus to death. The transformation of the Jesus movement into something more permanent in his memory was surely rooted in the maelstrom of emotions that was the immediate aftermath of the crucifixion, so one could hardly expect it to be straightforward.

Inevitably early explorations of the possibility that Jesus was something other than fully human used Jewish terminology. The most important was the concept of the Messiah, *Christos*, although this title had to be adapted from its normal meaning – of one who had come in power, and possibly in a military context, to save Israel – to deal with Jesus' apparent defeat on the cross. Paradoxically the cross itself became a symbol of victory (although not in art, where any representation of Christ on the cross was taboo for some centuries) and it was now believed to have been actively sought after by Jesus (or required of him by God) as a means of taking on the sins of the world and so bringing salvation. This in itself required humankind to be defined essentially in terms of its sinfulness. Paul was crucial here, both in dwelling on this sinfulness (above all in his Letter to the Romans) but also in recreating the crucifixion and the vision of a resurrected Christ in terms of cosmic drama. Paul was also important in defining the resurrection as an essentially spiritual event. Outside the gospels there is no mention of a physical appearance of Christ on earth; the emphasis is rather on God's raising him from the dead, apparently straight into heaven where, as 'the first fruits', he inaugurates the possibility of resurrection for all. His later appearances are as visions.

There remained the problem of finding a place for Jesus alongside, or subordinate to, the majesty of God. The extreme views ranged from those who saw Jesus as essentially human but adopted by God, in much the same way as the prophets had been, and those who saw him as a pre-existent figure who lived with God, was sent as an ambassador, the *logos*, to earth and then returned to sit at the right hand of God, having fulfilled his role through his suffering. John even hints that he is to be seen as equal to God the Father, an idea which naturally caused outrage, but which was, though no one could have predicted it, to triumph in the fourth century in the doctrine of the Trinity. The predominant view of the canonical texts of the New Testament is that Jesus is quasi-divine but always subordinate to the Father who sends him to earth from above, or raises him from his human existence.

The first Christian communities, those whose primary allegiance was to Jesus Christ, however they defined him, endured much in order to survive. They were always on the margins of Judaism and so vulnerable to attack from conservative Jews. There are also reports of persecution from the Roman authorities. The historian Tacitus documented Nero's targeting of Christians after the great fire in Rome in 64. He tells how Nero ordered Christians to be crucified, set alight or dressed in the skins of beasts and set upon by dogs. So brutal and vindictive were these atrocities that they resulted in a backlash in favour of the Christians. Although it has been hard to discover the extent of any persecution of Christians under Domitian in the 90s, there are hints in the sources that Christians suffered misfortunes and setbacks in this period. In Rome, Clement (see below) talks of 'the sudden and successive calamitous events' which have happened to his congregation in this period. Yet the biggest threat seems to have been internal – the 'false teachers' who are found in almost every Christian community. Yet what else could one expect? What was truth or falsehood in this fluid situation when there were bound to be different emphases on the way Jesus was perceived? There must have been many cases where one individual or faction decided that its interpretation was superior to others and attempted to impose it. Either schism, as in John's community, or internal wrangling would have been the inevitable result.

The *Didache* (whose author and place of origin are unknown) is an important text in showing how an early community defined itself. The author, who claims to be directly representing the apostles, draws heavily on Jewish tradition, especially on the rules for fasting which are similar to those required of Jews but are to be celebrated on different days of the week to emphasise a distinction from Judaism. Some of the prayers designated for the Eucharist are based on Jewish ones, yet Christians are also expected to say the Lord's Prayer three times a day. The text may even have been a manual of instruction for Jews that had been rewritten to meet the needs of Christians. The author appears to know of Christian traditions similar to those of Matthew (presumably from the same matrix of ideas that Matthew drew on) but he knows nothing of Paul even though he often expresses hostility to Jews. So this is an isolated community that is evolving out of Judaism and carefully defining barriers between itself and its host religion but without any inspiration from Paul.

The gateway into the community is provided through baptism in Jesus, 'the holy vine of David your servant', through whom God has made known the news of salvation. Baptism allows the convert access to the Eucharist. The writer is determined to find a common core of moral values that can bind the fledgling community together. Included among the sins to avoid are abortion and infanticide and overall the values are those of traditional Jews. Finding a basis for authority is crucial. The importance of respect for the priest is stressed, as against the lure of false prophets. An injunction to 'give high priority to the unity of the church and to reconciling those groups which are inclined to schism' must reflect the tensions which threatened this otherwise unknown group of believers. There is a hint that Jews ('the hypocrites') are taunting them for believing in a man, Jesus, who was cursed by the manner of his death.[2]

By AD 100 more stable communities were emerging. It may have been the very experience of hostility that helped give them their cohesion. In the very early days this cohesion was boosted by confident predictions that pagans and all others who rejected Christ would suffer eternal damnation. The Day of Judgement was proclaimed to be on its way and the transformation that would precede it could already be sensed by those committed to Christ. The Christians needed to preserve themselves until this Second Coming took place. Now, some decades on, with no evidence of an imminent Second Coming, a framework for survival had to be erected. An initiation ceremony, baptism by water, which in early days seems to have been a once and for all commitment with permanent effect (unlike the ritual purifications required of Jews in specific circumstances), was in place. There were formal gatherings, many of them in private houses. Some of these involved listening to the Hebrew scrip-tures and the new texts, gospels, letters and stories of the apostles which were circulating, others included a shared meal, the Eucharist, rooted in memories of the Last Supper. Ignatius, bishop of Antioch in the early 100s, refers to the Eucharist as 'the medicine of immortality and an antidote, that we do not die but live forever [sic] in Jesus Christ'. This reiterates Paul's belief that participa-tion in the Eucharist might lead to a transformation of the physical body into something more spiritual, even transcendent, before death.

Meanwhile confidence was maintained by definitions of the Christians as a 'royal priesthood' (1 Peter 2:29). Their leaders told them that they 'walked in the light', in other words had transcended the material world. There were precedents here, of course, with the Qumran community. The precepts by which Christians were required to live were, however, conventional ones.

Sober living, traditional family relationships, the maintenance of the social hierarchy, including the ownership of slaves, were all enjoined. Women were expected to continue in their traditional roles and not to participate openly in church activities. The Letter to Titus even demands allegiance to the imperial authorities.

One of the most important documents relating to the growing institutionalisation of the church is the First Letter of Clement, dated perhaps to 96. Clement was later described as bishop of Rome, in fact among the first of the popes, though it appears that early leadership in the Rome church was collegiate (the evidence suggests a number of small but distinct congregations) and he may have been only one of its leaders. The letter is perhaps best known for its reference to the martyrdom of Peter and Paul (Chapter Five). The letter does not specifically say where the martyrdoms took place but tradition taught that it had been in Rome and this is why Clement knew of them.

There have been painstaking attempts to assemble the evidence of the early church in Rome. It appears to have broken with synagogue worship by the 50s, perhaps even after disturbances that resulted in the expulsion of Christian Jews such as Prisca and Aquila from Rome. By the time Paul wrote to the Romans, he assumed that most Christians had come from pagan communities but had preserved knowledge of Jewish traditions within the community. Clement mentions a tradition in the earliest Roman church of Christians deliberately selling themselves into slavery so as to raise funds to support their fellow Christians. However, by the time he was writing, fifty years on, there were wealthier Christians. Clement exhorts them to help the poor while telling the poor that they in their turn should respect the rich. Hard though it is to reconstruct the early church in Rome, there is evidence of it here as a community attracting converts from across the classes by 100. There is yet no further evidence for the existence, let alone primacy, of Peter in the Roman church but, some time after 160, a modest memorial was built over a grave in a cemetery on the Vatican that was revered as his resting place. Constantine was to centre the first St Peter's directly above it.[3]

The primary aim of Clement's letter was to admonish the Christians of Corinth for the way one faction, described as 'worthless', had risen up against their own 'presbyters' (Greek *presbyteros*, an elder). Their disruptions, Clement warns them, are even worse than they had been in the days of Paul! Clement assumes some kind of authority over Corinth, certainly the right to supervise the community when things go wrong. The letter also refers to an apostolic succession, the idea that the apostles themselves passed on their authority to a new generation of priests, who would pass on their authority in turn. So long as the presbyters of Corinth live blameless lives, they deserve the respect of their contentious flock. The ideal has been betrayed by the squabbling Corinthians (Chapters Forty-two to Forty-four).

This letter is important evidence of an emerging church hierarchy. Even if the early Christian communities had been egalitarian, the traditional Jewish division between a priestly elite and the laity had reasserted itself. By 100 there are the first references to bishops as senior to presbyters and deacons. The Greek word *episkopos* originally meant an overseer and so its early use by Paul does not necessarily imply a bishop in the sense of an authoritative leader of a church community. By the early 100s, on the other hand, in the letters of Ignatius, the *episkopos* is treated as an important figure in his own right: 'You are clearly obliged to look upon the bishop as the Lord himself,' he writes. Ignatius tells of his efforts to set up one centralised church in Antioch from which baptisms and the Eucharist could be controlled. He complains that many of the Christian households of the city are inviting wandering charismatics to carry out their services and are resentful of his efforts at control. In his letters he expands on the need for the bishop to exhort his congregations to trust in their baptism, to care for widows and the poor and even to protect their slaves. He has praise for those who free them (a right which had always existed in Roman law). The bishop should oversee the finances of the community and approve all marriages. He is the focal point for a unified church community and a bastion against schism.

At some point (Eusebius specifically dates the event to 107 but it may be later), Ignatius was arrested by the authorities and transported, probably with other Christians, to Rome. Despite his captivity he seems to have been allowed to communicate with the churches of the larger cities he passed through and he pleads with them to respect the authority of their bishops. He encounters all kinds of dissenting groups – Jews who wish to maintain separate churches, others who see the Hebrew scriptures as having greater authority than more recent Christian texts which are now circulating, docetists who hope to keep their belief in a Christ who was not 'of flesh' and those who place insufficient, as Ignatius sees it, emphasis on the Eucharist as the unifying ritual of the church. He calls on them all to live in unity under their bishop. Yet the issue, which overshadows all as he nears Rome, is his impending martyrdom. He actively yearns for it and when influential members of the Roman Christians are urged to be allowed to plead for his release, he refuses to let them deprive him of his martyr's crown. This desire to die in the cause of Christ and the subsequent veneration of those who have done so are important features of this new phase in the history of Christianity.

Who were the early members of Christian communities? They appear to have been a diverse group. Many remained close to Judaism, certainly to its scriptures, even if they had by now rejected the need for circumcision, ritual diet and sacrifice. Clement uses examples from the Hebrew scriptures to support his chastising of the Corinthians. He lists all the Jewish prophets who found favour with God on account of their faithfulness. He recounts how Moses had solved the problem of dissensions among the priesthood by asking for a sign from God, the blossoming of a rod that showed that Aaron was the chosen priest. So here are communities still deeply rooted in Judaism. Others may have been from that elusive group, the so-called God-fearers who lingered on the edge of the Jewish communities without giving them full commitment. Then there was the wider Gentile community targeted by Paul. Some of these would have been used to cults involving initiation rites, collegiate activities including shared meals and belief in a spiritual world that somehow transcended the evils of the material one and so many features of Christianity might have been familiar to them. Greek was the language of the church – even in Rome. The earliest Christian text in Latin is dated to about 180. In the western empire, this meant that Christians were distinguished from their fellow pagans by language as well as belief.

The sparse records of the early Christians suggest that there were adherents from most strata of society, excepting only the aristocracy and the landless poor. In Paul's letters there is the dyer Lydia in Philippi and the city treasurer of Corinth, Erastus. Luke's patron, Theophilus, appears to be of high status while Barnabas, with Paul in attendance, seems to have gained an audience with Sergius Paullus, governor of Cyprus, without difficulty. Ignatius' correspondents in Rome must have been influential in the community if they were ready to plead with the authorities on his behalf. Other early leaders were householders able to host the Eucharistic meal in their homes. Yet there is also an abundance of references in the letters to the artisan class, such as the members of the Thessalonian church whom Paul addressed. Here James echoes Paul's approach when he castigates the very wealthy as oppressors ready to haul the poor into court. It is the poor not the rich that have faith, an ethos that is to be found, of course, in the gospels and in Jewish life. Many of the letters specifically mention the slaves, if only to command them to maintain their obedience to their masters. Some comparison can perhaps be made between Christianity and the cult of Mithras, where there were initiation rituals, shared meals and a similar mix of adherents, both slave and free. If the ferocity with which Christians later targeted Mithraic shrines is anything to go by, the two may have seen themselves as rivals for the same audience.

The position of women is more complex. Jesus was clearly open to them, ready to associate even with those who were considered dissolute by his apostles. Paul claims to give women equality with men before Christ. Yet, while there is no record of either man being married, one senses a completely different response to the presence of women. Jesus was adamant in his condemnation of divorce but he does not seem to have been preoccupied with the temptations of physical contact in the way that Paul was. Jesus does not withdraw from the crowds and is confident of his authority. He transcends sexuality. Paul is consumed with fears of his own unworthiness and refers often to the destructive power of lust. He regards celibacy as preferable to marriage for those who can control their desires (but marriage for those who cannot, 'Better to marry than to burn') and this approach becomes popular. In the Book of Revelation 14:4 the saints following the Lamb of God are all 'undefiled with women' and Ignatius also recognises celibacy as a higher state of being. This was in conflict with traditional Jewish views on the importance of marriage and family life. However, Christianity did provide roles for women that may have been denied them elsewhere. There is the specific injunction to widows in First Timothy: 'A widow in the full sense, one who is alone in the world, has all her hope set on God, and regularly attends the meetings for prayer and worship night and day. But a widow given over to self-indulgence is as good as dead' (1 Timothy 5:5). This circumscribed role was to lead to the consecrated Christian virgin who was given a respected status within her community.

It is often said that Jesus initiated a new era in the history of human ethics, revealing the love of God for humankind through his teachings and sacrifice on the cross. These values were, of course, deeply rooted in Jewish tradition and it is not easy to distinguish specifically Christian aspects of them. It is difficult to find historical evidence for Jesus' self-sacrifice, although this role may have been given to him shortly after the crucifixion. The challenge in understanding why God's love might be expressed in the appalling torture of his 'only Son' remains formidable. It seems to offend one's deepest ethical instincts. It is also difficult to reconcile the love of God with his apparent willingness to confine so many individuals to eternal punishment. Pagan philosophers noted that a god who needs to persecute can hardly have confidence in his own authority. The notion of a coherent set of Christian ethics is made more complicated by three distinct traditions, those of the Old Testament, Jesus and Paul, each with a different emphasis and focus and each with its own inconsistencies. How does one fit in, for instance, the 'miracle' by which Peter brings about the deaths of Ananias and Sapphira after they withheld money promised to the apostles (Acts 5:1–12)?

Is it possible to speak of a Christian identity in this period? Traditionally these early Christian communities have been portrayed as having a strong sense of mission and purpose. They were, it was said, already well on their way to defining what would later become 'the church', making an effective break with their Jewish roots in the process. Yet most of the texts speak of disputes and divisions and an ambivalent attitude to Judaism. The more that is known of the diversity of Judaism, the more it is understood that there could be distinct Christianities that evolved from different Jewish traditions. The empire itself was so fragmented and any new Christian community would have to adapt to local pagan conditions to survive. It seems difficult, then, to talk of any form of institutional church at this date. The picture is rather of many different conceptions of Jesus and ways of worshipping him, some more rooted in Judaism than others.

PART TWO: BECOMING CHRISTIAN

CHAPTER ELEVEN

Toeholds in a Wider Empire

THE ASTONISHING EXPANSION OF THE ROMAN EMPIRE BEGAN IN
the fifth and fourth centuries BC with the absorption of the mountainous
terrain of Italy. The challenges of these early campaigns established a
pattern whereby each victory led to the accumulation of plunder and
manpower that fuelled the next conquest. Sicily, the Carthaginian empire of
the western Mediterranean, and the whole Greek world of the east followed.
By AD 117, on the death of the emperor Trajan, the entire Mediterranean and
outlying areas such as Britain and Dacia, across the Danube, and the civilisations of ancient Egypt and the Near East were under Roman control. It was
Trajan's successor, Hadrian (AD 117–138), who understood that continuous
expansion was self-defeating. He consolidated the boundaries of the empire,
reformed the legions as a defensive force and concentrated on his real passion,
the culture of the Greeks. He loved to tour the major cities, scatter his largesse
on them and compete with their intellectuals as an equal.

In his great work on the Mediterranean, Fernand Braudel reminded his
readers that the Mediterranean was not a single sea.[1] Rather it was a succession of smaller seas and even within these there were smaller distinct communities. There was never a coherent Roman Empire or something describable
simply as 'Christianity'. Rather there was a mass of different cultures, patterns
of rule and spiritual movements. The first Christians related Christianity to
what they already knew. The Jewish roots remained the most nutritious.
However much the life and death of Jesus seemed to represent a turning point
in human history (and was certainly believed to be so by later Christians),
most of the ways in which Jesus was described were not unique to him but had
Jewish precedents. He was 'the son of David' of the gospels and the 'chief
priest' of Hebrews among many other titles.

After AD 100 Christianity had to find its own niches in a very different environment – the Greek-speaking eastern Mediterranean. It used to be argued
that Greek culture was stagnant in the second century AD, especially when

compared to the achievements of the classical era of the fifth and fourth centuries BC. In his *The Decline and Fall of the Roman Empire*, Edward Gibbon suggested that 'the name of Poet was almost forgotten; that of Orator usurped by the sophists [philosophers who sold their knowledge to students, thus, in the eyes of some, debasing themselves]. A cloud of critics, of compilers, of commentators darkened the face of learning and the decline of genius was soon followed by the corruption of taste.' In the early twentieth century, Christian scholars, notably Adolf von Harnack, agreed. Philosophy, Harnack argued, had become introspective, religious rituals had become meaningless and lost their vigour. Christianity, on the other hand, was apparently an active and attractive spiritual force that filled the void.

This claim of a moribund Greek world has long since been exploded. Archaeological research and a renewed interest in Greek literature of the period have shown that Greek culture was buzzing, dynamic and expansionist. Certainly the Greeks had been shattered by the experience of defeat and humiliation at the hands of the Romans in the second century BC but their conquerors valued Greek civilisation and by the second century AD confidence in their intellectual superiority had returned. In fact, it was under Roman rule that Greek culture penetrated more fully into the civilisations of the eastern Mediterranean than it had ever done in the aftermath of the conquests of Alexander.

Far from intellectual life being moribund, some of the finest Greek minds were at work in these years. The Alexandrian scholar Ptolemy compiled the most sophisticated Greek work on astronomy, the *Almagest* (from its Arabic title 'the Greatest') in the AD 130s. Ptolemy also made an immense contribution to the discipline of geography, especially in devising means of establishing coordinates and mapping a globe on a flat surface. In medicine, Galen was recognised as both an outstanding logician and a dedicated observer of the human body, establishing the paths of nerves and the functions of arteries. Plutarch of Chaeronea (*c*.AD 50–120) is credited with some two hundred works of moral philosophy, history and commentary (they were still regarded as classics two hundred years later but most have since been lost). His twinned lives of prominent Greeks and Romans showed that, despite tensions between the two dominant cultures of the empire, there were ways in which they could find accommodations. It was the quintessentially Roman emperor Marcus Aurelius who composed his 'Stoic' *Meditations* in Greek. The pagan Plotinus (AD 204/5–270) possessed what was probably the finest spiritual mind of the early Christian centuries. These figures were part of a rich intellectual world in which a knowledge of Homer and the Greek tragedians, the works of the great philosophers such as Plato and Aristotle and an understanding of the challenges of scientific and mathematical knowledge were expected of any well-trained mind.

One reason for the ease with which the Greeks were able to penetrate further east was that Roman rule was comparatively restrained. Provincial governors normally held their posts for only two to three years and in the more settled provinces their staffs were small. It was the local elites who were expected to keep order, as we have already seen in the case of Judaea where the high priest presided. This was a collaborationist empire, elites and the Roman governing class each recognising the importance to the other of maintaining status. Greek cities flourished, new ones were founded and the elites absorbed Greek cultural symbols in their buildings, language and the acquisition of *paideia*, the good breeding and behaviour that went hand in hand with an education in the Greek classics.

The best-known example of the relationship between emperor and a Greek-speaking province is to be found in the correspondence between Trajan and the younger Pliny, governor of Bithynia and Pontus, a province made up of two kingdoms absorbed by Rome in the first century BC. While the people of the province were Thracian in origin, its culture was overwhelmingly Greek: there were ancient Greek cities on the coastline and new foundations had been added inland. However, at the beginning of the second century AD, the prosperity of the region was being undermined by poor administration. Petitions had been sent to Rome with complaints of corruption against two of its governors. Too many major city building projects were started and then left uncompleted. The situation had to be taken in hand and the emperor Trajan sent Pliny, one of his most experienced senators, from Italy to examine the affairs of the troubled province. He arrived in 111. There are forty issues on which Pliny and the emperor communicated over two years and among them was the problem of how to deal with Christians.

The very fact that there was concern tells us a great deal. This was a good distance from the cities of Syria and the province of Asia where the early Christian communities had been recorded. Here they are seen as a distinct group; there is no hint of any residual link to Judaism. Pliny notes that it is not only the towns, but also villages and rural districts that are 'infected through contact with this wretched cult'. There are men and women of every age and class. (There is no other independent account from this period of such a flourishing Christian population.) When questioned, the Christians deny wrongdoing and they claim that their activities involve no more than meeting once a week before dawn to chant verses to Christ 'as if he were a God' and to bind themselves by an oath to abstain from theft, robbery and adultery. In a separate ceremony they engage in some kind of meal that involves food 'of an ordinary, harmless kind'. These meetings had already been banned under general measures that prohibited 'political societies'.

In reply, Trajan urges caution. There should be no hunting out of suspects. Anonymous accusations should be disregarded: 'they create the worst form of precedent and are quite out of keeping with the spirit of our age'. Only when a Christian is actually brought before him should Pliny deal with the matter. Even then Christians who have lapsed (a reminder that conversion did not necessarily last) or who are prepared to swear an oath to the traditional gods should be released whatever their previous conduct. If they do not recant, however, they should be executed after due warning while those who are Roman citizens should be sent to Rome for trial.

In this instance, being an active and unrepentant Christian was now seen as a capital offence. This was the same period, and in the reign of the same emperor, that Ignatius of Antioch was taken to Rome for execution as a Christian. So what exactly was the offence? The fact that no action would be taken against a Christian if he or she made an oath to the gods and showed reverence to the statue of the emperor suggests that a gesture of loyalty to the authorities was crucial. It is easy to understand why. Jesus had been executed as an enemy of the empire, a man accused, even if on a fabricated charge, of conspiring to be king of the Jews and thus a direct threat to the Romans. This echoes the hostile crowds in Thessalonica: 'These men all act against the edicts of Caesar, saying there is another king, Jesus' (Acts 17:7). Those administrators acquainted with Judaism would also have known that a messiah was traditionally linked to military and public upheaval and so for this reason alone those who followed such a leader were suspect. Only a very few years later a self-proclaimed messiah in Jerusalem, Shimon Bar Kosiba, was to lead a major revolt against Rome. So the concern was justified. (One cannot expect Jews, let alone Roman administrators, to have known how Christians had adapted Isaiah's 'suffering son' to create their distinct form of messiah.)

Further suspicion would have been aroused by the Christian practice of meeting in secret. In both the Greek and Roman worlds, associations (*collegia*) were widespread. Many, especially those concerned with the professions, were considered respectable and emperors allowed Jewish groups to gather to collect Temple tribute and soldiers to participate in the cult of Mithras. Burial clubs were also permitted. The rest were officially frowned upon. In the specific case of Bithynia, Trajan had insisted on a ban on all associations unless they had already been established under the local laws of a city. No Christian group would have at this period received such recognition and so would have fallen under the ban. Pliny mentions how he tortured two Christian slave girls, said to be deaconesses. The information he gained through this brutal treatment (which was standard in the examination of slaves) was no more than that their cult was degenerate and 'carried to extravagant lengths'.

This reflects the prejudices of an upper-class Roman. Roman religion was highly ritualised. There was an intense distrust of what was known as *superstitio*, a broad and somewhat flexible term covering any kind of exotic or over-exuberant religious activity. The Roman historian Tacitus, a friend of Pliny, regarded Judaism as a *superstitio*, although he grudgingly accepted its ancient origins gave it some respectability. It was in the Jews' rejection of the Roman gods that the *superstitio* lay but Tacitus also condemned the Egyptian worship of the god Serapis in Alexandria. For Pliny 'the extravagance' of Christians was part of the same pattern, an unsettling religious activity that deserved nothing more than contempt (he used the word *superstitio* in the letter to Trajan, here translated as 'cult'). The fact that slaves, and female ones at that, had some official position in the cult cannot have helped its cause.

So a cluster of factors accounts for the persecution of those Christians who persisted in the practice of their faith: they were seen as disloyal to the state, as members of an association at a time when these were declared illegal in Bithynia and as guilty of participation in a cult that offended Roman convention. However, until the empire-wide persecutions of the third century, the authorities refused to overreact against Christianity. At Dura-Europus a Christian community appears to have been worshipping peacefully in the 230s. In the African provinces there is no record of any execution of a Christian before 180. Hadrian and Antoninus Pius, emperor from 138–61, shared Trajan's distaste for witch-hunts. Eusebius quotes an imperial reply from Antoninus Pius to the proconsul of Asia, Minucius Fundanus, warning him not to prosecute individual Christians simply on petitions or 'mere clamour'. Antoninus Pius, who, in contrast to his restless predecessor Hadrian, stayed in Rome 'like a spider at the centre of a web', noted how Christians simply became more determined when attacked. In one response to a city council in Asia he reminded the councillors that Hadrian had written to provincial governors telling them only to take action against Christians if it was clear that they were actually scheming against the Roman government. Those launching unscrupulous prosecutions of Christians should themselves be pros-ecuted. The governor should hear accusations in person. In a large province this might mean waiting for some time for him to arrive at an outlying city, another restraint on impetuous accusations. In this period, AD 120–250, it was more likely to be mob hysteria than state initiatives that led to the rounding up of Christians.

While the references to Christians in pagan literature and official documents remain few, there is evidence that Christians were now seen as a distinct group, even if a discordant one. One opponent, writing about AD 200, describes Christians as 'a crowd that lurks in hiding places, shunning the light; they are speechless in public but gabble away in corners'.[2] How the communities grew is unknown. In his *History of the Church*, Eusebius provides an overview for the second century AD from a fourth-century perspective that suggests large-scale conversion by itinerant preachers: 'Staying only to lay the foundations of the faith in one foreign place or another, appoint others as pastors, and entrust to them the tending of those newly brought in, the preachers set off again for other lands and peoples with the grace and cooperation of God, for even at that late date many miraculous powers of the divine spirit worked through them, so that at the first hearing whole crowds in a body embraced with a whole-hearted eagerness the worship of the universal creator.' Here there is an echo of the Acts of the Apostles. Whole communities appear to have been converted en masse by the skill of itinerant ministers. So in the Acts of John, when the apostle John prays in the great temple to Artemis in Ephesus that the demon who lives there might be driven out by God, the altar of Artemis is said to have split into pieces and half the temple to have fallen down. The astonished crowds announce their conversion. The casting out of demons is seen as a particularly potent expression of divine support. In another text a martyr drowns at Caesarea in Palestine and an earth tremor sweeps the victim ashore. Overawed by the wrath of God against the persecutors, the whole town is converted. These can hardly have been real events but Celsus, writing his attack on Christianity in the later second century, also talks of Christianity spread by preachers who penetrate remote villages and country houses.

A series of apocryphal stories (meaning, in this context, texts, usually of a much later date, wrongly attributed to the apostles or other early Christians) of the apostles written in the second or early third centuries are often disregarded as of no historical value, yet they tell a great deal about how Christians saw themselves in this period. They share a common theme. An apostle arrives in a city, preaches and converts many. Usually a high-born woman is among the converts and she then calls on her husband to renounce sexual relations with her. The infuriated husband succeeds in return in having the apostle sentenced to death. The emphasis is not only on the distastefulness of sex, 'horrid intercourse' as the Acts of Thomas puts it, but on the apostle challenging the traditional social hierarchy and the subverting of the institution of marriage. Christians are presenting themselves as the representatives of a counter-culture.

One of the most interesting of these Acts, in this case one from the second century, is that of Thecla, a wealthy woman from Asia Minor who renounces the marriage offered her, breaks with her family and baptises herself. She then meets the apostle Paul (who is given a subsidiary role in the drama) and he commissions her to go and preach. The Acts of Thecla must have struck a chord with women; it was translated from the original Greek into Syriac, Latin and other languages. The crusty Tertullian, an arch conservative so far as women were concerned, condemned it for encouraging women to believe that they had the right to baptise others. It shows that there were some Christian groups where women assumed prominence, but very little is known of them.

More sophisticated pagans mocked the credulity of Christians. In his *The Passing of Peregrinus*, the second-century writer Lucian, one of the most fertile minds of the period, ridicules them. The hero of *The Passing*, an unscrupulous philosopher by the name of Proteus, worms his way into Christian circles in Palestine, persuades their gullible members that he is a prophet, offers interpretations of their texts and even composes some himself. He proves so successful that the Christians treat him as second only to Christ. His activities, however, land him in prison but his fellow believers rally around to defend him. Lucian describes the Christians as so credulous that they really believe they are going to live for ever, that they are justified in despising all the Greek gods and that they will be saved by 'that crucified sophist himself'. It proves all too easy for a sophisticated charlatan like Proteus to gain their allegiance.

Communities converted en masse are notoriously unstable and many of the new Christians must have lapsed (as Pliny's own comments suggest). Yet a charismatic preacher can create a sustained religious movement. The early twentieth-century Congolese prophet Simon Kimbangu, who came from a Baptist background, began preaching in the Belgian Congo in 1921 and within a period of only six months achieved an enthusiastic following. Kimbangu saw himself as a Christ figure: he had his own twelve apostles and preached ascetic renunciation. Crowds flocked from the plantations to hear him speak and hospitals emptied as the sick left them to be cured. The word spread that a *ngunza* (prophet) and *mvuluzi* (apostle, messiah) was among the Congo people. Kimbangu was said to raise the dead. His village, Nkamba, was renamed New Jerusalem. The movement was so powerful that it was seen to threaten the Belgian imperial authorities. European missionaries were furious that Kimbangu's preaching achieved far more than their own activities. When he managed to evade the first attempt to seize him, his followers announced that his escape was yet another miracle. He was eventually arrested and sentenced to death. Kimbangu was never executed but spent thirty years in prison where his pious behaviour gained him more converts. He died in 1951 but his movement continued without him. His Church of Jesus Christ on Earth was one of the first to be admitted to the World Council of Churches.[3]

If one is looking for a similar example in the early Christian world, then Gregory the Wonderworker appears to offer a parallel. Gregory came from an aristocratic background in Neocaesaraea in Pontus, the province where Pliny had served. He had been a student of the great theologian Origen in Caesarea in Palestine and had adopted the name Gregory, 'the reawakened one', after his conversion to Christianity. He returned to his home town in about 240 to become bishop. It was said that there were only seventeen Christians in Neocaesaraea when he returned and only seventeen pagans left when he died thirty years later. In the adulatory Life of Gregory, written by the Cappadocian Gregory of Nyssa in the 380s, he comes across as a true miracle worker. He expels demons, lifts enormous boulders, changes the course of a river and brings a plague to an end. When some pagans who had packed too tightly into a theatre called upon Zeus for more space, Gregory ensured that God struck them down by disease for such brazen idolatry. Yet there is no archaeological evidence for the spread of Christianity in Neocaesaraea in the third century: the city's coinage shows that pagan festivals were still in full swing in the 260s and the accounts of Gregory's success now appear exaggerated. It seems more likely that miracle working had become part of the literary presentation of any early church leader. Gregory's prestige probably derived from his power as an aristocrat able to get things done in an age of social breakdown. As an individual Gregory might well have offered an administrative and charismatic energy lacking in the provincial or local government, a sign of the growing importance of bishops in the civic networks of city life.

It is notoriously difficult to evaluate a conversion. An early model is, of course, Paul's dramatic revelation on the road to the Damascus, so powerful that Augustine is said to have used it to shape his own account of conversion in the *Confessions*, even though Augustine only came to his new religion after a long and fraught process of self-discovery. Conversion may not in reality have been traumatic or as sudden as Paul's, and it is easy to exaggerate the contrast between Christian and other religious communities. Many features of the early Christian congregations – the initiation rite of baptism and a communal meal such as the Eucharist – would have been recognisable in other religious fellowships. The reading of texts at weekly meetings was a well-established Jewish practice even if there is no record of any pagan cult having such an extensive reliance on sacred writings. Nor was the worship of a single all-powerful god unique to Christianity and Judaism. One study of Anatolia makes the point well: 'Outwardly, at least, there was much in common between the paganism of late Roman Asia Minor and contemporary Judaism and Christianity. God was an awesome, remote and abstract figure to be reached through the agency of divine intermediaries, such as angels, or human ones such as prophets. The language which men chose to describe the supreme god of both pagans and Christians was sometimes indistinguishable, and had close affinities with language that was taken over and elaborated in the philosophy of the age.'[4] Belief in a single supreme god penetrated to quite humble levels. Many tomb inscriptions mention *theos hypsistos*, 'the most high God', a term used by Jews from the second century BC. By the second century

AD, this might also refer to the god of both pagans or Christians. So, for the Anatolians, conversion might not have been as dramatic as Christian sources suggest. An inscription from the tomb of one Neikatoris from Mysian Hadriani proclaims that he 'had gained greatest honour among all men, and brought joy to the holy people of the highest God, and charmed them with sacred songs and readings, and who sleeps now immaculate in Christ's place'.

Nor did the church encourage sudden conversions. Two texts from third-century Roman sources, Rome and Carthage, show that an elaborate ritual was in place for converts in the western empire.[5] Supplicants for admission to the community would present themselves to the teachers with sponsors to vouch for their sincerity. They must distance themselves from pagan rituals and occupations that require them to respect these. In the process of instruction, which might take three years, catechumens would be continually interrogated for evidence of good conduct. They would be repeatedly exorcised as if there was a persistent fear that the devil would infiltrate the church through the medium of unworthy applicants. A successful commitment would be followed by 'hearing the gospel'. A final exorcism would lead to the day of baptism on Easter Sunday followed by the first participation in the Eucharist. This, then, is a slow process by which an individual moves from one state of mind and code of behaviour to another.

In the end, it is hard to say what drew people to Christianity in these first centuries. This was a world where spirituality was flexible, where new cults rose and fell and drew from each other. This was as true for those societies outside Greek culture as for those within it. A very distinct Syriac Christianity (Syriac is a dialect of Aramaic) flourished in cities such as Nisibis in Syria and Edessa on the frontier with Persia. Missionaries from these cities converted King Trdat of Armenia in 311 and he declared Christianity his state religion well before Constantine did the same in the western empire. Missionaries from Syria reached Ethiopia in the mid fourth century. Then there are the twenty bishops recorded in Persia in AD 235 who themselves led missions that took Christianity as far as Basra (in southern Iraq), Qatar and the modern Oman and Yemen. The royal family of Kerala in southern India might even have been converted in the early third century. By the end of the second century, and then only in a few areas, Christianity spread to the Latin west. So while the early Christianities were distinctive sects which were Jewish in origin but capable of adapting their beliefs in Christ to a Greek environment, they had the flexibility and vigour to expand well beyond that.

CHAPTER TWELVE

Open Borders

THE OVERLAPPING WORLDS OF CHRISTIANS AND JEWS

Christians first met in private houses. The earliest known example of a 'church' comes from the remote city of Dura-Europus on the Euphrates (in modern Syria). This had been a settlement of the Seleucids, one of the Greek dynasties that succeeded Alexander the Great, but from AD 160 the Romans had transformed it into a garrison town from where they could lead the defence of the eastern empire against a newly aggressive Persian empire. The inhabitants were a lively mixture – descendants of the original Macedonian settlers, migrants from the surrounding steppes and the trading city of Palmyra, Jews who retained links with the ancient Jewish communities of Babylonia, and a small group of Christians. From inscriptions bearing some of the Christians' names it appears that they were outsiders, Greek speakers who were probably in service with the Romans. In about 240 a house was converted into a church with a baptistery joined to it. Frescoes in the baptistery show Christ's miracles and what appear to be the two Marys approaching the empty tomb. There is a Good Shepherd and a representation of Adam and Eve. Its congregation is estimated at about sixty. In the church fragments of papyri were found which contain Christian Eucharistic prayers in Hebrew, even though the congregation was also worshipping in Greek. A red cross marked the door to the street and so here Christians seem to have been able to worship openly. The Romans were prepared to tolerate them, perhaps because of their contribution to the defence of the town.

Not far away, preserved when the Romans constructed siege works against a Persian attack, a synagogue was found, also decorated with frescoes, among them rare scenes of Moses receiving the Law and leading the Israelites out of Egypt. The synagogue congregation was much bigger than that of the Christians. The Jews were worshipping in both Greek and Aramaic. Wall paintings in either a church or a synagogue are otherwise unknown from this period. Here both draw heavily on Old Testament images but choose different ones.

Such finds show how complicated the relationship between Christianity and Judaism remained. Here, one finds an immigrant Christian community living alongside a larger and probably native Jewish group but apparently completely separate from it. In this same period, there was also a group known as the Ebionites, 'the poor ones', the name suggesting a group that saw their poverty as a mark of piety.[1] They claimed to be the authentic descendants of the first Christians, still Jewish and respecting Jesus as a major prophet. They rejected the virgin birth and the attempts of Paul to break with the Law. One can guess that there were many other compromised positions.

The destruction of the Temple in AD 70 certainly marks some form of turning point in the relationship between Judaism and the emerging Christian communities. There was another in AD 135 when a Jewish rebellion, by Shimon bar Kosiba (often known as Bar Kokhba), was decisively defeated by the Romans. Shimon had declared himself the longed-for messiah and his ruthless concentration on military victory was in line with earlier messianic traditions. Those Jewish Christians who refused to transfer their allegiance to this new messiah appear to have been executed (although the only evidence for this comes from Christian sources). The suffering in the environs around Jerusalem that followed the revolt was intense, and the Romans themselves appear to have taken heavy losses. Any remaining goodwill the Jews had enjoyed from their overlords had been lost.

This revolt may well have been the catalyst that encouraged the Christians to distance themselves from Judaism, leaving behind a few marginal Christian groups such as the Ebionites. The Romans added a further insult to the Jews by allowing a Gentile Christian bishop to be installed in the new colony (one Marcus of Caesarea, according to Eusebius). Christians pressed home their advantage by claiming that the humiliations of AD 70 and 135 were punishment to the Jews from God for their betrayal of Christ. Their own survival showed that they were now the favoured ones, even able to earn the goodwill of the authorities.

Whatever the catalysts that forced the breakdown, the process by which the two religions separated from each other was tortuous. The New Testament shows that there was a variety of ways in which Christians used or discarded their Jewish inheritance. The Letter of James is still set in a Jewish framework while, in contrast, the Letter to the Hebrews suggests that the Christians have superseded Judaism. Conflicts with Jews are well documented in the letters of Paul and the gospel of John. In the second century the surviving texts show a similar range of attitudes and confirm that one cannot talk in any generalised way of distinct Christian and Jewish communities. A major problem remains the almost total lack of Jewish sources in the four centuries after the comparative wealth of those of the first century, the Dead Sea Scrolls, Philo and Josephus.

At one extreme there is Theophilus, said to have been the sixth bishop of Antioch, writing in the second half of the second century to one Autolycus, a learned pagan whom he was trying to convert. In the opening paragraph of his letter, Theophilus confirms that he is a Christian and claims that it is a mark of Christians that they are anointed by 'the oil of God'. Theophilus is sympathetic to Judaism and he tells us that he was converted to Christianity from paganism through the books of the prophets. In other words, rather than becoming Christian first and then seeking support in the prophecies, he starts the other way around. He is heavily dependent on Jewish sources. He rubbishes Greek philosophy and the traditional Greek deities and preaches instead the importance of the Hebrew scriptures. The Law, he argues, is central to Christian morality and it is only in a few instances, the observance of the Sabbath, for instance, that Jesus changed it. It is a remarkable feature of this apparently 'Christian' letter that Jesus is hardly mentioned. The most direct reference is rather to the *logos*, where Theophilus draws directly on the gospel of John. He seems to have known the beginning of this gospel and also some of the teachings from the Sermon on the Mount but little more. There is no deeper reflection on the significance of Christ and it has even been noted that if Autolycus had been convinced by the letter he would have been just as likely to convert to diaspora Judaism as to Christianity.

One work of Theophilus, now lost, was an attack on Marcion who had died probably only a few years earlier in about 160. Marcion is one of the most interesting and effective figures of early Christianity. He came from Sinope, a prosperous Greek city in Pontus, where some reports say his father was the bishop. He must have grown up just at the time that Pliny was administering the province and he seems to have made a fortune from the shipping industry. He was clearly an impressive figure, a successful businessman, a brilliant and energetic organiser and an original thinker. Marcion was also aggressively ascetic. He was so hesitant in embracing materialism and so abhorred sexuality that he rejected marriage. The foetus was a 'repulsive coagulated lump of flesh, nourishing in the same slime for nine months'.[2] All his followers had to commit to celibacy. Determined to make an impact on the emerging Christian community in Rome, he arrived in the capital in the late 130s and pressed a large donation on them.

In contrast to Theophilus' muted references to Jesus, Marcion was an enthusiast for Christ. Christ was, of course, the Son of God, who had appeared in human form and who had preached a new gospel of divine goodness. Marcion's emphasis was on the 'new'. While many of his fellow Christians were searching the Hebrew scriptures for evidence of prophecies of Christ's coming, Marcion made the radical and shocking claim that they had nothing to do with Jesus at all. He was actually outraged by the immorality of the

Old Testament God. Jesus may have been 'the Son of God', but surely this could not be the temperamental god of the Hebrew scriptures, 'lustful in war' as he was. This god's role was as a demiurge (from the Greek *demiourgos*, a craftsman, the term that Plato had used in the *Timaeus* to describe the force that had created the world). His actions, said Marcion, had been restricted to this creation and to setting in place his own Law. His behaviour, as any serious reading of the scriptures made clear, showed that he could not be the true god of mercy and love. Marcion blamed him, in fact, for the suffering and crucifixion of Christ – it was this very act of betrayal of the innocent Jesus by the Hebrew god that released human beings from any allegiance to Judaism. A totally different and superior god, one as yet unknown to humanity, reigned above the god of the scriptures and it was he who was the father of Jesus. With Jesus' arrival the works of the creator god, the demiurge, could safely be discarded as no longer relevant. The gospel now ruled in its place.

Marcion's vision of a perfect transcendent god appears to come from Platonism. Plato had argued that there was a hierarchy of spiritual levels. So, in Marcion's version of Platonism, one could have a supreme deity, below which there were lesser gods such as the creator god of the Hebrew scriptures. Yet, while Plato had taught that the ultimate spiritual reality could only be grasped by a long process of reasoned thought which led up through ever higher states of knowledge, Marcion believed that this god had been directly revealed through Jesus, just as Jesus had revealed himself to Paul in a vision. Marcion was a docetist, that is, he believed that Jesus only used a human body as a medium. He could hardly have maintained his divinity if he had been encased in that 'sewer' that was the womb.

Unlike some of his contemporaries, Marcion refused to denigrate the Jews (he was even taunted by the more outspoken of his opponents for his sympathy for them). They had, after all, suffered under the inconsistent rule of the demiurge. It was the demiurge, not the Jews themselves, who must take responsibility for the crucifixion. Certainly Marcion saw the Jews as far inferior to those who had accepted Christ but he accepted that they too might ultimately be saved. In fact, he even found himself in a form of alliance with the Jews against those Christians who could see prophecies of the coming of Jesus in the scriptures. Jesus, Marcion argued, really was an unexpected arrival, totally unforeseen by the prophets of old.

It used to be argued that Marcion compiled the earliest canon of texts, choosing the letters of Paul and a single gospel to make the first New Testament. It is possible, however, that Marcion simply adopted the texts that had reached Pontus before he left for Rome. Marcion does not name the gospel he selected although there are later traditions that it was a truncated version of Luke. Quotations from it, however, suggest some relationship to either Matthew or Mark but it may have been an otherwise unknown gospel used only in Pontus. The letters of Paul he chose (ten in all), appear to be an early collection addressed to seven specific churches.[3] Seven was a symbol of the universal, as seen in the seven churches of the Book of Revelation. The seven churches of Paul's letters thus proclaim him as the apostle of the universal church and this is why some unknown compiler may have selected them as such. Marcion probably came across this collection but he tampered with the letters, omitting passages that he claimed were later additions.

Marcion was an impressive advocate of a Jesus Christ who revealed a message of salvation from a universal transcendent god. He believed that Paul was the only apostle who had fully grasped the nature of Christ's revelation. The Letter to the Galatians, in particular, showed that Paul had recognised the inadequacies of the Hebrew scriptures (see Galatians 4:3–5). The other apostles had not recognised Jesus as he truly was, the spiritual figure who had brought the world of the creator god and his Law to an end. Paul had been right to break with those Christians who had not realised the truth and had clung to Jewish custom

Marcion's thinking showed rigour and clarity and so provided a convincing analysis of many of the issues that were still fuzzy in the minds of those Christians who thought less deeply. He showed up the contradictions between the two Testaments, just when many Christians were trying to gloss over them. However, in the second century, the break with Judaism and the Law and the rejection of the god of the Hebrew scriptures were too radical for the Roman Christians and Marcion was expelled from their community. Unabashed, Marcion founded his own churches which spread so widely that in many parts of the empire they rivalled or even replaced mainstream Christianity and were still active three hundred years later. Even in the fourth century, Cyril, bishop of Jerusalem, had to warn members of his church to take care when they were looking for a church in a foreign town in case they ended up in one run by the Marcionites!

Marcion and Theophilus mark two boundaries of an emerging Christianity, acquiescence in a Jewish Christianity at one extreme and total rejection of the Jewish God at the other. There are a significant number of texts 'in between' that retain the links between Christianity and Judaism while arguing for the superiority of Christianity. One of the most remarkable documents in the debate is Justin Martyr's *Dialogue with Trypho the Jew*. Justin Martyr had a Roman background – he was brought up in a Roman colony in Samaria, probably in the early years of the second century AD – but he spoke and wrote in Greek. He was attracted first to the traditional pagan philosophers – Stoics, Pythagoreans and, most profoundly of all, the Platonists. However, he found none of these satisfying and was converted to Christianity by 'a wise old man' who showed him how Christ had fulfilled the Hebrew scriptures.

At some point, probably in the 140s, Justin travelled to Rome and was able to teach there, in the comparatively tolerant reign of Antoninus Pius. (He was martyred by order of the city prefect when persecution resumed in the subsequent reign of Marcus Aurelius.) One of his most important works was his *First Apology*, addressed to the emperor, in which he asks for Christianity to be judged on its own merits. He pleads that there should be no persecution of Christians simply because of their name or rumours about their 'atheism' or immorality. Addressing the emperor as a philosopher and lover of culture, he argues, rather provocatively perhaps, that the Greek philosophers, Plato foremost among them, had been inspired by Moses and the Jewish prophets. These had had the true wisdom, which is now represented by Christ. The Greek philosophers had squandered this inheritance through their intellectual squabbles and division into rival groups. Now the world must return to Christ.

In his *Dialogue*, Justin engages in a discussion with a Jew, Trypho, who like himself has a background in philosophy. The *Dialogue* is set in Ephesus where Trypho has fled as a refugee from the revolt of 135. The tradition of the dialogue, in which opposing views are presented in a conversational argument, goes back to Plato and so Justin would have been well acquainted with it from his own studies. Plato presents each side in full but 'his' side, as usually argued in the person of Socrates, inexorably progresses to philosophical victory. Justin is remarkable in that he too presents both sides, Jewish and Christian, fairly. Trypho holds firmly to his own beliefs even though, as the *Dialogue* progresses, Justin's voice becomes the dominant one. Trypho is no mere figurehead and at times one feels that Justin is unable to provide a coherent response to his arguments. Unlike later more polemical Christian 'dialogues', Justin does not end his work with Trypho admitting defeat and agreeing to convert. Trypho is always given serious arguments. While many opponents of Christianity spread rumours that Christians indulged in cannibalism or free sex, Trypho rejects them: 'those things about which the multitude speak are not worthy of belief; for they are most repugnant to human nature'. He has no need to stoop to abuse. It may well be that Justin is accurately reproducing dialogues he has had with sophisticated Jews.

The *Dialogue* provides an excellent overview of the differences between Jew and Christian in their attitudes to the scriptures. Trypho stresses the contradiction between the Christian assertion that they accept the authority of the scriptures and their refusal to follow some of their requirements such as circumcision and the laws on diet. The Law, Justin replies, was instituted as a means of punishing the Jews, as events have shown and, in any case,

Christians have taken on other burdens – including the threat of martyrdom. The crux of the argument centres on the apparent contradictions in Christian belief. Trypho reminds Justin that in Jewish tradition the messiah has never been a divine figure but always a human one and there was never any prediction of a messiah suffering crucifixion. What right have the Christians to claim that Jesus is a divine messiah? Furthermore, there is no Jewish prophecy that predicts that God will enter the world as a human being, especially through the weak device of a virgin birth. The ensuing discussion, which gets heated at times, shows that there can be no common ground between these two views. Jews cannot compromise on the unity of God: he simply could not have another significant divine force, his Son, beside him. Christians believe in a divine messiah, however much this breaks with Jewish tradition. The *Dialogue* shows what were now unbridgeable fault lines between the two faiths.

These fault lines are emphasised by a tussle over the interpretation of scripture. The *Dialogue* raises a number of issues that have often resurfaced in the history of Christianity. For a start, which text does one use? The Christians use the Septuagint but surely, Trypho argues, the original Hebrew is preferable, especially when discussing issues such as the virgin birth where Matthew has used a faulty translation of the Hebrew. (Justin is forced into replying that he believes the translation to be more trustworthy than the original!) Trypho accuses the Christians of interpreting the texts to suit their purpose, using allegory in an unjustifiably imaginative way to support their beliefs. One can understand why Jews felt angry with this. Why should their own scriptures be twisted to support the claims of an upstart religion that considered itself superior? Often, Trypho remarks, it is clear that a reference, to a king, for instance, is to a king in the text itself; in one case he cites Solomon. One could not pretend that here the term 'king' actually refers to Jesus. In short, in so far as it rested on Jewish prophecy the whole of Christian belief is built on weak foundations.

Justin hits back by staking the claim that the Christians have taken on the Jewish inheritance. Justin does not reject the richness of the Jewish past or pretend that the Jews had not once enjoyed the favour of God, but explains that that time has now passed: 'For the prophetical gifts remain with us, even to the present time. And hence you ought to understand that [the gifts] formerly among your nation have been transferred to us.' Gentiles who have accepted Christ can be judged on the same terms as the prophets of the past. 'Those who have persecuted and do persecute Christ, if they do not repent, shall not inherit anything on the holy mountain. But the Gentiles, who have believed in Him, and have repented of the sins which they have committed, they shall receive the inheritance *along with the patriarchs and the prophets, and the just men who are descended from Jacob* [my italics] even although they neither keep the Sabbath, nor are circumcised, nor observe the feasts.'

Justin is particularly important in developing a new conception of Jesus as *logos*, the Word. For Philo, *logos* was still seen in somewhat abstract terms, as an intermediary, between God and the world. Philo did not know anything of Jesus and one has to wait for Justin to stress that Jesus moves beyond Philo's *logos* in being a human being among other humans. 'Next to God, we worship and love the *logos* who is from the unbegotten and ineffable God, since also He became man for our sakes, that, becoming a partaker of our sufferings, He might also bring us healing.' Jesus has been freed from the confines of Philo's Platonic philosophy. As the passage suggests, Jesus remains subordinate to the Father. In the *Dialogue*, Justin refers to him as the 'First Principle created before all things' and he also describes Jesus as if he were a torch lit from the existing fire of the Father but, as with any transfer of fire, not diminishing the status of the original.[4]

Justin retains some respect for Judaism even if it has proved blind in failing to recognise the Messiah. He is not alone. In a remarkable text, which in its original form probably dates to a few years later than Justin, the *Pseudo-Clementine Homilies* (so-called because of the mistaken belief that they were by Clement, bishop of Rome), the writer goes so far as to excuse the Jews for failing to recognise Jesus. Jesus was hidden from those who followed Moses as a prophet. The Jews could hardly be condemned for this but they should also not condemn Christians for not recognising Moses. This generous approach assumes that there is one supreme God who has allowed two traditions to exist side by side in harmony.

However, alongside these works, which show some tolerance of the differences between Jew and Christian, there was an ominous development in Christian thought. It centred on the belief that the Jews were unworthy of their heritage and especially so as they had rejected Jesus. One finds its birth in Paul's First Letter to the Thessalonians, where the Jews are described as killing 'the Lord Jesus', and in the confrontation between Jesus and the Jews in Chapter Eight of John's gospel. In the so-called Epistle of Barnabas, which may have been written as early as the 90s but which is more usually dated to about AD 130, after the Roman suppression of a Jewish revolt in Alexandria that had split Christians from Jews, 'Barnabas' suggests that the Jews had never been the favoured nation. They had completely misinterpreted the circumcision of Abraham and believed that it was a physical requirement. What was called for instead was 'a symbolic circumcision' of the ear and the heart which would open believers to the Word of God and the prophecies of Jesus' coming. In Chapter Four, Barnabas recounts how God gave the covenant to the Jews but they lost it at once when Moses broke the tablets he had received.

Barnabas knew his scriptures well and argued that the prophecies in it were prophecies of Christ that the rejected Jews would, of course, never have been able to recognise. So the entire history of those who think that they are the Israelites is one of separation from God. The Christians had entered the void that their apostasy had left.

The theme that God is punishing the Jews for their pretence is taken up by Melito of Sardis, active in the last third of the second century. Melito is the first recorded pilgrim to Palestine, in the sense of one who went specifically to see 'where it was proclaimed and done'. He also refers to the Hebrew scriptures as the Old Covenant, the first time the scriptures were seen as a distinct body of texts that contrast with those of a New Covenant or New Testament. His hometown, Sardis, the ancient capital of Lydia, was an important Roman administrative centre. Excavations have also shown that it was the home of a substantial Jewish community whose members played a role in town government (although the large synagogue uncovered there dates from much later than the second century). It may have been this ebullient community that impelled a committed Christian like Melito to respond with a denigration of the Jews.

Melito's only surviving work is a Paschal Hymn, part of a liturgy that would be recited by a congregation. The text is presented as an argument. If one is making a sculpture or building out of wax, clay or wood, it begins, one starts with a model, then one gathers the material and finally one completes the work itself. At this point the model is redundant. Melito takes this as an analogy of the history of the Jews. They were no more than 'the model' now surpassed by the reality of 'the Lord'. 'When the church arose and the gospel took precedence, the model was made redundant, conceding its power to the reality, and the law was fulfilled conceding its power to the gospel.' Reaching back into Jewish history, Melito notes how the Passover lamb had to be sacrificed in order to liberate the Jews from the evils of Egyptian rule. So too, Jesus has to be sacrificed as 'the Lamb' in order for the Christians to be free of Jewish rule. Jesus had always been with the Jews, just as the Jews had always been with the Egyptians, but now they had betrayed him. While earlier writers, Matthew, for instance, placed responsibility for the death of Jesus on the Jews (Matthew 27:25), Melito goes further, launching a denunciation of the Jews for deicide, the killing of no less than God himself. 'O lawless Israel, what is this unprecedented crime you committed, thrusting your Lord among unprecedented sufferings, your Sovereign . . . The Sovereign has been insulted; the God has been murdered; the King of Israel has been put to death by an Israelite right hand.' Melito has gone beyond berating the Jews as killer of Jesus into making the crucifixion, a public and humiliating event, the most terrible crime imaginable.

Melito's rhetoric proved highly popular. Early translations of the hymn (from the Greek) have been found in Latin, Syriac, Coptic and Georgian. It was one of the founding documents of the tradition of *Adversus Judaeos*, polemic aimed at the Jews (the name comes from a text by Tertullian). This tradition brought together many of these themes: that the Jews had proved unworthy of their inheritance, which had now been transferred to the Christians, that the need for circumcision, the observance of dietary laws and celebration of the Sabbath had passed with the transfer, that the destruction of the Temple and the expulsion of Jews from Jerusalem reflected God's just punishment of them and that they would for ever, as a race, be defiled by the crime of deicide. It was these harsher judgements that prevailed, especially after the reign of Constantine when the church had imperial backing against the Jews. So one finds the dismissive invective of Ambrose of Milan and the crude diatribes of John Chrysostom, bishop of Constantinople.

The intensity with which the issues were debated surely reflects two lively traditions, one old and one new, battling with each other for converts. Some Christian communities had evolved a theology that allowed them to appropriate the Old Testament, interpret it as a prophecy of Christ and use it as a foundation for their own evolving New Testament. Yet there were still important groups such as the Marcionites who rejected the God of the Hebrew scriptures completely. In contrast, there were the Ebionites, 'the poor ones', self-proclaimed Christians in the late second century, who still accepted circumcision. Even as late as the late fourth century, John Chrysostom directed his invective at Christians who visited the synagogues because they believed that an oath made there was more likely to be respected. The fact that Christians could find in the synagogue many of the same scriptures that they were using in the Christian churches may well have made it difficult for them to understand why Judaism needed to be rejected. There were no clear boundaries between the two religions, no matter how much Christian leaders attempted to define them. Spiritual migrants passed from one side to another, often unaware, it seems, that they were doing anything untoward. In many respects Judaism in the first century AD fragmented and a cluster of successor religions emerged that would accommodate Jesus Christ to a greater or lesser extent.[5]

CHAPTER THIRTEEN

Was There a Gnostic Challenge?

WHAT, IF ANYTHING, EXISTS BEYOND THE MATERIAL WORLD WE experience around us? There was intense dispute in this period among Jews, pagans and Christians alike over what survived after death, a 'soul' perhaps, or even a reconstituted earthly body, and whether it could experience reward or punishment. Then there was the issue of who might be selected for special favour, what forms of commitment, belief or behaviour were necessary to ensure entry into a state of bliss rather than one of misery or even eternal punishment. Furthermore, how could one learn about the world beyond when there seemed no empirical evidence for a future existence? Did God reveal himself, and something about his realm, directly or did he use interme- diaries, human or divine (angels)? Was it possible for a spiritual emissary to appear in human form to tell of the world beyond? Answers varied from one period to another and even within the same religion. For some, especially those in the Platonist tradition, which was to have an important influence on Christian theology, the immaterial world 'above' was more real and stable than the volatile and shifting material world 'below'. It could be reached through an intense and prolonged period of reflection.

In the second century the issues were brought into the open by the conflict over what is known as gnosticism. Few subjects have been so intensively analysed, especially since the discovery of a cache of what were claimed to be gnostic texts at Nag Hammadi in 1945, yet the more the so-called gnostic texts are examined the more elusive their message seems to be.

As an introduction to gnosticism let us take one of the most popular texts, the so-called 'Apocryphon [or "Secret Book"] of John'. The original text may have been a meditation on how a human being could aspire to divinity but, as it survives in copies today, it was framed within an account of a vision by Christ himself to John, one of the sons of Zebedee, in the desert somewhere near Jerusalem. No less than three versions were found among the Nag Hammadi texts.

The vision begins with Christ telling John of an Invisible Spirit, which exists even beyond the realms of heaven. It is known in some sense through its 'thoughts', one of which is personified as a mysterious figure by the name of Barbelo. Barbelo is given many titles, among them Providence, but his prime role is as mediator between the Invisible Spirit and all else that exists. He appears in many forms: one is as a transcendent form of humanity, another is as the Mother, a female consort of the Invisible Spirit, through whom a child is born. There is another figure, the Perfect Human, Adamas, who appears to be a prototype for human beings as they will actually appear on earth. There are other entities – aeons, as they are often referred to – in the heavenly court. Every time a new aeon appears it goes through a process of being welcomed and accepted by the Invisible Spirit and Barbelo. For the time being these aeons all live in harmony with each other. This is a settled sphere of being.

However, there is a troubled spirit among the court and this is Sophia, or Wisdom. She proves an unruly figure, refusing to abide by the conventions of mutual acceptance that prevail. She in her turn brings forth a 'thought', an offspring so ugly that she has to take it out of heaven and hide it in a cloud. His name is Ialdabaoth, which appears to be a corruption of the Jewish 'Yahweh, Lord of Sabbaths'. He grows up entirely unaware of anything more about himself or his birth other than that Wisdom is his mother. Deluded as he is, he believes that he is God and there is no other god but him.

This causes consternation in heaven. A world is being created which is totally ignorant of the true Divinity. Ialdabaoth and his helpers put together the shape of a human being Adam. Each body part is the creation of one helper. However, the whole is sterile and it only comes alive when heavenly forces trick Ialdabaoth into breathing life into it. It soon shows that it is more intelligent than its makers. Ialdabaoth tries to remove the spirit that he has unwittingly planted in the human but he only succeeds in drawing out a woman, Eve, who responds to the man whose body she has just left. The couple go through a process of awakening to each other. Aware now that he has released living things he cannot control Ialdabaoth throws the couple out of Paradise. Here the myth of the Revelation and the Genesis account of the expulsion from Eden overlap.

To ensure that the punishment he wishes to inflict on the world persists Ialdabaoth has sex with Eve. She conceives and the result is Cain and Abel. Wakened himself to the power of sexual desire, Adam then begets his own son Seth with Eve. Seth carries the original spirit that was breathed into Adam so that this spirit survives in the material world, despite the attempts by Ialdabaoth to go on destroying it. Floods, plagues and earthquakes instituted by Ialdabaoth threaten the world in typical apocalyptic style. Barbelo in his role as Providence has to intervene to save the human race through the medium of Noah's Ark. These interventions ensure that some human beings retain the memory of the need to resist Ialdabaoth and the possibility of restoration to heaven. The 'Secret Book' itself is part of this memory and listeners to it are warned of the dire consequences for those who hear its teachings but refuse to accept them.

The 'Apocryphon' was probably the text of a single Christian community. There are references to baptism in it so presumably this served as an initiation ceremony for newcomers. Its beliefs weave together the story of an Unknown God ('the Invisible Spirit') with that of an original human spirit that has been submerged by the destructive powers of a subsidiary god. The world he has created is full of evil forces, not least of which is sexual desire, here seen in negative terms. However, for those who have absorbed the revealed teachings there remains the possibility of a return to heaven.

The 'Apocryphon' is comprised of a number of interlocking sources that are to be found, often in different guises, in other texts. The concept of the evil creator god appeared in Marcion but in the 'Apocryphon' the writer, unlike Marcion, has accepted the scriptures to the extent of weaving the Genesis stories into the myth. There are also Platonic influences. The idea of an intermediary, in this case Barbelo, is very much part of Middle Platonism and echoes the *logos* of John's gospel which is also some form of intermediary between the divine and man. The idea of a few having the secret knowledge is common in initiation cults, many of them older than Christianity. It is the Greek word *gnosis*, knowledge, which gives gnosticism its name, although the term 'gnosticism' as the description of a movement dates only from the eighteenth century.

Before 1945, what was known about gnosticism was largely drawn from texts written against it by orthodox Christian writers between the second and fourth centuries. (The term 'orthodox' is used here, somewhat anachronistically perhaps, to describe the writers whose works later became authoritative in the Christian tradition.) Several of these, notably Irenaeus, Tertullian and Epiphanius, will appear in later chapters as influential figures in their own right. However, it is very difficult to pin down exactly what Irenaeus and his supporters meant by gnosticism and whether in fact they merely used the word as a general term for heretics. The full Greek title of Irenaeus' most important work (normally known by its Latin name *Adversus haereses*) suggests it is an attack on those who 'teach what is falsely called "knowledge" '. Irenaeus may simply have been taunting rival Christian sects or even members of his own congregations for claiming that they were superior because they were claiming to 'know': 'They consider themselves "mature" so that no one can be compared to them in the greatness of their *gnosis*, not even if you mention Peter and Paul or any of the other apostles ... They imagine that they themselves have discovered more than the apostles, and that the apostles preached the gospel still under the influence of Jewish opinions, but that they themselves are wiser and more intelligent than the apostles.' This can hardly be seen as a reasoned attack and Irenaeus had to admit that the 'gnostics' themselves were not impressed by his criticisms. 'They ask, when they confess the same things and participate in the same worship . . . how it is that we, for no reason, remain aloof from them; and how it is that when they confess the same things, and hold the same doctrines, we call them heretics.'

It is hard to give any coherent definition of gnosticism but one can set out some of the features associated with the term. There is an awareness of a divine 'spark', which is confined to a few human beings, usually a privileged elite. (A similar view is found among the Stoics and the 'gnostics' may have borrowed it from here.) This spark fell downwards from heaven, usually through a crisis of creation during which a lesser god achieved power in the material world. The world this god has created is essentially flawed and even the bodies in which humans live are corrupted. In contrast, the spiritual world has a completeness, the Greek word used is *pleroma*, literally 'fullness', but human beings are unable to reach it unaided.

Recovery is possible because the transcendent God and his helpers in heaven are able to liberate the divine spark in those favoured. A redeemer figure, one able to release the spark features prominently, and this is often portrayed as Christ. In one of the Nag Hammadi texts Jesus talks to his 'brother', Judas Thomas: 'While you accompany me, although you are uncomprehending, you have in fact, already come to know, and you will be called the "one who knows himself". For he who has not known himself has known nothing, but he who has known himself has at the same time already achieved knowledge about the depth of all.'[1] However, if Christ had become fully human he would surely have been contaminated by the material world, so it was assumed that he appeared within a human body 'in the likeness of human flesh' as Paul had put it in Romans (8:3). ('Gnostic' texts often draw on Paul.) One version suggests that Jesus was a human being into whom Christ had been absorbed. Christ had then left the Jesus being before the crucifixion, which Jesus suffered, in its full agony. Finally, according to Irenaeus, gnostics believed that Christ returned to raise the body of Jesus from the dead. While many so-called gnostic ideas have parallels in ancient Middle Eastern religions and Platonism provides the concept of a higher spiritual life and a degraded and inadequate material one, this has been given a Christian setting

The complaints that the orthodox Christians heaped upon those they classed as 'gnostics' were varied. There was ridicule of the convoluted stories and myths (of which the 'Apocryphon of John' is a good example), which were contrasted with the comparative simplicity and clarity of the scriptures. The 'true' Christians could always be identified because they spoke with a united voice that derived directly from Jesus and the apostles. The 'gnostics' claimed a secret knowledge only because they were afraid of speaking openly. Jesus, in contrast, was open to all who showed faith. The gnostics claimed too to have acquired their heresy from a single source but their opponents suggested that this was Simon Magus, 'the father of all heresy', as revealed in Acts. The gnostics were also accused of wild and immoral behaviour. They so despised the body, it was said, that they abused it in every way possible or, alternatively, destroyed it through fasting.

By 1945 most agreed that it was unfair to define a movement by referring only to the description of it given by its opponents. The German scholar Walter Bauer had transformed the context within which early Christianity was discussed through his book *Orthodoxy and Heresy in Early Christianity*, first published in German in 1934 (but not in English until 1971). Bauer argued that the concept that there had been an original Christian orthodoxy that evil heretics had conspired to overthrow was profoundly flawed. Christianity had evolved in a number of different local cultures and in different ways. It was simplistic to argue that 'gnosticism' was a heresy, in the sense of a distinctive deviation from some established truth. It was misleading to talk of a struggle within Christianity when the concept of Christianity itself was so fluid. This was an important move forward as it helped liberate gnosticism from the predominantly negative aura that surrounded it. It could be examined as a movement in its own right and on its own terms. If Bauer was right, and early Christianity was made up of a variety of competing beliefs, then gnosticism itself might not be as monolithic or sinister a movement as it appeared. There might even be many 'gnosticisms' and the term might have no coherence at all. No further progress could be made, however, when there were so few surviving texts.

All this changed in 1945. In one of the most fascinating and influential developments in the study of early Christianity, thirteen codices containing a total of forty-six distinct texts, forty of which had never before been found complete, were discovered by two Egyptian peasants in a sealed clay jar at Nag Hammadi. They were translations into Coptic (the Egyptian language written using the Greek alphabet) of what were originally Greek texts and were quickly proclaimed to be 'gnostic'. The way in which the Nag Hammadi documents were concealed together shows that they had formed part of a library of a community, possibly of a nearby monastery. The fact that they were concealed suggests that they had been declared heretical but were considered precious enough by their owners to be preserved rather than destroyed. The date of their concealment, possibly the late fourth century (as an analysis of the papyrus on which they were written suggests), was just when the New

Testament canon was being finalised but also when imperial legislation required the burning of heretical books. This may well have been the reason why they were hidden.

The Nag Hammadi documents are a mixed bag. Perhaps the most celebrated of the texts has been the gospel of Thomas. However, there were also 'gospels' attributed to Philip and John, the sons of Zebedee, and to Jesus' brother James. These are full of intriguing details about Jesus that appear, as there is no other evidence to support them, to be largely fictitious, with the disciples' names used to give them spurious authority. The 'Gospel of Philip' has fragmentary references (from a papyrus with much missing) of Jesus kissing Mary Magdalene and the disciples complaining that he loved her more than them. The text has given fantasists a field day, culminating in bizarre and unsubstantiated suggestions that the two married and had children. There were also a 'Gospel of Truth', 'A Treatise on the Resurrection', three versions of the 'Apocryphon' described earlier and even a fragment from a paraphrase of Plato's *Republic* (which Plato had written in the fourth century BC).

Most of the works date from the second and third centuries AD although many of the texts draw on earlier material including the Jewish scriptures and possibly traditions from other eastern religions. Some of the texts are overwhelming in their obscurity, others have a clear message and set out alternative visions of Christianity that certainly do not agree with the traditional accounts of gnosticism. Take the 'Gospel of Truth', for instance. This is not so much a gospel as a meditation on Christ's mission to a troubled world. The gospel tells us that there is one supreme Father, God of all. (There is no mention of a distinct and inferior creator god.) The world lived in 'anguish and terror' as a result of humanity's ignorance of the Father until Christ came down on earth to bring salvation. He appeared as fully human – this is not a Christ appearing as a spirit in the body of a human being – but was not recognised because of the darkness in which men lived, and so was put to death. He now became 'a fruit of the knowledge of the Father'. His death and resurrection brought the possibility of knowledge to those who were prepared to understand. The world was made a place of light as a result of Christ's sacrifice and it seems that the 'knowledge' is available to all, not simply an elite. His followers are enjoined to 'feed those who are hungry and give repose to those who are weary'. There is no turning one's back on the world – it must be lived in with compassion and hope. The writer specifically tells his audience that they must not look back to the past.

The 'Gospel of Truth' is uplifting and inspirational. In its stress on the contrast between 'light' and 'darkness', it echoes the Qumran writings, passages in Paul and, of course, John. However, Irenaeus condemned it as blasphemous, apparently on the grounds that it differed from the gospels of the apostles. Here is an excellent example of a text that had been unknown beyond Irenaeus' condemnation but one that can now be read in full in its original version. It becomes obvious that Irenaeus' attack is unfair. Although the text is called a 'gospel' and does in fact contain 'good news', if seen as a homily or a meditation there is little one can object to in its teaching.

The 'Gospel of Truth' has been linked to a specific preacher, Valentinus. Valentinus was a Greek from Alexandria who moved to Rome in about 140 and set up a school of philosophy there. Like Justin Martyr he was able to teach within the comparatively tolerant atmosphere under the emperor Antoninus Pius. Valentinus built up a substantial following (one report suggests that he was even put up for election as bishop of Rome) and several of the Nag Hammadi texts are by his students so that scholars talk of 'Valentinianism' as a distinct movement even if the boundaries are not easy to define. If the 'Gospel of Truth' is his, he was well trained in Greek rhetoric and employed a sophisticated style of writing. It often seems that it is Valentinus and his supporters who are Irenaeus' main obsession and as Irenaeus is known to have spent some time in Rome the antagonism may have arisen when they became competitors for the same congregations. In his *Adversus haereses*, Irenaeus describes Valentinus as 'adapting the principles of the heresy known as gnosticism to the peculiar character of his own school'. In other words, rather than considering Valentinus' teachings in their own right, Irenaeus sees them as a development from a movement that he has already classified as heretical. He goes on to lambast Valentinus as arrogant and spiritually elitist. He and his followers believe themselves to be already saved in contrast to those lower in the spiritual hierarchy who can only be saved through faith and good works. Yet now that some of Valentinus' writings can be read, it appears that he might not be a gnostic at all.

One of the major criticisms Irenaeus makes against the Valentinians is that they indulge in every kind of immoral behaviour. He argues that the gnostics see themselves as a composite of spiritual and human natures, the latter of which they despise to such an extent that they feel free to indulge in every form of sexual defilement. Even if they pretend to be ascetic, it is normally only a sham. However, there is not a hint in any of the Nag Hammadi texts that such practices are encouraged. We see a wide range of attitudes to the body, some undoubtedly dismissive, but not necessarily more so than those practised by some of their opponents (for instance, Tertullian, whose misogyny will be discussed later).

Another group of documents, eleven of those from Nag Hammadi, have been termed 'Sethian' because of the prominent place they give to Seth, the son of Adam and Eve. As has already been seen in the 'Apocryphon of John', Seth is contrasted with Cain and Abel in that he has received the pure spirit from above and those descended from him preserve this. As the spirit is already embedded within humanity, even if only in a favoured few, the prominent role accorded Jesus by Valentinus, for instance, is not so vital. So Christ appears as a much more marginal figure and in some cases it is Seth himself who is the Saviour of humankind. Almost every aspect of Sethianism is contested: how it originated, how it developed and whether it ever maintained itself as a distinct movement. Sethianism is pessimistic about the material world and emphasises the inadequacies of the creator god. This distinguishes it from Valentinianism which is more positive about the world, sees Christ as offering salvation to all humanity, rather than to a small elite, and accepts the creator god of the Old Testament as the true God.

The Nag Hammadi documents have shown that 'gnosticism' was a much more complex movement, if it was a movement at all, than was originally thought. It is clear that the polemical attacks on the gnostics by Irenaeus and others provide a distorted picture. Irenaeus confronts groups such as the Valentinians whose beliefs may have differed little from his own version of Christianity. If one examines the Nag Hammadi texts without preconceptions, it is individuals such as Valentinus who become more prominent, not as followers of a pre-existing gnosticism, but as original and influential teachers in their own right.

This is not to deny that some texts do show most of the features that had been traditionally described as gnostic. One is doceticism, the idea that Christ is a spiritual figure who only appears to be human. In two Nag Hammadi texts, the 'Apocalypse of Peter' and 'First Apocalypse of James', both probably dating from the third century, Jesus escapes the crucifixion. Jesus explains to Peter, for instance, that a substitute, 'the first born, the home of demons and the stony vessel in which they dwell', was the one crucified. In the 'First Apocalypse of James' Jesus tells James at the resurrection that he did not suffer at all and the crucifixion was simply a means of exposing the impotence and arrogance of the world rulers. In the Acts of John, Jesus appears in different guises to different observers – as a child, a young man and an old man. He shifts appearance at will. Yet these texts are offset by others, the 'Apocryphon of James', for instance, in which Jesus tells James and Peter that he did indeed suffer on the cross 'that you may be saved'.

Again we see the diversity of early Christianity at a time when it was spreading from the Jewish world into Greek-speaking communities. This perhaps explains why there is a strongly anti-Jewish element in many gnostic writings: Judaism was a foreign and now derided culture for new converts. Many of these, Valentinus and Justin Martyr being good examples, were intelligent and well-educated Greeks who were used to the critical analysis of theological and philosophical issues. This was a time of lively intellectual debate and one can hardly expect Christianity to be segregated from this. As the church's hierarchy and theology were still in a state of flux, individuals were comparatively free to explore their own understandings of the religion and some gnostic ideas were the result of this.

One can see how some ideas classified as gnostic became embedded in Christianity if one imagines an educated mind confronting a Jewish text such as Genesis for the first time. Take Genesis 1:26–7, for instance: 'God said, "Let us make humankind in our image, according to our likeness . . ." ' The difficulty here for Jews and other monotheists was the plural – does it imply there is more than one god? For those who followed Plato, however, it was not such a concern as they believed that there were spiritual intermediaries between God and the material world. These could well be the 'us' of the Genesis verse. Philo interpreted the verse in this way: the 'us' refers to God's powers that have a distinctive subsidiary role in creation. So this verse supported an approach in which heaven is peopled with other divine figures, as many so-called 'gnostic' texts suggested. Here 'gnosticism' may be little more than the application of Platonic ideas to difficult scriptural passages.

Take as an example the Genesis story of the expulsion from Eden from a non-Jewish perspective. The god of Genesis is certainly not transcendent. He shows jealousy, vindictiveness and an apparent inability to foresee the results of a situation that he has created. He had warned Adam (at 2:17) that if he ate of the tree he would die. Yet Adam did eat and failed to die. In fact, he went on to found the human race! How could this god have made such a mess of things and ended up with just what he had hoped to avoid – a human race with the ability to thwart him? No intelligent enquirer into the Genesis text is going to fail to see these contradictions. One of the Nag Hammadi texts, the 'Testimony of Truth', contains a critique of the Genesis narrative. If the author of the Testimony was a Platonist believing that the Supreme Good is totally transcendent, above all emotion and the vagaries of the world, then his critique makes sense. In this context the belief that the god of the Old Testament is a lesser form of deity is entirely understandable. One can hardly pretend that Genesis does not present major theological problems about the nature and power of the creator god.

The Nag Hammadi texts offer many other challenges and few of them will ever be fully understood. However, one must keep in mind that elements of 'gnosticism' may have been the result of a thoughtful approach to the contradictions of the scriptural texts from those who believed in a transcendent god but did not find him in the Hebrew scriptures. Nor is there anything odd about 'gnostics' wanting to understand the inner secrets of nature. The Greek philosophers had been at work on the problem for centuries. This is not the last case we will meet where what comes to be classed as heretical is in fact a sincere attempt by committed Christians to deal with what appear to be intractable theological problems. Educated converts who confronted the unresolved tensions of early Christianity, and the large number of competing Christian groups, were likely to join schools where these issues were discussed at a sophisticated level. This was the custom among the pagan philosophers and Christianity was still open to such debates. Human nature being what it is, there is no wonder that many like Irenaeus who, as we shall see, had learned their Christianity from the martyrs, felt excluded! Where he was wrong was to see the gnostics as forming a movement that could challenge 'his' Christians. There was no group that could do that and those accused by Irenaeus would no doubt have been amazed to find themselves cast together.

The most celebrated of the Nag Hammadi texts is the 'Gospel of Thomas'. Fragments of this 'gospel' had been known before 1945 but the Nag Hammadi text was the first complete text. The gospel is not really a gospel at all in the sense of a life of Jesus, his baptism, travels, trial, crucifixion and resurrection set within a connecting narrative. It simply contains 114 sayings of Jesus. It begins: 'These are the secret sayings which the living Jesus spoke and which Didymus Judas Thomas wrote down. And he said, "Whoever finds the interpretation of these sayings will not experience death." '[2] Some seventy-nine of the 114 sayings, by one count, echo verses to be found in the four gospels, primarily the three synoptics. So the author of the gospel has either drawn on earlier documents which overlap with other 'sayings' traditions such as Q or has drawn out some of these and presented them in an original collection compiled much later.

The issue has caused great controversy. One school argues that the Gospel of Thomas is one of the earliest Christian documents and thus reflects a more authentic Jesus than is known in the canonical gospels. In this view, an 'orthodox' church suppressed Thomas and also the gnostic tradition it represents. This assumes, of course, that gnosticism, if this is indeed the underlying philosophy of the 'gospel', was well established in the first century. The rival school notes that many themes one would expect to find in a first-century 'Christian' text of Jesus' sayings, such as apocalypticism, are totally lacking in Thomas. There are gnostic elements in the sayings but they reflect the beliefs expressed in other texts known to be of the second century. There is no reason, this school argues, to see Thomas as a founding document of gnosticism. It proposes a date of between 140 and 160 for the gospel.

As the opening verses suggest, the sayings recorded by Thomas concern secret knowledge transmitted to an elite group. If this describes the earliest form of Christianity, Jesus does not appear to have come for all humankind but only for those lucky enough to hear him. Certainly Jesus sees himself as everywhere on earth – 'It is I who am the light which is above them all. It is I who am "the all". From me did "the all" come forth, and unto me did "the all" extend. Split a piece of wood and I am there. Lift up the stone and you will find me there' (Saying 77) – but this is not the historical Jesus surrounded by enormous crowds. He requires intimacy from his chosen followers: 'He who will drink from my mouth will become like me. I myself shall become he, and the things that are hidden will be revealed to him' (Saying 108).

Jesus talks of the insights achieved once one has found knowledge through him: 'When you come to know yourselves, then you will become known, and you will realise that it is you who are the sons of the living father. But if you will not know yourselves, you dwell in poverty [the poverty of materialism] and you are that poverty' (Saying 3b). The material world is worthless: 'Whoever has come to understand the world has found only a corpse, and whoever has found a corpse is superior to the world' (Saying 56). This suggests that 'knowledge' will reveal the essential sterility of the material world but bring at the same time recognition that there is something superior beyond it. The wonder, Jesus tells Thomas, is not that the human body gave birth to the spiritual, but that the spiritual deigned to dwell in a human body (Saying 29). At death, one rises as a spiritual being – in this the gospel is at one with the Treatise of the Resurrection. However, in contrast to some texts, and the gospel of John, for instance, achieving knowledge will allow one to live more fully in this world: 'The Kingdom of God is within you' (Saying 3). Knowledge transforms the knower on earth; he or she does not have to wait until death for this to happen. So this gospel is talking of the coming of the kingdom, even if only for a select few, on earth.

In short, it is hard to talk of a gnostic movement, still less of a gnostic church, in the second century. A preferable approach is to see Christian theology in this era as interplay between Gentile newcomers, many of them well educated in Greek philosophy, and more traditional Christians. There is something in the view put forward over a hundred years ago by Adolf von Harnack that gnosticism 'was ruled in the main by the Greek spirit and determined by the interests and doctrines of the Greek philosophy of religion'.[3] The 'gnostics' were often doing no more than asking the questions that intelligent outsiders could be expected to ask of a movement which was still not clear in itself about what it believed. Some of their answers were extreme, straying into the realms of myth-ridden fantasies; others were not so different from those of their co-religionists. Yet there is nothing in any of the texts which provided an anchor for any sustained community. It is hard to imagine how 'gnostic' sects might even have communicated with each other, let alone a wider world. There had to be an institutional structure if Christianity was to survive, even if this inevitably brought a narrowing of intellectual perspectives in the name of unity.

Postscript: The Gospel of Judas

The monastery of San Antonio in Polesine is to be found in a quiet corner of medieval Ferrara in northern Italy. It is a timeless spot where the Benedictine nuns welcome visitors with stories of the depredations of church property by Napoleon when he was in northern Italy as if it had happened yesterday. A remarkable sequence of frescos from the early fourteenth century survives in the chapels of the monastery's church. They resonate with the influence of Giotto but show an unexpected originality: on the Flight into Egypt, Jesus nestles against Joseph rather than Mary; in another scene he is shown releasing the souls from Limbo. One of the most startling is a crucifixion scene. The cross is already upright and a ladder is lent against it. Ascending the ladder is Jesus himself. Two soldiers perched on the crossbar await him, one with a nail in his hand. Jesus himself is taking on the responsibility of being crucified.

If Jesus was predestined to die on the cross and he participated in his own crucifixion, then the role of Judas, a figure so deeply derided in the Christian tradition, becomes more ambiguous. In April 2006, through the auspices of the National Geographic Society, which had acquired the fragmented papyrus, it was announced that a 'Gospel of Judas' had been found. It had probably been discovered in Egypt in the 1970s (it is in Coptic), as part of a codex including texts already known from Nag Hammadi, and hawked around dealers before being reassembled and translated. A text by this name had been known, once again from Irenaeus, as a gospel of 'followers of Judas' who believed that 'he alone, knowing the truth as no others did, accomplished the mystery of the betrayal'.

The gospel, as it was first presented to the press, appeared to present a subverted version of the traditional account of Jesus' betrayal with Judas now playing a 'good' role as the one who helps Jesus' mission to succeed.[4] He is distinguished from the weak apostles who have no idea of Jesus' true role, a possible echo of Mark's gospel. Almost immediately there was a challenge by other scholars who claimed that the first English translators had completely misread the place of Judas. In fact, they argued, a careful translation, of a text that was far from complete, showed that Judas was presented after all as he had always been, as the most devilish of the apostles.[5] There were even accusations that the original translators had been seduced by the chance of creating a sensation with their 'good' Judas. To this day academic and popular battles rage over the 'correct' understanding of early Christianity.

There are some important themes in the gospel on which there is general agreement. The apostles are shown as weak and ignorant to such an extent that they are mocked by Jesus. Later they report to him a dream in which they are sacrificing their own children. Again Jesus condemns them. Here the gospel appears to be challenging the rise of the doctrine of apostolic succession, by which authority is passed down through the apostles to each new generation of priests (one of the themes of Clement's letter to the Corinthians). The author is warning that the apostles do not deserve the status the church is now giving them. The condemnation of the dream suggests that the author of the gospel is confronting those Christians who offer themselves for martyrdom. A devilish Judas also has a part to play. The author of the gospel makes the point that the apostles are worshipping a lesser god in error. The true god of Jesus lives on a much higher plane. While some Christians were developing the doctrine of atonement, that god willingly sacrificed his son for mankind, the author of Judas sees this as impossible. No true god would ever do this. Jesus dies, not because God wants him to, but because the devil in the shape of Judas betrays him. The evil Judas has been restored.

The 'Gospel of Judas' gives a vivid, if disputed, picture of the internal struggles going on between Christian groups. The writer of the gospel is horrified by what he perceives as the evildoing of an emerging institutional church, especially its glorification of martyrdom and adulation of the apostles. However, he presents his attack as a secret revelation – that includes the knowledge imparted by Jesus that there exists a heavenly kingdom beyond the god of the Old Testament. So the gospel is important not so much for its depiction of Judas, but as a clear demonstration of the concerns raised by an emerging institutional church. The champion of this church was Irenaeus, bishop of Lyons.

CHAPTER FOURTEEN

The Idea of a Church

Prophecy ran deep in Jewish history and 'the gift of prophecy' was recognised by Paul as one way in which 'the Spirit' could manifest itself in an individual (1 Corinthians 12:10). In the *Didache*, the short manual of advice to Christian congregations, prophets are seen as pervasive in Christian life. Visiting prophets are to be seen as 'high priests' and if they can prove themselves the community should support them. The problem lies in distinguishing between false and true prophets. The true prophet, the congregations are told, does not ask for money for himself and behaves as he teaches. Even so, spotting the 'real' prophet was to prove a perennial problem in the churches.

In the 160s a new movement appeared in Phrygia (Asia Minor) that drew on direct prophecies from God. Known as the 'New Prophecy', its leader was one Montanus, a failed priest of the cult of Cybele according to his critics. Montanus was joined by two women, Prisca and Maximilla, who were said to have abandoned their husbands. (This is another instance where women appear to have fulfilled a prominent role in second-century Christianity.) The Montanists claimed that the Holy Spirit had chosen their vocal chords through which to express his message: that the world was at an end and the heavenly Jerusalem would descend, not to the site of the old Jerusalem, but to Phrygia itself. The Montanists claimed to be inspired by the martyrs and they spoke against the belief held by gnostics and others that there would be a spiritual rather than physical resurrection. Anyone who did not recognise the Spirit in the voices of these prophets was warned that they must be lacking in faith. The message spread quickly and was known in Rome, Lyons and Carthage. In a church that already contained an impressive range of texts, here was a charismatic movement that threatened to bypass and subvert them all.

Once again the problem had been raised of how one could define truth and falsehood. There was as yet no coherent explanation of what exactly had been revealed about God by Jesus Christ and whether this revelation had been for all time or was still in the process of unfolding. To some the Montanists appeared to be harbingers of an imminent judgement, to others they were no more than hysterical ravers whose utterings went beyond any form of reasoned belief. Yet even if the Montanists were rejected, where else among the texts and congregations of the church could one find a secure footing? Or was it simply a matter of letting Christianity spread as it willed, taking different forms in different social and cultural contexts?

There was no clear distinction between orthodoxy and heresy in the early church. Originally the Greek word *heiresis* simply meant choice, usually of a philosophical school that a student chose to follow. The process by which the word was transformed by Christians into its later meaning of 'wrong choice' is hard to follow because precise definitions of what heresy involved took so long to evolve and shifted with time. In retrospect, three elements of orthodoxy proved crucial. First was the recognition of an institutional framework for the church within which 'truth', however it came to be defined, could be protected. This was done by consolidating the positions of the bishops as possessors of a 'pure faith' that had been absorbed by the apostles from Jesus and then passed down from one generation to the next through what became known as the apostolic succession. The second was defining which texts were orthodox and which were not. This was a long process covering some three hundred years but an important step was made when the four gospels were made canonical and the others rejected. The third was extracting from the canonical texts, which were certainly not unanimous in what they taught about God and Jesus Christ, the essence of what could be seen as 'faith', those items of belief which were considered essential to Christianity. After much debate these articles of faith were to be enshrined in creeds.

To give 'orthodoxy' shape, it had to define itself against the alternatives, the 'wrong' paths taken by rival Christians, in other words the heretical. 'Heretics', many of them, of course, sincere Christians as committed to finding the truth as their 'orthodox' opponents, were painted in increasingly lurid colours. They were agents of Satan as enemies of God and would certainly burn eternally in hell fire for their arrogance in opposing 'the truth'. One of the earliest and most comprehensive attempts to set up an orthodoxy which defined itself partly through the condemnation of the heretical was Irenaeus' *Adversus haereses*, 'Against the Heretics', the Latin title of a work known in its Greek original as 'On the Detection and Overthrow of What is Falsely called "Knowledge"'. A rambling but important work, it is one of the founding documents of orthodox Christianity.

Irenaeus came from Smyrna on the coast of Asia Minor. As a young man he had been a devoted follower of the city's bishop, Polycarp, an account of whose martyrdom was one of the inspirational texts of early Christianity. Polycarp comes across as a practical leader and gifted teacher, 'a man who was of much greater weight, and a more steadfast witness of truth than Valentinus, and Marcion, and the rest of the heretics', Irenaeus tells us. Legend recorded that as a young man Polycarp had known John the Evangelist and Irenaeus treasured this personal link back through the generations to Christ. The impact on Irenaeus of Polycarp's martyrdom was profound and it left him convinced that the mark of the true Christian lay in the readiness to face martyrdom. He left Smyrna and travelled west, eventually becoming a priest in the Greek-speaking Christian community in Lyons. He also spent some time in Rome and it was probably here that he came across Valentinus whose teachings he was soon to denounce. While he was away in Rome, riots broke out in Lyons which led to the martyrdom of some forty Christians, including their bishop, Pothinus. Irenaeus was asked to become the shattered community's new bishop.

Irenaeus had read widely in earlier Christian literature including the works of some of his opponents. While he does not appear to have had a formal education in Greek philosophy he certainly knew something of the techniques of rhetoric and how to present an argument. There are quotations from Homer and Plato in his works. Even though the church had appropriated Jewish traditions and scripture Irenaeus believed it was now broken from Judaism and he rejoiced in this. 'But in Christ every blessing is found; and for this reason the latter people [Christians] had snatched the blessings from the Father of the former people [the Jews], just as Jacob stole his blessing from Esau.' He singles out as heretics the Ebionites, who professed Jesus but who continued to follow a Jewish way of life and refused to believe that Jesus was born of a virgin.

Instead Irenaeus is conscious of a church that has transcended its Jewish roots and is empire wide, as his own migration from Asia Minor witnesses. In his writings he specifically mentions Christian communities in Germany, Spain, among the Celts and in Egypt and Libya. He refers to Christians involved in trading activities and even some working in the imperial service. He praises the overall peace of the empire and the freedom its subjects have to travel. This suggests that the persecutions which took place in 177 in Lyons, horrifying though they appear to have been in the sources, were the result of local rather than empire-wide tensions. In fact, the period between the death of Marcus Aurelius in 180 and 202 when the emperor Septimius Severus initiated a new bout of persecution appears to have been relatively trouble-free for Christians and Irenaeus' comments may have reflected this.

Once he had settled back at Lyons, Irenaeus found he was beset by rival Christian preachers. 'Gnostics' tended to set up their own 'schools' within congregations and Irenaeus was particularly irritated by the activities of one 'Marcos the Magician', a follower of Valentinus, in his own. *Adversus haereses* was the response.

What is remarkable about Irenaeus' work is the confidence it shows in the church's mission. Accounts from only a few years before, those of Justin Martyr, for instance, show a church on the defensive, having to 'apologise' for itself (the word used here in the sense of 'defend'). One might have thought that the brutalities that had been inflicted on the community of which Irenaeus was now bishop would have cowed him. Yet he describes a church with a strong tradition of faith that is clearly well defined and stable enough to be upheld against those within the church, notably the heretical 'gnostics', who are assailing it.

There is, Irenaeus argues, only one God and his presence is consistent throughout the scriptures. Irenaeus weaves these into a coherent narrative. When God created the world and Adam and Eve he intended that humankind would grow in obedience and wisdom so that eventually the words of Genesis, that 'man would be created in his own likeness and image', in other words, would become as if divine, would be fulfilled. A phrase Irenaeus often uses is of humankind approaching 'near to the uncreated'. Alas things went wrong early on. Adam and Eve were like children, easily persuaded by Satan that they could seize maturity for themselves without divine help. So they fell and the human race remained in a state of immaturity. To coerce humankind towards the ultimate obedience needed, God introduced the Law. This was a learning period as God was accustoming humanity to himself so that human beings would grow in understanding. The Old Testament, as it had become since its appropriation by the Christians as the source of their own prophecies, was thus a vital part of the story. Neither God nor the text itself can be diminished.

The period of rule by the Law lasted until a state of relative maturity had been reached. Then God decided that a new phase in history could begin with the sending of Jesus Christ to earth. Christ has always been in existence, as the Spirit has been, and the terms Wisdom, in the Old Testament, and 'the Word' in the New (here Irenaeus followed the gospel of John) refer to him. (The linking of Wisdom, used widely in the Old Testament to *logos*/Christ was an important development, even though some church fathers preferred to associate Wisdom with the Holy Spirit.) While Christ was revealing God to the world (again following John) it was essential that he was fully human in order to redeem the sin of the human Adam. To counter the docetists, those who preached that Christ only appeared to be a man, Irenaeus stressed that Jesus was visible and palpable, an actual demonstration of life. There was no need to follow the gnostics in despising the material world or human existence.

This link between Adam and Christ, Christ as the second Adam, draws on similar images in Paul's Letter to the Romans. The disobedience of Adam and Eve had been reversed by the obedience of Mary in agreeing to take on the burden of bearing Christ and the obedience of Jesus himself in suffering on the cross. The Holy Spirit is given an important role by Irenaeus. It was through the Spirit that the prophecies were uttered, the coming of Christ was proclaimed, the virgin conceived, Christ was raised from the dead and the Second Coming would be put in hand.

Irenaeus often refers to the coming of Christ as a 'recapitulation'. The Greek original normally means the summing up of an argument, a pause while the points made are reviewed, but Irenaeus also seems to use it in the sense of 'a gathering in'. All has been changed with the coming of Christ. Yet the final revelation will not be complete until the Last Judgement when the just will be restored to their full divinity in the image of God, promised in Genesis. Irenaeus was at pains to argue that the resurrection would be of the flesh. He refused to follow his 'heretical' opponents who argued, using texts from Paul to do so, that the material body would not be reconstituted in the afterlife.

Irenaeus bitterly attacked 'heretics' for using the scriptures selectively, especially in the way they disregarded or even discarded some of the texts. 'By specious argumentation, craftily patched together, they mislead the minds of the more ignorant and ensnare them by falsifying the Lord's words: thus they become wicked interpreters of genuine words.' In a shorter and later work, the only other work from among several recorded of his that survives, the *Proof of the Apostolic Preaching*, he again stresses the importance of the Old Testament as a body of prophecies about the coming of Christ. He reiterates the unity of the Christian message: the scriptures, the teaching of Christ, the activity of the Spirit and the teaching of the church are all linked and reinforce one another.

The New Covenant that Jesus Christ has brought needs to be preserved through proclamation. Again the Spirit is essential in guiding the church onwards: 'Where the church is, there is the Spirit of God; and where the Spirit of God is, there is the Church and every grace, and the Spirit is truth.' The mechanism by which the teachings are preserved is the church. Christ's message has been passed to the apostles and then on to their successors. The apostles 'have handed down to us one God, announced in the Law and the Prophets to be the maker of heaven and earth, and one Christ who is the Son of God.' The idea is not unique to Irenaeus as it was a term used of the philosophical schools that also passed their teachings down from founders and something similar is to be found in Clement's letter to the Corinthians. The prime purpose of the bishops is to keep the message intact and pass it on. Irenaeus does not elaborate on the authority of bishops beyond this.

However, in order to make his theology 'fit' with history Irenaeus often distorts the past. He believed that to be fully representative of humankind, Jesus had to live through every phase of human life including old age. This forces him to argue that Jesus lived to be an old man, even to the reign of Trajan (which began in AD 98). It is not clear whether he believed that this was a resurrected Christ who had lived on as such for many years or whether the crucifixion took place when Jesus was old. Irenaeus claims that it was the apostles who passed on the tradition that Jesus lived to be an old man, even though the gospels make it quite clear that he was crucified in his thirties and, according to Luke, was only present in a resurrected form for forty days. Irenaeus ignores this contradiction.

There is another distortion. In order to explain how apostolic succession works, he provides a list of bishops of Rome. He saw the empire's capital as home to the most prestigious of the churches. In fact, there was no presiding bishop that Ignatius could address when he wrote to the city's Christians in 107. When one looks at Irenaeus' list one can see that it is made up. Irenaeus claims that Peter and Paul founded the church in Rome, even though Paul's own Letter to the Romans does not mention Peter and makes it quite clear that the church was already in existence when Paul wrote to it. The names of their successors – Linus, Anacletus, Clement, Euarestus and Alexander – seem to have no other historical support and the list has been described as 'probably a pious fiction'.[1] So one needs to be cautious about accepting Irenaeus' claim that his hero Polycarp had actually met the apostle John. (The dates make it unlikely. No apostle could have been born much later than AD 10 and Polycarp died c.155 so John would have been improbably old if he did meet the young Polycarp.)

How did the apostles and their successors relate to the emerging Christian scriptures, to what was eventually to become the New Testament? For Irenaeus the criteria for admission to the canon of scriptures is, hardly surprisingly, the relationship of a specific text with the apostles, among whom he includes Paul. He went on to limit the gospels to four, the first time this had ever been done. He did not attempt to explain why the specific four gospels he has chosen deserved their inclusion. Rather, he based his view on the naturalness of four – four quarters of the earth, four winds and even, in an early creative use of the Book of Revelation, four living creatures (Revelation 4:7). The authors he provided for his chosen texts may have had no more basis in fact than his choice of early bishops of Rome. It was now a hundred years after they had been written and there is no evidence other than Irenaeus' attributions in support of his claim.

Irenaeus traces heresy back to the father of heresy, Simon Magus (Acts 8:9–13), and so, just as he creates a tradition of apostles handing on the 'true' faith, he has rival traditions of those handing on heresy – a genealogy of heresy, as it might be called. Inevitably these heresies comprise a ragbag of ideas and writings, many of which are anonymous. He introduces the idea that heretics were arrogant in their attempts to subvert the truth and he uses a good analogy that describes a mosaic made out of precious stones that depicts a king, here seen as a symbol of the church. Yet heretics break up the original, rearrange the stones in the form of a dog or a fox and then claim that this is what the king/church should look like.

The idea that there were four gospels and no more or less than this must have presented a challenge to the church. The problem was that the significant differences between the portrayals of Jesus, especially the massive discrepancy between John and the synoptic gospels, would have made it difficult for any congregation used to one gospel to be prepared to accept another. Not surprisingly, some felt that the confusion could only be resolved by amalgamating the four gospels into one. Tatian, a Greek Christian from Syria who had become a student of Justin Martyr in Rome, set about creating a single version of the four gospels, known as the *Diatessaron* ('through the four'). It may have been written in the author's native Syriac (although it was probably soon translated into Greek). Tatian omitted the genealogies of Christ in Matthew and Luke (these contradicted each other and could hardly be reconciled) but reproduced much of the rest of the gospels, though in a revised chronological order. With duplicate verses omitted, the harmonised gospel was just over 70 per cent of the length of the original four. The *Diatessaron* became very popular in Syria and the east. It was only in the fifth century that the four gospels reappeared in their original state when it is recorded that Theodoret, bishop of Cyrrhus, a city on the Euphrates, collected up about two hundred copies of the original *Diatessaron* in the 450s, destroyed them and replaced them with versions of the canonical gospels. Even so, it is fascinating to note that the Koran refers to a single Christian gospel and this may well be the *Diatessaron*.

In contrast to the heretics whom he denounces, Irenaeus claims that the church has 'one soul and one and the same heart, proclaims and teaches and hands on those things with one voice, as if possessed of a single mouth'. This ideology drew its strength from the Platonic belief that, ultimately, truth was made up of a harmonious unity. This is, of course, questionable. The creation of Christian orthodoxy was always to involve arbitrary and artificial boundaries and some uneasy compromises between different traditions (and, as will be seen, between the scriptures and pagan philosophy). It could not have been otherwise when the major issues of theology, the relationship between God and Jesus, the ways in which Jesus' human and divine nature co-existed and whether there was a physical or spiritual resurrection, were philosophically intractable. It was the idea that there could be a single truth and the possibility that it might be defined and passed on within an institutional framework and upheld that was important. Irenaeus had provided a model for survival and, in the long term, it proved more attractive than the closed and esoteric communities that challenged it.[2]

CHAPTER FIFTEEN

To Compromise or Reject

CONFRONTING THE MATERIAL WORLD

THE DAILY LIFE OF CHRISTIAN COMMUNITIES IN THIS PERIOD
remains murky: the evidence is simply scant.[1] There is no surviving
Christian art from before 200, almost no funerary inscriptions from before
the third century. The earliest church history, that of Eusebius, concentrates
on lists of bishops and graphic accounts of persecutions. So it is difficult to
recreate the lives of second- or third-century Christians. Some Christian apologists wished to emphasise the similarity of their lives to their pagan counterparts. As Tertullian the ebullient church father from Carthage puts it in his
own *Apology*: 'We live together with you in this world, including the Forum,
including the meat market, baths, shops, workrooms, inns, fairs, and the rest
of commercial intercourse, and we sail along with you and serve in the army
and are active in agriculture and trade.'

A late second-century source, the Epistle to Diognetus, starts in much the
same vein. The unknown Christian author writes that Christians cannot be
distinguished from pagans by their language, the places where they live, in cities
both Greek and barbarian. They appear to follow 'the customs of the natives
in respect to clothing, food, and the rest of their ordinary conduct'. The differences, he goes on, are more subtle. Christians live on a different plane as
strangers in a foreign land. 'They are in the flesh, but they do not live after the
flesh. They pass their days on earth, but they are citizens of heaven.' He notes
that while they marry and beget children like their fellow citizens, 'they do not
destroy their offspring'. They eat together but do not share a common bed –
presumably a reference to sexual continence. 'They obey the prescribed laws,
and at the same time surpass the laws by their lives.' He goes on to complain
that despite their lifestyle, 'they are assailed by the Jews as foreigners, and are
persecuted by the Greeks . . . They love all men, and are persecuted by all.'

This idea of Christians living in 'a foreign land' where they are despised, and
which they, in their turn, are exhorted to despise, is also to be found in the *c.*140
text known as the *Shepherd of Hermas*, from Rome. Hermas is told, by a man

dressed as a shepherd who has been sent to him from heaven, that the king of his country (God or Christ) might call him home at any time so that he must not accumulate property on earth. 'Therefore, instead of fields buy ye souls that are in trouble, as each is able, and visit widows and orphans, and neglect them not; and spend your riches and all your displays, which ye received from God, on fields and houses of this kind.' Here one has the outlines of a specifically Christian attitude to life, based on restraint and charity. It is assumed, as in many other early texts, that Christians will ascend straight to heaven.[2]

Concern for sexual continence ran deep in the Christian tradition. Jesus was unusual for a Jew in being unmarried although it is Paul who most actively expresses distaste for sexual behaviour. This was reinforced by the Platonic tradition that despised the desires of the human body as diverting the attention from the philosophical contemplation needed to understand the immaterial world. While the vast majority of Christians must have married, a respect for celibacy remained and sometimes this is expressed in a positive way. The Acts of Thomas, a text originally written in Syria but which was circulating in Greek translations by the middle of the third century, describes the travels of the disciple Judas Thomas from Antioch eastwards through Syria to Mesopotamia and India. For Thomas, commitment to Christ is essentially the offering of a pure body, healed by Christ from a state of unworthiness. Conversion is often linked to recovery from serious illness or the exorcism of a demon. After conversion, celibacy is expected and along with it a commitment to those still suffering. Healing of the body and healing of the soul go hand in hand. The Acts assume that women will have as active a ministry as men and this may reflect a more egalitarian Christianity on the eastern borders of the empire than that to be found further west.

The fragmentary evidence relating to Christian marriages, especially those in the Latin west, suggests that they were as patriarchal as Roman ones. The father is given absolute authority within the family and this is now expressed within a specifically Christian context. The submission that the wife makes to her husband is similar to that which the Christian should make to 'the Lord' while the husband's love for his wife should echo that of Christ's for the church. Tertullian reiterates the importance of patriarchy and assumes that it is the father who sets the Christian tone of the household beneath him, extending his control to the slaves, stressing, as seen in earlier texts, that it is their Christian duty, as well as their legal obligation, to submit to their masters. It appears that many were forced to convert so as to create a fully Christian household.

A Christian wife also has her duties. In a treatise written to his wife, Tertullian outlines the problems a woman experiences if her husband is not a Christian. Her pattern of prayer will be disrupted by his insistence that she attend the baths with him, his banqueting plans will interfere with her fasting, he will divert her with his own business when she wishes to attend to the poor. She will need to attend pagan festivals with him and he will forbid any Christian activities in the house. Socially conservative though he was, Tertullian even argues that it is better for a Christian to marry another Christian below his social status than a pagan. Disparity of belief was accepted as grounds for divorce (see 1 Corinthians 7) even though this appears to have conflicted with Jesus' own commands on the matter. Others, the writer of the *Shepherd of Hermas*, for instance, allowed divorce as the formal end of a marriage but not the remarriage of a divorced spouse.

Christian family behaviour in this period was distinct in its condemnation of abortion and the abandonment of newborn children. The practice of exposing babies, especially girls, was widespread in the Roman world. Sometimes these unlucky children were saved. Hermas, for instance, claimed to have been rescued from abandonment although he was then raised as a slave. (By the time he is writing he has become a freedman.) However, the vast majority of these babies must have died. Jews had always abhorred infanticide and Christians followed them. The Christian view was elaborated by stressing that abandonment was akin to murder.[3] This was an important ethical advance on pagan, if not Jewish, custom, especially when Christianity became the predominant religion of the empire and laws against infanticide were enforced. Outside this development very little is known of Christian children at this period and it was not until later, for instance, that infant baptism became the norm, although in Hippolytus' *Apostolic Tradition* of *c*.215 children, including those 'who are unable to speak for themselves', are among those admitted to baptism alongside their parents.

It is right to talk of the Judaeo-Christian ethical tradition because Christians adopted so many facets of Jewish life. This was seen in the requirements to support the poor, especially those who were widowed or orphaned. This was linked to concerns that wealth was corrupting in itself so that giving to the poor not only helped the recipients but liberated the giver as well. In his *Similitudes*, Hermas discusses how rich and poor can live in mutual dependence. If the rich give to the poor, the poor will pray to God, who is more sympathetic to their prayers than he is to those of the rich, to favour the rich who will then help the poor even more! Hermas makes the analogy with an elm tree, which is fruitless, alongside which a vine runs unproductively along the ground. If the vine is hooked up to the elm, the elm will support its flourishing!

In his *Apology*, Tertullian gives a vivid picture of how a Christian community of his day, the early third century, carried out its proceedings. The emphasis was on the common ownership of goods. Christians share everything except their wives, Tertullian tells his pagan audience. A contribution to a common fund is expected each month when Christians gather for worship and there are designated groups – orphans, shipwrecked sailors and abandoned slaves – who are its recipients. Justin Martyr concurs: 'What is collected is deposited with the president, who succours the orphans and widows and those who, through sickness or any other cause, are in want, and those who are in bonds and the strangers sojourning among us – in a word he takes care of all who are in need.' One report of the church of Rome tells of its support of over fifteen hundred widows in the mid-third century. This centralised giving must have been an important factor in sustaining the growing Christian communities.

The *Apostolic Tradition* of Hippolytus, apparently written in Rome in about 215, gives specific details of the requirements for acceptance into a Christian congregation. Hippolytus describes how those who come forward for instruction are summoned before their teachers and questioned about why they are attracted to Christianity. They must give full details of their marital status and occupation and if they are slaves must confirm that they have the permission of their masters to attend instruction. The slaves have to promise further that they will continue to please their masters if these are pagan. There must have been fears that their conversion might be seen as an act of subversion and rebound on the Christian community. As regards occupations, pimps and prostitutes are out, of course, sculptors must give up any creation of statues of the pagan gods, actors cease altogether to attend the theatre. Teachers are also expected to give up their jobs as these involve passing on worldly rather than spiritual knowledge. They can continue only if they have no other occupation. Charioteers, gladiators and priests of the pagan cults will be rejected as will anyone who dabbles in magic.

Those accepted are admitted as catechumens. There follows a three-year course of instruction that may be shortened for good conduct. Any catechumen martyred in this period becomes baptised through his or her own blood. For the rest, the ceremony of baptism is preceded by a fast and the exorcism of demons by the bishop. Baptism is by total immersion in flowing water: Jesus' baptism in the Jordan provides the model. The rite of baptism involves the renunciation of Satan and then three separate acceptances of belief, in effect an early creed. The catechumen must assent to belief in God Almighty, then to belief in 'Jesus Christ, the Son of God, who was born of the Holy Spirit and the Virgin Mary, who was crucified under Pontius Pilate, and died, and rose on the third day living from the dead, and ascended into heaven, and sat down at the right hand of the Father, the one coming to judge the living and the dead', and finally to belief 'in the Holy Spirit and the Holy Church and the resurrection of the flesh'. While the resurrection of the flesh may still have been in dispute in the Greek east, here it seems to have been accepted as an article of faith.[4]

Those who have been baptised can attend the Sunday services and participate in the Eucharist. Justin Martyr in his *First Apology* of c.150–55 describes the particulars of the sacrament in some detail: the priest presiding over the sacrament gives a thanksgiving over the bread and wine (mixed with water) and then distributes it. 'Not as common bread and common drink do we receive these; but in like manner as Jesus Christ our Saviour, having been made flesh by the Word of God, had both flesh and blood for our salvation, so likewise have we been taught that the food which is blessed by the prayer of His word, and from which our blood and flesh by transmutation are nourished, is the flesh and blood of that Jesus who was made flesh.' Justin notes that the ceremony has been passed down to the Christian communities through the apostles and reiterates the central place it has in Christian worship. It seems to have been accepted that ingesting the consecrated 'bread and drink' gave life to the recipients and may have been associated with the spiritual transformation of their physical bodies. The Eucharist must surely have served to give Christians an added spiritual dimension. The elaboration of rituals, sexual continence and fasting before communion, and the presentation of the ceremony as a spectacle (as can be still found in a Catholic high mass today) developed in the centuries that followed.[5]

In the early fourth century, probably before Constantine had extended toleration to the church, a council of nineteen bishops met at Elvira in Spain. Its proceedings, and the eighty-one canons it promulgated, provide a picture of a Christian community which had to define its own values within a predominantly pagan society. The first concern of the bishops appears to be the continuing attractions of both Judaism and paganism and the need to define effective boundaries against them. Anyone who offers a sacrifice to the gods is permanently excommunicated, and any Christian who sits down to eat with Jews is also kept from communion. Ten years of penance is required for even watching sacrifices and those who follow the pagan custom of burning candles in cemeteries during daylight will be excommunicated. Christian girls must not marry pagans, by so doing they are committing 'adultery of the soul'. Nor may they marry Jews or 'heretics'. Any parent who allows such a marriage will themselves be banned from communion for five years.

(It was the offering of sacrifices that caused most concern. It seems to have been the touchstone that defined admission to the community. The significance of the rejections needs to be emphasised. Sacrifice, the ritual killing of an animal on an altar in front of a temple, was not simply a religious ceremony. It was intimately connected to the protection and survival of the city and a centuries-old relationship with the gods. By condemning sacrifice one was turning one's back on what it meant to be a citizen or a member of an ethnic community. No wonder Christians saw themselves as foreigners – they had made themselves so by their commitment to Christ.)

The normal penalties for infringing the rules of conduct are a period of penance, sometimes as much as ten years, or excommunication. (In many cases the excommunication was permanent but in some cases if the miscreant was on his or her deathbed, fellowship of the church could be restored.) A male adulterer may be pardoned on his deathbed if he renounces his partner: if he recovers and resumes the relationship he can never be readmitted to the church. Women who leave their husbands for another man can never be readmitted to the church, even on their deathbeds. Consecrated virgins who break their vows and do not repent are permanently excommunicated. If they do repent and refrain from further sex, they may be offered communion but again only on their deathbeds. In comparison to the harsh treatment of sexual misdemeanours, other offences attract less condemnation. Seven years excommunication from the church for a woman who intentionally beats her slave girl to death, five years if the death is not caused intentionally, seems lenient.

The canons showed a growing concern with sexual behaviour. In many ways, they reflected the traditional behaviour expected of women although for men the code was more rigorous than pagan convention demanded: a Christian who commits a sexual offence is given a penance the first time but is excommunicated completely if he offends again. All clergy must now be celibate. Those who have wives must refrain from having sex with them and even evidence of sexual immorality in the past is enough to prevent ordination. The only women allowed to live in a cleric's house are his sisters or daughters and then only if they have consecrated themselves to virginity. Those committing themselves to perpetual virginity made up a small but growing number of Christians. The practice offended conventional family values, which required the daughters of the family to be used to cement alliances with other families, but there were benefits in that the virgins were given a status of their own which may have been higher than that of a wife in a patriarchal society. In the fourth century, however, some Christians preached an intense revulsion of all forms of sexuality, with women being cast in the role of temptresses if they did not make a public renunciation of their sexuality.

One senses a growing feeling of common identity, not only through shared values but through the creation of communities that ritualised and expressed those values in charitable support. These were much more important than the arcane explanations of the more intellectual sects. In this period, it was a matter of defining boundaries, working out the ways in which a fellowship in Christ could be distinguished from contemporary Judaism, still in number a far greater movement than Christianity, and paganism. As the communities established their presence, thoughtful pagans began to express their concerns. One of these was Celsus.

The Earliest Christian Art

THERE IS NOTHING FROM BEFORE AD 200 WHICH CAN BE RECOGNISED as distinctively Christian art. This is partly because Christian communities were small and poor but it is possible that traditional Jewish conventions about portraying images may have inhibited them. Any public display of Christianity would certainly have invited retaliation. There is, in fact, a canon of the Council of Elvira (c.314) that specifically forbids the painting of church walls, a stricture still followed by the Donatists in north Africa as late as the early fourth century. While the baptistery at Dura-Europus is decorated, the neighbouring meeting hall is not.

Rome is the home of much of the earliest art, which decorates the tombs of the Christian dead in the catacombs. There are a few other examples scattered around the empire, the frescoes from the baptistery in Dura-Europus, dating to 240, some sculpture which may have come from a marble tomb in Asia Minor and fragments of frescoes from Thessalonika and sites in North Africa. Some third century sarcophagi survive from Gaul where Roman styles have been adapted to Christian themes. All these, with the rare exception of Dura-Europus, are funerary art.

Catacomb art is usually very rudimentary, rushed and awkward in style, often little more than a symbolic shape or figures, stamped on to the tomb as a gesture of hope. The sarcophagi, on the other hand, must have been commissioned by wealthier Christians and their carving is of high quality. In many cases it is hard to know whether pictures of grapes and vines or sheep are purely decorative, as they would be in pagan art, or have a Christian meaning. Certainly the vine, associated with the Eucharist or with Christ himself, easily makes the transition from paganism. Another well-known Christian symbol is the fish. If one takes the first letters of 'Jesus Christ, Son of God, Saviour' in Greek they spell out the Greek *ixthus*, fish, so the association is very clear. Scenes of fishermen are common: Clement of Alexandria talks attractively of Christ as 'the fisher of men, of those saved from the sea of evil, luring with sweet life the chaste fish from the hostile tide'. Fishermen in boats, which of course suggest the early apostles, also symbolise a link to water and baptism.

The most common figure of all in early Christian art is the Good Shepherd. This was already known as a pagan symbol but it fitted well with Christian readings (notably the gospel of John). One of the rare links between art and a text is to be found in the *Shepherd of Hermas* (*c*.140) in the vision of a man 'of glorious aspect, dressed like a Shepherd, with a white goat's skin, a wallet on his shoulders and a rod in his hand'. Another popular image is the *orant*, a figure, usually female, standing face front with her hands raised, the traditional representation of the virtue *pietas* in classical art. Often an *orant* is shown alongside the Good Shepherd as a standard Christian tomb image. Many early Christians would have been converted in schools of philosophy, such as the ones run by Clement of Alexandria or Origen, so it is not surprising to find images of teachers or philosophers with their pupils. These presumably drew on real life but the teacher also stands for Christ. Early hymns link Christ to the sun, the light that contrasts with the darkness, but representations of Christ as the sun god, *Helios*, are rare.

Themes from the Old Testament are more common than those from the New, probably because it was easier to find copies of the Hebrew scriptures to read from when the New Testament was still in formation. Jonah, thrown up by the whale after three days in darkness, a symbol of the resurrection, is very popular, as are the Old Testament characters who were rescued by the intervention of God – Noah, or Isaac at the moment of sacrifice. One of the earliest themes from gospel sources is the raising of Lazarus. Others record Christ's miracles but there are no known images of his birth, Passion or resurrection, all common in later centuries. The hope of salvation and the raising to new life bind these images together.

By the late third century, on a sarcophagus from Santa Maria Antiqua in Rome, the dead man is shown as a philosopher among a cluster of what have become common themes. Water flows from the River Jordan where Christ is shown being baptised. The water runs along the relief reaching a scene of Jonah being tossed overboard and then reclining on earth after he has been thrown out from the whale. Meanwhile the dead man is flanked by an *orant*, probably his wife, and a Good Shepherd.

CHAPTER SIXTEEN

Celsus Confronts the Christians

THE EARLIEST SYSTEMATIC ATTACK ON CHRISTIANITY TO SURVIVE IS 'On the True Doctrine' by Celsus.[1] It tells us what educated Greeks found difficult about Christianity. Nothing is known about Celsus other than what his writings tell us and they give no hint as to where he came from or where he wrote. They probably date from the 180s – much the same period as Irenaeus. Celsus was clearly well educated in the ideas of his time but he was not a particularly sophisticated thinker. In fact, his temperament comes across as conservative and he was happy to repeat the religious philosophy of his day without any critical analysis of it. His work only survives because the great theologian of the third century, Origen, chose to reply to it and in doing so reproduced some 70 per cent of the original. So what still exists can be pieced together in a truncated but continuous narrative. In comparison, other sophisticated attacks on Christianity, notably that by the third-century philosopher Porphyry, were destroyed altogether by later Christians.

Celsus is a Platonist, typical of his period in believing that there is a Supreme Good or God, who exists as a transcendent being above all things and beyond all emotions. God is essentially benevolent: 'God takes care of the universe; that is to say that providence never abandons it, and it does not become more evil.' 'All has been made by God so that the world itself may be complete and perfect in all its parts.' God does not need to be worshipped but he has set in place an ordered society and as such deserves respect. Celsus is adamant that humankind does not have a privileged role in creation: 'Things have been proportioned, but not for the sake of man – rather for the good of the universe as a whole.' Here Celsus admits to being influenced by the Stoic principle that everything in the world, material and immaterial, is linked.[2] He records how ants appear to operate intelligently: they set up a stratified society, work hard, punish idlers and even have their own graveyards. There is an underlying good order to the world which can be appreciated through the use of reason and, judging from Celsus' example of the ants, through observation. Certainly evils exist – 'they are a part of the nature of matter and of mankind' – but the amount of evil is constant, as is the amount of good, and it is extremely difficult to know whether what appears to have an evil effect on one individual might not have a good one on another.

Just as there is an underlying order to the material world, so should there be a similar order in human society. Celsus sees reverence for the emperor as complementary to the reverence for God. Yet, one should not be subservient. Human beings have the power of reason and they should use it: 'One ought first to follow reason as a guide before accepting any belief, since anyone who believes without testing a doctrine is certain to be deceived.' Plato, he goes on, accepted that the good could only be known to a few but 'he does not ask people to stop questioning or to accept that God is like such and such'. Celsus sums up the relationship between God and intelligence as follows: 'God is not mind, intelligence, or knowledge; but he causes the mind to think, and is hence the cause of the existence of intelligence, the possibility of knowledge.'

However, finding the truth is not easy. Celsus is aware of Plato's analogy of the cave (from *The Republic*) in which individuals growing up inside a cave see only shadows but then have to embark on a painful journey towards reality, here symbolised by the light of the sun. One of Celsus' criticisms of the Christians is that they bypass this long journey by accepting Jesus too readily as 'the light'. They spend too much time in the outer world, listening to deceivers and magicians and they place too great an emphasis on miracles. 'They [Christians] think one cannot know God except through the senses of the body.' Rather they should be studying the poets and philosophers who have gone beyond the world of the senses and looked into the inner soul.

It is not clear what made Celsus so fascinated and appalled by the Christians. He had certainly studied the movement in detail and even read from the gospels. He acknowledges that the Christians are distinct from society, in that they worship in secret, condemn the pagan gods and 'are agreed that they must remain perpetual apostates from the approved religions'. He believes that their numbers are growing and he worries that knowledge of their myths, such as the virgin birth, the crucifixion and the resurrection, are becoming more widespread than the works of the philosophers. What holds the Christians together, he suggests, is fear of persecution and the rejection of Judaism but he is also aware that there have been many forms of Christianity. He cites the Marcionites, the gnostics and Christians who wanted to go on living by Jewish law. He mentions by name a number of Christian sects led by women that are recorded nowhere else. He knows of the debates going on within Christianity although his assertion that 'Christians, it is needless to say, utterly detest each other' is rather sweeping. His own explanation for the disagreements is that Christian beliefs lack solid foundation and so disputes are inevitable.

Understandably Celsus has little time for the God of the Old Testament and his criticisms echo those of the gnostics described earlier. If God is beyond all human emotions and has no human attributes, as Celsus believes, then a god who moves over the waters, has hands with which to create and speaks cannot be God. The Christians speak of God 'being angry, jealous, moved to repentance, sorry, sleepy, – in short, as a being in every respect more a man than a God'. Celsus acknowledges the 'gnostic' view that the Old Testament god was an evil creator god but, in that case, why did the true God allow him to take charge?

In line with Trypho in Justin's *Dialogue*, Celsus refuses to believe that the Old Testament is filled with prophecies which foretell Christ. Rather the prophecies seem to tell of a great prince, a leader of nations, not 'a low-grade character like Jesus'. There are many thousands of others who might qualify to be the one prophesied. How can one distinguish Jesus from all the other magic workers who can also expel demons and cure disease?

One of Celsus' major concerns is that Jesus is the messenger of a malevolent god. God has already shown that he can be destructive of his creation – Celsus cites the tower of Babel and the destruction of Sodom and Gomorrah. Now Jesus brings the message that the majority of humankind will suffer eternal punishment at the judgement with only an elect few being saved. Apart from the objection that the destruction of the world is hardly worthy of God, Celsus finds the principle that one section of mankind is elevated above others unsustainable. As has been seen, as a good Stoic he believed in the unity of matter and one cannot privilege some human beings in this way. He spotted a trend. By the time of Augustine two hundred years later, Christians were arguing that they had the right to dispose of the rest of creation as they wished. God created humankind as the superior species and humans had the right to use animals, which had no souls and lacked the power of rational thought, exactly as they wanted.

Celsus finds the incarnation of Jesus equally incomprehensible. The Platonists accepted that there were intermediary figures between God and the material world but Celsus feels that the adulation given to Jesus is hardly that due to an intermediary – Christians speak of him as if he were another god. In any case, why does God, who is accessible through reason, need to show himself in the form of a human being? Why does he have to degrade himself by mingling with human flesh? If he were divine surely he would not have looked just like a human being? 'It is plainly impossible that a body containing the essence of divinity itself would be like anyone else's.' Even if he did have to appear in human form why did he wait so late in history to show himself in this way and then in such an out of the way place? Jesus' life does nothing to improve the dignity of God. He allowed himself to be humiliated as no true god would. He was not recognised as divine in his lifetime even by his own followers, who failed to maintain their allegiance to him when he was arrested. So the Christians' claim that the arrest and humiliation of Jesus are all the more reason to believe that he was the Son of God is just perverse to Celsus. The Christians confuse everyone further by claiming that the wisdom of men is nothing but foolishness with God. This challenges Celsus' own approach to intellectual life. He derides the way in which Christians aim their message at those without wisdom by saying that they will have the 'real' wisdom if they believe in Christ. Humility is important in that one should not accept that one can fully understand God, but the Christian form of humility involves little more than self-abasement, something very different.

Celsus is particularly concerned with the way that Christians have withdrawn from society. He believes that the rituals of worship and sacrifice that underpin everyday life in the pagan world cannot simply be disregarded. If Christians wish to participate in society then they should respect the gods of the society in which they live. It can be compared to living in someone else's property and not paying rent for it. Their denigration of existing custom and their lack of respect for authority are equally inexcusable: 'If everyone were to adopt the Christian's attitude, moreover there would be no rule of law: the legitimate authority would be abandoned; earthly things would return to chaos and come into the hands of the lawless and savage barbarians; and nothing further would be heard of Christian worship or of wisdom, anywhere in the world. Indeed for your superstition to exist, the power of the emperor is necessary.' If Celsus was writing in the reign of Commodus (180–92), as seems to be the case, this rings true. Whatever Commodus' many other faults, little persecution of Christians is recorded in his reign.

Celsus goes on to query the power of the Christian God. He notes how Christians will strike statues of Zeus and Apollo claiming that they will be protected from any retaliation because they are Christians. Yet, surely, if he, Celsus, struck a statue erected by the Christians there would not be a reaction either. If the Christian God were a true protector he would not allow Christians to be persecuted. There is no evidence that there was any retribution for those who crucified Jesus. 'What are we to think of a God so negligent that he not only permitted his son to suffer as cruel a death as thus Jesus did, but who allowed the message he was sent to deliver [probably that of the Second Coming] to perish with him?' The emperor would gain nothing by adopting the Christian God as a protector of the state because the evidence shows that both Jews and Christians have suffered rather than prospered under God's 'care'. Likewise, Christians talk of the great struggle between God and Satan but why is God not able to overcome the devil?

Celsus resents the way that Christians simply respond to being challenged with bland statements such as 'Do not ask questions, just believe' and 'Your faith will save you'. He admits that there are some intelligent Christians who are prepared to see the meaning of Christ in allegorical terms but the majority are simply credulous. He particularly berates preachers who concentrate their efforts on 'the foolish, dishonourable and stupid ... slaves, women and little children'. He claims that when in private houses they target 'wool workers, cobblers, laundry workers and the most illiterate country bumpkins ... Children are told that they must not believe their own teachers or parents but that they will only be happy if they believe in Christ'. He cannot understand the Christian obsession with sinners and contrasts Christianity with other mystery religions that aim to recruit among the pure and righteous.

'On the True Doctrine' provides a vivid picture of the culture clash between Christianity and traditional Platonic beliefs in the late second century. Even if Celsus' sweeping condemnations may be somewhat polemical and elitist, he does highlight the difficulty that conventional Greeks and Romans experienced in understanding Christianity. Many of the issues he discusses were, of course, being argued about within the Christian communities themselves but Christians continued to offend the more conservative members of society by their widespread rejection of traditional ritual and their lack of loyalty to the emperor. Yet as Christianity spread, there was increasing pressure to make compromises with mainstream society, not least with the rich variety of Greek intellectual life that Celsus accused them of rejecting.

CHAPTER SEVENTEEN

The Challenge of Greek Philosophy

A T THE VERY BEGINNING OF CHRISTIAN HISTORY, PAUL LAID DOWN A challenge to 'the wisdom of the wise': 'I determined not to know anything among you save Jesus Christ and him crucified.' (1 Corinthians 2:3). He initiated a negative response to philosophy, especially to the rigour of rational thought, which has persisted in strong or weak forms throughout Christian history. Yet for the Greeks the use of rational thought was intrinsic to serious learning and it was precisely the emotional, faith-centred commitment to Christ that most disturbed them. If Christianity was to attract more highly educated Greeks it would have to come to some form of reconciliation with classical learning.

At the higher end of the social hierarchy this was one of the best-educated and most intellectually alive generations ever known, heir to the classical philosophers who had defined most areas of knowledge from mathematics to science in a form which we still use, and still capable of original thought. It is impressive that intellectuals, both pagan and Christian, between the second and fourth centuries, were at home with poets, philosophers, playwrights and historians stretching back to Homer a thousand years before. Central to higher education was training in rhetoric. This was not merely an education in how to speak and construct an argument. It took place within a moral framework. The great classical rhetorician Isocrates (436–338 BC) had stressed how easy it was for rhetoric to become no more than emotional manipulation if the speaker did not observe high standards in the material he used and the way he used it. The training involved choosing a wide variety of texts and discussing the moral and historical significance of each. With such an education completed, the student could now embark on a professional career exploiting all the opportunities where effective speaking was needed. This included, for Christians, the art of making sermons. Augustine was the city orator in Milan before he converted to Christianity.

A more rigorous training in philosophy was available for the truly dedicated intellectual. This involved finding a teacher and joining his school, perhaps for several years. It was often a fruitful relationship. Students formed lifelong attachments to their teacher and to each other. Not only was the teacher responsible for their moral welfare (he would dismiss the dissolute), he would often foster his students in their careers, recommending them for posts in the imperial bureaucracy or in teaching. After the suppression of pagan thought in the fourth century and the collapse of the western empire in the fifth, it was to be a thousand years before, in the Renaissance, such a varied, rigorous and benevolent education was to be available again and even that did not have the breadth in the natural sciences that the classical world had enjoyed. Perhaps one had to wait until the Encyclopaedists of the eighteenth century or even the scientific advances of the nineteenth for that to happen.

Most teachers taught within a specific school. Plato (c.429–347 BC) remained the most appealing philosopher. His dialogues were so accessible and the broad tenor of his ideas so easy to grasp that, in the words of Cicero, 'everyone, even those who do not accept their teachings or are not enthusiastic disciples, reads Plato and the rest of the Socratic school'. Fundamental to his philosophy was the contrast between the volatile, changing and emotionally unstable material world and the changeless world of the Forms or Ideas above. Starting with the mastery of the logic of mathematics the student began a challenging journey of understanding what these Forms might be. So by contemplating all the different ways in which courage is manifested in this world, one might eventually grasp the essence of the Form of Courage which existed in a much more real way in the immaterial world. The Forms themselves had their own hierarchy so that an ultimate, 'the Good', contained all the aspects of 'good' manifested in the Forms below it.

By the second century Platonism had developed so that the Good, or 'the One' took on a life of its own as a benevolent entity reaching out to the world below, through intermediaries (the lower Forms, often called daemons (from the Greek *daimon*)) and being accessible in return through contemplation and rational thought. In the *Handbook of Platonism*, for instance, the mid-second-century philosopher Alcinous argues that, while it is almost impossible to contemplate God ('the One'), one can think rationally what God might or might not be, consider the relationships that man has with God so as to appreciate the reciprocal relationship, of God to man, and use intuition to establish some form of personal relationship with God. Alcinous concludes that while God is eternal and perfect and above all created matter, he is responsible for creation in so far as he brought order to an existing disorder and continues to foster further progress. His creative impulses were put into action by the daemons. This was a much more metaphysical philosophy than Plato had taught and it is normally known as Middle Platonism to distinguish it from the original inspiration. The Platonists were wary of the material world, suspicious of emotion and dismissive of sex and sensuality in general. So good philosophising and virtuous living went hand in hand.

Aristotle (384–322 BC) was a student of Plato and his early works show the influence of his master but gradually he developed his philosophy in different directions. He came to reject Plato's theory of Forms, or eternal ideas which existed for all time, and which could be grasped, eventually, by the reasoning mind, in favour of detailed observation of what could be seen in the material world. At one level this involved the accumulation of empirical facts and reasoned thought on them (he was the founder of biology and zoology as disciplines) but he was also the acknowledged authority on logic. His influential *Categories* contained the fundamental questions that should be asked about any subject: what is its essence, its qualities and relationships to other objects? In particular he pondered on the process of change. Fundamental to his thought was the belief that living beings grow towards the potential unique to their species. Each species has its proper end – for human beings that is the state of *eudaimonia*, or flourishing. The whole is bound up in a world whose supreme being, the Unmoved Mover, keeps all the heavenly bodies revolving in perfect harmony. To contemplate the divine and to appreciate the underlying good order of all things is the highest state of *eudaimonia*. Aristotle developed these ideas to include sophisticated works on ethics and politics.

Aristotle faced two problems in this period. The first was that his texts were always difficult to read, especially in comparison with the dialogues of Plato. They were often no more than lecture notes and had to be explained by commentators. The second was that his stress on empirical observation and logic was out of step with the age. His ethics focused on making pragmatic decisions within a wider context of self-knowledge, the weighing up of moral alternatives and moderation in all things. For many this involved an unacceptable compromise with the material world and its desires. This does not mean that there was a lack of scientific advance in this period – Galen's brilliant use of logic in medicine, Ptolemy's astonishing astronomical models and his pioneering work on geography make that obvious. There were some important defenders of Aristotle such as the philosopher Porphyry in the third century but, in general, all-encompassing spiritual solutions were more attractive to scholars than the dogged and meticulous sorting of facts and the application of reason to them. It was an age in which there was continual probing of new spiritual opportunities even if, in general among the elite, there was increasing belief in a single rational force which would not act perversely.

The Stoics were another influential school. They understood the material world, the *cosmos*, as encapsulated within the force of reason, *logos*. Everything from the divine to human beings, animal life and the material world was linked to each other in a great cycle of change, birth, flourishing, death, in a conflagration, and rebirth. Human beings themselves contained a spark of the *logos* (and it may have been from the Stoics that the gnostics gained this idea of entrapped *gnosis*) but it was only the *logos* that survived each transformation. The Stoic Chrysippus had provided the fullest articulation of Stoic thought in the third century BC but there were always difficult questions of logic, free will and ethics to discuss and Stoics were famous for their readiness to take their philosophy in new and penetrating directions. They affected to despise wealth and to bear the changing fortunes of life with dignity. The first-century Stoic Seneca committed suicide rather than endure the tyranny of Nero, while the Stoic emperor Marcus Aurelius doggedly carried out his duties as commander on the frontiers despite having no background as a soldier. Christians, with their own experience of steadfastness in the face of persecution, could respond to this. They could also see the conflagration expected by the Stoics in the awesome descriptions of the Coming of Christ at the Last Judgement. Had not Jesus said, at Luke 12:49, 'I have come to set fire to the earth, and how I wish it were already kindled'? The Book of Revelation promised much the same.

There were smaller tributaries that ran into the major rivers of Greek philosophy, adding new currents or stirring up waves in the mainstream. The more mystical were attracted to the Pythagoreans, whose school was the oldest of all, having been founded in the late sixth century BC by Pythagoras who had emigrated from Asia Minor to southern Italy. His followers considered themselves a religious community dedicated to passing on the wisdom of their founder. In particular they saw numbers as representing an underlying reality. The Pythagoreans lived ascetically and were concerned with discovering the patterns and relationships, expressed numerically, of course, which underpinned the natural world.

The aim of engaging with this lively tradition of competing philosophies was to reach the goal of all education, *paideia*, excellence in behaviour through the process of a training in rational thought. Christians might seem a world apart from this elite community but by the middle of the second century we find the first Christians to have converted after rejecting a traditional education in philosophy. Tatian, the author of the *Diatessaron*, talks of himself, in his *Address to the Greeks*, as 'he who philosophises in the manner of barbarians, born in the land of the Assyrians, educated first in your principles, secondly in what I now profess'. In other words, despite being an 'Assyrian' (it is not quite clear what he means by this), he has acquired a Greek education but abandoned it for the 'barbarian philosophy' of Christianity. Christianity, he tells us, is superior because Christians behave better than philosophers do. He gives examples of the philosophers' 'vain boasting', gluttony, elitist prejudices (here Aristotle is cited) and other dissolute or devious behaviour. Moreover, he claims, they are endlessly fighting among themselves. 'Wherefore', he warns, 'be not led away by the solemn assemblies of philosophers who are no philosophers, who dogmatise one against the other, though each one vents but the crude fancies of the moment.' The Christians, in contrast, Tatian argues, worship one all-powerful God and do not need to dispute between themselves.

This was hardly a philosophical retort. In particular, Tatian failed to appreciate that it is through such disputations that progress in philosophy is made. More measured is an account from Justin Martyr of his experiences with the pagan philosophers before he found Christ. He describes how he moves from school to school, dissatisfied by each philosophy until a wise man introduces him to Christ. One of the reasons Justin gives for his conversion is his belief that the prophets had the truth and it was the Greeks who had acquired it but then lost it by splitting up into warring groups. He claims that Moses had passed on information about the creation of the universe to Plato who had reproduced it in his *Timaeus*. (There is an echo here of Philo's 'Who is Plato but Moses speaking Greek?') Justin goes on to claim that Christ was the Word (*logos*) and those who accepted the *logos* in the days before Christ were, in fact, honorary Christians. He includes Socrates among them. This was an important development in that it was now possible for Christians to argue that the insights they might find in pagan philosophers had been planted there by the prophets and were not to be rejected.

Nevertheless there remained many Christians who were deeply distrustful of pagan philosophy. One of its most determined opponents was Tertullian. Very little is known about this doughty traditionalist. He was born in Africa in about 160, apparently the son of a centurion, and spent most of his life in Carthage. He converted to Christianity in middle age – he began writing his Christian tracts in about 195 – and then after 205 drifted towards Montanism. He seems to have died at a great age, perhaps as late as 240. He is important as the first major Christian writer who composed in both Latin and Greek and who coined many Latin words, such as *trinitas*. His colourful rhetoric, his uncompromising stand on morals and his defence of faith make him an interesting if somewhat unsettling figure. He would shock the more conventional by his subversive statements such as this from *De carne christi*: 'The Son of God was born: there is no shame, because it is shameful. And the Son of God died: it is wholly credible, because it is ridiculous. And, buried, He rose again: it is certain, because impossible.' So faith was often more important than reason with the result that his attitude towards pagan philosophy was dismissive. It is the philosophers who were the channel through which heresy infiltrated and corrupted Christianity.

Tertullian lays out his case in Chapter Seven of his *Praescriptio haereticorum*, the 'Prescription against the Heretics'. Every heresy has its roots in a school of pagan philosophy. For instance, he argues that the idea of the aeons, so beloved of the gnostics such as Valentinus, comes straight from Plato, who, as we have seen, did indeed teach of intermediaries. Where else did Marcion find his heretical idea that a supreme god reigned above the creator god of the Old Testament but from the Stoics? Those 'heretics' who talk of the death of the soul have taken this from the Epicureans, who deny the existence of the gods, while all the philosophers deny the resurrection of the body, a doctrine to which Tertullian was strongly committed. Tertullian has a particular hatred of Aristotle: 'Unhappy Aristotle! who invented for these men dialectics, the art of building up and pulling down; an art so evasive in its propositions, so far-fetched in its conjectures, so harsh in its arguments, so productive of contentions – embarrassing even to itself, retracting everything, and really treating of nothing!' Tertullian continues with a peroration that encapsulates his rejection of all pagan philosophy. 'What indeed has Athens to do with Jerusalem? What concord is there between [Plato's] Academy and the Church? What between heretics and Christians . . . Away with all attempts to produce a mottled Christianity of Stoic, Platonic, and dialectic composition! We want no curious disputation after possessing Christ Jesus, no inquisition after enjoying the gospel! With our faith, we desire no further belief. For this is our primary faith, that there is nothing which we ought to believe besides.'

Tertullian marks an extreme, a contemptuous rejection of the possibilities of a rational underpinning for what is held 'in faith'. For those with broader minds, on the other hand, it was apparent that there were possible bridges between Christianity and philosophy. The tenor of Greek philosophy, whether its roots were Platonic, Aristotelian or Stoic, was towards one supreme god, even though the changeless God of the Platonists, the Unmoved Mover of Aristotle and the *logos* of the Stoics seemed to have little in common with the emotionally charged god of the Old Testament. Nevertheless Philo, and following him Justin, had already tried to relate Judaism to Platonism and this foundation could be built on.

One connection between Platonists and Christians was established through Plato's text the *Timaeus*. Here Plato dealt with the problem of the creation of the world. He imagined a divine craftsman, the demiurge, who made an orderly world out of a previous confusion: 'Desiring that all things should be good . . . he took in hand all that was visible, which was not at rest but in discordant and disorderly motion, and brought it from its disorder into order.' This could be reconciled with the account in Genesis: 'And the earth was without form and void, and darkness was upon the face of the deep. And the Spirit of God moved upon the face of the waters.' Justin Martyr complained in his *First Apology* that Christians were being persecuted when they were actually agreeing with Plato in claiming that 'all things have been produced and arranged into a world by God'. Again Plato's 'God, being generous, desired that all things should become as like as might be to himself . . . that all things should be good' might be equated with 'God saw that all he had made . . . was good', again from Genesis. Yet it was unclear from the *Timaeus* whether the world came into being as a direct creative act or had existed eternally in disorder (so that the demiurge simply brought it into order). Most Platonists did not worry much – they just assumed that the material world was of 'divine' origin – but others argued that it had existed eternally in disorder until the 'creation'. Many early Christians were quite happy to agree. As Justin put it, 'God in his goodness created everything from formless matter' (1 Apology 10.2).

An alternative approach, first seen in the works of the second-century Alexandrian Basilides, suggested an act of creation *ex nihilo*, from nothing. The possibility of 'nothingness' always perplexed the Greeks but the idea of creation *ex nihilo* was later taken up by Theophilus of Antioch who challenged Plato on the grounds that if matter had existed for eternity then it would also be divine and that God's power was diminished if his act of creation involved no more than the bringing of order. The reality of his power was shown in his ability to make whatever he wished out of what did not exist. Theophilus interpreted the first verses of Genesis to support his case. Here he was followed by Irenaeus who, in his campaign against gnostics, wished to avoid any suggestion that the demiurge was a lesser form of god. Irenaeus argued that God of the Old Testament had the will to do whatever he wanted and he did not need any matter from outside himself to do so. Creation *ex nihilo* became orthodox Christian doctrine but this does not seem to have diminished the status of the *Timaeus*. In early medieval Europe, when most works of classical philosophy had been forgotten, it was the only work of Plato that was still known.[1]

Two other facets of Platonism were to prove especially important in the debates to come. Plato had written extensively on the soul. It was the most noble part of a human being, even if held in bondage by the human body and its desires. In Socrates' meditation on his coming death as recounted by Plato in the *Phaedo*, Socrates is convinced death is not to be feared because the well-disciplined soul lives eternally. Plato went further and argued that the soul of each individual existed before birth and this could be proved by the way it 'recollected' the fruits of reason. Crucially the soul could be developed during life by strengthening one's powers of thought and this in its turn meant living an ethical life. For many Christian thinkers this equated with the hope that the soul might reach such a state of perfection that it would be united with God in heaven. Origen follows Plato closely in arguing that the soul existed before its arrival in a human body and that this body was a temporary and degrading home from which it might escape through its own efforts. Other writers, Irenaeus, for instance, again anxious not to diminish the power of the Old Testament God, disagreed and claimed that the soul was totally dependent on the will of God for its continuing existence. There remained intense debate within Christianity over whether the body rose with the soul and if so when and in what form, its real one as seen on earth or an idealised, spiritual, one.

The second significant facet of Platonism was the relationship between Plato's intermediaries and Christ. As we have seen, the term *logos* was used widely in pagan philosophy and had already been adopted by Philo to refer to 'an ambassador' from God. Whether John in his gospel took this conception directly from Philo or not, Christians were by now used to the idea of *logos* becoming flesh in the person of Jesus Christ. The question that had to be explored was whether there were other intermediaries, on the lines suggested by Plato, other quasi-divine Forms that emanated from God. Christians could certainly think of some from their scriptures, notably the Holy Spirit which was seen as a distinct divine entity with its own sphere of activity. Then there were the angels, as in the case of Gabriel who arrived to tell Mary of the coming of Christ. Of course, all these intermediaries were the servants of God, sent by him to carry out his desires. Where did Christ fit alongside the other intermediaries? The dominant belief until the early fourth century was that he was a form of superior intermediary, still subordinate to God but above the Holy Spirit and the angels. This was to be dramatically challenged in the fourth century by an alternative view that broke with this Platonic and scriptural inheritance by claiming that Jesus and the Father were 'of one substance'.

Clement of Alexandria, a Christian who was deeply sympathetic to pagan philosophy, provides an insight into these issues.[2] Clement had been born in Athens of pagan parents in about 160 and arrived in Alexandria, the other great centre of Greek intellectual life, in search of further education. He attended the school of a Christian, Pantaenus, and eventually became its leader. When a bout of persecution broke out in Alexandria in the reign of the emperor Septimius Severus in 202–3, Clement fled into exile and died sometime before 215. His works show that he was widely read across the whole range of Greek literature and philosophy. In his most famous work, the rambling *Stromateis*, or 'Patchwork', Clement tells us that philosophy is 'a sort of preliminary discipline for those who lived before the coming of Christ' and adds, 'Perhaps we may say it was given to the Greeks with this special object; for philosophy was to the Greeks what the law was to the Jews – a schoolmaster to bring them to Christ.' Now, of course, in the Christian era, progress is possible: 'That which the chief of philosophy only guessed at, the disciples of Christ have both apprehended and proclaimed.' The philosophers had only perceived a slender spark of Christian knowledge; now this was capable of being fanned into flame. In contrast to his contemporary, Tertullian, Clement sees pagan philosophy as an essential part of Christian education.

Clement is the first Christian to name Philo as an inspiration and he follows Philo in using both the scriptures and Platonism as the sources for his own theology. Clement follows the Platonists of his day in seeing God/the Good as sending forth the Forms which share a common relationship to each other but which reflect back to him. Jesus is – and here Clement follows John – the *logos*, which is bound into this reciprocal relationship with God but is also accessible to humanity in a way God himself could never be. An important issue that Clement addresses is the relationship between faith and knowledge.

Faith, *pistis* in Greek, is a complex term and Clement acknowledges the different ways in which it could be used. It might provide the starting point for reasoned judgement or a form of perception or something that could be anticipated. Without faith one could never begin the journey to knowledge. One of Clement's favourite verses from the scriptures was, and here Augustine was to follow him, translating from the Septuagint version of Isaiah 7:9, 'Unless you believe, you will not understand'. Baptism was crucial in opening up a new phase of intellectual life: notably it allowed the reception of knowledge from above. As Clement puts it in his *Paedagogus*, 'The Instructor', 'we who are baptised, having wiped off the sins which obscure the light of the Divine Spirit, have the eye of the spirit free, unimpeded, and full of light, by which alone we contemplate the Divine, the Holy Spirit flowing down to us from above'. Once you have your core of faith then you can proceed either by logic or spiritual intuition to knowledge. Clement distinguishes between the 'true' gnostic, the one who really has mastered the deepest truths, using reason when it is possible to do so, and the 'false' gnostic who is easy to recognise because he does not use reason and lacks a wider intellectual vision.

Crucial to Clement's theology was his belief that all Christians must progress towards greater virtue, which he saw as the ultimate expression of God. The nature of virtue could be grasped through reason. This was certainly a Platonic approach but while Plato had talked in *The Republic* of those trapped in the cave learning to live in the light of the sun, Clement substituted Christ for the sun – it was Christ, 'the light of the world', who had turned sunset into sunrise. This is typical of the effective way that Clement adapted philosophy into a Christian mould, using his two most important mentors, John and Paul, in support of his cause. The description of Jesus as 'the light of the world' derives, of course, from John's gospel.

Clement's moderate approach and his thoughtful advocacy of faith based on reason compares well with the more frenzied denunciations of other church fathers. He is optimistic about the possibility of Christians finding God. The virtuous Christian might even reach divine status if he imitates Christ: 'He who listens to the Lord, and follows the prophecy given by Him, will be formed perfectly in the likeness of the teacher – made a god going about in flesh.' The drag of original sin which, according to Augustine, destroyed any hope of salvation unless God chose to intervene, is not for Clement. He gives advice on sexual behaviour, certainly with a sober insistence on continence, but without the active distaste for sexuality that Paul and many of his followers expressed. He scorns those who offer themselves for martyrdom – they should be seen as guilty of their own deaths: 'He who kills a man of God sins against God, he also who presents himself before the judgement-seat becomes guilty of his death. And such is also the case with him who does not avoid persecution, but out of daring presents himself for capture. Such a one, as far as in him lies, becomes an accomplice in the crime of the persecutor.'

Clement and Tertullian stand at opposite poles in their accepting and rejecting attitudes to Greek philosophy. Each point of view, one from Greek-speaking Alexandria and one from Latin-speaking Carthage, represents a response to pagan society. The conflicting beliefs over the nature of God, the supreme benign force of the Platonists or the emotional and often vituperative god of the Old Testament, seem irreconcilable. The two approaches represent two very different psychologies and it is perhaps too easy to idealise one, the intellectual openness of Clement, as against the merciless intolerance of the other. They could live together for the time being because there was as yet no framework that could impose consensus, yet the warnings were there for the future. While a secure intellectual base for Christian theology was needed, it was going to be immensely difficult to find.

CHAPTER EIGHTEEN

Origen and Early Christian Scholarship

THERE COULD HAVE BEEN FEW BACKDROPS MORE CONDUCIVE TO intellectual creativity than the great city of Alexandria. Founded by Alexander in 332 BC, Alexandria flourished as the major port of the eastern Mediterranean, its lighthouse one of the 'Seven Wonders of the World'. The Ptolemies, the Greek dynasty that succeeded Alexander, had been major patrons of culture and the city soon became the leading centre in the Greek world for science and mathematics. The library was the most impressive in the world even if its ambition of having a copy of every single Greek text was never realised, while the Mouseion, 'the place of the Muses', acted as a meeting place for scholars. The Mouseion was ridiculed by some as no more than a talking shop for intellectuals but the Romans sustained it after they had incorporated Egypt into the empire in 30 BC and the accredited scholars still enjoyed tax exemptions and free meals. The astronomer Ptolemy spent most of his life there in the second century working on his studies of the stars and the natural world. The city was, of course, embellished with fine buildings. A massive temple, the Serapeion, dedicated to the Egyptian god Serapis, stood on Alexandria's highest hill. For many it was the most impressive shrine in the entire eastern Mediterranean. While he was growing up, Origen, the subject of this chapter, would have seen it being rebuilt in an even grander form. No less impressive was the Caesareum, alongside the harbour. Built in honour of Julius Caesar by his lover Cleopatra, the last of the Ptolemies, this temple was the seat of the Roman imperial cult and in the fourth century was to become the city's Christian cathedral.

As with any prosperous and prestigious port, Alexandria had a vibrant mix of cultures. The Greeks were dominant but there was also one of the largest communities of Jews in the Mediterranean as well as a busy quarter of native Egyptian weavers. Sometimes tensions boiled over: there were riots in AD 115–17 that targeted Jews, and others against Christians in 248; Alexandria had the reputation of being a violent city. However, for much of the time the population lived together in relative peace and there was some mingling of intellectuals from the different communities. The Jew Philo's respect for Greek culture and philosophy has already been discussed and Philo's brother Alexander was a close friend of the scholarly emperor Claudius. The brilliant 'gnostic' Valentinus had come from Alexandria. In the third century, the links between Christian and pagan intellectuals remained close as we have already seen in the life of Clement. This was a city where a tradition of tolerant debate made it possible for Christians to use philosophy creatively and Origen was foremost among them.

To many Christians of the third and fourth centuries, Origen was an intellectual hero. The scholarly Gregory of Nazianzus believed he was the greatest mind in Christian history; Eusebius of Caesarea, the biographer of Constantine, gave him a central place in his *History of the Church* and Jerome described him in his *Famous Men* as an 'immortal genius, the greatest teacher of the Church since the apostles'. Like Clement, Origen was an Alexandrian and some reports, now disputed, suggested he might have been Clement's pupil. He was born in about 184, the son of Christian parents. His father was martyred but had already put in place for his son a broad education in both the scriptures and philosophy. By the age of seventeen Origen was the leading teacher of a school of Christian catechism. Until the late 240s there was comparatively little persecution of Christians in the empire so for most of his life Origen was able to write freely and to watch a church growing in numbers and stature around him. He is even known to have corresponded with the emperor Philip the Arab who was sympathetic to Christianity. Origen also travelled widely – he was in Rome about 216, in Antioch between 231 and 232 and in Athens in 233 and 245. In about 231, when he was already famous in Alexandria, he moved to Caesarea in Palestine. The bishop of Alexandria appears to have resented his growing status. It was in Caesarea that his excellent library remained for later generations to exploit. He never rose high in the church hierarchy, although he was eventually ordained as a presbyter in Caesarea. He was tortured in the persecutions initiated by the emperor Decius and died in 254.

There is a legend that, troubled by sexuality as a young man, Origen castrated himself. Certainly he was ascetic by temperament but not obsessively so. He offended the more austere by saying that divorced couples should be able to remarry, as this was better than the alternatives. There is none of the polemic in his writings such as that found in the works of Tertullian and Jerome. He lived under the shadow of martyrdom and was not afraid of it but, like Clement, he did not believe it should be actively sought out, not least because those who wish to secure the salvation of sinners should never tempt others to commit a crime. Yet he expected dedication from his fellow Christians and ridiculed those bishops who were taking advantage of their position to build up personal wealth (he gives examples of bishops bequeathing church lands to their relatives) or social contacts. The more effective bishops were by now skilled networkers and they could often do much, in the traditional role of patron, to help the poorer members of their congregations with tax or law cases. Yet this gave them a social status that Origen believed many were exploiting for their own benefit. He was also dismissive of those Christians who still attended the local synagogues or the theatre.

Origen was a brilliant and much-loved teacher. A panegyric to him survives by one of his pupils, Gregory the Wonderworker. Gregory not only praises Origen's sweetness of temperament but applauds the breadth of his curriculum. Reading was expected to be wide and Gregory goes on to note that Origen excluded nothing except works of atheists (by whom he meant the Epicureans). Geometry 'he presented lucidly as the immutable groundwork and secure foundation of all' and, through astronomy, 'he lifted us up to the things that are highest above us, while he made heaven passable to us by the help of each of these sciences, as though they were ladders reaching the skies'. These served as an introduction to the higher levels of philosophy that were orientated towards the understanding of God. 'For he asserted further that there could be no genuine piety towards the Lord of all in the man who despised this gift of philosophy, a gift which man alone of all the creatures of the earth has been deemed honourable and worthy enough to possess, and one which every man whatsoever, be he wise or be he ignorant, reasonably embraces, who has not utterly lost the power of thought by some mad distraction of mind.'

Origen responded with his own praise for Gregory. 'Your natural abilities enable you to be made an esteemed Roman lawyer or a Greek philosopher of one of the most notable schools. But I hoped that you would entirely apply your ability to Christianity. Indeed, in order to bring this about, I beg of you to take from your studies of Hellenic philosophy those things such as can be made encyclic or preparatory studies of Christianity . . . apply the things that are useful from geometry and astronomy to the explanation of the Holy Scriptures.' The close relationship between philosophy and Christian belief is well put. The idea that one should move through pagan philosophy into Christianity was to survive in Christian circles until the Christian emperors of the late fourth century began to suppress paganism.

Origen was a prolific writer. A patron, Ambrosius, was good enough to provide him with an army of scribes so that he could produce works and copies of them at high speed. It is estimated that he wrote some thousand different texts, although most of the library that was preserved at Caesarea disappeared after he was declared heretical by the emperor Justinian in the sixth century. Of the hundred of Origen's letters known to Eusebius a century later, only three survive. Fragments remain of the massive commentaries Origen wrote on the books of the Bible, especially his Commentary on John, the gospel to which he, as a philosopher, was most naturally drawn. The fullest statement of his beliefs, *De principiis*, 'On the First Principles', is largely known from a Latin translation by Rufinus made in the 380s. By this time Origen's creative theology was beginning to offend the church authorities and Rufinus glossed over difficult passages (with the assertion that a heretic had inserted them later!) so it is not complete.

At the beginning of *De principiis*, Origen sets out his commitment to Christ: 'All who believe and are assured that grace and truth were obtained through Jesus Christ, and who know Christ to be the truth, agreeably to His own declaration, "I am the truth," derive the knowledge which incites men to a good and happy life from no other source than from the very words and teaching of Christ.' He accepts that the teaching of Christ has been passed down accurately through the apostles. He then lists some essential beliefs which were now accepted by the church: that there is one God, that Jesus Christ had been sent by him and that the Holy Spirit is equal in honour and dignity to Father and Son. The scriptures had been written through the Spirit of God. Origen agreed that the world had been created by God, rather than just brought into being from an existing formless mass (here he broke with the Platonists as he was always prepared to do if his commitment to Christ demanded it). He believed that souls survived after death when they would be subject to reward and punishment. Outside this tradition he felt free to speculate and, as much of Christian theology was still in flux, it was here that his brilliance was given full sway.

First and foremost Origen was a major commentator on the scriptures. The Septuagint was the text that Christians should read but Origen felt that it could be improved by comparison with the original Hebrew and other translations. It is also possible that he was concerned by the continuing vitality of the Jewish community in Alexandria and felt that Christian theologians needed to have access to a version that was as close as possible to the original Hebrew in order to combat them in debate. So he embarked on one of the greatest works of scholarship of the era, the *Hexapla*.[1] He accumulated a series of texts of the Old Testament in the original Hebrew, a transliteration of this in Greek letters and four Greek translations including the Septuagint and a very literal translation made by one Aquila. He put them alongside each other in order to study them and comment on the variations. His Hebrew was not advanced and so he must have had some help. It was a mammoth undertaking, requiring large quantities of parchment and an extraordinary dedication to getting it all in order. It remained the most sophisticated research tool for biblical criticism for centuries afterwards. A few fragments of copies have survived.

Next Origen had to define a framework for the interpretation of the scriptures. Were they the literal word of God or should one search for deeper spiritual meanings? Origen had no doubt that the text of the Bible was divinely inspired, by the Holy Spirit, but his instinct was always to look behind the literal interpretation. His education in the pagan classics would have introduced him to similar approaches to Homer and other ancient authors and he knew too that he had to offer interpretations which did not invite ridicule from those used to more sophisticated texts. (This may sound condescending but when Augustine first read the scriptures he considered them barbaric in comparison to the classical works he had been used to.) In so far as the main aim of the Old Testament was to prophesy the coming of Christ, the focus had to be on the understanding of how each passage did this. This required commitment and the correct spiritual approach, otherwise misinterpretations were possible: 'Thorns grow in the hand of a drunkard' as Origen put it, quoting Proverbs (26:4). The more troublesome of the texts, those referring to the wrath of God, for instance, he believed had been deliberately placed to deter those who were prepared to approach the scriptures without the required spiritual commitment to their study. He berated those such as Marcion who read the Old Testament in such a way as to suggest that God was evil.

When he began the exegesis of a text, Origen read it literally and often provided a wealth of background information to explain the original context. His breadth of learning was extraordinary. He used medical ideas from Galen and Hippocrates, drew information on the natural world from the Greek scientists, acquired details of Jewish practice and ceremony from Jews: he even went in search himself for the original Bethany, the site of the resurrection of Lazarus. His approach here is that of the Platonist. One examines the material world, which is a pale imitation of the 'real' world beyond, so as to grasp the nature of that world more fully. So the literal interpretation is the stepping stone to the spiritual. When Moses comes down from Mount Sinai with his face covered with a veil, this symbolises the veil that hides the true meaning of the scriptures from the Jews. While the story of Jonah spending three days in the whale might be true, it is an allegory of the three days that Christ will spend in hell before the resurrection. The famous Song of Songs may appear to be about the love of Solomon for his bride but for Christians its allegorical meaning is of the relationship of Christ with his church or the individual believer. The 'bride' stands for the soul.

This allegorical approach allowed Origen to explain away the contradictions encountered by anyone attempting a literal interpretation of the Bible. If one takes John's gospel, for instance, one finds Jesus confronting the moneylenders in the Temple at the beginning of his ministry while the other evangelists place it at the end. So a literal interpretation of the gospel texts would result in a contradiction in the historical sequence. Origen suggests that John has changed the sequence deliberately so as to make a spiritual point. So it is a 'spiritual truth in historical falsehood' and acceptable as such. Often his imagination soars. When discussing the Second Coming, Irenaeus had argued that it would happen as predicted with Christ actually reappearing on earth. Origen thought that it could be believed in a very different form, either as the extension of the gospel to all parts of the world or in the mystical sense of the coming of the *logos* to the human mind so that it could illuminate the meaning of scripture. Such an approach was useful in confronting Marcion and the gnostics. One could simply argue that, unworthy as they were, they had missed the real meaning of the text.

While Origen must be seen as the first major Christian exegesist, and one of the greatest in terms of the thoroughness and profundity of his work, his approach presents problems. He leaves no place for any human input into the Bible. It is as if the Holy Spirit, rather than the writer of the text, has worked relentlessly to use every word for a spiritual purpose. Origen gives a spiritual meaning even to the containers in which the sacrificial meat is cooked in Leviticus. Many of his interpretations, those on the Second Coming, for instance, appear arbitrary. It is as if Origen knows the end point that, as a committed Christian, he is aiming for and develops his interpretation to suit it. This is a fair criticism (and it can be made of many theologians), yet what is remarkable about Origen is that he recognises that his own understandings can only be provisional. In the beginning of *De principiis* he defines the search for truth as an *individual* quest: 'Everyone [*sic*], therefore, must make use of elements and foundations of this sort, according to the precept, "Enlighten yourselves with the light of knowledge," if he would desire to form a connected series and body of truths agreeably to the reason of all these things, that by clear and necessary statements he may ascertain the truth regarding each individual topic – either those which he has discovered in holy Scripture, or which he has deduced by closely tracing out the consequences and following a correct method.' This is a healthy approach in that it allows discussion to continue, an essential requirement if any progress in exegesis is to be made.

Origen's most interesting studies focus on the relationship between man and God and the specific role of Christ in that relationship. God is essentially a Platonic god and Origen follows many Christians in preferring the emotionless figure that transcends all to the emotional God of the Old Testament (whose 'human' attributes have to be explained away through allegory). At the beginning of time – and here Origen borrows from his 'compatriot', Philo – God created a large but limited number of souls. As the name he gave them, *logica*, suggests, they were endowed with reason and free will. The freedom of the individual was a crucial part of Origen's theology – if God himself had the freedom to do whatever he willed, so too did those who were his immediate creation. Yet therein lay the problem. The souls could use their freedom either to stay close to God or to move away from him. Those who stayed close were fulfilling what God hoped of them, eternal contemplation of himself, and might appear as angels or stars. Those who moved further away faced deterioration. They were transformed from the fine ethereal and invisible body (of the angels) to something much coarser, the human body. The material world was not evil for Origen; it was a springboard from which an ascent back to God could take place. God had provided the demands and tribulations of everyday life as an incentive for escape. Origen was positive here in that he believed that the goodness of God would act as an attractive force. 'For although, in the diseases and wounds of the body, there are some which no medical skill can cure, yet we hold that in the mind there is no evil so strong that it may not be overcome by the Supreme Word and God.' In contrast the Platonists believed that any ascent to a higher state of understanding had to be entirely through one's own efforts.

So where did Christ fit in? Origen believed that one soul remained so close to God as to retain its full spirituality. This was Christ and he was sent in human form to earth to show the possibilities of spiritual completeness. The incarnation remained a mystery to Origen. 'Of all the marvellous and splendid things about him [Christ], there is one that utterly transcends the capacity of our weak mortal intelligence to think of or understand, namely how this mighty power of the divine majesty, the very word of the Father and the very Wisdom of God . . . can be believed to have existed within the compass of that man who appeared in Judaea.' He had to find a compromise. Christ was distinct from those souls trapped in a human body in that he had no erotic urges and did not need to excrete. His mind remained embedded in divinity. However, this left a problem that was to haunt later Christians, whether this Christ could suffer on the cross. If not, was this an act of salvation at all? Despite his lack of understanding of the incarnation, Origen believed that Christ's coming to earth brought about a profound revolution for those prepared to recognise his coming and the impact it should have on their whole being. 'What does it profit me to say that Christ has come to earth only in the flesh He received from Mary, if I do not also show that he has also come in my flesh?'

Origen meditated deeply on the problem of how the soul might exist after death. Like the Platonists and many other Christians of his day, he could not see how the material body could ascend with the soul. Paul had after all made it clear that the body is raised as a spiritual body. 'Because', argued Origen, 'if they believe the apostle [Paul], that a body which arises in glory, and power, and incorruptibility, has already become spiritual, it appears absurd and contrary to his meaning to say that it can again be entangled with the passions of flesh and blood, seeing the apostle manifestly declares that "flesh and blood shall not inherit the kingdom of God, nor shall corruption inherit incorruption". Instead Origen suggested that the body of a risen soul, such as it was, would reflect the new environment it was entering. He took the sea as an analogy. If a body needed to live under water, it would have to develop gills and other 'fishy' things. There would be similar adaptations if the body were to survive in the immaterial world. One possible model is the transformed body in which Moses and Elijah appeared with Jesus at the Transfiguration. Yet, despite the changes, the 'body' would not lose its identity. An analogy might be made with an individual's genetic code. This maintains its distinct identity whatever changes takes place in its material form. This sophisticated idea of a body in flux which can maintain its own identity within different worlds avoids many of the problems encountered by those who preached that it would be the actual body of the deceased that would be reconstituted.[2]

When he considered the nature of God, Origen could not see him as anything but loving. He refused to believe in evil as a dark force, an entity in itself. It could better be seen as a withdrawal from goodness. As human beings have free will, any evil act is a deliberate act of will. God is not by nature punitive – it is human beings who bring judgement on themselves and so it is possible for anyone to be saved from eternal hell fire. Imaginatively Origen stretched this concept to include Satan. Even the will of the devil to do evil could be thwarted by the power of God. Furthermore, how could ordinary human beings, mere mortals, thwart God so completely that the latter really has no option but to punish them for eternity? An eternal hell would be, in effect, a symbol of God's impotence and this could hardly be believed. It was on this issue that Origen broke with the bishop of Alexandria, Demetrius (who believed in eternity of hell) and it may have been the catalyst for his departure for Caesarea. It is known that Demetrius reacted with fury to the news that Origen had been ordained there.

Origen also did important work on the Trinity. He was influenced by a Neopythagorean philosopher, Numenius of Apamea (fl. AD 150–76), who had conceived of a second God proceeding from 'the One'. This analogy could be applied to Christ who proceeded from the Father in a similar way. No one could equal God, who was above all things. 'The God and Father, who holds the universe together, is superior to every being that exists, for he imparts to each one from his own existence that which each one is; the Son being less than the Father, is superior to rational creatures alone (for he is second to the Father); the Holy Spirit is still less, and dwells within the saints alone.' The Father's power is universal, the Son's power is equal to that of the rational creatures of whom he is one (even if the only one to enjoy perfection) and the Spirit's power extends to those souls that have achieved salvation. The Trinity is therefore a hierarchy and this accords well with the scriptures where a mass of texts supports the concept of Jesus' subordination to the Father. Until 300 this reflected the mainstream teaching of the church even if the nature of the subordination of Jesus and the Holy Spirit was impossible to define with any clarity.

Origen was not a polemicist by instinct – it was simply not in his nature to indulge in the vicious attacks on 'heretics' and 'schismatics' that many of his fellow church fathers revelled in. Nevertheless his patron Ambrosius was successful in persuading him that he should refute the powerful assault on Christianity by Celsus. *Contra Celsum* is a long and detailed work in which Origen shows considerable ingenuity in taking each of Celsus' points and refuting them. The response is heavily rooted in scripture. 'He [Celsus] wilfully sets aside, I know not why, the strongest evidence in confirmation of the claims of Jesus, viz., that His coming was predicted by the Jewish prophets.' Origen berates Celsus for failing to understand the sophistication and antiquity of Jewish civilisation, citing Josephus' *History* as his source. The prophecies are clear for all to see and much of *Contra Celsum* relies on quotations from the scriptures to show that the life, death and resurrection of Christ were all foretold and came to be. The fact that the apostles risked their lives for their belief in a resurrected Christ is evidence enough that they had genuinely seen it. *Contra celsum* is an impressive work and added to the *Apologies* of Justin and Tertullian shows that Christians were now prepared to make sophisticated defences of their beliefs.

Origen offers a model of Christian scholarship that is open to learning across the spectrum of disciplines. He could see how breadth of learning could help achieve a greater understanding of God and Christ. He is overwhelmingly positive about the goodness of God. God wills those souls who have fallen into the material world to make the ascent back to him. Origen had the courage to interpret scripture in imaginative and original ways. Of course, he had opposition from those who lacked his optimism and intellectual brilliance and he could be exasperated by it. 'The stupidity of some Christians is heavier than the sands of the sea', was one response. He was, and knew himself to be, a member of an elite.

As a more authoritarian Christianity developed in the next century, Origen's optimistic ethos came under scrutiny. The pre-existence of souls, the subordination of Jesus to God the Father, his belief in the limited nature of hell, all aroused suspicion. It was one of the paradoxes of Christian history that as Christians came to live in greater freedom, their own perception of the power of God became more pessimistic. The unceasing attacks of the barbarians and the disintegration of social order in the third and fourth centuries may have been partly responsible for this but a different tone was contributed by the Latin-speaking church which was now becoming established. By the time of its spokesman Augustine a hundred and fifty years later, all humankind was suffering divine displeasure for the sin of Adam and eternal hell was fully deserved by most. This was a completely different approach to that of Origen and by the sixth century he was officially declared to be heretical. It was a tragic fate for one of the finest Christian theologians to have lived.

CHAPTER NINETEEN

New Beginnings

THE EMERGENCE OF A LATIN CHRISTIANITY

WHILE ALEXANDRIA WAS THE LARGEST CITY OF THE EASTERN Mediterranean, Carthage, capital of the Roman province of Africa was, after Rome, the largest city in the west. Capital of the old Carthaginian empire which had been humiliated and destroyed by the Romans in the third and second centuries AD, it had been revived as a Roman colony and its port was the link between the increasingly grain-rich provinces of the African mainland and the hungry masses in Rome. Some two-thirds of Rome's grain came from Africa by the first century AD. With the original Carthage razed to the ground, the city re-emerged as the quintessential planned Roman colony, the Romans acting as an elite ruling over the native population. A vast civic centre had been built and the city planned around it. The circus (for chariot racing) was one of the largest in the empire and there was an immense bath complex, second, at the time of its construction, only to that built by the emperor Nero in Rome. Gradually the local Punic speakers were being absorbed into Roman life as was typical in Roman cities of the west where the integration of local native elites was encouraged.

Christianity was introduced to the city by Greek traders and it is not until after 180 that the very first references to Latin-speaking Christians appear. These accounts are of martyrdoms – of which the most celebrated was the death of Perpetua in the city. Certainly it was a harsh city for Christians to survive in and there is a rigour and austerity to Christian life there which conflict with the more relaxed attitudes of the Greeks. Christians from the native population may have brought with them attitudes from the worship of the Punic gods Baal and Tanit, implacable deities who welcomed human sacrifice. Tertullian is typical of the Roman Christians of this period in his obsession with discipline, heretics and rigid adherence to 'a rule of faith'.

While Tertullian declared himself opposed to Greek philosophy, his words always have to be taken with caution. His preoccupation with rhetorical invective threatens to conceal a considerable intelligence and breadth of learning.

He certainly knew something of the great Greek historian Herodotus and had read widely in Plato. He was able to write in Greek and his earliest treatises are in that language. His first audiences must have been Greek-speaking Christians. His language also sparkles with imagination and vivacity. As a man who loved a battle, he was relentless and brilliant in the deployment of every rhetorical device in the humiliation of his opponents. The most profound influence on him was the Stoics. It can be assumed, from the quality of his education, that he came from a well-off background and like many of his class he was attracted by the selfless endurance in the face of fate that the Stoics preached.

Yet there were other influences on Tertullian. He had a good understanding of the terminology of law, which suggests a legal training. The word *praescriptio* was used in the law courts to denote an objection against a case that was out of order. So when Tertullian called his major work against heretics the *Praescriptio haereticorum*, he was suggesting heretics did not deserve any kind of hearing. His mastery of Latin was such that he was able to use the language creatively to develop terminology that was to be important in the formulation of Christian doctrine. While he transferred Greek terms into Latin, as with *ecclesia* for church, he also invented new ones, such as *sacramentum* (and so 'sacrament') for the Greek *mysterion*. He coined *trinitas* and put in place the vocabulary of later Trinitarian debate with the terms *substantia* and *persona*, the substance of a single Godhead within which there were distinct personalities. One of his most successful conceptualisations was the *anima naturaliter Christiana*, the soul that in its humble and uneducated state (another dig at the philosophers) is naturally attuned to an awareness of God. 'Tertullian successfully, even brilliantly, pioneered the cultured Latinisation of Christian discourse.'[1]

What attracted an educated man of comparatively high social status like Tertullian to the new faith? In a society where philosophy and learning were less valued than they were in Greece, the loss of status for those who converted must have been strongly felt. It meant immediate exclusion from the round of civic festivals that gave city life so much meaning. Yet Tertullian's treatise against luxury of dress, *On the Adornment of Women*, suggests that he knew many extravagant women of his class who had already converted to Christianity. When he warns the governor of the province against instituting a persecution of Christians, he tells him that he will offend 'many of the governor's own order and other leading personages'.

Tertullian's church is one in which ritual has become important for its own sake. In his *De corona*, a discussion of whether a soldier should have refused to wear a laurel wreath because he was a Christian, Tertullian explores the nature of convention and ritual and notes that there are many Christian rites and customs that are not even mentioned in scripture. The rite of baptism, he tells us, is far more elaborate than the one Jesus experienced while the Eucharist is now often taken at daybreak independently of a communal meal. Yet these rites should be observed because they have become embedded in church practice. 'If, for these and other such rules, you insist upon having positive Scripture injunction, you will find none. Tradition will be held forth to you as the originator of them, custom as their strengthener, and faith as their observer.' This suggests that, in Carthage at least, the church was developing its own liturgy independently of the gospels (which, at this time, were only available for Latin speakers in crude translations). As with traditional Roman worship, the liturgy had become sanctified by repetition over time.

Just as he expects order in his rituals, Tertullian also requires commitment to a set of doctrines. The teaching of Christ is embodied in the 'rule of faith'. In Chapter Thirteen of *Praescriptio haereticorum*, Tertullian sets out the rule as a creed. It includes the belief in one God, who created the world out of nothing and sent his Son, the Word, who had already been recognised as such by the patriarchs and the prophets, to earth. Born of the Virgin Mary, Christ preached 'the new law', was crucified and ascended into heaven on the third day. The Holy Ghost was now sent to earth 'to lead such as believe'. Eventually Christ 'will come with glory to take the saints to the enjoyment of everlasting life and of the heavenly promises, and to condemn the wicked to everlasting fire, after the resurrection of both these classes shall have happened, together with the restoration of their flesh . . . This rule, as it will be proved, was taught by Christ, and raises amongst ourselves no other questions than those which heresies introduce, and which make men heretics.' So, for Tertullian, issues such as the creation of the world and the resurrection of the body, which were still disputed in the east, have become orthodox belief. Note too, in contrast to Origen, the belief in everlasting hell fire.

Tertullian suggests that orthodoxy is so firmly established that those who challenge it must by their very nature be heretics. He sees himself in the vanguard of the fight to preserve the traditions of the church and, in the longest of his works, *Against Marcion*, he revels in the demolition of Marcion's theology. For Tertullian, and here he echoes Irenaeus, there is 'a deposit of faith', passed down in an unchanging and unchallengeable form through the apostles and the very act of questioning it is itself to be condemned. Tertullian insinuates that heretics live undisciplined lives, not only personally (he talks of the immorality of their women), but because of their curiosity. They are totally unscrupulous in their beliefs so long as these challenge the truth. 'They huddle up anyhow with all comers; for it matters not to them, however different be their treatment of subjects, provided only they can conspire together to storm the citadel of the one only Truth. All are puffed up, all offer you knowledge.'

This waspish attitude to life extends to Tertullian's view of asceticism, women and sex. He was deeply concerned with the power of the devil to subvert the faithful especially after they had just made their baptism. If they sin at this important juncture in their lives, then they must go through a second repentance. The penitent is expected to 'nourish prayers with fast, to groan, to weep, and to bellow day and night to the Lord God; to fall prostrate before the presbyters and kneel before the altars of God; to enjoin upon all his brothers the embassy of his own entreaty . . . the less you spare yourself the more will God spare you'. Tertullian was deeply misogynistic. Women are 'the devil's gateway'. His *On the Veiling of Virgins* addresses the issue of some young girls in his congregation who had committed themselves to virginity. Their fellow-believers encouraged them to free themselves of the veils they would normally have worn, in order to show the superior status they had reached through their renunciation. Tertullian was having none of it. Even in their new state, they were still alluring. Like many ascetics, he compared sexuality to a permanent bubbling cesspit of desire. It became the sin that transcended all others and women were indeed the means through which the devil encouraged downfall. They could not escape this role and he ordered the veils to be put back on.[2]

Tertullian's austerity extended to welcoming martyrdom, even seeming to suggest that it is a necessary sacrifice to appease God (perhaps there is an echo of Punic worship here). As he puts it in his *An Antidote to the Scorpion's Sting*, 'Does God covet man's blood? And yet I might venture to affirm that He does, if man also covets the kingdom of heaven, if man covets a sure salvation, if man also covets a second new birth.' When confronted by the text used by Origen to show that Jesus recommended that his disciples, and hence their successors, flee persecution (Matthew 10:23), Tertullian replied that it applied to that instance alone and to no other. Instead he gave primacy to a verse he attributed to Paul: 'I am glad of my suffering on your behalf, as, in this mortal frame of mine, I help to pay off the debt which the afflictions of Christ still leave to be paid for the sake of his body, the Church' (Colossians 1:24). The 'good' Christian, in Tertullian's view, therefore actively wills his sacrifice. In the concluding chapter to his *Apology*, which is addressed to the magistrates of Carthage, he makes the point explicitly: 'It is quite true that it is our desire to suffer, but it is in the way that the soldier longs for war. No one indeed suffers willingly, since suffering necessarily implies fear and danger. Yet the man who objected to the conflict, both fights with all his strength, and when victorious, he rejoices in the battle, because he reaps from it glory and spoil . . . Nor does your [the persecutors'] cruelty, however exquisite, avail you; it is rather a temptation to us. The oftener we are mown down by you, the more in number we grow; the blood of Christians is seed.'

In the *Praescriptio* Tertullian accepts that the rule of faith has been passed on down through the churches founded by the apostles. This presented enough problems for the church now that the lines of succession had stretched for two hundred years. Yet, paradoxically, as he grew older, Tertullian found less and less fulfilment within the institutional church and he turned towards the Montanists, those who claimed that God was talking to them directly through the Holy Spirit. From about 208, he seems to have committed himself to this movement and he remained a Montanist for the remaining ten or fifteen years of his active life. There is no evidence that Tertullian was excommunicated but later Latin theologians approached him with caution. His fellow-Carthaginian Cyprian seems to have used his work without any acknowledgement and Augustine was ambivalent towards him. He has never been canonised. Nevertheless he has been called 'the first theologian of the west'[3] and it is hard to see who else might challenge him for the accolade.

Tertullian must have been an awkward member of any community; it is easy to imagine him irritating anyone who wished to live anything like a normal life and his attraction to the personal revelations of God's message claimed by the Montanists may well reflect his rejection by the bishops of his native city. In Tertullian's eyes, bishops were essentially administrators, taking on the tasks of baptism simply because this provides order in the organisation. They do not enjoy spiritual power by virtue of their office. This minimalist approach disregarded the earlier teachings of Ignatius and Irenaeus on the authority of the bishop but these were to be reasserted by the next important figure of Carthaginian Christianity, the bishop Cyprian.

Cyprian must have come from very much the same social background as Tertullian, although his roots appear to be Punic or Berber, his status as a well-educated and prosperous man a tribute to the success of Romanisation. At his conversion, he tells us in his *Life*, he rejected 'worldly ambition', probably a reference to the civic posts that a man of high class would naturally aspire to, and he made over his estate near Carthage to the poor. Not much more is known until he became bishop of the city in 248 or 249, only two or three years after his conversion. In the account he gives in *The Life*, he suggests that he was propelled into the position over the heads of older clergy by the acclaim of the *plebs*, the mass of Christians. This was very typical of the way a magistrate would be appointed in Roman colonies where the citizens had a vote. The community he took over seems to have been expanding although there is no evidence that it was wealthy or secure enough to have its own public buildings.

Once in post, Cyprian purged his writing of classical allusions and engaged in a deep study of the scripture. He was literalist in his interpretations of texts and, even though he never named him, relied heavily on Tertullian's works, which were no doubt those closest to hand. He comes across, however, as a much less intense personality, writing with genuine affection to his close friends and talking more warmly of the loving nature of God than Tertullian ever did. In his understanding of his role as bishop, he drew on traditional Roman models. The office was described in similar terms to that of a Roman provincial governor. As Cyprian puts it in one of his letters, the bishop was the judge representing Christ, just as a governor might represent the emperor. He even describes his diocese as a *provincia*, the allotted territory within which a governor's rule was absolute, while those who opposed him were described as rebels and revolutionaries, very much as a Roman governor would see them. His staff was graded, from the readers, through the letter carriers, deacons and presbyters, who instructed catechumens and could celebrate the Eucharist, to the bishop himself. He assumed that a gifted Christian would make the ascent just as a Roman citizen traditionally followed the *cursus*, the route up through the various magistracies to the top position, and he would channel his patronage towards those he favoured as a Roman patron would.

It appears, then, that Cyprian adapted the political structure he would have known well in Carthage to Christian purposes. Yet there was an important difference in that God had to be accorded the supreme role, the heavenly equivalent of an emperor. God's power was awesome, especially when directed against those who challenged the authority of his bishops. Heresies and schism were the result of a failure to recognise that 'there is but one bishop and judge who acts in Christ's stead for the time being'. Against Tertullian, who had denied that bishops had the power to grant absolution, Cyprian argued that in fact it was only the bishops who could absolve by virtue of the power they had obtained by God through their office.

The issue soon became a live one. In 250 a new emperor, Decius, ordered that all should show their commitment to the state by sacrificing to the pagan gods. Cyprian was horrified by the number of his congregation who gave in. Anxious not to offer any provocation, he decided to withdraw from Carthage. 'What I fear is that my presence may provoke an outburst of violence and resentment among the pagans, whereas it is particularly a duty of ours to ensure that everyone is left undisturbed.' However, many of those Christians who had stood firm were thrown into prison and Cyprian began to receive criticism for his abandonment of them. In his absence some of the presbyters who had remained in Carthage, urged on by those imprisoned, began to pardon those who had lapsed in the face of persecution. This was a direct affront to Cyprian's authority as bishop and he reacted firmly by excommuni- cating the miscreants. As the persecution lost its intensity, he summoned a council of bishops to Carthage to support his authority. Hardly surprisingly, the bishops made common cause against the presbyters in insisting that a bishop alone could authorise penance.

How was this to be effected and on what terms? Could a compromise be reached between recognition of the seriousness of the betrayal of one's faith and compassion for the weakness of the individual? While excluded from the church the lapsed were deprived of any personal security they might have enjoyed as members of a close-knit community and were faced with the threat of their souls suffering eternal torment. Yet forgiveness was not to be granted easily. As one of his letters puts it: 'People coming back from the altars of Satan approach the Lord's sacred flesh, their hands still foul and reeking.' A period of repentance was needed. 'Let no one commit his ship again to the deep, when it has been broken and holed by the waves, until he has carefully repaired it. Let no one put on a torn tunic unless he has seen it mended by the trained craftsmen and treated by the fuller.' It was eventually agreed that those who had only compromised their faith in a minor way (such as obtaining a certificate which said that they had sacrificed even if they had not) could be given immediate forgiveness by a bishop (but only by a bishop) while those who had gone so far as actually to make a sacrifice must make greater penitence before forgiveness. They would only be forgiven immediately if they were close to death.

In *De unitate*, 'On the Unity of the Church', a document he brought to the council, Cyprian reasserts the authority of the bishops as equal members of a united church. He waxes eloquent: 'The episcopate is one, each part of which is held by each one for the whole. The Church also is one, which is spread abroad far and wide into a multitude by an increase of fruitfulness. As there are many rays of the sun, but one light; and many branches of a tree, but one strength based in its tenacious root; and since from one spring flow many streams, although the multiplicity seems diffused in the liberality of an overflowing abundance, yet the unity is still preserved in the source.' He goes on to assert that 'he can no longer have God for his Father, who has not the Church for his mother'. There is no salvation outside the church: 'Whoever breaks with the Church cuts himself off from the promises made to the Church; and he who turns his back on the Church of Christ will not come to the rewards of Christ: he is an alien, a worldling, an enemy.'

This was coherent enough but the unity of the church was to prove difficult to sustain. As the status of bishops rose, it was essential to find a process for their appointment that had wide approval. Many dioceses involved their congregations in elections and Cyprian himself had gained his see through the support of the laity (who, he argued, had been inspired in their choice by God). Yet it was also wise for a bishop to have the support of his neighbouring fellow bishops and these would often gather in the vacant diocese to participate in the election. In 251 there was a vacancy for the bishopric in Rome, after the previous bishop, Fabian, had been martyred in the Decian persecution. Both candidates, Cornelius and Novatian, wrote to Cyprian asking for their support and each then claimed that they had been 'elected' with the support of other Italian bishops. Cyprian wavered but then recognised Cornelius, partly on the grounds that his election appeared to have taken place first but also because Cornelius shared his view that a bishop should be able to forgive those who had lapsed. Novatian insisted that clemency was never justified – only God at the Last Judgement could decide the issue.

Thwarted in his ambition to become bishop of Rome, Novatian set himself up as a rival bishop to Cornelius. For many of his followers this was a step too far and they abandoned him and asked to be readmitted to the church of Cornelius and Cyprian. Yet did those who had been baptised by Novatian have to be baptised again? Cyprian took a hard line. He argued that by setting himself up as a rival bishop, Novatian was guilty of schism. Schismatics, as *De unitate* made clear, were outside the church. Those now joining the official church had simply never been registered as Christians at all and now had to be baptised as if for the first time. Cyprian secured the support of a local council of bishops and, with Cornelius acknowledged as the bishop of Rome, his position seemed secure. Despite some disagreements in other parts of the empire there was a chance that the church could be united on the issue.

However, in June 253 Cornelius died and his successor Stephen took an opposite view. It did not matter, Stephen argued, that the original bishop carrying out the baptism was unworthy; it was still a baptism as the Holy Spirit could bypass the unworthiness of the celebrant. He was simply a medium through whom the Spirit passed. Nowhere in either scripture or the practice of the apostles was there any backing for the idea of a second baptism. So those abandoning Novatian did not have to seek rebaptism. Cyprian risked being rebuffed but he reacted cautiously. He gained further backing for his position from another council, this time of seventy-one bishops from the African provinces, and then wrote a conciliatory letter to Stephen hoping that the power of the Holy Spirit would bring the church to consensus on the matter. The letter he received back, however, was, as he put it, 'arrogant, irrelevant, self-contradictory, ill-considered and inept'. Although the letter does not survive, Stephen, secure as bishop of the ancient see of Rome, the successor of no less than the apostle Peter, was clearly not going to be dictated to by a provincial bishop.

A battle was on. Cyprian began a programme of intense networking. A new council, this time of eighty-seven bishops, was summoned to Carthage to support him and he received backing from as far afield as the Greek bishoprics of Asia Minor. Tensions mounted further. Stephen told the bishops of Asia that he was no longer in communion with them. One bishop from Cappadocia retaliated with a highly abusive letter to Stephen: 'Look, for instance, at the quarrels, the dissensions you have provoked throughout the churches all over the world! Look at the magnitude of the sin you have heaped upon yourself by cutting yourself off from so many flocks! While imagining it was in your power to excommunicate everyone, you have in fact succeeded in excommunicating yourself alone, from everyone else.'

Stephen died in 257 and, when a new wave of persecution was launched by the emperor Valerian, the issue was left unresolved. In this persecution Cyprian stayed in the city with his flock. The city's governor did not want to risk an open confrontation with Cyprian and he sent him into exile. Later he was brought back to Carthage and executed in 258. The matter of authority lay dormant until it flared up again after the next major bout of persecution in the early fourth century.

The legacy of Cyprian's reign remained an ambiguous one. He had used his status and the prestige of his own bishopric to enhance the authority of the office. Bishops were to become increasingly powerful figures in the years to come and *De unitate* a seminal document for the authority of the church. Cyprian had also shown that there could be a hierarchy of bishops with a senior bishop, a metropolitan as they became known, acting to coordinate the activities of the other bishops in his area through common council. With Carthage as the largest city in North Africa and Cyprian himself an imposing personality, it was an understandable development. Yet as the row with Stephen showed, the relationship between Rome and the provincial bishops was still fluid. When a major theological issue arose, and the question of rebaptism was surely one, had Rome the right to impose its views on everyone else? Cyprian's own writings show that he was confused on the matter. Some texts suggest that he respected the primacy of Rome, others that, when confronted by Stephen, he was deeply reluctant to compromise. He told one bishop that Peter himself 'did not claim to usurp anything for himself insolently and arrogantly', the implication being that he had a right to disregard Rome if Peter's successors behaved 'arrogantly'. The question of how church authority was to be exercised and through whom was still unresolved but the Christians of North Africa had instituted a particularly rigorous form of Christianity and its later impact on western Christianity, through Augustine, the bishop of Hippo, was to be immense.

CHAPTER TWENTY

Victims or Volunteers

CHRISTIAN MARTYRS

THE EARLIEST VOICE OF A CHRISTIAN WOMAN TO SURVIVE IS THAT of Perpetua, a martyr who was persecuted in Carthage in the early third century. Perpetua was a well-born woman of twenty-two, mother of a baby boy whom she was still suckling when she was arrested as a catechumen. (She was baptised when in prison.) In the Passion account of herself and a slave girl Felicity[1] no reason is given for her arrest and it causes great distress within her family. Her father pleads for her to show reverence to the traditional gods but she steadfastly refuses. She is sentenced to death in the arena and meanwhile is thrown into prison together with three male Christians and Felicity, the slave of one of them. Here she has a series of visions, most of which envisage a welcome into heaven. In one her older brother, who had died of cancer of the face, is shown healed and refreshed by water from a golden bowl. In another she fights an immense and repulsive Egyptian in the arena and triumphs over him. She realises that it is no less than Satan whom she has conquered.

After the first part of the Passion, which is in Perpetua's words, the focus turns to the narration by a sympathetic observer of the execution itself. The Christians spend some months in the prison, during which Felicity, who was pregnant at the time of her arrest, gives birth to a daughter. Their martyrdom is delayed until the emperor's birthday when there are special games. The martyrs are then taken to the arena. The women are stripped and wrapped in nets and taken into the arena where they are savaged by beasts before being dispatched by gladiators. Perpetua guides the gladiator's sword to her own throat. The crowd roars with callous approval as the spectacle unfolds. Somehow the mangled bodies were recovered and in the fifth century were recorded as being buried in the main basilica in Carthage.

The original meaning of the word 'martyr' is witness and it was used in classical Greek not only as a legal term, the witness in the court, but to depict many kinds of observer. In the gospels it refers to those who witnessed the suffering of Jesus on the cross and his resurrection. It is not until the second century AD that it is recorded in the sense of someone who is prepared to die for his or her faith. There were, of course, precedents of Greeks and Romans who died for their beliefs. Even Christians were prepared to recognise that Socrates, condemned to death by an Athenian jury in 399, was some kind of martyr. His insistence on speaking freely had proved too disturbing to his fellow citizens and the account of his death by Plato enjoyed a cult status. There were Roman heroes such as the conservative republican Cato who preferred to take his own life than live under what he believed would be the dictatorship of Julius Caesar, or the Stoic philosopher Seneca who felt the same about Nero. However, there was no hint in these cases that they believed a better life lay ahead; it was rather that continuing to live under tyranny was unbearable.

A more direct influence on Christians, and certainly on the way the martyr narratives were composed, might have been the Maccabean 'martyrs'. The Seleucid king Antiochus IV, a Greek, entered Jerusalem in the 160s BC and launched a campaign of persecution against the Jews in which he attempted to force some to eat pork. The stories of Eleazer, 'one of the chief scribes', and the seven brothers, are recounted in the apocryphal 4 Maccabees.[2] It may date from the second century AD and it contains an account of martyrdoms that are very similar in style to those of the Christians. The accused are arrested, brought to trial, ordered to eat pork, tortured when they refuse and finally put to death. The brothers talk of resurrection to a new life: 'By our suffering and endurance, we shall obtain the prize of virtue and shall be with God on whose account we suffer.' There is an echo of this story in the account, probably written by Irenaeus, of the death of slave girl Blandina in Lyons (see p. 209). She refers to her spiritual children in very much the same way that the mother of the seven brothers refers to her sons, suggesting that Christians must have known the text. Stephen, normally seen as the first martyr, tells his angry listeners that there was never a prophet who was not persecuted. He too sees himself as heir to a Jewish tradition of persecution, here of Jewish prophets rejected by their own people (Acts 7:51–3).

Yet there is something unique about Christian martyrdom. None of the pagan martyrs seems to have sought death in the way that whole groups of Christians did, in some accounts pleading with magistrates to be executed: 'Allow me to be bread for the wild beasts, through whom I am able to attain to God. I am the wheat of God and am ground by the teeth of wild beasts, that I may be the pure bread of Christ', as Ignatius of Antioch put it, as he was taken off to Rome for execution, frightened that his supporters in the city might intercede to save him. In his *Meditations*, Marcus Aurelius reflects on the rational (Stoic) soul, which is at peace with itself and so ready for death when it comes. He contrasts this with the obstinacy of Christians, suggesting that they meet death without dignity and with 'tragic show'.

Tertullian, the most relentless of the advocates of martyrdom, argued that if the martyrs of the pagan world were prepared to sacrifice their lives for false ideals, Christians should be expected to be even more willing as they were dying for the truth. Even so, the motives for the desire remain obscure. For many, the commitment to Christ meant sharing in his sacrifice on the cross. There was a personal identification with Christ and his suffering, perhaps intensified by the experience of absorbing the body and blood of Christ at the Eucharist, that was very different from the refusal of the Maccabees to offend the Law. As Ignatius puts it: 'if, as unbelievers say, His suffering was but a make-believe . . . then why am I in chains. Why do I pray that I may fight with wild beasts?' He is assuming the death of Jesus was not a humiliation but a triumph worthy of emulation. The slave girl Blandina takes on the aura of Christ himself: onlookers 'saw in the person of their sister [who was hung from a pole] him who was crucified for them, that he [Christ] might convince all who believe in him that all who suffer for Christ's sake will have eternal fellowship in the living God'.[3] The writer of the Letter to the Colossians, possibly Paul, suggests that martyrdom is repaying the debt. 'I am glad of my suffering on your behalf, as, in this mortal frame of mine, I help to pay off the debt which the afflictions of Christ still leave to be paid for the sake of his body, the Church' (Colossians 1:24). There is no record at all of how the impulse towards martyrdom was generated – whether small groups built up each other's courage or whether charismatic leaders created mass hysteria.

This eagerness also reflects the power of the afterlife. Martyrdom would have been inconceivable without the certainty that there was a world into which martyrs would be welcomed. Cyprian records their beliefs: 'In persecutions the earth is shut up but heaven is opened. Antichrist threatens but Christ rescues: death is brought in, but immortality follows; the world is taken away from the slain, but paradise is revealed to the redeemed: temporal life is extinguished, but eternal life is restored. What an honour, and what security, it is to go gladly from this place, to depart gloriously from amongst oppressions and afflictions – to shut one's eyes for a moment and to open them again at once to see God and Christ.' Many of the accounts describe martyrs actually laughing as the nails are driven in or the fire lit beneath them. According to the Christian poet Prudentius, when Lawrence was being roasted to death on a grid in Rome, he quipped to his executioners, 'This part of my body has been burned long enough. Turn it round and try what your hot god of fire has done.' These accounts need to be read with caution. The agonies of these tortures could hardly have been experienced with such aplomb and the repetition of the laughter and joy in different accounts suggests that it was intrinsic to the genre, added to the narrative whatever the reality.

The stage on which the martyrdom took place allowed a dramatic literary presentation. The empire was not a shabby dictatorship of the kind seen so often in the twentieth and twenty-first centuries where dissidents just vanish, often by the thousand. Justice in the Roman Empire, unless in response to revolt when any kind of retaliation was permissible, was formal and public. Only a provincial governor could order an execution and there had to be some kind of trial with an interrogation of the accused before sentence was passed. This, of course, gave the martyr a platform from which to proclaim his or her faith. While there were cruel and corrupt governors, many struggled to keep some fairness to the proceedings. What is remarkable about the early martyr accounts is the willingness of the authorities to be lenient; it is often the refusal of Christians to compromise which leads to their deaths.

The format is well illustrated, for instance, by a vivid account of the martyrdom of St Polycarp, bishop of Smyrna, and his followers, possibly in 155. The proconsul (of the province of Asia) continually urged Polycarp to recant and even gave him the opportunity to explain his beliefs to the crowds. However, Polycarp seemed set on martyrdom, as did his companion Germanicus: 'For the most noble Germanicus strengthened the timidity of others by his own patience, and fought heroically with the wild beasts. For, when the proconsul sought to persuade him, and urged him to take pity upon his [advanced] age, he attracted the wild beast towards himself, and provoked it, being desirous to escape all the more quickly from an unrighteous and impious world.'

The magistrates were embarrassed when their authority was ridiculed and often the governor tried to interrogate prisoners in private or hold a number of short trials that were abandoned as soon as the accused began to proclaim his or her faith. It was the aftermath that was brutal. The Romans had perfected the public execution as both humiliation and entertainment. The condemned was as 'a slave to the penalty' as one source puts it. He had no rights and was just an object to be played with. The day in the arena began with the hunting of wild animals and then in the middle of the entertainment came the executions, which included, of course, all the criminals sentenced to death. The prisoners were bound or nailed to stakes or placed in stocks on a raised platform, then they were savaged by beasts. Those who had not died were dispatched by gladiators. A new 'Christian' mythology emerges which has a powerful emphasis on the minutiae of violence. Martyrdom becomes a form of spectacle in itself.

A particularly harrowing example from the second century survives in a letter from Lyons that Eusebius includes in his *History of the Church*. Lyons was the administrative capital of Gaul and a prosperous city at the junction of important rivers and roads. It had attracted a large community of migrants including some Greek-speaking Christians. Christians had already been banned from public places in the city (they were charged with bringing 'into this country a new foreign cult') but in 177 a mob rounded them up and dragged them before the local governor. Some forty, including the congregation's bishop, Pothinus, were condemned to death by beheading or execution in the arena. The brutalities imposed on the martyrs and their steadfastness under persecution are recorded in grotesque detail. The death of the slave girl, Blandina, was especially inspiring to her co-religionists: 'After the whips, after the beasts, after the griddle, she was finally dropped into basket and thrown to a bull. Time after time the animal tossed her' until finally she was hung from a post and savaged by wild beasts until she died. What local tensions led to this outburst of persecution is unknown but Christians were often immigrants seeking artisan work and this may have been a factor in the violence. The authorities were giving in to popular pressure to eliminate outsiders.

As Christianity spread to the upper classes, governors were even more reluctant to send Christians into the arena. Confronted by a man of stature such as Cyprian, the first response was exile. However, Cyprian insisted on returning to Carthage where he was beheaded, the traditional punishment for a Roman citizen, in the garden of his own house, relatively protected from the public gaze.

The case of Pionius shows just how hesitant a governor could be to order an execution. Pionius was a native of Smyrna, the city where Polycarp had been martyred ninety-five years before. In fact, Pionius claimed to have had a vision of Polycarp, who became a spiritual mentor to him throughout his ordeals. The Decian persecution of 250–1 had begun and Pionius and his companions were determined to make a public display of their resistance to carrying out a sacrifice. They bound themselves in chains even before they were arrested to show that they fully accepted their fate. As they were led off, Pionius spoke eloquently to a crowd of Jews and pagans and aroused their sympathy. There was fear that if he was brought into the arena there would be disturbances among his supporters. Polemon, the temple official in charge of the sacrifices, tried to find a compromise, even suggesting that Pionius sacrificed only to the emperor rather than to the gods. Pionius refused and the case was eventually brought in front of the governor who again tried to persuade Pionius to sacrifice or eat some sacrificial meat – to no avail. Pionius was ordered to be burned. In one of his speeches Pionius inveighed against the Jews and they joined with the pagans in calling for his death.

The sheer horror of the proceedings and distaste among more sophisticated Christians such as Clement and Origen meant that there was intense debate over the justification for offering oneself in what appeared to be a suicidal sacrifice. In Book One of his *De corona*, which deals with a Christian soldier who refuses to wear the laurel wreath and is martyred, Tertullian ridicules his fellow Christians who consider the action unnecessarily provocative: 'Their pastors are lions in peace, deer in the fight', but he cannot conceal that there was deep unease among the Christian communities at those who allowed themselves to be martyred. For many bishops, the adulation that martyrs received was a threat to their own authority. Far from being Tertullian's 'seed of the church' martyrs must often have been an embarrassment.

Clement of Alexandria presents the argument against martyrdom in its most sophisticated form in the fourth book of his *Stromateis*. He goes back to the original meaning of the word martyr – witness. The true witness, he argues is the one who openly confesses his faith to glorify God and inspires others to conversion. There is no need to involve death in this and certainly not to seek it. In fact, he goes on, anyone who does so is the cause of another's (the persecutors') sin. Surely, the crucifixion of Jesus had in itself atoned for all sins and no more self-sacrifice was needed. Christ himself had advised his disciples to flee from persecution (Matthew 10:23), proving that the rush to martyrdom was completely unjustified. It was little more than suicide.

The martyr narratives are so powerful that they have left an impression of widespread persecution of Christians. However, in his *On the Deaths of the Persecutors*, Lactantius, writing in the early fourth century, notes no persecuting emperor between Domitian and Decius, granting 150 years of what he calls 'peace in the church'. There were certainly outbursts of pure vindictiveness against Christians, such as that of Nero in 64, described by Tacitus, when Christians were tied up in animal skins and taken to the beasts or set alight like torches but this, apparently, only aroused sympathy for Christians. The early accounts show that magistrates seldom initiated campaigns of persecution but that crowds often pressurised them into doing so. Many Christians went on living openly as such even during the persecutions. Perpetua had Christians around her who were able to visit her in prison without hindrance. Irenaeus returned to Lyons to become bishop there after the outburst of persecution in the city; whatever local tensions had caused it seemed to have died down.

The persecution initiated by the emperor Decius was more sweeping but it was not primarily an attack on Christians. Decius was an elderly senator who emerged as emperor in 249 after his troops had killed his predecessor. He looked back to tradition to boost his position. He added the name of the great soldier-emperor Trajan to his own, used coins that echoed earlier imperial models and requested through an edict that all return to worship of the traditional gods. An inscription found in Italy refers to him as 'restorer of the sacred things'. There is no mention of Christians in the edict at all, although Jews were specifically exempted from having to sacrifice. There was no organised assault on the church and many of the leaders were able to go into hiding as Cyprian had done. The limited evidence suggests that it was easy to avoid having to sacrifice simply by lying low. It was only those whose loyalty seemed in doubt who were asked to provide a certificate, the *libellus*, issued by the temple officials once a sacrifice had been made and the sacrificial meat consumed. Thousands of Christians gave in and many others obtained certificates through bribery or sympathetic officials without actually sacrificing. Those who refused were normally imprisoned rather than executed but they often suffered torture or deprivation of food or water to make them conform. Those who publicly confessed their Christianity and refused to sacrifice gained great honour. They were visited in prison by Christians and even interested pagans, and were assumed to have special divine powers, especially to forgive sins.

The Decian persecution ended with the death of the emperor in June 251 and peace returned. The next recorded persecution, that of the emperor Valerian, was more specifically targeted at Christians. Valerian was facing new crises in the empire. The important frontier post of Dura-Europus had fallen to the Persians in the autumn of 256 and Valerian decreed that the favour of the gods must be restored to the embattled empire. He ordered that no Christian services be held and that Christian cemeteries where worship took place be seized. Bishops were targeted and summoned before the governors. In Alexandria, Bishop Dionysius was told he could worship his Christian god but only alongside those of the state. He refused. The God of the Christians, Dionysius told his interrogator, was of a completely different order to those of the pagans. A year later the arrest of all church ministers was ordered. Any senator or knight who was Christian would be deprived of his status and property as would upper-class women (the *matronae*). Civil servants were to be reduced to slavery and sent off to work on the imperial estates. Cyprian died in this persecution, as did the bishop of Rome, Sixtus II, who was tracked down to the catacomb of Callistus and killed there. (A tombstone over his presumed resting place can still be seen.) The persecution only came to an end when Valerian suffered his own humiliation after being captured by the Persians at Edessa. The new emperor, Gallienus, was sympathetic to Christians and an order of 261 survives in which he restores 'their places of worship' to the Christians of Egypt. There followed a period of peace for the church with only scattered accounts of persecution. The emperor Aurelian was even approached to arbitrate in a dispute over the bishop's house in Antioch.

The empire-wide persecutions of Decius and Valerian were a new departure. Cyprian saw them as punishment from God for the laxity of the church: 'Among the priests there was no devotedness of religion; among the ministers there was no sound faith: in their works there was no mercy; in their manners there was no discipline. Not a few bishops ... became agents in secular business, forsook their throne, deserted their people, wandered about over foreign provinces, hunted the markets for gainful merchandise, while brethren were starving in the Church.' It is hard to know how to take this description of his church by such a prominent bishop (which echoes similar concerns of Origen), but it warns against oversimplistic descriptions of Christian communities of the third century as well organised and committed.

In the 290s, after thirty years of tolerance, pressures built up again on Christians. The emperor Diocletian was one of the most remarkable men the empire had ever seen. Of low birth, possibly the son of a slave, he rose through the ranks of the army to seize power in a coup in 284. He put in place a sweeping programme of political, economic and military reform. Crucial was the reorganisation of the empire under four emperors – two senior ones, the Augusti, and two juniors, the Caesars (Constantius and Galerius). The empire was divided territorially between them and a much more effective structure of local administration instituted. Taxes were collected more efficiently and channelled towards the army. At last the Persians were beaten back from the borders of the eastern empire with a great victory in 297, led by Galerius, that saw peace preserved there for almost a century.

Galerius was strongly anti-Christian. He began by purging his army of Christians (whose loyalty to the state could be doubted when they refused to sacrifice) and then put pressure on his fellow emperors to launch a more coordinated campaign. Diocletian was hesitant to join in. He recognised that transferring resources to persecutions did little to strengthen the empire. He finally agreed that persecution could go ahead only if it involved no bloodshed. In February 303 Christians were banned from using the courts and those who were civil servants were to lose their jobs. Church property and copies of the scriptures could be seized for burning. It proved impossible to confine the persecution within these limits. At a time of social and economic tension, crowds got out of control – in Phrygia a Christian town was surrounded by troops and everyone one in it killed. In 305 Diocletian abdicated leaving Galerius free to impose far harsher penalties on Christians – either death or committal to the mines, which offered little more chance of survival. Egypt, North Africa and Palestine all recorded martyrs. Eusebius tells how the methods of execution varied from province to province: by axe in Arabia, hanging by the feet over a slow fire in Mesopotamia, mutilation in Alexandria, torture to death by roasting in Antioch. An account of the martyrdom of Crispina, a matron of Theveste in the province of Africa, follows the standard accounts of decades earlier. The governor tries again and again to force her to recant her faith. He has all her hair cut off in an attempt to shame her but it has no effect and, as a Roman citizen, she is eventually beheaded.

Although, towards the end of life when he was in agony from bowel cancer, Galerius relented and called off the persecution, his Caesar, Maximin, carried it on. Eusebius, whose *History of the Church* was inspired by the sufferings he saw around him in Egypt, records an imperial rescript (the emperor's reply to a petition concerning the status of a law) which attributes the fertility of the empire, the peace of the seas and protection from earthquakes and typhoons to the favour of the gods which must not be lost. As with Trajan two hundred years before, Maximin had no interest in persecuting those who had renounced their faith. Their return to the old ways should be rejoiced in 'as if a storm had calmed or an illness been cured'. Those, however, who persisted in practising Christianity were to be banished from their towns. Maximin bolstered his message by commissioning anti-Christian propaganda, notably a doctored account of the trial of Jesus before Pilate that was to be posted up in every village. (One could always cast Christians as followers of a man who had threatened the peace of the empire.) This moderate approach did not seem to work. Local crowds felt free to go on the rampage against Christians. Eusebius records a mass of executions in Egypt that only encouraged more to offer themselves for martyrdom.

In the west, the persecution was not enforced. Christians were still relatively rare in western Europe but the emperor Constantius admired their courage and refrained from condemning them. Gradually the emperors were coming to realise that the church was so deeply entrenched that it could not be removed. Moreover, its hierarchy of bishops provided a model of effective authority that might well be copied. Maximin, in fact, reorganised the pagan priesthood so that there should be a high priest in each province, the equivalent of a metropolitan bishop, overseeing the revival of pagan worship. A much wiser man, Constantine, the son and heir to Constantius and proclaimed emperor on his death in 306, was to go further in co-opting the Christian hierarchy into the state and so changing the history and nature of Christianity for ever.

When Polycarp was being burned, it was recorded by an observer that 'the fire took the shape of a vaulted room, like a ship's sail filled with the wind, and made a wall round the martyr's body, which was in the middle not like burning flesh but like gold and silver refined in a furnace. Indeed we were conscious of a wonderful fragrance, like a breath of frankincense or some other costly spice.' Again the text of *The Martyrdom of Pionius* ends with the scene at the funeral pyre in which a body is transformed: 'After the fire had been extinguished, those of us who were present saw his body like that of an athlete in full array at the height of his powers. His ears were not distorted; his hair lay in order on the surface of his head; and his beard was full as though with the first blossom of hair. His face shone once again – wondrous grace! – so that the Christians were all the more confirmed in the faith, and those who had lost the faith returned dismayed and with fearful consciences.' The intactness of the martyr's body becomes part of the mythology, the symbol of the triumph of the body over death through the miraculous intervention of God. 'The bones of a martyr are more precious than stones of great price, more splendid than gold,' writes Eusebius.

A tradition that the blood of executed criminals has some special potency, particularly in the cure of epilepsy, seems to have transferred to Christianity.[4] When friends of a martyr would desperately want to take responsibility for the body, the authorities soon realised that Christians believed the martyred body had spiritual power. There were fights over the remains of martyrs with the authorities attempting to destroy the bodies so that Christians could not reclaim them. The bodies of the Lyons martyrs were burned to ashes that were then thrown into the Rhone so that they could not 'rise again'. There were deeper forces at work. By the fourth century, the relics of these spiritualised bodies were being used to effect cures. A handkerchief that touched the bones of martyrs discovered by the bishop of Milan, Ambrose, had cured one man's blindness before they had even reached the city walls and Ambrose was quick to distribute parts of his find to favoured bishops. The cult of relics, one of the most influential developments in the history of medieval Christianity, had begun.

The Christian writer Lactantius, who described the agonies of Galerius as he lay dying of cancer, believed that his afflictions were a just punishment from God. Within a few years, Lactantius, who was to become the tutor of Constantine's son, was able to record the triumph of the Christian God over those who had abused him: 'They who insulted over the Divinity, lie low', he rejoiced, 'they who cast down the holy temple are fallen with more tremendous ruin; and the tormentors of just men have poured out their guilty souls amidst plagues inflicted by Heaven, and amidst deserved tortures. For God delayed to punish them, that, by great and marvellous examples, He might teach posterity that He alone is God, and that with fit vengeance He executes judgement on the proud, the impious, and the persecutors.' Here was divine support for new persecutions, but this time the victims would be those who opposed Christianity.

The Spread of Christian Communities

I N HIS *HISTORY OF THE CHURCH*, EUSEBIUS, BISHOP OF CAESAREA on the coast of Judaea, sees the period from Gallienus to the outbreak of persecution by Diocletian, one of over forty years, as a period of peace and growth. The goodwill the emperors showed to Christians was such that Christians were now employed in the imperial households; in some cases they were apparently preferred to their non-Christian counterparts, perhaps because their sober living made them more trustworthy servants. There were cases, Eusebius tells us, of Christians becoming provincial governors, but even pagan ones allowed Christians to meet freely. The growing congregations began planning major new church buildings.[1]

The archaeological and epigraphic evidence to back up this assertion of growth is fragmentary, especially as regards buildings. Of the hundreds of thousands of known inscriptions from the empire, no more than a tiny minority relate to Christianity. There is only one Christian inscription from the whole of Gaul before the reign of Constantine – a gravestone that refers to the 'divine race of the heavenly Fish'.[2] Again there is a single Christian pre-Constantinian inscription from Athens. In Africa, not even Carthage has any archaeological evidence of Christianity. Only in Rome do the catacombs provide evidence of widespread activity. It is exceptionally difficult to build up much of a picture of the Christian communities from these limited sources. The case of Gregory the Wonderworker shows that Christians often exaggerated their success and Eusebius' accounts of 'mass meetings' and 'enormous gatherings' of Christians in these years have to be viewed with caution. While most authorities agree that between 7 and 10 per cent of the population of the empire were Christian by 300, this figure glosses over the unequal pattern of settlement and the intractable problems of defining who was or was not a Christian at this period. Eusebius is now seen to have defined Christianity as a much more organised movement than the evidence suggests it was.

Just how hard it is to define what is meant by a 'Christian' community can be seen in Edessa, a city on the borders of the empire in Mesopotamia.[3] An early third-century Christian philosopher of the city, Baidaisan, drew, in his teachings, on a wide range of traditions including Judaism, Stoicism and Persian. He was never ordained but he was influential enough to convert the local ruler to Christianity and his school was carried on by his son after his death. His primary target was the Marcionites who were especially strong in Edessa and said to be the largest Christian group in the city even as late as the 360s. Other Christian groups in Edessa saw Baidaisan as a heretic. In the fourth century new strands of Christianity arose in Edessa, based, it seems, on the apocryphal story of three aristocratic martyrs of the early second century. This invented cult existed alongside another of three villagers who had died more recently, in the Diocletian persecution. By the 360s the most influential Christian in the city was Ephraim, a refugee from the city of Nisibis that had been ceded to the Persians. He stood for Nicene orthodoxy and became famous for his hymns that were written in Syriac. He left polemics aimed at followers of Baidaisan, Marcion and Arius as well as Jews.

The situation in Syria was made more confused by the spread of the teachings of another of Ephraim's targets, the Persian prophet Mani, who was active between 240 and his death in Persia in 276. Mani presented himself as the Holy Spirit whose arrival had been promised by Christ in the gospel of John. He drew on the Acts of the apostle Thomas to preach Christ as the Good Physician. The divine spirit imprisoned in each earthly body could be released through the power of the Healer. Manicheism relied heavily on Christian imagery and welcomed the apostle Paul into its mythology. The movement spread throughout Syria and then further west into the empire. Augustine was a Manicheist before he became an orthodox Christian. In the late third and early fourth centuries, Manicheism was probably spreading faster than Christianity, even though its roots in Persia made it suspect to the Roman authorities.

The church in Rome in the third century was even more diverse because so many of its leaders were immigrants. Marcion came from Pontus, Justin from Palestine, Valentinus from Alexandria, Irenaeus from Smyrna and the Montanists from Phrygia. They brought their own cultures and theologies with them and many others attempted to set up their own schools in what was a tolerant atmosphere for much of the second and early third centuries. Congregations centred on different immigrant groups and adopted different approaches to doctrine and many survived from generation to generation in mutual exclusion. One immigrant, Theodotus, who arrived from Byzantium in about 190, successfully ran a congregation which believed Jesus was fully human and had only been adopted by God at his baptism. The Theodotians were known for their learning and acute criticism of scripture and the congregation was still there in the late fourth century.

The result was that Rome became the home of a fragmented Christianity with rival sects denouncing each other as heretical. The sheer size of the city, with possibly a million inhabitants, meant that different churches probably never interacted with each other. The bishop of Rome had enormous difficulty in asserting his authority within the city and it is certainly premature to talk of 'popes' in anything like the sense we use today. The liturgy remained in Greek until the 380s when Latin was imposed by Bishop Damasus. Alexandria was another city with a variety of competing Christianities, with apparent tension between teachers who built up their own Christian schools and bishops who resented this threat to their authority.

Traditional accounts of the history of Christianity have tended to assume that congregations were stable and expanding in the third century. This is not what the sources suggest. Celsus described Christians as at war with each other and even if he was exaggerating to make his case against the upstart religion, he was echoed by the denunciations from Carthage by both Tertullian and Cyprian of their fellow Christians in the first half of the third century. In Tertullian's case the lack of commitment of bishops was enough to make him leave the institutional church. Eusebius tells a similar story of the late third century. Alongside his account of Christian growth, he records how 'those who were supposed to be pastors cast off the restraining influence of the fear of God and quarrelled heatedly with each other, engaged solely in swelling the disputes, threats, envy and mutual hostility and hate'. This, says Eusebius, lost the favour of God who – and this echoed Jewish tradition in which the God of Israel withdrew his favour from his own people and punished them – unleashed the persecution of Diocletian.

This was a troubled church and the aftermath of the persecution left it even more split between those who were ready to welcome lapsed Christians back into the church and those who were devastated by the betrayal. Any account suggesting that the spread of Christianity was characterised by smooth undisturbed progress is simplistic.[4] The best one can do to give an overview is to describe some of the areas that are said to have had Christian communities in AD 300, even if it is not always clear what form of Christianity one is talking of.

The greatest concentration of named sites is along the coasts of Syria and Judaea. These include ancient Christian cities such as Antioch and the important maritime port of Caesarea, the diocese of Eusebius, where Origen moved to in the early third century. One of the few cities in the empire believed to have had a Christian majority in this period is Maiuma, the seaport of Gaza. Christianity appears to have been attractive to the transient populations of these coastal cities. Then there was an important scattering of Christian communities in Asia Minor, including those in Phrygia. Stephen Mitchell, in his meticulous study of Anatolia in the early Christian centuries, has tried to locate and quantify these Christian communities from the inscriptions on surviving tombs. It is hard to distinguish between pagan and Christian as they were buried alongside each other, and both observed local burial customs. A curse that 'violators [of tombs] would be accountable to the living God' is only used by Christians. A study of such gravestones in the upper Tembris valley in Phrygia gives an estimate that 20 per cent of the population were Christian by 230, 80 per cent by 300. The only three other cities in the empire believed to have had a Christian majority are in Phrygia. Again one has to be cautious in saying what this means as there were still followers of the 'heretical' Montanists in Phrygia in the fourth century, as well as Novatianists.

In Isauria, a province of central Anatolia known for the unruliness of its people, Mitchell suggests a Christian population of perhaps a third before 260 but a figure of 80 per cent was only reached in the fourth century, when there was a major increase in Christian numbers after Constantine's grant of toleration. Thirteen bishops from Isauria attended the Council of Nicaea in 325. Just as noteworthy, however, is the large number of cities in Asia Minor that show no evidence of Christianity at all. As Mitchell concludes, 'the progress [of Christianity] was irregular and the map of Christian progress resembles an irregular patchwork quilt, not a simply monochrome blanket'.[5] There are a number of cases where determined pagan city councils resisted the spread of Christianity or were able to challenge it effectively through backing the persecutions of the early fourth century.

Egypt was well settled with Christian communities: bishoprics stretched up along the Nile. Thanks to its bone-dry climate and long tradition of literacy, Egypt is the major source of preserved early Christian manuscripts – including the oldest surviving fragments of the gospels and the Nag Hammadi documents. Texts were sucked in from the rest of the empire by receptive audiences. Irenaeus' polemic against the heretics, which he wrote in Lyons, had turned up in Egypt within twenty years. Most documents were in Greek but from the second and third centuries AD, Christian texts were translated into Egyptian and transcribed in Greek letters – the Coptic writings that became such a feature of Egyptian Christianity and its liturgy and are still being produced today. The figures from an analysis of 'Christian' names from Egyptian papyri support the story of steady growth. They suggest that about 12 per cent of the total population of Egypt perceived themselves as Christian by 280 and 17 per cent in 290. Oxyrhynchus, famous for its great cache of papyri found in the city's rubbish dump, is known to have had two basilicas by the end of the third century. Following the grant of toleration in 312, the

The early texts of Christianity

1, 2 and 3 Fragments of Matthew's gospel (*above left*) have been found in the rubbish dumps of the Egyptian city of Oxyrhynchus. There is a more complete early third century text of Luke, part of the Bodmer papyri found on an early monastic site in Egypt (*above right*). Near by were found the famous late fourth century Nag Hammadi texts (*below*). Note the transition to the *codex*, or bound book, from the papyrus roll.

4 This late third century Christian epitaph from the Vatican Hill mixes traditional pagan and Christian symbols. The Greek word *ichthys*, "fish" and the fish images signify Jesus as saviour, but otherwise the shape and Latin wording are traditionally Roman.

5 An early (late second-century) banquet scene from the catacomb of Saint Callistus in Rome which draws on Roman precedents. The loaves and fishes, and the catacomb setting, confirm it as a Christian liturgical or Eucharistic meal.

6 Christ appropriates the iconography of the sun-god Helios in his chariot, perhaps to show that Christianity has replaced this popular cult. Mosaic from the third-century Vatican cemetery in Rome.

Christ as Good Shepherd

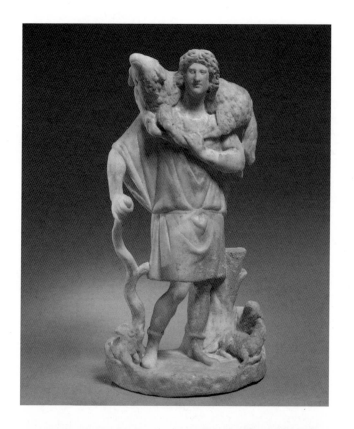

7, 8 and 9 The Good Shepherd was a traditional figure in Greco-Roman art which appears to have been adopted by Christians in the second century (perhaps following John 10:11). This late third century figure (*opposite above*) was made in Asia Minor, possibly Phrygia, while the mosaic panel (*opposite below*) comes from the magnificent early fourth century floor of the basilica of Aquileia in north-eastern Italy. By the fifth century, Jesus is shown divested of his burden and, in the Mausoleum of Galla Placidia in Ravenna, he is transformed into a costume of gold and purple as his sheep graze around him (*above*).

10 In their lifetimes, Peter and Paul represented different strands of Christianity and are shown in conflict. By the fourth century, traditions of a common martyrdom in Rome lead to their appearance together, here, on a belt buckle found near Naples, in a gesture of loving friendship.

11 Paul also stands by as Peter receives a scroll of the Law from a heavenly Christ. The iconography is that of an official approaching an emperor, typical of this period of Christian art. From the Mausoleum of Santa Costanza, Rome c. 350.

The Story of Jonah

12 and 13 The story of Jonah is one of the most commonly represented in early Christian art. He not only reappears alive after three days (compare the resurrection accounts) but his intact flesh after the regurgitation suggests myths of the unblemished bodies of martyrs. His nudity within water may also reflect the practice of baptism by total immersion. Here, in a mosaic from Aquileia (*left*), the 'whale' sucks him in, while, in a roughly contemporary statuette from Asia Minor (*below*), he is shown being cast out.

14 This wooden image, from the door of the church of Santa Sabina in Rome, dated to *c.* 430, shows a Christ who appears crucified but without a cross. Christian art seldom shows Christ suffering on the cross before the tenth century, perhaps because of the shame involved or because of the theological difficulty in showing a suffering deity. A cross without Christ was, however, acceptable and so was written or spoken reference to the crucifixion.

15 In this exquisite *pyxis*, carved from an elephant's tusk, Christ is shown in the dual role as authority figure and teacher: he is seated on a throne and the raised right hand is a traditional teaching gesture. Peter and Paul flank him with the other disciples. Early fifth century, provenance unknown.

16 In this mosaic from San Pudenziana in Rome (*c.* 390 but possibly later), Christ dressed in gold and purple and enthroned in a jewelled chair representing the traditional authority of the magistrate. The earliest known 'Christ in Majesty', it echoes the dominating fully frontal images of the emperors of the period.

17 The transformation of Christ into a warrior (see the words of Ambrose on page 253) is shown in this late fifth-century mosaic from Ravenna. Without any New Testament texts to support the theme, the allusion is to the Old Testament Psalm 91 in which God will protect by treading on a lion and an adder.

18 Sarcophagi were expensive to produce and so represent the beliefs of wealthier Christians. This late third-century example from Rome shows Jonah, nude as usual, on the shore, the deceased as a philosopher, his widow in the traditional pose of pietas, and Christ both as the Good Shepherd and at his baptism, though here as a child. The nude Jonah may refer across to the baptism scene.

19 Here the Passion of Jesus is integrated into traditional Roman iconography. On the right side Jesus is taken before Pontius Pilate who is shown as a traditional Roman authority figure. On the left of the central panel, Jesus is crowned with a wreath of victory. He is not shown suffering on the cross but his triumph over death is shown, symbolically, by the chi-rho monogram. From Rome, *c.* 350.

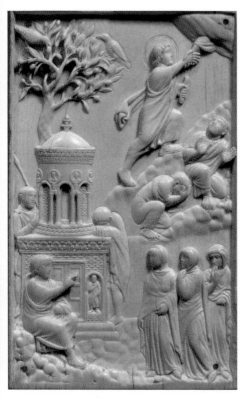

20 and 21 Traditional Roman iconography showed a deified emperor ascending into heaven, his right hand grasped by a right hand from above. This is echoed in this early fifth-century ivory where three women approach the tomb to be told by a stranger that Jesus has risen *(above left)*. The illustration matches the narrative of the Nicene creed where Jesus 'rose again on the third day in accordance with the scriptures and ascended [apparently directly] into the heavens'. As noted in the text (p. 39), the physical appearances of Jesus on earth before the ascension might not have had the prominence in early Christianity that is given to them today. The importance of the ascension of Elijah as a model is suggested by this early fifth century panel *(above right)* from the church of Santa Sabina in Rome (see p. 34). Note too Elijah's raised right hand.

22 The basilica of Santa Sabina in Rome (*c.* 420) shows how well the traditional Roman audience hall adapted to Christian purposes. Santa Sabina is symbolically important in the new Christian empire because it reuses columns from pagan temples. It is a very early example of arches used between columns, a standard feature of later church building.

23 The rise of the Virgin Mary as Theotokos, 'bearer of God', is well shown by this sixth-century presentation of her with the baby Jesus from the basilica of Sant' Apollinare in Ravenna. She is dressed in imperial purple and is seated on a bejewelled throne. Note the right hands of both raised in the traditional philosopher's expression of his right to teach (compare the earlier images of Jesus).

24 These ivory gospel book covers were made in northern Italy in the late fifth century. They provide a superb example of fifth-century iconography in which canonical and non-canonical images exist side by side. Note the symbols of the four evangelists in the top corners: Matthew as a winged man, Luke as an ox, Mark as a lion and John as an eagle. They derive from the Book of Revelation (4:6-8) with the four animals there being allocated to evangelists in a commentary by Jerome of *c.* 398. The front cover stresses Jesus' humanity and shows scenes from his and his mother Mary's life. The upper frame of the left vertical panel shows the annunciation at a spring, from the *Protoevangelium* of James (see p. 278). The lower horizontal panel shows the Massacre of the Holy Innocents with Herod issuing the order. There had been much embarrassment over this incident but by the fifth century

sermons proclaimed that the babies had achieved baptism (in blood) and martyrdom simultaneously, and had avoided the miseries of an extended life. The centre piece has the sacrificial lamb, framed within a wreath of grapes, wheat and fruit: symbols of the Eucharist. The other cover emphasises Christ's divinity, shown through his miracles, teachings and his presence in heaven. Note the marriage feast at Cana in the bottom panel and the raising of Lazarus from the dead in the lower left-hand panel of the vertical frame. The right-hand frame shows two images of Christ sitting on a globe, as a symbol of his universal authority, with an image of the institution of the Eucharist between them. In the centre the Cross, standing on a hill representing paradise, proclaims Christ's victory over death. The open doorway on each central panel symbolises entry to the gospels within the covers.

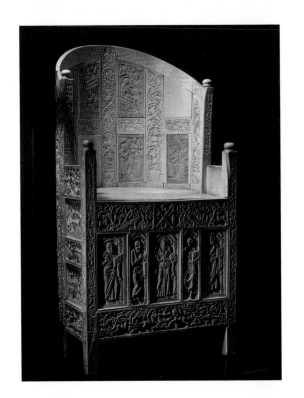

25 This wonderful bishop's throne with its richly decorated ivory covering was made for Archbishop Maximinian of Ravenna, who completed the church of San Vitale in Ravenna, in the mid-sixth century. On the façade, John the Baptist is shown flanked by the four evangelists while the other panels show scenes from the Old Testament and the life of Christ. The whole is enclosed within friezes of fertile vines on which animals graze. Perhaps made in Constantinople (which had just regained Ravenna from the Arian Ostrogoths).

26 This bejewelled cross was given by the Byzantine emperor Justin II to the city of Rome at the time of Pope John III (561-74). Similar crosses are shown in mosaics but this one had added significance because it contained a relic of the True Cross behind the central medallion. The reliquary was to become one of the most opulent forms of Christian art.

Christian population jumped to 70 per cent by 325. While the Christian population appears to have been sparser than that of many parts of Asia Minor, it was increasing nonetheless. Eusebius describes in detail the agonies of 'immense numbers' suffering martyrdom in Egypt during the Diocletian persecution.

Other parts of the eastern empire show very little impact of Christianity at all. There are only six recorded communities along the long coastline of Cyrene and only a few on the shores of the Black Sea. Greece and the Balkans have surprisingly few foundations. The province of Dalmatia has only one recorded community, and the large province of Achaea, which included Athens, only five. Origen spoke of the Athenian church community as 'meek and quiet'. The Christian congregations known to Paul – at Thessalonica, Corinth and Philippi – have hardly any funerary evidence to suggest their continued presence and it cannot be assumed. A letter from Paul did not guarantee the survival of its recipients as a congregation.

Eusebius tells of Christianity spreading among Greeks and non-Greeks alike but the Latin west shows the same picture of uneven growth. There are only three known clusters of communities in the early fourth century. One centres on Carthage and its surrounding territories. Cyprian was able to summon over eighty bishops to a local council, even if the evidence suggests many dioceses covered little more than a single village. As Cyprian's own story shows, Christianity had reached the higher social classes here. Yet the concentration is not typical. Of the other provinces of North Africa, Numidia is well represented but Mauretania has only one recorded community and the long coastal sweep of Africa Proconsularis only four. African Christianity had developed a distinctive personality and, as with most of the empire, was to see an explosion of growth in the fourth century, as well as providing the background for the major schism of Donatism.

The church in Rome is poorly documented before the fourth century but the catacomb remains confirm that communities were growing. In Rome, for instance, the catacomb of Peter and Marcellinus records eleven thousand new burials in this period, extending its passageways by some two kilometres. There were perhaps twenty-five churches in the city by 300. Bishop Cornelius of Rome gathered some sixty bishops from Italy for a council in 251 – less than Cyprian could attract to his, but an indication that his authority was recognised locally at least. There were a number of Christian communities along the coastline of Campania, between Rome and Naples. The size of the two-halled basilica church at Aquileia in north-eastern Italy and the splendour of its floor mosaics, all of which date to about 315, make it clear that there must have been a well-established congregation there ready to be housed in such magnificence when toleration came.

The very earliest reference to any church in Spain comes in a letter to Spanish bishops written by Cyprian as late as 256 but, by 300, a concentration of western bishoprics is to be found in Baetica in the south of the country, the site of the Council of Elvira. Twenty-six communities are recorded while in the neighbouring province of Lusitania there are only two, and only twenty-two in the vast province of Tarraconensis. The whole of Gaul had only twenty-two recorded communities and most of what is known about Christianity comes from the letter describing the martyrdoms in Lyons of 177 preserved by Eusebius. In so far as the composition of the Lyons congregation can be reconstructed, it was made up of Greek speakers from the east including a native of Pergamum and two Phrygians. The inscription relating to Christ as 'the heavenly Fish' echoes similar references and depictions in the catacombs and Phrygia, underlining the links between the communities across the empire.

The vast majority of Christians were urban workers. Those artisans specifically mentioned on funerary inscriptions include linen weavers, traders, mat makers, mule keepers, stone cutters and tailors but there is a growing number of 'middle class' occupations: small landowners, bailiffs on the imperial estates and, at the higher end, the manager of the imperial dye factory at Tyre, a freed slave who had risen to become chamberlain of the household of the emperor Commodus, and civil servants in the households of both emperors and provincial governors. This is overwhelmingly a church of artisans with a minority of wealthy and more literate leaders. There is some evidence, from the gravestones of Phrygia, for instance, of growth outside the cities and it has been suggested that one reason for the survival of so many Christians during the Diocletian persecutions is that they could now find refuge in the countryside.

So can one pinpoint the reasons for Christian growth? The evidence of patchwork development of Christianity in Anatolia, the flourishing of some communities, the failure of others to make an impact, are a reminder that good leadership was probably vital for success. The historian may be frustrated by Eusebius' concentration on personalities at the expense of the nitty-gritty of everyday Christian life, but he does make an important point. However much Cyprian and Tertullian complained of the inadequacy of the bishops, there were still powerful men around asserting their authority within city life. The third century was an age of social breakdown and some civic structures were certainly weakened by the turnover of emperors and the repeated attacks of barbarian tribes on the empire's frontiers. Bishops were emerging as the men who could get things done. Increasingly, and Cyprian is an excellent example, they were of higher social status and imbued with the traditions of civic responsibility. Naturally some of them abused their positions (and presumably their communities disintegrated, as happens in similar circumstances today) but the many references to bishops taking charge of charitable work, distributing the collections and acting as arbiters in disputes, show that they were fulfilling an important social function. There was a good reason to join a church for social protection.

This could not have been the whole story. Christians were expected to cut themselves off from all the religious rituals of civic life: a canon of Elvira required penance to be done for even watching a sacrifice. Social cohesion was achieved through defining a community that stood apart from the rest of society and promulgated its own values. It is interesting how often its opposition to abortion and infanticide is mentioned in apologetic texts. The stress on sexual continence was another defining factor. Again, the promise of eternal salvation must have played its part in fostering cohesion. In this period, Christians assumed that their very membership of the church would ensure their place in heaven. There was an extraordinary moment in Carthage in 252 where Cyprian actually welcomed a plague because it would speed Christians more quickly to heaven (while Jews and pagans would head to hell). Christian identity was reinforced by its rituals – the solemn ceremony of initiation through baptism and the weekly Eucharist. Baptism marked a symbolic transition after which sanctity could be sustained through participation in the absorption of the body and blood of Christ.

An important development in the third century was the creation, or in many cases invention, of histories for Christian communities. Some of these went back very far indeed. King Abgar of Edessa was said to have communicated personally with Jesus and been converted by a disciple sent to him. The apostles travelled widely to found churches – Peter to Antioch and Rome, the apostle John to Ephesus, the evangelist Mark to Alexandria. It was common for congregations to claim that their founding bishop had been consecrated by an apostle. These claims were consolidated by traditions of local martyrs. Edessa may have invented its earliest martyrs but there were many better documented ones, in Carthage, Smyrna (Polycarp) and Lyons, for instance. Rome was surrounded by shrines raised to their memory, either on the reputed place of their martyrdom – Peter on the Janiculum Hill, Paul on the road out to Rome's port, Ostia, Agnes in Domitian's stadium (now Piazza Navona) and Lawrence on the Via Tiburtina – or at their place of burial.

While the sources leave us with a picture of diverse Christianities in this period, it is possible, perhaps largely through hindsight, to spot the emergence of an institutional framework with links established between communities through the bishops. The spread of religious movements across the empire was not uncommon; the Christians would have to confront the far-flung Mithraists and the Manicheists as rivals in the fourth century. Yet Christians appear to have had a more coherent idea of a universal church. When Paul of

Samosata, the bishop of Antioch, was deposed by his neighbouring bishops and clergy in 268 for his views that Christ was born a man but then united to God at his baptism, the bishops sought support for their views by dictating a letter to the bishops of Alexandria and Rome. They asked the bishops to write to Paul's replacement so as to establish communion with him. One cannot talk of any real unity of the church at this time but the idea that Christians shared a common purpose may have played its part in raising the status and improving the cohesion of Christianity. A Christian travelling from one part of the empire to another would find a welcome in a host community. Martyr cults also spread as the major Christian cities became the focus of pilgrimages and relics were dispersed. A cloth which had touched the shrine of Peter or Paul became part of an 'international' currency of relics.

It is easy to exaggerate the success of Christianity by 300: 90 per cent of the empire's population were not Christian and there were vast areas of the empire where there is no community recorded. We cannot assume that growth would have continued at a significant rate. There is no record of sustained growth of Christianity in the Persian empire in the fourth century – in fact, the church there was persecuted as a reaction to Constantine granting toleration to his empire's Christians and appears to have declined. It was the sudden and unexpected boost of support from the emperor Constantine that was the catalyst which transformed Christianity into a social and dynamic force in the empire. In doing so it broke dramatically with its roots.

PART THREE: THE IMPERIAL CHURCH

CHAPTER TWENTY-TWO

The Motives of Constantine

'Let me now obediently sing aloud the new song because after those terrifying darksome sights and stories, I was now privileged to see and celebrate such things as in truth many righteous men and martyrs of God before desired to see on earth and did not see, and to hear and did not hear ... a day bright and radiant, with no cloud overshadowing it, shone down with shafts of heavenly light on the churches of Christ throughout the world.'[1] So, in the final chapter of his *History of the Church*, Eusebius rejoices at the toleration and patronage given to Christians by Constantine. Eusebius became a confidant of Constantine, wrote speeches for him, and after his death composed an adulatory life of his hero.

The transformation of the church that followed Constantine's involvement still shapes Christianity as we know it today. There is no knowing if the numbers of Christians would have continued to grow if they had been left to themselves but now the numbers expanded so fast that Eusebius complained of the hypocrisy of converts who had only joined because the going was good. Soon the church's authority figures, the bishops, were recruits to the service of the state. Their social and legal status grew enormously as did their wealth. Vast churches, glittering with gold and mosaics, were to be found in the major cities of the empire. Although the church continued to care for the poor, and was used by the state to do so, the transfer of resources to prestige building projects proved permanent, as walking through the streets of any medieval European city or viewing the megachurch complexes of the modern United States shows.

The role the emperors played in defining church doctrine was to prove enormously important. It was vital to have uniformity and good order although the church itself had no mechanism for achieving, let alone enforcing, a consensus on the intractable theological problems that consumed the energies of its more intellectual leaders. This was to be done by emperors – first by Constantine but, more effectively, by Theodosius in the 380s. Their interventions were followed by confrontations with Judaism and paganism. Eventually a predominantly Christian state became established in both halves of a disintegrating empire. It went hand in hand with transfer of interest from the gospels, whose portrayal of a spiritual leader crucified by the Roman authorities fitted uneasily with the new regime, to the Old Testament, which had far more texts supporting an empire whose survival depended on success in war and, in so far as authority needed to be reinforced over a sinful population, the letters of Paul. Augustine's Paul became the cornerstone of western theology.

Constantine emerged from the breakdown of Diocletian's system of four impe-rial rulers. When his father, Constantius, died in York in 306, Constantine had been acclaimed as new emperor by his troops. He had no right to accept the promotion but he was ruthless in his opportunism. He knew how important it was to have the gods on his side: he soon had his court panegyrists proclaiming that as Constantius had ascended to heaven, the heavens had opened and he had been welcomed there by none other than Jupiter himself. Then the sun god Apollo had appeared in a vision to promise Constantine thirty years of rule while the image of Sol Invictus, the Unconquered Sun, a cult popular with his troops, appeared on his coins as late as 320. He claimed that his right to rule came from his descent from an earlier emperor, Claudius Gothicus (268–70). There is no evidence that Constantine exhibited any early allegiance to Christianity although he certainly showed religious instincts which tended towards monotheism.

The new Augustus of the eastern empire, Galerius, was forced to acquiesce in Constantine's status, recognising him first as a Caesar and then as Augustus, one of the two senior emperors. Even when Galerius finally succumbed to bowel cancer in 311, his successor, Licinius, accepted Constantine and married Constantine's half-sister to formalise a new imperial order. Constantine's terri-tory included Britain, Gaul and Spain and he made his imperial headquarters on the northern border at Trier where his audience hall still stands. To the south, in Italy, another usurpation had taken place. One Maxentius, the son of Diocletian's Augustus, Maximian, had been proclaimed emperor by the Roman senate, and so ruled over Italy and, after defeating a rival, the African provinces. His usurpation was never accepted by Constantine or his fellow emperors in the east. A showdown was inevitable.

In 312, Constantine, who had honed his military skills with campaigns against Germanic and British tribes, led a carefully planned invasion of Italy. The north of Italy was secure behind him when he reached the outskirts of Rome in October. Maxentius met Constantine on the ancient Via Flaminia where it crossed the Tiber. He had replaced the Milvian Bridge with a bridge of boats, taken up position beyond them and stood to fight. It was a disaster. Maxentius' forces broke, the bridge of boats collapsed as his men retreated back over it and Maxentius drowned. Constantine entered Rome in triumph. His victory was trumpeted on the Arch (315) that still stands by the Colosseum in Rome flaunting its reliefs of the successful campaign. The emperor is shown alongside a chariot of the sun god that ascends to heaven while, in an inscription, the victory is attributed to the 'the highest divinity'.

However, other stories began to circulate. They suggested that it was not Jupiter, Apollo or even the Unconquered God of the Sun who had brought victory but the God of the Christians. Lactantius, close to Constantine as his son's tutor, told of a dream Constantine had had the night before the battle in which he had been told to place a sign of Christ (presumably the Chi-Rho, the first two letters in Greek of Christ's name) on the shields of his men. He had obeyed and won his victory. Twenty-five years later, a conflicting story appeared in Eusebius' *Life of Constantine*. Eusebius claimed that Constantine had told him under oath that some time before the battle a cross of light had appeared in the sky to Constantine and his troops together with the words, 'By this sign you shall conquer'. Christ then appeared to tell Constantine to put Christian images on his standards.

The most likely explanation for these stories is that Constantine had already decided to bring Christianity under the auspices of the state and realised that the best way of doing this was to associate his dramatic victory with the Christian God. There was no precedent in the New Testament for the association of Christ with war other than a single reference in the Book of Revelation to a warrior, normally believed to be Christ, in a bloodstained garment on a white horse. When Eusebius wrote up the battle he had to find texts in the Old Testament, among them the overwhelming of Pharaoh's chariots in the Red Sea, as a prophecy of the collapsed Milvian Bridge. So was born an uneasy relationship between Christianity and the imperial state that relied heavily on Old Testament texts.

In 313 Constantine met Licinius in Milan. Together they issued an Edict of Toleration which extended to all in the east the same tolerance Constantine had already offered to Christians in the west: an end of persecution, freedom to follow their own religion and, now, restitution of property. The edict specifically recognised the right of all to follow their own cults in the hope that 'the highest divinity, to whose worship we pay allegiance with free minds, may grant us in all things his wonted favour and benevolence'. The edict did nothing to privilege Christianity above other religious beliefs but it acknowledged that continued persecution was fruitless and that Christians needed to be welcomed fully into Roman society. This was the high point of religious toleration within the empire.

There was much more to Constantine's Christianity than this. He soon showed that he was ready to give positive support to the bishops. Such patronage was not unusual; emperors had always favoured specific gods or used cults of their own personalities, Rome or the imperial family, as a means of consolidating their rule. Constantine now relieved the clergy of all civic duties, including taxes, a major concession, in the belief that the clergy 'shall not be drawn away by any deviation and sacrifice from the worship that is due to the divinity . . . for it seems that, rendering the greatest possible service to the deity, they most benefit the state'.[2] Again this did not make Christianity the imperial religion. Constantine remained unbaptised (although this was normal practice when it made sense to leave the washing off of sins as close as possible to death) and he continued to use pagan symbols, such as the image of the sun god on his arch in Rome. Although Eusebius was to present every policy of the emperor as a sign of Christian commitment, many of Constantine's later decrees were phrased in terms of a neutral monotheism which pagans could interpret as no more than a general support for a supreme deity. His laws on marriage were seen by Eusebius as Christian in intent but they were typical of what any conservative Roman might support.[3] Eusebius also claimed that the emperor banned sacrificing, which was, in any case, in decline as a ritual, but it seems to have continued and the claim may only reflect Eusebius' hopes that Christianity had finally triumphed over paganism.

Constantine, however, might have had a deeper personal commitment to Christ. There were occasions when he lectured his court on the evils of polytheism, the importance of worshipping Christ and the need to repent. The so-called *Oration to the Saints*, a speech that was probably composed in Latin in the 320s and then translated into Greek for audiences in the east after he had seized power there, may well be a standard speech he delivered to audiences he encountered on his progresses around the empire but in it he attributes his good fortune as ruler to Providence and the protection of Christ. 'Be it my special province to glorify Christ, as well by the actions of my life, as by that thanksgiving which is due to him for the manifold and signal blessings which he has bestowed.' The *Oration* provides an important guide to Constantine's thought in that it links polytheism to social disorder. A single god was a more effective symbol of authority.[4]

Constantine could hardly challenge the polytheism of the vast majority of his subjects but he could bolster the bishops. They were now important figures in their city communities at a time when other authority figures were under pressure. So Constantine went beyond releasing them from civic duties to boosting their powers in other ways. His church-building programme gave them control of local patronage. Some bishops were given grain supplies to hand out to the poor, responsibilities that fitted well with their traditional role as organisers of relief for their own congregations. They were granted legal powers that extended to the right to free slaves on the same grounds as other magistrates and to hear a wide range of cases. These moves were all the more effective because bishops were now so well known in their cities and were often in office for years.

The integration of bishops within the legal and institutional structure of the empire extended to include uniformity of belief and discipline within the church itself. As early as 313, a group of bishops from the African provinces had petitioned Constantine for help. It was the unresolved issue of how to deal with the *traditores*, those who had betrayed their faith under persecution. Out in the country areas, hardline survivors of Diocletian's persecution were determined to show no mercy to those clergy who had lapsed and they refused to accept the validity of any of their sacraments, even those administered before the persecutions. In the cities, and among those of higher social class, there was a more relaxed atmosphere, forgiveness was thought possible and the validity of early sacraments recognised. Battle lines were drawn, perhaps as much on social as doctrinal grounds. Each group elected its own bishop – Donatus for the hardliners and Caecilian for the moderates. At first Constantine passed the petitions on to advisory councils of bishops meeting in Rome and Gaul, but he gradually became more involved – he enjoyed meeting petitioners in person – and he was instrumental in deciding against the Donatists. He even went back on his policy of toleration and there was a short period of renewed persecution of the Donatists before he relented and let them be. In Africa the imperial church, that of the Caecilianists, remained a minority drawn from the richer classes in the cities, but they received the goodwill and patronage of the emperor. Constantine was shaping a church ready to compromise with the state. For the Donatists, the empire continued as it had always been, something marginal and often antagonistic to Christian life, and the martyrs created by Constantine's 'Christian' state were as revered as the victims of earlier persecutions.

Constantine's wider ambitions remained unsatisfied and he now set his sights on securing the eastern empire. Licinius was gradually excluded from imperial decision-making, his head disappeared from coins issued by Constantine and the annual appointments to the consulships were now Constantine's choices alone. In 324, as the relationship broke down, Constantine found the excuse to invade the east. Once again the placing of the Chi-Rho on the imperial standards was said to have brought success in two major battles. Constantine soon removed his rivals. The captured Licinius was killed in 325 as was his ten-year-old son, Constantine's own nephew. Worse was to come. In 326, Constantine ordered the execution of his illegitimate son, Crispus. Crispus had proved a worthy commander in his own right and had held a consulship. Later gossip, from pagan sources, supplied the story that Constantine's wife Fausta was jealous of Crispus' preferment and feared that her own legitimate sons would be passed over. So she falsely accused Crispus of trying to rape her. Constantine accepted the story but was so appalled when he learned of the deception that he ordered the drowning of Fausta in a scalding bath. It is also alleged that his mother Helena was involved and one pagan report suggests that she was sent by her confessor on her famous pilgrimage to the Holy Land as a penance.

As Constantine consolidated his control over his new territories he realised that disorder among the Greek Christians was as widespread as it was in the west. The eastern empire was much more heavily Christianised with some hundreds of bishops. Intellectual life was competitive and different Christian communities and a mass of fringe groups such as the Manicheists vied with each other for converts. If the bishops were to be used in support of Constantine's rule, then their authority over their subordinates had to be upheld. The bishop of Alexandria, Alexander, for instance, faced two challenges. One was from a rival bishop, Melitius, who claimed he had been given the right to make his own ordinations in the diocese by the previous bishop of Alexandria, Peter, during the persecutions and he refused to surrender the privilege. The second was the famous confrontation with Arius, a presbyter in the city itself.

Arius was a charismatic figure, with a popular appeal – he expressed some of his teachings in catchy tunes and he had a loyal following in the city. The roots of the controversy are tangled. Arius claimed that he was representing traditional teaching in his views that Christ must, at some point, have been a later, but distinct, creation of God the Father. God's majesty made it impossible for him to share his nature with anything in the material world while Christ, as an inferior if still divine creation, could do so. Christ's inferior status was confirmed by his own words in the gospels, the frequent admissions that he only did the will of his Father who had sent him and whose purpose he did not fully know. Alexander, in contrast, preached 'one Lord Jesus Christ, begotten out of the Father, not in any bodily way but in an unutterable and inexplicable fashion'.[5] This was hardly clear. It assumed that Jesus had always been part of the Godhead but was also begotten of his Father in a way that Alexander could not explain. The historian Socrates, writing a hundred years later, records that Arius challenged Alexander with the heresy of Sabellianism, that Jesus had been a temporary manifestation of God. Naturally Alexander decided to bring Arius into line. He summoned the Egyptian bishops to Alexandria and had them condemn him.

Arius refused to give in. He made off to the imperial city of Nicomedia where the bishop, one Eusebius, who had developed similar ideas from a teacher they had shared, backed him and gathered his own bishops in support.

Arius also had the sympathy of the historian Eusebius, whose own bishopric was the important coastal town of Caesarea, Herod's foundation, where Origen had taught. Eusebius had been strongly influenced by Origen's theology and had absorbed the idea that Christ was a later creation and subordinate to the Father (see p. 192). Another council of bishops meeting at Antioch in 325 appears to have taken Alexander's side and condemned Eusebius of Caesarea as a heretic.

For Constantine these were 'idle and trivial' speculations and did not have anything to do with the Divine law, 'leadership doctrines' or heresies. They could be resolved by following 'the Divine Commandment which enjoined on us all the duty of maintaining a spirit of Concord'. However, in this case, as Constantine's adviser the Spanish bishop Ossius discovered when he visited the region, the dispute was causing mayhem. 'Confusion everywhere prevailed: for one saw not only the prelates of the churches engaged in disputing, but the people also divided, some siding with one party, and some with the other. To so disgraceful an extent was this affair carried, that Christianity became a subject of popular ridicule, even in the very theatres.'[6] Constantine had to abandon his instinct to let the bishops sort things out for themselves and intervene directly. In 325 the bishops were summoned to the imperial residence at Nicaea with transport laid on to convey them there. Constantine hoped to settle not only the disputes over Arius but consolidate the authority of bishops and come to an agreed date for Easter, an issue which was causing more upheaval with rival communities celebrating the feast on different dates.

Those who assembled, probably between 200 and 250, although later legends fixed their number at 318,[7] reflected the spread of the church. The largest contingent, some hundred bishops, came from Asia Minor, fifty arrived from Syria and Palestine and about twenty were from Egypt. Hardly any bishops came from western Europe, the bishop of Rome pleading ill health and sending only observers. Even so, the council could claim to be ecumenical, 'of the inhabited world'. All views were represented. Alexander came in person, of course, with his deacon Athanasius, a formidable contributor to later debates on Arianism. Eusebius of Nicomedia, the metropolitan bishop for Nicaea, spoke for Arius who, as a mere presbyter, could not participate. Eusebius of Caesarea was also there and left one of the fuller accounts of the council. It must have been an extraordinary gathering. Many bishops were said to carry the marks of their beatings and tortures at the hands of the persecutors. Now they were being welcomed by the emperor who, dressed in glorious robes and glittering with diamonds, would have been the nearest thing to divinity they had ever seen.

Medieval representations of the council show Constantine dominating the proceedings, as could be expected of the host and benefactor of all those seated before him. He could hardly miss the opportunity to stage-manage the assembly to achieve his ends. His instinct was always for order. In a letter to the peoples of the eastern empire the year before, he had described Christianity as 'the Law', the basis of a regulated way of life under the auspices of a single god. Whatever the theological issue, Alexander as the established bishop of the largest city in the east was more likely to have his backing than a presbyter who stirred up trouble by peregrinating through the eastern Mediterranean. The trick was to find a formula that supported Alexander's authority but around which the bishops with different perspectives could gather. Constantine's opening speech was masterly in framing the agenda to this end. He said nothing about theology other than claiming that the perils of dissension were a greater threat than war. The settlement of the issues would not only please God but would be of immense favour to the emperor. Anyone who stepped out of line would be sure of Constantine's anger.

Yet some kind of theological consensus had to be forged. A major speech was given by Eusebius of Caesarea. He had the reputation for being the most learned man of his generation and he must have wished to restore his standing after his condemnation in Antioch. It was a carefully phrased oration that talked glowingly of Christ's divinity without specifically saying how and when he had been created. It was enough for his condemnation as a heretic to be overlooked. Yet the creed he suggested seems to have failed to convince because it left the central issue, of whether Christ had existed eternally or as a later creation, unresolved.[8] Arius would have been able to claim that there was nothing in the formula with which he disagreed. Eusebius of Nicomedia, perhaps the senior bishop there, aroused greater anger when, according to one report, he produced a document which backed Arius. There was now confusion as charge and counter charge followed each other until Constantine intervened. As Eusebius reports, he tried, in halting Greek, to bring about unity, 'urging all towards agreement, until he had brought them to be of one mind and one belief on all the matters in dispute.' His means of doing so was a bombshell. He suggested, possibly on his own initiative, perhaps at the instigation of Ossius, that the correct way of describing the relationship between Father and Son was to declare them *homoousios*, 'of one substance'. The motive was probably to isolate Arius through inserting a phrase that his supporters would never accept.

It was, in fact, a clumsy way of expressing support for Alexander. The term *homoousios* was not to be found in scripture and quite what it meant, other than to express some kind of very close relationship between Father and Son which precluded a later act of creation, was difficult to define. Worse still, Paul of Samosata had used the term to describe the relationship between Christ as *logos* and God, and he had been declared heretical in the 260s. While one might be able to make some distinction between Paul's use of the word and its use at Nicaea, the odour of heresy lingered.

These reservations disappeared in the excitement of the moment. The cajoling of Constantine, his insistence on agreement and the sheer glamour of the occasion must have swept almost all to consensus. Not only was the *homoousios* formula accepted but a number of anathemas aimed at Arius were also included in the creed that was passed. Any claim that there was a time that Christ had not been, that he was created, that he was of a different substance from God or that he could alter or change from the state in which he had been eternally, was condemned. Almost everyone signed up to it. Eusebius of Caesarea, who joined the majority, was deeply unsettled by the whole occasion and had to write to his congregation explaining why he had assented to the *homoousios* formula. He glosses over the problem as if it were of little import but his embarrassment is obvious. Arius and two bishops were formally excommunicated and Eusebius of Nicomedia was also deposed from his bishopric, apparently after he refused to sign the anathemas at the end of the creed.

Of course, as with many decisions made under pressure and in a charged atmosphere, as was certainly the case at Nicaea, the radical nature of what had been done became clear only when the bishops had departed. Constantine had achieved a praiseworthy consensus in the short term but with a formula that began to dissolve soon afterwards. The council, writes Mark Edwards, 'had canonised a term [*homoousios*] which being new, unbiblical and uninterpreted, could hardly fail to irritate the conscience'.[9] There were immense philosophical problems in understanding how the two divine personalities related to each other if they were of the same substance but also distinct as Father and Son. Another term inserted during the debate was 'begotten', in that Christ was 'begotten, not made'. Here again the aim was to condemn Arius' idea that Christ was a later creation. So 'make' was rejected but some form of replacement had to be found. 'Begotten' was chosen, but surely 'begetting' involved an independent act of creation? The desire to overwhelm Arius had led to the sacrifice of theological good sense.

No one knows where the basic text of the Nicene creed originates; one report suggests Palestine, another Asia Minor. It was probably provided at short notice, possibly by Eusebius of Caesarea who did indeed claim that it was his local creed. The final version, with its additions, was compromised by the overwhelming desire to isolate Arius. One of the anti-Arian anathemas, the condemnation of the idea that the Son of God might be another *hypostasis*, or personality, within the Godhead, left it unclear whether Jesus was distinct from the Father at all – in other words it smacked of Sabellianism. More reflection would probably have avoided this. Nor was there any assertion of a Trinity. The only reference to the Holy Spirit was 'And I believe in the Holy Spirit'. The assembled bishops had missed their chance to describe any relationship between the Spirit and Father and Son. One has to agree with Richard Hanson, the author of the fullest study of the affair, that 'the Creed was a mine of potential confusion and consequently most unlikely to be a means of ending the Arian controversy'.[10] All this is understandable in the context of a council that was concerned more with backing the authority of the bishops and the state than with theological precision. No one could have imagined that the creed, even when modified at the Council of Constantinople in 381, would become the core of the Christian faith.

The following is the creed passed at Nicaea:

We believe in one God Father Almighty Maker of all things, seen and unseen:
   And in one Lord Jesus Christ the Son of God, begotten as only-begotten of the Father, that is of the substance [*ousia*] of the Father, God from God, Light of Light, true God of true God, begotten not made, consubstantial [*homoousios*] with the Father, through whom all things came into existence, both things in heaven and things on earth: who for us men and for our salvation came down and was incarnate and became man, suffered and rose again on the third day, ascended into the heavens, is coming to judge the living and the dead:
   And in the Holy Spirit.
   But those who say 'there was a time when he did not exist', [e.g. Arius and his followers] and 'Before being begotten he did not exist', and that he came into being from non-existence, or who allege that the Son of God is of another *hypostasis* or *ousia*, or is alterable or changeable, these the Catholic and Apostolic Church condemns.

It did not take long for Constantine to realise that the additions caused further confusion in the church. To his credit he sought to bring Arius back into the fold. He met the presbyter himself, encouraged him to sign an acceptable statement of beliefs and urged the new bishop of Alexandria, Athanasius, to readmit him to the church. Athanasius refused, to the fury of Constantine, who banished him from his see and exiled him to Gaul. Constantine had little time for those who spurned compromise. The bishop of Constantine's new capital Constantinople had to be asked to carry out the ceremony. He was about to comply but on the way to the ceremony Arius collapsed and died in a public latrine. His opponents saw this as the vengeance of God on a heretic. Still Constantine persisted in his rapprochement. It was none other than Eusebius of Nicomedia who, restored to his see, administered baptism to Constantine as he lay dying in 337, so much had Constantine reversed the theological stance of his own council.

The other canons of the Council of Nicaea show Constantine's concern to bring greater order to a church. Each area was confirmed as having a metropolitan bishop – in Rome, Alexandria, Carthage, or Antioch, for instance – to whom other bishops of the region were subservient. In Alexandria, Melitius' existing ordinations were accepted but he could make no more without the approval of Alexander. Bishops could not move from see to see. Once they had been appointed they had to stay where they were. A tolerant attitude was granted to those who had lapsed – even those who had sacrificed would be readmitted to the church after a period of exclusion followed by penance. Although the matter is only recorded in a letter of Constantine, there was also agreement that the date of Easter would be fixed according to the custom of Rome (where the date was decided with reference to the lunar calendar) rather than Asia. The Asians still tied the feast to the Jewish Passover, an interesting example of the continuing Christian links with Jewish tradition, with the result that Easter usually failed to fall on a Sunday. Constantine, in contrast, rejected a feast which was celebrated 'in accordance with the practice of the Jews . . . Having sullied their own hands with a heinous crime [the death of Jesus], such men are, as one would expect, mentally blind.' His championing of Christianity, tolerant though it was at one level, was already resulting in the exclusion of other religious beliefs.

One of Constantine's first initiatives was to commemorate his success at the Milvian Bridge with a triumphal building. This was to mark his new commitment to Christianity and provide a suitable setting for the bishop of Rome. Sensitive as he had to be to the continuing vitality of pagan life in the ceremonial centre of Rome, his first church was built on imperial land at the southern edge of the city. The form of the church of Christ the Redeemer, now St John Lateran, was conventional, the basilica an all-purpose meeting hall which could be used for audiences or the administration of law. Its apse, traditionally highly decorated, had acted as the backdrop for emperors or magistrates and the *cathedra*, or ceremonial chair, of the bishop was placed there, at the eastern end as was the custom for pagan buildings. The people of Rome would not have been offended by the building style itself, or even the opulence of its decoration, but they must have wondered what ceremonies went on there. An octagonal baptistery, still intact today, was placed alongside the basilica. Close by, in the remains of an imperial palace, Constantine's mother Helena had her own church (now Santa Croce in Gerusalemme). It was later to enshrine the *titulus*, the board hammered to the True Cross, which she had claimed to have unearthed on her pilgrimage to the Holy Land. The battered piece of wood is still on display although the legend that she found the cross itself is not recorded before 395.

It was on this pilgrimage that Helena had put in hand shrines in Bethlehem and on the Mount of Olives, the traditional site of the ascension. Constantine had already shown great interest in the Holy Land. He had ordered the clearing of a site in Jerusalem where rumour suggested pagan buildings had been placed above the tomb of Christ. As if by a miracle a cave emerged from the debris. A vast church of the Holy Sepulchre, much praised by Eusebius who visited the Holy Land himself, was commissioned. It was probably the first time that a church had been surmounted by a cupola, a style that was soon to become pervasive with glittering examples in Antioch (the Golden Octagon initiated by Constantine himself before his death) and Constantinople (Santa Sophia, possibly Constantine's commission but not completed, in its first version, until 360).

Another initiative of Constantine involved building churches over the burials of martyrs. On the Vatican Hill in Rome, the presumed resting place of Peter had been honoured since the late second century and Constantine ordered a great basilica to be placed on the site, the first St Peter's, with transepts so that there was a large area around the shrine itself. This was another architectural innovation that was to become standard in large Christian churches. Other shrines outside the walls of Rome attributed to Constantine commemorate the burial places of St Lawrence and Sant' Agnese on the Via Nomentana. All these churches were given fine decoration in gold and mosaic, and sumptuous fittings.[11]

Once, when he was asked about his relationship to the church, Constantine replied that he was a bishop for those outside the church, not for those already inside, and it is true that he usually kept his distance from the institution. The bishops attended him, not he their churches. They often offended him by their intransigence. 'You, the bishops, do nothing but that which encourages discord and hatred and, to speak frankly, which leads to the destruction of the human race,' was one remarkable outburst.

Constantine's foundation of Constantinople maintained the distance. Although strategic considerations must have predominated in his choice of the small Greek city of Byzantium as his new eastern capital, the emperor showed little interest in creating a Christian city there. (Byzantium had no known Christian heritage and did not even provide a bishop for the council at Nicaea in 325). He followed Greek rituals when setting out the new foundations, brought in pagan statues from as far afield as Rome to line the streets (to the puzzlement of his biographer, Eusebius), while an image of himself alongside a figure of Tyche, the pagan goddess of chance, was paraded around the hippodrome on the inaugural day in 330. A statue of Constantine was given a halo as if he still conceived of himself as some sort of sun god. The temple of the protecting goddess Rhea remained in place and it was only gradually, after the emperor's death, that she was transcended by a cult of the Virgin Mary. The first churches in Constantinople were dedicated to such spiritual abstractions as Wisdom

(Santa Sophia), Peace (Sant' Irene) and 'the Holy Power'. There was a church dedicated to the Holy Apostles, the dedication marked by twelve symbolic tombs. However, Constantine announced that this would be his mausoleum and he would be buried there as the Thirteenth Apostle. The appropriation of this title bordered on blasphemy but was another reflection of the way in which Christianity was being transformed by his support.

These ambiguities of Constantine's reign have made it difficult to assess his religious beliefs. Eusebius, in a panegyric of Constantine, delivered to the emperor in person in 336, describes him as 'invested with a semblance of heavenly sovereignty ... He directs his gaze above, and frames his earthly government according to the pattern of that Divine original, feeling strength in its conformity to the monarchy of God.' Constantine, Eusebius went on, was above all forms of emotion and desire, free of cruelty and any kind of base feeling. In truth, there is no evidence for any commitment from Constantine to building a heavenly kingdom on earth, still less for any personal piety. Constantine's relationship with Christ will always remain unclear but it certainly did not temper his ambition to destroy his rivals or restrain the brutality with which he eliminated them. In many of his pronouncements, Christ appears only as a symbol of order and unity, God's 'only begotten, pre-existent Word, the great High Priest of the mighty God, elder than all time and every age', as Eusebius put it. The human Jesus of the gospels is missing.

In fact, in his panegyrical *Oration* of 336, Eusebius comes close to claiming that Constantine is the temporal equivalent of Christ. While Christ is 'the Preserver of the universe who orders these heavens and earth, and the celestial kingdom, consistently with his Father's will', Constantine fulfils the same role on earth. The reign sees the inauguration of the Byzantine concept of the Christian ruler, appointed as such by God. God's appreciation of his emperor is shown through the granting of military victory and the effective control of his territories: '. . . the only Conqueror among the Emperors of all time to remain Irresistible and Unconquered, Ever-conquering and always brilliant with triumphs over enemies, so Godbeloved and Thriceblessed, so truly pious and complete in happiness, that with utter ease he governed more nations than those before him, and kept his dominions unimpaired to the end'. Roman imperialism and Christianity have merged. The church gained enormously from the experience but the carpenter's son who had died as a rebel on the cross now risked being forgotten in the transformation of Christians from outsiders to insiders housed in rich buildings and tied in with the successes of the empire in war.

Debating the Nature of God

THE CHURCH DESPERATELY NEEDED NEW TALENT TO MEET THE MANY demands that Constantine had placed on it. The release of the clergy from the heavy burdens of local taxation and patronage meant that the class who most contributed these, the *curiales*, was now attracted to Christianity. Many of its members were used to administration, overseeing building projects and distributing the grain supplies to the poor and all these roles were increasingly the preserve of the church. This was also a highly educated class. Philosophical argument was at the core of traditional education and converts from paganism now had a new set of intellectual challenges to engage them. The years between 312 and 381, when the emperor Theodosius imposed doctrinal uniformity on the empire, are fascinating for the way in which some of the finest minds of the period grappled with the problem posed by Nicaea, that is how to define the relationship between God the Father and Jesus the Son.

In traditional histories of the church, it was, and in some cases still is, taught that Nicaea had promulgated a creed which reflected 'the truth', even the established tradition of the church, and this was subverted by 'Arian' heretics until Nicaea was reasserted by the assembled bishops at the Council of Constantinople, called by Theodosius in 381. This view, which originated in the accounts of the winners in the debate, such as Athanasius and Jerome, will no longer do. Nicaea was a muddled formula, adopted in the heat of the moment to achieve the political purpose of isolating Arius and this was recognised, not least by Constantine, as soon as the dust had settled. The church historian Socrates, writing a century after Nicaea with access to documents now lost, had letters of the bishops before him in which they expressed their confusion over the term *homoousios*.

It was hard enough to make a philosophically coherent case for the pre-existence of Christ but even more difficult to say with any authority when this pre-existence might have begun. While there was a wealth of relevant New Testament texts, in the gospels, where Jesus talked about his relationship with the Father, and in the letters of Paul, where the apostle expressed his own thoughts, these were far too varied to forge into any kind of coherent theology. The twenty-seven texts of the New Testament had not been selected for their compatibility on this question and everyone could find passages from scripture to support their views.

One of the reasons, in fact, that theological debate became so heated and incapable of resolution was that many of the issues involved had never been contemplated by any of the Old or New Testament writers and texts were distorted into meanings that were never intended. The chance that a single word from the scriptures would ever be able to encompass its complexity of a divine Father's relationship to his divine Son was remote. When a term such as *homoousios*, which was not even to be found in scripture, was imposed on the discussion, matters became even more convoluted. There would always be something artificial about the debates that followed. It was the historian Socrates who described the Nicene debates as 'like a battle fought at night, for neither party appeared to understand distinctly the grounds on which they calumniated one another'.

The theologians of the early church were all subordinationists, in that they believed Jesus was, in some way, subordinate to the Father. Subordinationism was strong because it had a mass of support from scripture, from the Old Testament, through the gospels and including the letters of Paul. It also fitted in well with Platonism, which now provided the philosophical backbone to Christian theology. Arius' conception of the Trinity, in which the Holy Spirit was subordinate to the Son who was, in his turn, subordinate to the Father echoed Plato's hierarchy of the Forms.

Those who still supported the Nicene creed of 325 faced a formidable theological challenge as they could hardly renounce the terms *homoousios* and 'begotten' without rejecting the creed altogether, yet these two terms seemed to clash with each other. How could an entity of one substance beget another of the same substance without diminishing itself or, if not, proclaiming its superiority to the one begotten? Did not 'begetting' suggest that God was involved in some kind of sexual activity? Were not fathers always of higher status than their sons? These problems proved so intractable that, in the short term, the subordinationist mainstream resumed its flow. Yet the story of the next fifty years is one in which a counterattack against the subordinationists, eventually supported by a determined emperor, Theodosius, led to the reassertion of Nicaea as the orthodox faith of the empire.

There were a number of smaller councils in the 340s and 350s and they were mostly representative of the subordinationist position. It was only in the Latin-speaking west that any sympathy was shown for a formula akin to Nicaea, one that talked of the equal majesty of Father and Son but the west was still isolated and Christianity much less popular there than it was in the Greek-speaking world.

One of the more impressive expressions of the mainstream subordinationist view is to be found in a creed drawn up by a small council of bishops at Sirmium (in the Balkans) in 357. The participating Greek-speaking bishops refused to endorse any formula relating to the creation of Jesus. 'It is clear that only the Father knows how he begot his Son, and the Son how he was begotten by the Father' was their sensible response. They were wise enough to recognise that this was an issue beyond human knowledge.

The bishops went on to reject the word *homoousios* on the grounds that it had never appeared in scripture. Instead, it seemed obvious to them that the Father was superior to Jesus. 'It cannot be doubted by anyone that the Father is greater in honour, in dignity, in glory, in majesty, in the very name of Father' and 'that the Son is subjected in common with all the things which the Father subjected to him'. One of the key points in the subordinationist position, reiterated in this creed, was that God could not suffer. If Jesus Christ was 'one in substance with the Father' then he would not be able to suffer either. So he had to be inferior to the Father at the very least in the capacity to suffer for mankind on the cross. The possibility of a valid salvation through his agonies could only be ensured if he was of a different, less elevated, substance than God the Father. This remained one of the strongest arguments against Nicaea. The creed of Sirmium was, in short, a coherent statement of subordinationist belief that appeared to be reconcilable with the scriptures and human salvation.

The compelling quality of subordinationism is well illustrated by the missionary journeys carried out by Ulfilas. Ulfilas was the son of Christian parents who had been captured by the Goths and he had been brought up among a Gothic tribe settled north of the Danube, the boundary of the empire. He spoke both Gothic (a now extinct Germanic language) and Greek and so was able to bridge the two cultures, his Greekness being sufficient for him to be consecrated as a bishop by Eusebius of Nicomedia (probably in 340–1). He then went off to work as a missionary among the Goths until he was driven back into the empire when one of the Gothic kings began a persecution of Christians. Ulfilas now worked with Goths settled in the empire and he produced a Gothic translation of the Bible, remarkable in that he left out some of the most warlike texts of the Old Testament on the grounds that his congregations needed no further encouragement to be warriors! Ulfilas was a convinced subordinationist. In a creed attributed to him, he states that the Holy Spirit is 'but the minister of Christ . . . subordinate in all things to the Son and the Son [is] subordinate and obedient in all things to his God and Father'. So all the converted Goths became subordinationists and remained so for centuries, long after the empire had turned back to Nicaea.

One reason for the success of subordinationism in the middle years of the fourth century was that all three of Constantine's sons, Constantine II, Constans and Constantius, were subordinationists. Their joint rule did not last long and by 351 Constantius had emerged as sole ruler of the empire. While he did not persecute pagans, Constantius wished to unite the Christians of his empire around a single subordinationist creed. He called on a group of bishops to advise him and they drew up the Dated Creed, so-called because the date, 22 May 359 in the western calendar, was inscribed on it. The creed, like that of Sirmium, renounced *homoousios*. Instead Jesus was described as 'the Son of God', distinct from Him but 'begotten before all ages', presumably therefore at some early point in the process of creation. The difficulties of having to explain how a Father and his begotten Son could exist eternally without a moment when the Son was unbegotten were thus avoided. The creed went on to describe how the Son had come down to earth to fulfil the will of his Father and then was taken up to heaven after his crucifixion to be seated at the right hand of the Father. As a replacement for *homoousios*, the creed declares that the acceptable terminology is that the Son is '*homoios* ['like'] the Father in all respects, as the Holy Scriptures also declare and teach'. There is a short statement of belief in the Holy Spirit but the Spirit is not included with Father and Son in a Trinity.

Constantius now called two councils of bishops in the hope that he would obtain the support of the church for the Dated Creed. One, of western bishops, some 400 strong, met at Ariminum in Italy, the other, with about 160 participants, met at Seleucia Isauria (in modern Turkey). Constantius was taken aback by the outcome. The bishops at Seleucia brought many of their personal antagonisms with them, quarrelled over every term in the creed and spent most days in divided sessions. The western bishops rejected the creed as deviating too far from Nicaea. Constantius was forced into acting firmly. The councils were closed down, a further gathering of bishops was summoned to Constantinople and here, in 360, Constantius pushed through his Dated Creed. The subordinationist Homoian terminology had now received official recognition and one might assume that the Nicene creed was dead. However, any hopes that Constantius had of sustaining his own creed vanished when he died in 361 and was succeeded by his pagan nephew, Julian.

These debates are depressing in the conceptual nit-picking and personal antagonisms which they reveal. One can see why a term such as *homoios* was selected in the hope of gathering a consensus around it, but it was hopelessly vague and few could give it unequivocal support. One only had to ask in what specific ways the Son was 'like' the Father and in what ways he was not to launch an interminable debate. It was at the Seleucia council that one group suggested *homoiousios*, not 'of the same substance' but 'like in substance', to describe the relationship but this proved no more acceptable. The crucial point was that no single term would ever be adequate because there were was no coherent experience or empirical evidence on which to base it. Constantius had shown that only the imposition of a formula from above would bring peace.

The very process of debate was challenged by Athanasius, the turbulent bishop of Alexandria who had refused Constantine's demand to readmit Arius to the church. Athanasius had been restored to his see in Alexandria in 346 and he presented himself as the champion of the embattled Nicene cause. He was not an intellectual and distrusted those who brought pagan philosophy into theology; their speculations were no more than 'fancies of human invention' as he put it in an episcopal letter of 352. Only the scriptures counted. Had not Christ commanded his disciples to call him alone their teacher (Matthew 23: 8–10)? The path to truth lay in clearing one's mind of any sensual desire and then relying on faith in the words of Christ.

Athanasius provided a figurehead in the Egyptian monk Anthony who had lived for decades in the Egyptian desert. In Athanasius' *Life of Anthony*, Anthony is presented as an unlettered man, a committed Nicene who rejects learning but who confounds philosophers by sheer force of personality whenever they come out to the desert to debate with him. The *Life of Anthony* circulated widely, inspiring many others, including Augustine. It is ironic that letters of the real Anthony have been discovered which show that, in contrast to the fabricated anti-intellectual of Athanasius, he was well educated and able to write profoundly on asceticism.

Athanasius' theology was rooted in his personal horror at the sinfulness of humankind. So desperate was humanity's need for salvation, he claimed, that God had to present an emanation of Himself, as the Son, to ensure redemption. A created intermediary would never be up to this awesome task. So 'when we see the Son, we see the Father' (drawing on John 14:9). Athanasius strengthened his Nicene position by relying on those few texts which supported his own view, notably John 10:30, 'I and the Father are one', ignoring those which differed from it and castigating his opponents with sweeping polemic.

While in his early works Athanasius used only terms from scripture to describe the relationship between Father and Son, eventually, in the tract *De decretis* written in 356 or 357, he revived the term *homoousios*. The catalyst appears to have been another sentence of exile, this time at the hands of Constantius who had been urged by subordinationist bishops to replace such a prominent opponent. (Athanasius took refuge in the Egyptian desert.) Athanasius now grasped that he would clarify his position and rally what support he had if he unashamedly returned to the Nicene formula. He made one important advance on Nicaea. He recognised that the status of the Holy

Spirit had been left unacknowledged in the Nicene creed and he insisted that it must be given some form of higher status alongside Father and Son.

Athanasius' position was strengthened in two ways. The first was his continuing contact with the bishops he had met during his first exile in the west. We are handicapped by our lack of knowledge of western theology in this period. In the eyes of Greek contemporaries, it did not amount to much: 'You will not find that any one of the western nations have any great inclination for philosophy or geometry or studies of that sort', was the dismissive comment of the emperor Julian on the matter and many Greeks argued that Latin did not have sufficient subtlety as a language to deal with theological issues. One recent exhaustive study of the Nicene disputes has to admit that 'our knowledge of Latin Christology and Trinitarian theology in the west between 250 and 360 is extremely limited and certainly not such that we can make certain judgements about its overall character'.[1]

What fragmentary evidence survives suggests that the western bishops did believe in a Trinity in which Father, Son and Holy Spirit co-existed in some form of a single Godhead. This could be equated with Athanasius' Nicene theology. The most sophisticated attempt by a Latin theologian to go further was made by Hilary, bishop of Poitiers. Hilary is a rare example of a westerner who understood enough Greek to read Athanasius in the original. He created a Latin terminology for a Nicene Trinity that was persuasive enough to attract a group of western bishops who were sympathetic to Nicaea. In the 370s they were to receive a formidable boost from the support of Ambrose of Milan, the dominant figure in the western church in the late fourth century.

Secondly, Athanasius realised that the best form of defence was attack. If one argued for the primacy of scripture over philosophy, then the subordinationists held the advantage through the mass of texts that supported their position. Paradoxically Athanasius, who claimed to put scripture before philosophy, was acutely vulnerable if the debate was rooted in the scriptures. So he hit on the device of classifying all subordinationists as followers of Arius and then lambasting all as heretics. Tract after tract followed against the Arians. Here Athanasius was at his most unscrupulous. Anyone who opposed him on political or religious grounds was declared to be an Arian. The devil was said to have inspired the Arians' use of scripture. The Arians were so wicked that they could only be compared to the Hydra, the monster whose severed head spawned a hundred others. They were no better than Jews or corrupted by the philosophy of the pagans. The cumulative effect of this invective was so great that the dispute became known as the Arian controversy, even though Arius had been only one representative of the subordinationist tradition. It did nothing to raise Athanasius' reputation as a theologian among his contemporaries. This was power politics not philosophical debate.

Meanwhile, the empire was undergoing dramatic change and disruption. Julian, who succeeded Constantius in 361, had been born a Christian but the squabbling over doctrine repelled him. The historian Ammianus Marcellinus tells us that he believed that Christian infighting was so bitter that the religion would simply destroy itself. He returned to the old gods. In his *Contra Galilaeos* ('Against the Galileans') Julian used his considerable knowledge of the scriptures to highlight their contradictions. Why is there no recognition in the synoptic gospels of Jesus' divinity, for instance? The use of Old Testament prophecies as harbingers of Christ is arbitrary and unjustified. Why did God create Eve if he knew that she would thwart his plans for creation? Within this critique, Julian made a sophisticated plea for religious toleration, on the grounds that each culture needed to define the supreme divinity in its own way.

Julian withdrew the right of Christians to teach outside their churches and revived a variety of pagan cults but it is unlikely that he would ever have displaced the church. His own philosophy was too intellectual and an exuberant polytheism was too amorphous to have created an effective anti-Christian force. In any case Julian was killed while campaigning against the Persians in 363 and his successor, a staff officer Jovian who was acclaimed by the army, was a Christian. Jovian himself did not last long – he died only eight months into his reign after he had been forced to make a humiliating surrender of territory to the Persian empire – yet Christianity was restored to its position as the favoured religion of the empire and all future emperors were to be Christian.

There survives an important oration made before Jovian by a pagan orator, Themistius. Themistius had two concerns, the fear that a restored Christianity would lead to a backlash against pagans and a deep anxiety that Christian infighting was undermining the stability of the empire. He pleaded for mutual tolerance. Themistius stressed the impossibility of anyone, an emperor included, controlling the human soul. Persecution of the body could never destroy the freedom that was intrinsic to its identity. Instead God had implanted 'a favourable disposition to piety' in human minds but had left each to follow its own path. God actually enjoyed being worshipped in a number of ways, a positive appreciation of the tolerance of God that later disappeared from western thought. In any case, Themistius went on, a society was only healthy if it allowed free competition between individuals and ideas.

This freedom to debate was honoured by the emperors who succeeded Jovian: a tough army general Valentinian I, who ruled over the western empire between 364 and 375, and his brother Valens who assumed responsibility for the east. Valentinian was reputed to be Nicene in his sympathies but he refused to impose his views on the church so long as individual bishops kept good order. When bishops did ask him for support, he simply told them that it was none of his business how the church was run. Valens was more openly partisan – in his case towards the Homoian, Christ as 'like' the Father, creed imposed by Constantius in 360. However, he recognised that any arbitrary suppression of Nicene bishops was likely to be counter-productive. He tolerated the ageing Athanasius, removing him briefly in 365 but then allowing him to return to his see for his final years (Athanasius died in 373). Effective Nicene bishops such as Basil of Caesarea (the capital of Cappadocia) were left in place.

This meant that discussion could flourish. In view of what was to follow in the 380s these years were the swansong of creative theology in the ancient world. The three most famous theologians of the period are the Cappadocian Fathers, Gregory of Nazianzus, Basil of Caesarea and Basil's brother, Gregory of Nyssa. Their achievement lay in their ability to use Greek philosophy to develop a terminology within which a Nicene Trinity could be expressed. While Athanasius might have led the onslaught against subordinationism, the Cappadocian Fathers gave the Nicene cause intellectual respectability.

All three were steeped in pagan philosophy. Basil even wrote a tract urging all Christians to master pagan texts before they embarked on the study of the scriptures.[2] To grasp some idea of their learning one can spot the allusions to classical literature in the works of Gregory of Nazianzus. From Homer, in the eighth century BC, through to Plutarch, in the second century AD, almost every major author, including the historians such as Herodotus and Thucydides, the poets, the philosophers Socrates, Plato and Aristotle, and the playwrights are represented. Gregory has read deeply in Philo and Origen as well as the scriptures. When one reads Gregory's *Theological Orations* of 380 one is also struck by his range and consummate use of analogy. He meditates on the human mind, ranging over the problems of communication between parent and child, the transmission of sound from one mind to another, how the mind can be simultaneously self-reflective and imaginative enough to tour the universe. He speculates on the process of human growth within the womb, how first the soul becomes established in the body, then the intellect becomes part of the soul and finally the ability to reason becomes attached to the intellect.

The Cappadocians showed great respect for Athanasius as a battering ram for the Nicene cause even if they could not warm to his writings. They could hardly approve of his open rejection of the pagan philosophy that they so enjoyed. It is not clear where their acceptance of Nicaea originated but the catalyst may have been a confrontation between Basil and Eunomius, one of the most interesting Christian intellectuals of the period. Eunomius, the son of a poor farmer from Cappadocia, prided himself on his use of reason and the precision with which he analysed issues. His conclusions were shocking to many. Eunomius argued that even the nature of the Godhead could be understood through reason and it was impossible to conceive of the substance of God being shared in any way with any other entity. So Eunomius rejected the Nicene formula completely and instead emphasised the radical differences between the Father and the Son. He highlighted the obedience of the Son, who was 'the perfect agent for all the creative activity and decisions of the Father'. Among these creations was the Holy Spirit who was thus at the head of the created order in the material world. In 360 Eunomius and his followers had been condemned by Constantius. They had positioned themselves well outside his formula of *homoios*. However, undaunted by imperial disfavour, they set up their own groups of bishops in a sweep of dioceses from Constantinople to Libya.

Basil is known to have debated with the Eunomians in 359 and in the mid-360s he wrote a number of tracts *Contra Eunomium*. It was as if their radicalism pushed him towards Nicaea. Furthermore, Basil was concerned in particular to bring the Holy Spirit into the Godhead and, in contrast to the Eunomians, in some form of equality with Father and Son. His most enduring work is his *On the Holy Spirit* of 375, a much more sophisticated work than that of Athanasius – its terminology reappears in the revised version of the Nicene creed which the bishops drew up at the Council of Constantinople in 381. Basil argues that the gift of the Spirit can only be received through rejecting the passions of the flesh and that the Spirit will bring 'enlightenment which enables the recipient to discover the truth'.

The major achievement of the Cappadocians was to define how each distinct *hypostasis*, personality, of Father, Son and Holy Spirit, could exist within the single Godhead. They had the intellectual advantage over Athanasius in that they were able to draw without inhibition from pagan philosophy. Much of their terminology seems to derive, for instance, from the Neoplatonist philosopher Plotinus, the greatest spiritual mind of the third century and among the finest philosophers of the classical world. Plotinus had also posited three divine entities, 'the One', an all-pervading 'Intellect', which conveys the Platonic Forms to the material world, and a 'World-Soul'. They shared a common substance, yet each had a distinct role, and here again Plotinus used the word *hypostasis*. So he provided a pagan framework that could be incorporated into Christianity. Yet the only way in which any one formula could be declared as supreme above the others was by imposition from above.

By 380, Constantinople was a predominantly Christian city and it had gained a reputation for buzzing with theological discussion. When Gregory of Nyssa visited in 381 he found that even the bath attendants were discussing the relationship of Father to Son. It is important to capture this moment, the last in the empire's history when different Christian traditions were free to express themselves.

The majority of the Christian population was still Homoian subordinationist, led by the bishop of the city, Demophilus, who had taken office in 370.

The Homoians still distinguished themselves from the Eunomians but, twenty years on from his rejection by Constantius and undaunted by the attacks on his theology by Basil and others, Eunomius was still full of energy. In 380, in fact, he is known to have been preaching to enthusiastic crowds at Chalcedon just across the Bosporus from Constantinople. His so-called *Second Apology* survives from these years as does a statement of his views made for the emperor Theodosius in 383.

In these Eunomius ruthlessly analyses the division between Father and Son, stressing again the impossibility of anything of the Father's substance being passed on to the Son. Eunomius may have irritated everyone by the relentlessness of his logic (he was taunted by his enemies for having Aristotle as his bishop!) but he played a vital part in helping to clarify the issues, especially by exposing the vagueness of the term *homoios*. He certainly had a point. There are no less than twelve known Homoian creeds, including one by the missionary Ulfilas. Gregory of Nazianzus remarked that '*homoios* was a figure seeming to look in the direction of all who passed by, a boot fitting either foot, a winnowing with every wind'.[3]

While Eunomius was expounding his views in Chalcedon, a small congregation of Nicene believers, drawn mainly from the administrative elite of Constantinople, was receiving a series of high-level orations from Gregory of Nazianzus who had been appointed their priest. The five so-called *Theological Orations* are the fullest and most coherent statement of Nicene orthodoxy. Gregory starts by explaining that only those who have reflected deeply on theology can expound it – a rebuke to the chattering bath attendants and others who were debating the issues on the streets. He proceeds by talking each major issue through, often courageously so by quoting the subordinationist case through its scriptures and attempting to refute each text. He admits that there are weaknesses in the Nicene case: he struggles, as did every Nicene, with the problem of how a Jesus 'one in substance with the Father' could suffer and he has to confess that there is no agreement on the nature of the Holy Spirit. His attempts to deal with the verses from the gospels that talk of Jesus' inferiority to the Father are not always convincing. Even so the orations remain a *tour de force* and were recognised as such for generations to come.

Yet as the debates continued in Constantinople, a shadow hovered over the city. In January 380 a new emperor of the east, a Spanish general named Theodosius, had issued an edict, not a law as such but a statement of his intent, from Thessalonika. Directed specifically at the people of his capital it announced that henceforth they must believe in a single deity 'of the Father, Son and the Holy Ghost under the concept of equal majesty and of the Holy Trinity'. Any other belief was 'demented and insane' and would incur both the wrath of God and the secular punishment of the emperor.

CHAPTER TWENTY-FOUR

The Stifling of Christian Diversity

THEODOSIUS' ROOTS WERE IN THE CHRISTIAN ARISTOCRACY OF Spain. He had been appointed emperor of the east in 379 at a moment of great crisis. Valentinian, probably the last Roman emperor to be able to mount effective assaults on the barbarian tribes, had died in 375. His successor in the western empire, his son Gratian, was only sixteen. Valentinian's brother, Valens, still ruled over the eastern empire but in 378 he was killed in a devastating defeat at Adrianople by an army of Goths. The victorious Gothic bands were never strong enough to take any major cities but they had humiliated the empire and they now disrupted much of its administrative framework in the Balkans as they plundered the countryside. It was at this desperate moment that Gratian appointed Theodosius, who had already proved himself as a successful general while in his twenties, as Valens' successor.[1]

Theodosius was still not baptised in 379 but he had an austere faith and had absorbed, as his edict suggested, belief in a Trinity of Father, Son and Holy Ghost of equal majesty. When he arrived at Thessalonika in 380 to lead the counter-attack against the Goths, he was baptised by the city's bishop, Acholius, who was firmly committed to Nicaea. As a Latin speaker, Theodosius probably knew little of the rich tradition of theological debate in the east, but he believed in bringing his new Christian subjects more fully under state control. The edict from Thessalonika was the first intimation of the new policy.

Theodosius approached the challenge of imposing uniformity of belief astutely. He announced the outlines of his 'creed' and promulgated it as a law before he sought the comments of the bishops. This was to be a political rather than theological coup. So, as soon as he had entered his capital, Constantinople, for the first time, in November 380, he summoned Bishop Demophilus and asked him to renounce his Homoian beliefs in favour of the formula of 'equal majesty'. To his credit, Demophilus refused. He was deposed and Theodosius turned to Gregory of Nazianzus whose *Theological Orations* were compatible with the emperor's own beliefs. Even though his 'Nicene' congregation made up only a small minority of the city's Christian population, Gregory was astonished to find himself the new bishop. To ensure his safety from the Homoian masses, troops had to line the streets and even take up guard inside the Church of the Holy Apostles where his enthronement took place.

Theodosius now moved to impose his faith across the eastern empire. In a surviving *epistula*, a formal letter imposing a law, issued to the prefect of Illyricum in January 381, Theodosius insisted that only those who affirmed 'the faith of Nicaea' could now be appointed bishops. The details of what this meant were left somewhat vague in the letter. Father and Son had to be accepted as 'under one name' but there was no specific mention of *homoousios*. The Holy Spirit was given no special status – it was simply stated that 'it should not be violated by being denied'. However, there were sweeping condemnations of 'the poison of the Arian sacrilege' and 'the crime of the Eunomian heresy'.

There was no mercy shown to those who were now classified as 'insane and demented heretics'. They had to surrender their churches to those clergy who came within Theodosius' definition, lose any tax exemptions they had and they could not build replacement churches within the city walls. Any open protest was to be met with expulsion of the dissenters from the city. A few months later, even the building of churches outside the walls was forbidden. There is a record from some years later of the resolute Demophilus still conducting open-air services for his expelled Homoian congregation. It is not known whether similar laws were issued to the prefects of other parts of the east but the letter to Illyricum concluded with a declaration of its aim 'that the whole world might be restored to orthodox bishops who hold the Nicene faith' and there are records of expulsions of Homoians in provinces outside Illyricum.

With the law now in place, Theodosius summoned to Constantinople a council of bishops who were known to be committed to Nicaea to endorse it. These had already made themselves known at an assembly held in Antioch by Meletius, the city's Nicene bishop, in 379, but it was a limited group. There were no bishops recorded from Illyricum or Egypt and the representatives from western Asia were followers of one Macedonius whose loyalty to the Nicene creed was such that they would not accept the divinity of the Holy Spirit. The Nicene creed asked no more than to 'believe in the Holy Spirit' and the 'Macedonians' clung rigidly to this limited phrase. Any attempt to revise the creed so as to give the Holy Spirit equality with Father and Son was bound to offend them.

The council began with a setback. Meletius died soon after his arrival. Not only had the council lost an apparently efficient and charismatic president, but a dispute immediately broke out as to who should be his successor as bishop of Antioch. This might have been resolved if the presidency of the council had not been taken over by the newly appointed bishop of Constantinople, Gregory of

Nazianzus. Gregory may have been a consummate theologian but he was hopelessly out of his depth in a leadership role. He endorsed an unpopular candidate, one Paulinus, as Meletius' replacement in Antioch, refused to back down when defeated and instead berated the council for not backing his personal interpretation of the Nicene formula which insisted that the Holy Spirit be given an elevated status as 'one in substance' with Father and Son. He resigned, leaving a bitter description of his fellow bishops as 'a mob of wild young men'. A walkout of the 'Macedonians' followed. Gregory, accused by his opponents, who had been strengthened by the arrival of some bishops from Egypt, of occupying his see unlawfully, in that he was still bishop of the remote Cappadocian town of Sasima, resigned the bishopric of Constantinople. It was now that he wrote that he had never attended a church council which 'produced deliverance from evils rather than the addition to them . . . rivalries and manoeuvres always prevail over reason'.[2]

Theodosius must have been taken aback by the uproar. He was, however, a pragmatic ruler. He seized the initiative by appointing a senator, Nectarius, as the council's new president. Nectarius was popular within the city and the bishops appear to have accepted him although he was only a catechumen and not yet baptised. It paid to have some form of bulwark against the dispossessed Homoians whose discontent must have been obvious to the visiting bishops. He was soon baptised and consecrated bishop of Constantinople. His theological deficiencies were remedied by instructing him in the Nicene faith. Theodosius now drove home his advantage. Constantinople was declared the second bishopric of the empire after Rome. It was an astonishing move but his policy was to link the ecclesiastical administration to the political and Constantinople deserved precedence as 'the second Rome'. The two most powerful bishoprics of the east could do little to stop him. Antioch was still vacant and the bishop of Alexandria, Timothy, had only just been installed. To keep them in their place, it was declared that no bishop could meddle in affairs outside his diocese. This was essentially a political coup against the church – Constantine would have approved.

At some point before the council was dissolved in July 381, it issued a revised version of the Nicene creed. The episode is shrouded in mystery because the new creed is only known from a declaration at the Council of Chalcedon in 451 when it was accredited to the council of 381. It is the version that is used today with the Holy Spirit elevated as 'the Lord and Life-giver'. There is no specific mention of the Trinity and certainly none of the consubstantiality of the Holy Spirit. As suggested earlier, the words appear drawn from Basil's *On the Holy Spirit*, although Basil himself had died in 379. There is no sign of any acknowledgement of Athanasius. It is probable that the creed could never have been promulgated in Constantinople while the council was in session because of the continuing hostility to Nicaea from the local population.

The creed which was passed at Constantinople in 381 runs as follows:

We believe in one God Father Almighty, maker of heaven and earth and all things, seen and unseen;

And in one Lord Jesus Christ the Son of God, the Only-begotten, begotten by his Father before all ages, Light from Light, true God from true God, begotten not made, consubstantial [*homoousios*] with the Father, through whom all things came into existence, who for us men and for our salvation came down from the heavens and became incarnate by the Holy Spirit and the Virgin Mary and became a man, and was crucified for us under Pontius Pilate and suffered and was buried and rose again on the third day in accordance with the Scriptures and ascended into the heavens and is seated at the right hand of the Father and will come again to judge the living and the dead, and there will be no end to his kingdom;

And in the Holy Spirit, the Lord and Life-giver, who proceeds from the Father, who is worshipped and glorified together with the Father and the Son, who spoke by the prophets;

And in one holy, catholic and apostolic Church;

We confess one baptism for the forgiveness of sins;

We wait for the resurrection of the dead and the life of the coming age, Amen.

The anathemas against Arius have been dropped in this version and the Holy Spirit given a higher status, although there is no mention of a Trinity in which it is a consubstantial member. Those who preach 'one baptism' have won out over those who believe in rebaptism, and the resurrection of the dead is now accepted. Note also the insistence that there is a single catholic (in this context 'universal') church based on the apostolic succession.

With the conclusion of the council, Theodosius issued a new set of *epistulae* to his civil servants asking them to impose the new faith. Again this was defined somewhat vaguely, as belief in Father, Son and Holy Spirit as one in majesty, power, glory, splendour and divinity. Some distinction between the three was maintained by acknowledging each as a *persona* (all imperial laws were issued in Latin and this was the closest equivalent to the Greek *hypostasis*). Theodosius had learned the lesson that any attempt to use a more precise terminology was likely to be thwarted by renewed debate and instead he nominated bishops for each diocese who would issue certificates of orthodoxy to their clergy without which they could not be promoted to bishoprics. It was a neat way of distancing himself from further wrangling.

Not surprisingly disorder broke out as the new laws were enforced. The church had built up so much wealth and enjoyed so many privileges that expelling the 'Arians' from their churches was explosive. One pro-Nicene historian, writing in the next century, talks of '[Arian] wolves harrying the flocks up and down the glades, daring to hold rival assemblies, stirring sedition among the people, and shrinking from nothing which can do damage to the churches'. The unrest was so extensive that Theodosius wavered. In 383 he called another, smaller council, perhaps more remarkable than the selective assembly of 381 in that he asked representatives of all the main schools to attend. There was Nectarius, of course, in his new role as bishop of Constantinople, Demophilus and even Eunomius himself. The Macedonians sent one of their bishops. The emperor asked each leader to provide a statement of his own beliefs. He hoped that some kind of consensus could be reached by comparing them. Once again, however, the discussions became acrimonious. The historian Sozomen records that the laity present were infuriated by the way the bickering between bishops discredited them before the emperor. Losing patience, Theodosius announced that he would accept only the creed of Nectarius (which had been drawn up for the former pagan by Nicene theologians) and that all other views were heretical. He issued a new set of laws against heretics.

Theodosius can hardly be blamed for his attempt to bring the empire into some kind of order and he doubtless felt that he was justified in doing this through the imposition of his Christian faith. He had the coercive power to do so and ultimately the church had no means of opposing his will. In effect, Theodosius had backed one faction, the Nicene, and isolated the rest. There was no way that those excluded, Eunomians and Homoians, could combine against him. By offering the wealth of the church to the victors, he was cementing his laws within a bedrock of privilege and patronage. The incentives for conformity were powerful.

Why did the emperor chose to support a Trinity of equal majesty rather than a subordinationist alternative? Certainly Theodosius represented the beliefs of his fellow aristocratic Christians in Spain and probably much of the western empire. The former provincial governor, Ambrose, now bishop of Milan, was ardent in the Nicene cause. Yet there were deeper ideological reasons why this class was so sympathetic to a Godhead in which Jesus was elevated into the divinity. The problem for anyone, emperor, senior administrator or aristocratic landowner, who was concerned with upholding the hierarchical structure of the empire, was that the Jesus of the gospels was a rebel against the empire and had been executed by one of its provincial governors. He had preached the immediate coming of the kingdom in which the poor would inherit the earth, hardly what the elite wished to hear at a time of intense danger. There was an incentive to shift the emphasis from the gospels to the divine Jesus, as pre-existent to the Incarnation and of high status 'at the right hand of the Father'. One can see the shift in Eusebius' description of Christ in his *Oration to Constantine*, 'the great High Priest of the mighty God', quoted earlier. The Jesus of the gospels had again been ignored.

One of the most extraordinary manifestations of this elevation of Christ is to be found in *De fide*, a defence of the Nicene faith written by Ambrose, bishop of Milan. In *De fide* Ambrose equates victory in war with acceptance of the Nicene creed and points out that the Homoians are always losing battles because they insult God through their heresy – an argument which was to be extended by later Nicene historians to provide an explanation for the Homoian Valens' defeat at Adrianople. Remarkably, Ambrose announces that Christ is the 'leader of the legions', a bizarre distortion of the historical reality but one that reflects the imperial ideology within which the church now operated. By 390, in the church of San Pudenziana in Rome, Christ is shown 'in majesty' as an imperial magistrate. The equation between Nicene orthodoxy and the administrative classes can be supported by details of the only independent Nicene congregation recorded – that ministered to by Gregory of Nazianzus in Constantinople and made up largely of civil servants and the city's elite.

The imposition of the Nicene creed was motivated as much by politics as theology. Imposed through imperial law, accepted by a council presided over by a hastily converted senator, it was the theological formula which most fully met the needs of the empire for an ideology of good order under the auspices of God. Yet histories of Christian doctrine still talk of the Nicene solution as if it had floated down from heaven and had been recognised by the bishops as the only possible formula to describe the three members of the Trinity. In reality, Theodosius brought the belief from his native Spain to the eastern empire where the matter was still unresolved and then imposed it by law before calling a hand-picked council on the matter. One result of this was that the church was unable to provide reasoned support for the Nicene Trinity and it is still referred to in the Roman Catholic catechism as a mystery of faith, a revelation of God 'that is inaccessible to reason alone'. Athanasius and the Cappadocian Fathers became the bulwarks of orthodoxy, their opponents denounced as heretical. Only recently has Theodosius' considerable role in settling the great theological debates been recognised.

CHAPTER TWENTY-FIVE

The Assault on Paganism

THEODOSIUS WAS A PRAGMATIST. BY 382 HE HAD ACCEPTED THE inevitable and come to an agreement by which the Gothic victors of Adrianople were allowed to settle in Thrace and declare themselves allies of the Roman state. While this brought peace, the forced compromise did not augur well for the future of the empire. There was another major blow to the empire in the summer of 383 when the commander of the British legions, Magnus Maximus, revolted against the rule of Gratian, the young emperor in the west, and crossed over to Gaul. Gratian's credibility was shattered as his authority collapsed across the north-western empire and he was assassinated by his own men as he marched north to confront the usurper. This left his young brother, Valentinian II, still only twelve, as nominal emperor in the west. In 387 Maximus moved on into Italy forcing Valentinian and his mother Justina to flee eastwards to Thessalonika in search of Theodosius' help. Theodosius' counter-attack proved successful. Maximus was killed and Theodosius moved into Milan which, thanks to its central position in northern Italy, had become the imperial command post of the western empire. He was now effectively the ruler of the whole empire and he began grooming his two sons, Arcadius and Honorius, for the succession.

In Milan Theodosius encountered Ambrose, the formidable bishop of the city. Ambrose had been a local provincial governor who had become bishop in 374 at a time of disorder among the Christian factions there.[1] Ambrose was typical of the administrative class in that he was an enthusiast for Nicaea. He was also a champion of church authority and had shown no inhibitions about imposing his will within his own diocese and in the western church whenever he had the chance. He did so without scruple. In 381, at a small council that he stage-managed at Aquileia, Ambrose had browbeaten the much-respected subordinationist bishop of Ratiaria, Palladius, into submission. Two years later a delegation arrived from Rome to petition with Valentinian II for the restoration of the Altar of Victory to the senate house in

Rome from where it had been removed by Christians. Its leader, the pagan senator Symmachus, had pleaded for tolerance on the grounds that it was essential to respect the different paths by which the truth might be found. More emotionally, he asked for respect for the religious beliefs that his ancestors had followed for centuries: 'Allow us, as old men, to leave for posterity what we received as boys.' Ambrose's retort, relayed to the emperor, was sharp and unrelenting: 'The only salvation comes from the Christian God: all pagan gods are devils.' The young Valentinian acquiesced to his bishop's demands.

Valentinian and his mother Justina, the widow of Valentinian I, were Homoians but when they had tried to secure a church for their own worship in the city in 385, the Nicene Ambrose had once again been obstructive. He organised demonstrations, occupied churches, and in one remarkable coup announced the discovery of the bodies of two martyrs from the persecutions of earlier times. The fresh blood on their bones and the miracles these effected were, he announced with considerable imagination, evidence of the support of the Nicene God. He manipulated the credulity of his congregation so effectively that Valentinian and Justina were completely outmanoeuvred. It was at this moment of their humiliation that Maximus chose to invade Italy in 387.

With Maximus defeated and the Nicene Theodosius now in Milan one might have hoped that Ambrose would have been satisfied. Yet his ambition was to achieve a personal ascendancy over the emperor and he searched for a way in which he could dress this in a theological cloak. In 388 news reached the emperor that a Christian mob led by its bishop had sacked a Jewish synagogue in Callinicum, a city on the Euphrates. Theodosius had ordered the bishop to restore the building. Ambrose was having none of it. He declared that there must be no building where Christ was denied and that it was unjustified to ask a bishop to betray his conscience by restoring a synagogue. He even said that he would be prepared to assume responsibility for the burning of the building himself. Theodosius quietly backed down.

The initiation of such violence against Jewish and pagan shrines was not new. Many of the 'miracles' accredited to Martin of Tours, an associate of Hilary of Poitiers, in the 370s in Gaul involved the destruction of pagan shrines. Several of Theodosius' senior officials in his eastern administration had come with him from the west and brought their own fanatical impulses with them. Maternus Cynegius, appointed prefect of the east by Theodosius, is associated with the destruction of the great temple complex at Edessa. These officials were supported by roving bands of monks. The pagan orator Libanius complained in an oration of 386 of 'the black-robed tribe who hasten to attack the temples with sticks and stone and bars of iron . . . utter desolation follows, with the stripping of roofs, demolition of walls, the tearing down of statues'. The archaeological evidence of destruction is extensive.[2]

Theodosius' initial reaction to Callinicum suggests that he was increasingly worried by this vandalism. He may have acquiesced to Ambrose's demands over Callinicum in 388 but in 390 he ordered monks to avoid cities and retire instead to the deserts. One reason for restraint was that paganism was still strong, particularly in cities such as Rome where the senatorial aristocracy remained largely unconverted. Provocation made no sense when the empire was still so unsettled. In 389, the emperor visited the ancient capital. The incentive for the visit was the need to present his son Honorius to the senate, still made up of the pagan aristocracy, in the hope that his legitimacy as Theodosius' eventual successor in the western empire would be recognised. Theodosius was greeted with all the traditional reverence accorded to respected emperors; he was compared to Augustus and Trajan, and even to the pagan gods, Jupiter and Hercules. In return Theodosius overlooked the support the senate had given Maximus. The peaceful consolidation of his power had priority and he awarded some of the more prominent senators posts in the imperial administration of Italy and North Africa.

By 390 Theodosius might have had cause for satisfaction. He had defended the borders of the empire from invasion and seen off the revolt of Maximus. Some form of peace with the Goths had been achieved. He had organised the church under his auspices and the empire was now officially Nicene. It was therefore tragic that an incident in Thessalonika threatened his image as the serene emperor. The governor of this important city, Butheric, a Goth who headed a garrison of Gothic troops, had arrested a popular chario-teer on a charge of homosexual rape. The crowds had erupted and Butheric and several of his officials had been murdered. Theodosius ordered retalia-tion. It appears that his temper had got the better of him, although it may be that his orders were elaborated by one of his officials, Flavius Rufinus, known to be ruthless, as they travelled eastwards. The result was a vicious massacre of the insurgents, many of whom were rounded up in the hippodrome and slaughtered. Even more serious than the loss of life was the spectre of an emperor who had lost his self-control. Emperors were expected to exist as if they were above the turmoil of everyday life and his display of petulance was unforgivable.

What happened next is difficult to assess as only Ambrose's account survives. In this, Ambrose refused Theodosius communion until he had made public penance in the cathedral. Theodosius did, in fact, come to the cathedral but it may have been on his own initiative to use the building for a stage-managed public display of *humilitas*, the most effective way he knew of redressing the situation. Whatever the truth, Ambrose was able to publicly declare, at Theodosius' funeral in 395, that the emperor had recognised the moral supremacy of the church over the actions of an emperor.

It was soon after this that Theodosius embarked on a sweeping programme aimed at the suppression of paganism. It was an unexpected development, especially in view of his conciliatory attitude to the aristocrats in Rome. Traditionally, this volte-face has been seen as a response to Ambrose's consolidation of his victory over the emperor but, in 391, when the first laws were promulgated, Theodosius was heading back to Constantinople and so was outside Ambrose's ambit. A more plausible explanation lies in the growing power of Flavius Rufinus. Rufinus' official title in Milan had been *magister officiorum*, 'head of the offices', a powerful position in the court. Rufinus is known to have been fanatical in his Christian belief and determined to take one of the top posts in the eastern administration. This meant ousting Tatianus, the praetorian prefect, who was a pagan. The harsh laws of 391 to 392 against paganism appear to be related to the power struggle, those of 391 having been passed when Theodosius was on the way back to the capital with Rufinus. Sacrificing was forbidden, as it had been before, but now entry to pagan shrines was banned as well. In April 392 the monks were released from all restrictions on their movements and once more were free to rampage among pagan shrines.

In the summer of 392, Tatianus was deposed and the triumphant Rufinus, who inherited his post as praetorian prefect of the east, issued a wide-ranging law against paganism. Any activity associated with pagan rites was suppressed and any symbol of paganism was banned. Officials could even enter homes in search of offensive material. There was simply no precedent for such a sweeping law. To find an equivalent one would have to go back to mid-fourteenth century BC Egypt when the pharaoh Akhenaten was banning all rivals to his god Aten. Akhenaten's campaign collapsed with his death; Theodosius' proved permanent.

The immediate results are well documented. While it is true that many pagan cults and festivals were in decline, they were still being celebrated. Recent excavations at Olympia suggest that games were thriving at the 291st Olympiad in 381 while archaeological research confirms that the temples in the Roman forum were being restored in the 380s. By the 390s, on the other hand, Jerome was reporting that 'the gilded Capitol falls into disrepair, dust and cobwebs cover all Rome's temples . . . The city shakes on its foundations, and a stream of people hurries, past half-fallen shrines, to the tombs of the martyrs.' Jerome approvingly recorded the sacking of a temple of Mithras and indeed excavations under the church of St Prisca on the Aventine Hill have uncovered a ruined Mithraeum on which the church was built. (The destruction of temples to Mithras is well documented – with their initiation rites, internal hierarchies and welcoming of free citizen, slave and freedman, they appear to have been rivals to the Christian communities.) Symbolically the most important moment came with the demolition in Alexandria of the Serapeion, regarded as the greatest complex of religious buildings outside Rome, by a Christian mob led by their bishop, Theophilus.

These years saw the beginning of the end of the pagan world. The Olympic games had been inaugurated in the eighth century BC; they were held for the last time in 393. In Egypt, the use of hieroglyphics had survived through centuries of Greek and Roman rule: the very last date from 394 and it was to be over fourteen centuries before anyone could again read them. Eusebius had already rejoiced that Christ had 'redeemed even the souls of the Egyptians from such a disease of lasting and continued blindness'. Throughout the empire shrines were destroyed, temples recreated as Christian churches, and buildings such as bathhouses (naked public bathing was now frowned upon) vandalised. Porphyry, the bishop of Gaza, visited the imperial court in 400 and managed to persuade the emperor Arcadius to provide him with troops to sack the main temple in the city. As the temple burned, neighbouring homes were raided for books and 'idols' that were either burned or thrown into the public latrines.

There was a final drama in Theodosius' reign. Valentinian had been isolated in Gaul and in 392 he appears to have committed suicide. His senior general Arbogast elevated one Eugenius as a replacement emperor. Eugenius had links to the eastern court and Arbogast may have hoped that Theodosius would acquiesce to the promotion. There was never much chance of this as Theodosius' dynastic ambitions for his son, Honorius, as well as his campaign to enforce Christianity, risked being thwarted by the usurper. Furthermore, while Eugenius was nominally a Christian, he showed himself receptive to paganism, and his promotion released an outburst of resentment against the anti-pagan laws. The old cults were revived in the Latin west, the Altar of Victory was returned to the senate house in Rome. Theodosius had little option but to return to Italy to confront Eugenius. The two sides met at the river Frigidus in September 394. It was a closely fought battle and Theodosius was lucky to win it. Many of his Gothic allies were killed in the first onslaught and it was said that it was only the icy blasts of the notorious *bora* that swept across the battlefield at a crucial moment the next day that brought him victory.

The battle of the river Frigidus was rewritten, notably by the fifth-century historian Theodoret, as the triumph of Christianity over paganism, the appearance of the *bora* itself a miracle from God. Ambrose was, of course, an important propagandist for this approach to events. He had his chance just a few months later, in January 395, on the death of Theodosius. The funeral oration he gave in one of his grand new churches in Milan is a fascinating one.[3] Ambrose creates the idea of a Christian dynasty, inaugurated by Constantine. Here is the earliest recorded account of the finding of the True Cross by Constantine's mother, Helena. Ambrose even tells how Constantine incorporated a nail from the cross in his horse's bridle so fulfilling the prophecy of Zechariah, 14:20: 'In that day that which is upon the bridle of the horse shall be holy to the Lord Almighty.' Theodosius, and now his sons Honorius and Arcadius, carry on God's will. In a sermon relying heavily on Old Testament texts, the victories of Theodosius are compared to that of Elisha over the Syrians in the Book of Kings. Ambrose cannot resist dwelling on Theodosius' repentance after Thessalonika: 'He wept publicly for his sin . . . he prayed for pardon with groans and with tears . . . What private citizens are ashamed to do, the emperor was not ashamed to do.' This subjugation of the emperor to the will of God and the church had, Ambrose assured his listeners, ensured his glory in heaven. This supremacy was embedded in western theology in the works of Augustine and Thomas Aquinas and the precedent of Thessalonika was used for the excommunication of the Holy Roman emperor Henry IV by pope Gregory VII in the 1070s.

The survival of Theodosius as emperor had been remarkable, especially in view of the vulnerable position he found himself in in 379 and the continuing challenges to the empire from usurpers. He had showed himself to be immensely resilient and able to compromise when necessary. His attempt to bring the church under the auspices of the state was understandable even if in his comparative moderation he was outmanoeuvred by determined churchmen and the more fanatical of his Christian officials. Yet he presided over a turning point in the history of western thought. The result of the Council of Constantinople (for which read Theodosius' laws), was 'to reduce the meanings of the word "God" from a very large selection of alternatives to one only' with the result that 'when Western man today says "God" he means the one sole, exclusive [Trinitarian] God and nothing else'.[4] Freedom of debate on the nature of the supernatural was under threat. For the pagan world this meant an assault on secular philosophy, for Christians on the many alternative ways of exploring God and his relationship with Father and Son and hence the possibility of high-quality and creative theological discourse.

The Nicene faith that had been imposed on the empire was never theologically coherent. The confusion over how one substance could exist in both 'unbegotten' and 'begotten' forms without losing its 'sameness' had not been resolved. The Council of Constantinople had failed to clarify the confusion. In fact, when one remembers the impressive debates which had taken place since 325, their contribution to the making of the creed of 381 was meagre. Yet, once Theodosius had applied the coercive powers of the state to the matter, the church had little option but to acquiesce to the Nicene formula. In return for this the church had achieved a structure and status that would enable it to survive through the ensuing centuries. When the Nicene creed was finally adopted in the west (by Rome only in 1014), it had become a ritualistic text and the theological inconsistencies it contained were beyond the reach of reasoned debate.

It was perhaps inevitable that Theodosius would also launch an assault on paganism, even if the immediate catalysts for his campaign are not obvious. One can hardly proclaim that there is only one correct form of Christian belief but at the same time allow all its pagan rivals to continue unmolested. Christians themselves were fuelled by the Old Testament texts that encouraged them to destroy the altars of the infidels. While emperors were reluctant to condone disorder they were hardly in a position to prevent it when they had done so much to shape an expansionist church as an integrated part of the empire. What was now lost was a tradition of intellectual diversity which was centuries old. No longer was the world seen as a place to be actively explored and understood; it was assumed instead to be the unchanging creation of God. The Jesus of the gospels had been elevated into the Godhead and centuries of subordinationist belief wiped out. Many histories of Christianity still fail to acknowledge that subordinationism was the dominant and virtually unchallenged theology of the early church.

'No one is honoured before him'

THE RISE OF THE BISHOP

'THE PEAK OF NOBILITY IS TO BE RECKONED AMONG THE SONS OF God.' This extraordinary statement made by Hilary, bishop of Arles between 429 and his death in 449, sums up the dramatic change of status that Constantine brought to the bishops. Hilary is echoed by John Chrysostom, the bishop of Constantinople: 'Prefects and city magistrates do not enjoy such honour as the magistrate of the church; for if he enters the palace, who ranks the highest, or among the matrons, or among the houses of the great. No one is honoured before him.' The resources that were now available to the church underpinned this elevated status. The patronage of the emperors, the surrender of their riches by ascetics, the offerings of the faithful, contributed to the creation of a wealthy community. Ammianus Marcellinus describes how the bishops of Rome 'are assured of rich gifts from ladies of quality; they can ride in carriages, dress splendidly and outdo kings in the lavishness of their table'.

Clearly this was not the whole picture. The number of bishops multiplied in these years – it is estimated that there were two thousand in the empire by the mid-fifth century. In those parts of the empire that had experienced schism, northern Africa, for instance, where even as late as 411 over three hundred Donatist bishops turned up to a council held at Carthage, there might have been two or more rival bishops in a small town. The remoter of the cities were unpopular assignments. When Basil of Caesarea appointed his friend Gregory of Nazianzus to the town of Sasima in Cappadocia, Gregory was deeply offended. One can imagine the condescension in his voice as he describes 'an utterly dreadful, pokey little hole, a place wholly devoid of water, vegetation and the company of gentlemen'. He refused to move there, retiring to a monastery instead. He was as dismissive of his fellow bishops in such areas, complaining of former labourers, money changers, sailors still smelling of bilge water and blacksmiths who had not yet washed the soot off their backs, 'dung-beetles headed for the skies' as he snobbishly put it. Whatever the brilliance of his mind, it had not tempered the disdain of his class towards those without *paideia*.

The church now offered a viable and prestigious career with many bishops being recruited directly from the civil service. Ambrose of Milan and Paulinus of Nola had both held governorships in Italy; the bishop of Cyzicus, Eleusius, had served in the imperial civil service; the father of Gregory of Nazianzus, another Gregory, had been a magistrate before becoming bishop of Nazianzus. Martin of Tours and several of his fellow bishops in Gaul had been army officers. Augustine held the prestigious post of city orator in Milan before his conversion. There were even cases of distinguished civil servants being 'awarded' a bishopric as an end-of-service post. Often the traditional roles of the elite were absorbed in the work of the bishop. Basil of Caesarea is found negotiating tax exemptions for petitioners in much the same way a patron would have done in earlier days.

Yet the core of a bishop's responsibilities lay where they had always been, with the care of their junior clergy and congregations, the administration of the sacraments, 'discharging the venerable mysteries', as one fifth-century bishop put it, and the overseeing of the needs of the Christian poor. The effective bishop had to add spiritual charisma to any administrative skills he might have. There had been much discussion by the earlier church fathers over the nature of a bishop's authority. Clement of Alexandria had taught that it could only grow out of a life based on an imitation of Christ. His instincts as a philosopher led him to define three roles: one of contemplation, one of fulfilling the commandments and one of leading others towards virtue. Origen went further in stressing the importance of the ascetic lifestyle, in essence the transferring of bodily desires into a mind that transcended them and released new spiritual and mental energies as a result. The problem lay in reconciling these holy men with the messy politics and power struggles of everyday life in the church. Spiritual power and administrative ability did not often mix. Those who had transcended the material world were not always eager to engage in the networking needed to secure election as a bishop and the ascetic living a withdrawn life in the desert was always a potential threat to the authority of the more worldly bishops.

A good example of a bishop who retained his saintliness despite the pressures to exploit the status of the position is the aristocratic Paulinus, a former governor of Campania (*c.*354–431). Paulinus renounced his vast estates, was ordained and eventually became bishop of Nola, in southern Italy, where he created a shrine to the local saint, Felix, alongside a hospital and other benefactions to the local community, including an aqueduct. He thought deeply about how to convey the teachings of Christ and his hero Felix to pilgrims to the shrine. On each of Felix's anniversaries he would compose a poem for his visitors that praised the more humble of Christian virtues. Paulinus is the first known clergyman to use the decoration of his church for instruction of the illiterate. Over the apse was a mosaic depicting the Trinity, with God as a hand from above, Christ as a Lamb and the Holy Spirit as a dove. In a portico facing an adjoining courtyard, a cycle of frescoes from the Old and New Testaments was designed to offer simple moral guidance 'for those not able to read and long accustomed to pagan cults'. Figures from the Old Testament were included to provide examples of holy living with accompanying texts for those who could read.[1]

For others, however, the public display of their status seemed to dominate. Many bishops' palaces echoed those of provincial governors with their audience halls and separate rooms for banqueting. Their churches were even more magnificent. While city life was on the whole losing vitality (this has to be a generalisation as many cities in the east were still flourishing into the sixth century but Ambrose, for instance, describes the once prosperous cities along the Via Emilia in northern Italy as 'corpses') there was a massive shift of resources towards church building. Many initiatives were local. Eugenius, bishop of Laodicea, a former provincial administrator who married into a senatorial family, had the opportunity to build a new church in Constantine's reign. In his epitaph he proclaimed that he 'had built the whole church from its foundations and provided all the adornments around it, namely the colonnades, the porticoes, paintings, mosaics, the fountain and the atrium'. Others had the support of the emperor. So the brilliantly decorated Golden Octagon in Antioch, completed in 341, was next to the imperial palace and acted both as a cathedral and a focus for the emperor's ceremonial occasions when he was in residence.

The greatest builder of all was Ambrose in Milan. He had inherited a vast cathedral built earlier in the century but he ringed the city with new basilicas built on the burial places of martyrs, following a pattern already established in Rome. This was an ambitious programme and established the bishop as a major employer of labourers, especially craftsmen skilled in stoneworking and mosaic-laying. It was typical of the man that he is the first bishop recorded to have built a church, the Basilica Ambrosiana, for the reception of his own bones. He was innovative in making relics a prominent focus of all his churches, obtaining *brandea*, cloths which had touched sacred bones, in this instance, those of Peter and Paul, for his Basilica Apostolorum. Theodosius gave him relics of the apostles John, Andrew and Thomas, for his foundations. This was a new and important way of advertising a church and city's presence to the wider world and those churches with the most prestigious relics became the focus of pilgrimage. This meshing of spiritual and political power was to prove essential for the long-term survival of the church, especially in the west when the structure of imperial government collapsed there.

A building programme less centred on self-glorification was the 'new city' that Basil built outside Caesarea (in Cappadocia) for the poor and lepers. This was begun in about 370 and was gradually extended over the next decade so it contained not only a large church but an impressive residence for the supervisor of the complex and his clergy (so grand, Basil writes, that magistrates themselves would be happy to reside there), hospices for visitors and the sick and accommodation for nurses and physicians. In his Funeral Oration for Basil (delivered in 379), Gregory of Nazianzus compares the city with the Seven Wonders of the World, suggesting it surpasses them because, unlike pagan shrines, it provided its patron with a swift ascent to heaven.

This Funeral Oration is often considered the finest of the age and marks the culmination of classical rhetoric, now transferred to a Christian setting. The speakers had learned their craft in the very best schools. John Chrysostom had been a pupil of the famous Antioch orator Libanius; Basil of Caesarea and Gregory of Nazianzus trained in Athens; Ambrose and Jerome were educated in Rome. Augustine studied rhetoric for three years in Carthage before becoming a teacher of rhetoric and then the city orator in Milan. These vast churches provided the bishops with a stage on which they could exercise their oratory and this enabled them to use congregations to achieve their spiritual and political ends. When there were tax riots in Antioch in 387 and statues of the emperor were defaced it was Bishop Flavian who hurried to Constantinople to plead, successfully as it turned out, with Theodosius for mercy. So here was a refocusing of an ancient art to new ends.

Perhaps the most accomplished orator of the age was John, known since the seventh century as John Chrysostom, John of the Golden Mouth. John was a superb speaker, coming down from his *cathedra* into the body of the church to magnify his effect. His sermons with their vivid imagery (he complained of how the rich were using silver chamber pots for their excrement while the poor maimed their own children in the hope of alms) brought continuous applause. John had made his reputation in Antioch with his dramatic sermons during that tense period in 387 when the city waited to see if the emperor would retaliate against those who had defaced his statues during the aforementioned tax riots. This, John warned his nervous audiences, would be how the Last Judgement would feel and they should learn from the experience. On a more scholarly level, he was one of the first preachers to explore Paul's letters in depth, again through a long series of sermons, and so helped give the apostle the prominence in Christian thought that proved permanent. (Augustine, as will be seen, was involved in much the same task in the west.) John's approach to the scriptures was literal, in contrast to the more allegorical Origenist approach adopted in Alexandria, and his sermons resonated with his audiences so well that some nine hundred, most of them from his time in Antioch, from where he was transferred to Constantinople in 397, have been preserved.

There were difficult boundaries here. The incentive to use rhetoric to arouse emotions often proved too great. The major targets, especially after 381, were pagans, heretics and Jews and the invective used against them was sweeping and polemical. The Jews were particularly hard hit. Many Christians still attended the synagogues or, in defiance of Nicaea, celebrated Easter on the same day as the Passover. John Chrysostom was furious. A series of sermons that he preached in 386 in Antioch is shocking in its tasteless denunciations of the synagogues as equivalent to brothels or dens of thieves. Accusing the Jews of every kind of perversity (including, of course, the murder of Christ) John dredged his way through the Old Testament in search of any displeasure shown by God to Israel, often taking texts out of context to do so.

These oratorical campaigns became part of the new Christian ideology. In 415, Severus, the bishop of Mahon in Minorca, set on fire a synagogue filled with its congregation after they had refused to debate with him. Many bishops played a leading part in the destruction of the pagan world. Alexandria, in particular, was known for its tempestuous bishops and the volatility of its population. The combination could be explosive. In 392 a Mithraeum had been demolished to make room for a new church. This caused a riot against the Christians in which hostages were taken and concealed in the complex of the Serapeion, the vast temple that dominated the city. The bishop of Alexandria, Theophilus, ascended the steps of the building and read out a letter from the emperor apparently denouncing the pagan gods. (This was presumably derived from Theodosius' anti-pagan legislation of that year.) It is not clear whether the pagans scattered or killed the hostages but Theophilus gave the signal to attack the statue of the god Serapis and then the buildings were razed to the ground. Part of the great library of Alexandria was included.

These stories of violence conflict with traditional pictures of bishops as respected upholders of good order.[2] Although there were many factors that made city life violent – scarcity of food, increases in taxation, or the flooding in of refugees – some were related to the rise of the church as an alternative centre of authority which found itself competing with other longer established communities in the cities. With the support of emperors from Constantine onwards the church felt that the tide was flowing in its favour. There was a confidence, even a self-righteousness, in the way bishops assailed their opponents. Once again the Old Testament provided a mass of texts that condoned the violence by providing examples of a jealous God wreaking vengeance on his enemies: 'Ye shall destroy their altars, break down their images, and cut down their groves . . . for the Lord, whose name is Jealous, is a Jealous God,' as Exodus puts it (34:13–14).

When the news of the destruction of the Serapeion reached him, Theodosius attempted to regain the initiative. He dismissed the city prefect, Evragius, for not preventing the violence and urged his successor to deal firmly with the rioters. Bishops who were determined to destroy paganism now had to act more carefully. Porphyry, the bishop of Gaza, went as far as to visit Constantinople to ask for imperial troops to help demolish the most important pagan temple there. By now Theodosius' son Arcadius was on the throne and, like his father, was reluctant to support such blatant destruction. He was prevailed upon by his empress, Eudoxia, and even her baby, the future Theodosius II, apparently made a sign that was taken as a gesture of approval. The tearing down of pagan statues became a badge of Christian holiness and Porphyry's triumph in Gaza was written up soon after his death in a hagiographic biography.[3]

There was another catalyst for violence. As bishops held their thrones for life, in contrast to the local governors who were often replaced after a year or two, promotion was slow and the death of a bishop might be the only moment when ambitious clerics could gain control of their local churches and their resources. Almost every election of which we have records was a violent one. Gregory of Nazianzus deplored a conflict that had broken out over even so unattractive a bishopric as Sasima. 'It was a no man's land between two rival bishops . . . . an occasion for the outbreak of a frightful brawl. The pretext was souls, but, in fact, it was desire for control, control of taxes and contributions which have the whole world in miserable confusion.' Damasus achieved the bishopric of Rome in 366 only after pitched battles in the streets following which 138 bodies were found in a basilica. Ambrose was appointed bishop of Milan, even before he had been baptised as a Christian, primarily to prevent unrest between squabbling factions. Bassanius, bishop of Ephesus, found himself assailed by a mob at Easter 448. He was taken from his church, beaten up and thrown into prison. A rival was installed and later some of Bassanius' supporters were found lying dead by the church door.

One of the most vicious power struggles was that which took place on the death of Theophilus in Alexandria in 412. His nephew Cyril was determined to succeed but faced intense opposition. He emerged triumphant but then launched violent attacks on his former opponents. These spread to the Jewish quarter of the city where synagogues were seized and Jews driven from their homes. The city prefect, Orestes, complained to the emperor (Theodosius II) about the disorder and the relationship between the church and state authorities broke down completely.

The matter had to be resolved if the secular administration was to retain its authority. It was an ancient custom that in times of unrest the city prefect would consult the philosophers of the city, who would give their counsel. They were promised *parrhesia*, complete freedom to speak their mind. Cyril claimed that the Christians had now assumed the role of advisers but Orestes snubbed him by choosing to consult the most respected of the pagan intellectuals of Alexandria, Hypatia, a woman of great integrity who was also an impressive mathematician and thoughtful commentator on the nature of religious belief. It was said that she backed Orestes in his refusal to support Cyril. Cyril in his turn spread rumours that Hypatia had cast spells on the Christians. In the rising tension, a deacon called Peter organised a lynching party. Hypatia was hauled from her carriage, her body was dragged through the streets and she was dismembered and burned. A seventh-century source describes how Cyril was hailed as 'the new Theophilus' in that he had followed the example of his predecessor and had now destroyed the last symbol of paganism in the city.

It was indeed a crucial moment in the conflict between traditional pagan thought and Christianity. The fate of Hypatia has been seen as the symbolic end of the era of Greek mathematics. It was particularly tragic as Hypatia had welcomed both Christians and pagans to her school and after her death many of her pagan students left for Athens to study there. As calm returned, even Christians began to realise the enormity of what had happened and we find the church historian Socrates, normally a supporter of church authority, openly criticising Cyril. The shocked emperor Theodosius tried to bring things back into order by commanding Cyril to reduce his 'bodyguard' to five hundred. It may be that it was outrages such as this that gave rise to a law in which Christians (named as such) who 'dare to lay violent hands on Jews and pagans who are living quietly and attempting nothing disorderly or contrary to law' are subject to heavy penalties.

The two areas where bishops provided the most effective service to the wider community were the law and care of the poor. Constantine had seen the opportunity to extend the role of the bishops as local magistrates.[4] A law of 318 deals with the procedures under which a case could be transferred from the secular to the ecclesiastical courts. At first this could take place if both parties agreed but later one party alone could take the initiative, in effect allowing a Christian to have his case judged by a man of his own faith. There is some evidence that the poor found it easier to have recourse to these courts and they became popular. Ambrose was to complain that he had to judge cases involving money, farms and even sheep. Augustine is found arbitrating between landlords and peasant tenants.

Very little is known of the legal procedures used by the courts. The basis of all jurisdiction remained Roman law. Many bishops had, of course, absorbed a legal training as part of their education. Ambrose was doing no more than transfer into an ecclesiastical context the skills he had already practised as a provincial governor. In the early fifth century the church courts took on an increasing responsibility for the enforcement of morals and the laws against pagans and heretics. Yet many of the cases involved arbitration and bishops appeared ready to adopt a specifically 'Christian' approach to their duties, especially in talking of the need to temper the harshness of traditional law with Christian charity. Others, notably Augustine, went further in backing judgements with reference to scripture. The Old Testament provided a host of references to the justice of the king, especially in upholding the rights of the oppressed. There is an emphasis in some records of the episcopal courts taking on reconciliation, in marital cases, for instance. Again there is fragmentary evidence from the 430s that the state encouraged the church courts to deal with the protection of orphans.

One traditional role of the clergy that remained intact was their concern for the poor. Jesus had taught that care for the sick and needy was central to the Christian mission. 'For now, by God's will, it is winter', preached Augustine. 'Think of the poor. Think of how the naked Christ can be clothed. Pay attention to Christ in the person of the poor, as he lies in the portico, as he suffers hunger, as he endures the cold.' The Old Testament precedents of the just king hearing the cries of the oppressed may have been an influence here.

There were, of course, pagan traditions by which 'bread and circuses' had been provided for the masses, not least to maintain social harmony. The emperors knew too well that hardship and subsequent rioting had resulted from any delay of the grain ships arriving in Rome each year. One of the most important developments of the age, initiated by Constantine, was the extension of the charitable functions of the church to encompass this established provisioning of food for the poor. There was, however, a different emphasis. Grain handouts by the emperors and other patrons tended to be targeted at a particular city and distributed primarily to buy off discontent in the hope of preserving the security of the elites. Christians talked instead of the poor as a group to be privileged with help because of their poverty.

It is hard to know whether the numbers of poor were increasing in this period. Standards of living in the empire were comparatively high compared to what they would become after its collapse and recent archaeological evidence shows many communities still thriving. However, marginal groups were acutely vulnerable. The Mediterranean climate was variable and famine often struck, made worse, the physician Galen reported, by the rapacity with which city dwellers stripped the rural areas for their own needs. The disruptions caused by wars and invasion were leading to a refugee problem. When Christians turned their focus on the poor, as they did with an intensity that had been lacking in pagan society, they found a mass of destitute, 'shivering in their nakedness, lean with hunger, parched with thirst, trembling with exhaustion and discoloured by undernourishment', as one preacher put it.[5] John Chrysostom estimated that 10 per cent of the population of Antioch lived in absolute poverty.

The poor had, of course, to compete with others for funds. The vast building programmes ate into resources that might have been spent on charity. One calculation of the cost of the gold alone for the apse vault of St John Lateran equates it to the provision of food for a year for twelve thousand poor. The revenues for the lighting of the basilica would have fed another fourteen hundred.[6] When Cyril of Alexandria launched a major programme of bribery to ensure that the emperor Theodosius supported him in a theological dispute in 431, the gold and other exotic gifts involved could have fed and clothed nineteen thousand poor for a year. This was the inevitable consequence of a church that now saw itself as a major player in a society where wealth and opulent display brought prestige and influence. Even ascetics who surrendered their wealth did not necessarily commit it to the needy. The enormously rich Melania settled on one of her estates in North Africa and began renouncing her wealth by endowing a local church so extravagantly that 'this church which formerly had been so very poor now stirred up the envy of all the other bishops in that province'.

However, what was achieved should not be dismissed. Basil of Caesarea's great complex was symbolic of numerous smaller projects, where bishops took it upon themselves to be 'the governor of the poor'. As the role became more institutionalised, each diocese seems to have drawn up its own list of deserving poor (the *matricula* as it was known in the Latin west) so that three thousand widows and orphans received help in fourth-century Antioch and there were 7,500 named poor in Alexandria in the early seventh century. The great parchment volume on which Gregory kept his list of poor in Rome survived until the ninth century. The special role of the bishops in helping prisoners is highlighted in an early fifth-century law in which the emperor orders the local governors to give clergy free access to prisons. There are even cases of clergy interviewing inmates to select those deserving of appeal, while Bishop Paul of Gerasa built a new prison to separate prisoners who had not yet been tried from those convicted.

Bishops were faced with many challenges. The church was attempting to expand its own boundaries against resilient and often resentful communities of Jews and pagans as well as the many Christian groups that had now been excluded by Theodosius' laws. It is fascinating to see the range of strategies they employed. On the one hand Ambrose survived, if precariously, his confrontations with the emperors. In Constantinople, on the other, John Chrysostom succeeded in building up a mass of support from the poor through the power of his sermons but, when challenged by rival bishops who exploited the offence he had caused the empress Eudoxia (see p. 299), the rioting that broke out in his favour only damaged his case. Unlike Ambrose, he had never learned how to build up a wider community that he could control to his own ends. He finished his life in exile. Other bishops, like Basil of Caesarea, were more successful in combining the traditional role of patron with a programme of charitable works that made their position unassailable. The Homoian emperor Valens respected the Nicene Basil so highly for his efficiency and keeping of good order that he even used him on official business.

The coming of Christianity involved much more than the extension of the teaching of the gospels to society. It required major shifts in the way power was exercised and wealth distributed – in ways that often seemed in conflict with each other. None of this involved a radical reordering of society. Very gradually bishops became the core of a conservatively structured society and with lasting effect. Twenty-six senior bishops of the Church of England are still entitled to places in the British House of Lords and over the centuries have often acted as upholders of aristocratic tradition.

The Art of Imperial Christianity

V ERY SOON AFTER CONSTANTINE'S EDICT OF TOLERATION OF 313, Aquileia, one of the richest cities of northern Italy, commissioned a great double basilica. One part was for catechumens, the other for those already baptised. Its floor was covered with rich mosaics only rediscovered under medieval silt in the early twentieth century. The themes are very similar to those of earlier Christian art: Jonah and the whale, fishermen and the Good Shepherd. Yet this was now an opulent and public display. Money from both Christian and imperial sources was poured into Christian buildings, their decoration and all the fittings, including jewelled gospel books, their illuminated pages and gold or ivory reliquaries.

There are a very few examples of halls set aside for Christian worship from before 312. After his 'conversion', Constantine adapted the traditional Roman audience hall, the basilica, to form the first public churches at the Lateran Palace (now St John Lateran) and over the burial place of St Peter. Early examples that survive in Rome are Santa Sabina and Santa Maria Maggiore, both from the early fifth century. Santa Sabina reused discarded Roman columns but is among the first buildings to join them with arches, an important development for later church architecture. Often an *atrium*, a covered entrance hall, stood in front of the entrance to the basilica. Paulinus of Nola recalls how pilgrims would wash themselves at the *atrium* to St Peter's before entering the shrine.

A very different centrally planned building form evolves for churches built as mausolea, or over the burial places of martyrs. While the first St Peter's is essentially a basilica shape with transepts, Santa Costanza, the mausoleum of Constantine's daughters Constantina and Helena just outside Rome, is circular with an ambulatory running below the central dome. The same format is used for baptisteries which were now built separately from churches to reflect the special nature of the ceremony and the large numbers of adults converting. Many baptisteries were octagonal, as it was believed that the world began on the eighth day (after seven days of creation) and Christ was resurrected on the eighth day of the Passion. The finest examples are the baptisteries built in Ravenna by both orthodox and Arian communities in the second half of the fifth century. Other centralised buildings were constructed over the site of the nativity in Bethlehem (again in an octagonal shape) and at the earliest Church of the Holy Sepulchre in Jerusalem. The most extraordinary architectural achievement in this form is San Vitale in Ravenna, again an octagon through the arcades of which one enters an ambulatory and a single chancel where the mosaics commemorating the recovery of Ravenna by Justinian and Theodora are displayed. Even more magnificent, with its great dome suspended on four pendatives, is Santa Sophia, the imperial church in Constantinople (completed in its present form by Justinian in 563).

All inhibitions about decoration had now vanished. In St John Lateran, five hundred pounds of gold were needed simply to gild the apse. Mosaics were set so that the lighting set off varied reflections. There were so many lamps in St John Lateran that estates were set aside to provide income for their maintenance. In the Church of the Nativity in Bethlehem the mosaics were so fine that over four hundred were needed for each ten centimetre square.

The traditionalists were not happy. 'Let them have their basilicas glittering with gold and ornamented with the ostentation of expensive marble, held up by the splendour of columns; let them also have extensive property, from which one runs the risk of losing the true faith . . .' as one put it. Christians had to formulate new approaches to art to justify the massive expenditure. In the New Testament the only text which could be used in support was the gold, frankincense and myrrh offered Jesus as an infant and the heavenly city filled with precious stones described in the Book of Revelation. The Old Testament was more helpful. The Song of Songs has a mass of imagery of jewellery, gold and ivory. The 'beloved' himself, often seen as a personification of Christ, has a head of gold.

Platonism underpinned the approach to treasure, as in so many other spheres of Christian theology. Plato had believed that the material world could only be an imitation of what went beyond, but it was possible to have hints from what could be seen on earth of the glories of heaven. Pseudo-Dionysus, writing around 500, argues that 'if a form for heavenly beings is to be found among precious stones one must think if they are white that they are images of light, if red of fire, if yellow, of gold, if green, of youth amid the flower of the soul. For each form you will find an image which will lead the soul aloft.' One of the most evocative symbolic representations of treasure comes from the Arian baptistery in Ravenna.

Christian iconography developed to meet the needs of a religion linked to empire. The transformation in ideology can be seen in representations of Christ. Traditional images such as that of the Good Shepherd vanish as Christ becomes absorbed into imperial iconography. In the Christ as shepherd in the Mausoleum of Gallia Placidia in Ravenna from the first half of the fourth century, 'the shepherd' is shown with a golden cross, gold tunic and purple mantel. Another development is Christ as *traditio legis*, the passer on of the new covenant. The coming of Christ has led to the supersession of the Law and Christ now hands on the new covenant to Peter or Paul as his representative on earth. A good example, from the middle of the fourth century, comes from Santa Costanza in Rome.

By 390 in San Pudenziana, also in Rome, Christ is transformed into a Roman magistrate, the earliest 'Christ in Majesty'. The fully frontal Christ, to become such a powerful element of Byzantine art, echoes portrayals of the emperor in relief sculpture of the period. In fact, one might say that Christ has become transformed into the emperor's own God. He can even be shown as a warrior. The Christ in majesty is a heavenly figure who has transcended death. One of the most interesting features is a reluctance to show Christ suffering on the cross. There are scenes from the last week of the Passion, as on the Junius Bassius sarcophagus, but not of the crucifixion itself. The carved panel of 'the crucifixion' on the door of the basilica of Santa Sabina shows Christ with his arms outstretched but no cross at all. Often a Chi-Rho becomes the symbol of the cross as victory. One reason perhaps is the difficulty of knowing whether Christ as part of the Godhead can be shown dead or, if alive, as suffering.

As the Nicene creed becomes orthodox and Christ is subsumed into the Godhead, the Arian Goths, in contrast, preserved a more human 'subordinate' Jesus. In the 'Arian' church of Sant' Apollinare Nuovo in Ravenna, the scenes from Christ's life show him in two sequences first as a young man and then as a bearded older one to make the point that he aged as a human would. When the Byzantines took over the church in the mid-sixth century, they portrayed their Christ on a throne in majesty to make the contrast. The Virgin Mary is also by now elevated to an imperial figure on a throne.

In so far as one can see a trend in Christian art between 300 and 600, it involves first the integration of Christian symbols into imperial iconography and then the transformation of the church into a transitional setting for those who wish to focus on heaven. Paulinus placed an inscription on the entrance to his shrine for St Felix at Nola which makes the point well: 'Christ's worshippers take the path to heaven by way of this lovely sward. An approach from bright gardens is fitting, for from here is granted to those who desire it their departure to holy Paradise'.

An Obsession with the Flesh

'PARCHMENTS ARE DYED PURPLE, GOLD IS MELTED INTO LETTERING, manuscripts are dressed up in jewels, while Christ lies at the door naked and dying.'[1] The ascetic scholar Jerome was among many who were appalled by the new opulence of the church. Only a hundred years earlier bishops had been in hiding, their sacred texts were being seized and any display of open ostentation would have been destroyed. Now the church was flaunting its wealth and actively seeking to dominate city life. Jerome wrote that the history of the church was one of decline, 'from the apostles down to the excrement of our time'. Cassian, one of the most influential early writers on monasticism, noted how the contrast between the commitment of the apostles and the laxity of the contemporary church provided an incentive for a withdrawal from the world. Those who did not identify more fully with the sufferings of Christ might lose their chance of salvation. As she lay dying, Macrina, the ascetic sister of Gregory of Nyssa and Basil of Caesarea, prayed: 'Thou that didst break the flaming sword and didst restore to Paradise the man that was crucified with Thee and implored Thy mercies, remember me, too, in Thy kingdom; because I, too, was crucified with Thee, having nailed my flesh to the cross for fear of Thee, and of Thy judgments have I been afraid. Let not the terrible chasm separate me from Thy elect.' Macrina fears she is missing out on the suffering required of her.

The Greek word *askesis* means discipline or training. It was used when the body underwent abstinence in order to achieve athletic or spiritual ends. The ascetic does not necessarily despise the body as such but recognises that it is vulnerable to outside pressures and these must be actively challenged. Any corruption by wealth or the surrender to greed and sexuality are to be avoided. The philosopher of asceticism was Plato, many of whose dialogues explore the ways in which the emotions subvert the search for ultimate truth. This requires the elevation of the soul and the recognition that only the application of reason can lead one on to knowledge. The most sophisticated

Christian proponent of this view was Evragius of Pontus (died 399) who followed Origen and, through Origen, Plato, in writing of the natural state of the soul before its fallen state when desire and ambition corroded it. This natural state – Evragius termed it *apatheia* – can be regained through an active mastery of specific temptations, the 'seven deadly sins' of later Catholic orthodoxy. Evragius was by far the most influential contributor to the literature of eastern asceticism.

The Christian asceticism of the fourth century went far beyond mere philosophical speculation in its intensity and violent rejection of any form of material comfort. It found inspiration in the sufferings of Christ on the cross and the early experiences of the Israelites. The most important model from the Old Testament was Moses. God had revealed himself to Moses in the Burning Bush on the edge of the desert and had given him his commandments on Mount Sinai. There followed forty years of wandering in the desert before the Israelites reached the Promised Land. So those who follow God obediently through hardship will achieve some form of bliss. Basil of Caesarea and his brother Gregory of Nyssa both used Moses as a pattern on which to conduct a life of, first education, then a period of contemplation and finally a period of leadership. In the New Testament John the Baptist emerges from the desert as 'the voice crying in the wilderness' which can be linked back to the prophecy in Isaiah (40.3). Then Jesus spends forty days in the desert fighting with the devil and retreats there for contemplation. In Paul there is a greater emphasis on the destructive powers of sexuality, an important ingredient in the Christian ascetic mix and one largely missing from the Old Testament.

The commitment to asceticism can be explored through the tortured life of Jerome, later honoured as one of the four Doctors of the Church and the translator of the Hebrew and Greek scriptures into Latin.[2] Jerome, the son of well-off Christian parents from Stridon in Dalmatia, was sent to study in Rome and appears to have followed the conventional route of mastering grammar, rhetoric and possibly philosophy in the 360s. None of this undermined his Christian beliefs and he was baptised in the capital. He was a restless youth, preoccupied with sexuality, touchy, yet needing the company of others. There were few moments in his long life when he ever seemed emotionally at peace and when he did live in society he seems to have offended others easily. Even if this was an age in which asceticism was popular, it needed a certain type of personality to embrace it. Jerome was obsessed with finding a haven for his troubled soul. Having fallen out with his family at home, he set out to the east in search of fulfilment. He reached Antioch in Syria and then decided to settle in the desert.

For the ascetic elite, it was the Egyptian rather than the Syrian desert that was the most prestigious destination. There was a dramatic contrast between the dark, fertile soil of the Nile valley and the red soil of the wilderness beyond. The Egyptians had always portrayed the desert as the haunt of demons and Christians believed that they were taking their souls to a battlefield when they retreated there. Jerome would have known of Athanasius' *Life of Anthony* that tells how Anthony was continually assailed by a mass of imaginary beasts and the temptations of the devil disguised as a naked woman. Already the Egyptian desert was filling up with hermits and small monastic communities. The Syrian desert was experiencing the same influx and was gaining a reputation for being inhabited by eccentrics who displayed their commitment through living on top of pillars (the famous Simeon Stylites), loading themselves with chains, or choosing to live on a few dates and muddy water.

Jerome lived in the desert for two or three years. In later works of art he is usually portrayed as alone against a setting of parched rocks (although sometimes, in medieval iconography, with a friendly lion from whose paw he had removed a thorn), but it was not a complete withdrawal. A friend from Antioch came out to visit him on a regular basis, bringing him his letters. He accumulated a large library and he even had access to copyists who could provide him with texts he needed. As a Latin speaker he was at first an outsider in Syria, so he mastered Syriac – already a language widely used for Christian texts and into which many others had been translated – in addition to Greek. Next he embarked on Hebrew. This was still very rare for a Christian but he found a convert from Judaism to teach him and soon surpassed Origen in his command of the language.

Several of Jerome's letters survive from this period and show him as a lonely man, furious whenever his attempted contacts with others were rejected. He struggled with his desires: 'Although my only companions were scorpions and wild beasts, time and again I was mingling with the dances of girls. My face was pallid with fasting and my body chill, but my mind was throbbing with desires; my flesh was as good as dead, but the flames of lust raged in it.' As with many ascetics of the period, his sexual imagination fed on his isolation.

After leaving the desert Jerome spent two years in Constantinople studying with Gregory of Nazianzus. He proved too pedantic a thinker ever to engage fully with the intricacies of Greek philosophy. One can see from his writings how he clung to Nicene orthodoxy but failed to think creatively beyond it. Even so, any contact with Greek philosophy must have been a broadening experience and he revered Gregory. He was also introduced to the works of Origen, the greatest exegete of the previous century, although he seems to have become far too dependent on them, with unhappy results. Many of Origen's commentaries on the scriptures are only known because they appear, slightly modified, under Jerome's name!

Jerome now had a chance to return to Rome. Paulinus, the bishop whom Gregory had unsuccessfully supported as Meletius' replacement in Antioch, wished to travel to the capital to plead with its bishop, Damasus, for support. Jerome joined his retinue alongside another prominent ascetic, the rigidly Nicene Epiphanius, bishop of Salamis in Cyprus. Jerome's role may have been no more than interpreter for these two Greek speakers but once Damasus, a cultivated man, met him, he realised how useful someone of Jerome's learning could be, especially in dealing with difficult problems in the scriptures. So began the relationship that led to Jerome taking on the task of producing a complete translation of the scriptures into Latin from Greek and Hebrew originals.

Although Damasus' court was known for its luxury, many aristocratic women in Rome had now rejected wealth. Jerome offered himself as their mentor. A widow, Marcella, who had set up a 'monastery' in her home on the fashionable Aventine Hill, was his first contact. Marcella had read the *Life of Anthony* and learned about the ascetic celebrities of the Egyptian desert from an exiled bishop of Alexandria. A woman of some learning, she wanted to know more about the scriptures, especially passages that troubled her. Attracted to her circle was the recently widowed Paula, who was scattering her vast wealth on charitable projects, and Paula's young daughters, Blesilla and Eustochium.

The relationship between this austere and socially inept scholar and these acolytes, who, if not worldly in their behaviour, were used to society, was never likely to be an easy one. Although they appear to have made their own commitment to virginity, Marcella and Paula in effect deciding not to remarry, the girls were very young to have entirely renounced marriage. There may not have been much joy in an arranged marriage with the attendant risks of dying in childbirth, but opting out completely threatened the mores of the traditional Roman family and risked the virgins ending up as social outcasts. In Milan Ambrose caused intense resentment when he tried to persuade local girls to commit themselves at the altar to perpetual virginity. 'You offer a bridegroom? I have found a better. You may tell tales of his fortune, vaunt his pedigree, extol his power. I offer someone with whom nobody can compare,' he told one protesting family when their daughter took refuge at his altar.

Jerome revelled in his new status. In his letters to his protégées, he behaved as if he alone understood the dangers of life, the threat of heretics, the possibility of sexual transgression, all the snares the devil lays. He pestered Blesilla so often about her behaviour that her relatives became furious with his intrusions. Finally, Blesilla, still recovering from an earlier illness, subjected herself to a rigorous programme of fasting and mortification, the strain of which led to her death. Paula was devastated but Jerome made things worse by proclaiming how much better off Blesilla was in heaven and how shocked she would be to look down from her bliss to see her selfish mother in tears.

Undeterred by the widespread disgust he aroused, Jerome turned his attention to Eustochium who had already as a teenager committed herself to perpetual virginity. The girl was subjected to Jerome's most weighty and prurient letter on the glory of her status. It is a confused tract that sets out virginity as the preferred state of God. The sexless lives of Adam and Eve in Paradise are the ideal and it is an understandable consequence of their transgressions, he says, that their life on earth should begin with the corruptions of sex! 'I cannot bring myself to speak of the many virgins who daily fall and are lost to the bosom of the church, their mother: stars over which the proud foe sets up his throne and rocks hollowed by the serpent that he may dwell in their fissures.' Like many sexual ascetics, Jerome sees sex everywhere. A glass of wine or a rich meal inflames lust. Even consorting with married women was to be avoided by the professed virgin who should spend her time with other fasting women or in prayer in her room. 'When lust tickles the sense and the soft fire of sensual pleasure sheds over us its pleasing glow, let us immediately break forth and cry: "The Lord is on my side: I will not fear what the flesh can do unto me." ' Jerome even suggests that the only good result of a marriage can be the production of more virgins. Marriage 'is the thorn from which roses are gathered'. What is the reward for Eustochium's abstinence? Here Jerome creates a picture of Jesus as the lover from the Song of Songs seducing Eustochium in her bedroom. This is a theme that had been found in Jesus' sayings in the Gospel of Thomas: 'It is the solitary who will enter the bridal chamber', as if renunciation on earth will somehow lead to sexual fulfilment in heaven.

These letters were widely distributed but Jerome could not claim a monopoly on the subject of sex. There were more balanced Christian approaches. One Christian layman, Helvidius, set out a reasoned exposition of the New Testament texts on the virginity of Mary to make it quite clear that the gospel writers taught that she had lived with Joseph as his wife and had further children. He cited earlier Christian authorities who agreed with him and then asked the vital question – what was wrong with being a good wife? God's approval of marriage could be seen in the marriages of Abraham, Isaac and Jacob. Why was there a problem in Mary losing her virginity and becoming a mother?

Jerome could not resist a response. These were years in which the status of Mary had risen and her life story had been fleshed out beyond the meagre details in the gospels. The *Protoevangelium* of James (probably the second half of the second century) had told of Mary's own conception as the child of Joachim and Anna. At six months she was already walking and she was sent at age three for service in the Temple. It was noticed how she had solemnly entered the building without looking back at her parents and had danced on the steps of the Altar. The priests, sensing that there was something special about her, had selected Joseph, here presented as an elderly man with children of his own, as her protector. The annunciation by Gabriel follows and the narrative describes how Mary gives birth in a cave outside Bethlehem. When a Salome, her sister according to some traditions, cannot believe that she has retained her virginity and examines her, her hand is withered as a result of her disbelief.

Other texts fill out Mary's later life to suggest that she was with Jesus throughout his life. It was said that she was really present at the Last Supper but so busy managing the servants that she is not mentioned. Then, after the crucifixion, she lives with John in Ephesus but rather than dying she falls asleep, the Dormition, at which the apostles miraculously assemble around her bed. She is assumed into heaven, the apostles standing in despair as she ascends upwards. The vast numbers of surviving sermons which detail this story show that for many Christians the imagined life of Mary had became as real as that of the Jesus of the gospels. Scenes from the *Protoevangelium* were shown on mosaics and frescoes. So in the great basilica of Santa Maria Maggiore in Rome, the fourth-century mosaic of the annunciation shows her spinning the wool for the veil of the Holy of Holies in the Temple.[3]

Jerome's response to Helvidius is vituperative. He denigrates him personally, misrepresents his views and presents his own interpretation of the gospel texts so as to suggest that 'the brothers and sisters' are, in fact, cousins. Mary remained a virgin throughout her marriage, he asserts, as indeed did Joseph. Jerome draws on the letters of Paul to decry marriage as a destructive force that distracts attention from the worship of God. Jerome's views were later elaborated to insist that Mary remained physically a virgin, even during the birth of Christ. As such they became enormously influential and fed into the movement that declared Mary *Theotokos*, 'bearer of God', at the Council of Ephesus in 431. Jerome discovered an alternative text, from Ezekiel (44:2), which he took out of context to support her perpetual virginity: 'This gate will be kept shut. No one will open it to go through it, since Yahweh the God of Israel has been through it, and so it must be kept shut.' Mary was increasingly contrasted with the temptress Eve and one result of her elevation was to cast women as either virgins or whores. The impact on later Christian attitudes to sex was immense.

At a humbler level, the new emphasis on virginity did give a new status to those who openly renounced marriage. In many cases these were widows who chose not to remarry and many of these found important roles as givers of charity and founders of monasteries. The immensely wealthy Olympias, a widow after only twenty days of marriage to the city prefect of Constantinople, took to a life of renunciation, passing on her riches to the church. 'Her dress was mean, her furniture poor, her prayers assiduous and fervent, and her charities without bounds,' as one account put it. The penetrating, if often hagiographic, accounts of these lives are an important literary development and here asceticism had given an opportunity for women to be valued. Perhaps the most sophisticated life is that of Macrina by her brother Gregory of Nyssa. The respect Gregory shows to his sister as he describes her dying days demonstrates how he had transcended the conventions of an upper-class upbringing. Even though he is one of the most highly educated men of his age, he acknowledges that Macrina's lack of learning (she refused to read any pagan works) is no bar to her finding salvation.

Olympias and Macrina lived in settled homes surrounded by other committed women. Some women were more adventurous. The two Melanias from Rome, one the grandmother of the other, led lives on the move. Both were immensely wealthy. The elder Melania proclaimed that the deaths of her husband and her two sons liberated her to serve the Lord and she had been one of the first westerners to settle in Palestine. She gave help to Nicene supporters persecuted under Valens and so her theological credentials were, after 381, impeccable. With Rufinus, a friend of Jerome's from his childhood studies in Rome, she founded a monastery on the Mount of Olives. She later returned to Rome to persuade her granddaughter, who lived with her husband in chastity, to move east. The younger Melania is recorded in Sicily, North Africa, Egypt, Syria and in Constantinople, where she became a friend of Eudocia, the pious empress of Theodosius II. Her wealth extended to buying islands for monasteries, the freeing of some eight thousand slaves and the care of captives. An even more vivid record of a woman's travels survives in the diary of a Spanish nun, Egeria, who spent three years on pilgrimage to the Holy Land in the 380s. It is remarkable how easily Egeria was able to travel – she must have been wealthy enough to have her own retinue – and she shows a keen interest in archaeology of the sites she visits and their links to scripture.

Jerome was about to have his own pilgrimage to the Holy Land. When Damasus died in 384, the feeling against Jerome in Rome boiled over. There was some form of official condemnation that forced him to leave the city. His reputation was damaged further when it was heard that Paula and, later, Eustochium had left to join him. The gossip about their relationship was probably no worse than that in similar situations today but Jerome, always quick to take offence, was outraged at the insinuations buzzing around Rome. Jerome associated his rejection with those endured by Christ and Paul and cast Rome, to which he would never return, as the Babylon, the harlot arrayed in purple and scarlet, to be found in the Book of Revelation.

When Paula had joined him, they embarked on an extensive tour of the Holy Land. Jerome had an exhaustive knowledge of the scriptures and he was determined to visit every site from Bethlehem and Jerusalem northwards to Galilee to absorb its atmosphere and connect to the texts he knew so well. Paula proved a willing companion, taking to a donkey when necessary in more remote areas. Jerome recorded her emotional responses as she encountered the stone floor from which Christ had been resurrected or the stained column on which the flagellation had taken place. Already relics, real or contrived, were gripping the Christian imagination. Every moment in the nativity story, from the fields where the shepherds had heard the angels to the site of the massacre of the Holy Innocents, had been identified. Paula was overcome when she was allowed to kiss 'the' manger in Bethlehem. These were the years when Christianity was able to spread itself as a religion of sacred places and the Holy Land achieved a resonance that was to inspire the crusades for its recovery six hundred years later.

Jerome and Paula decided to settle in Bethlehem and it was Paula's money that financed the founding of two monasteries, one for either sex. She would preside over the women's with impressive austerity: 'A clean body and clean clothes betoken an unclean mind,' was one of her more forbidding announcements. Jerome was to head the other. He was to live there for the rest of his life.

There is no precise definition of a monastery in this period. The Greek word, first coined by Philo, suggests the buildings of those who live alone (*monos*, alone) but this covered an enormous variety of living arrangements. Some monks seem to have seen themselves as itinerant shock troops bent on the destruction of paganism. It was gangs such as these that Theodosius banned, if only temporarily, from cities in 390. Most monasteries were more stable. In Egypt supporters of the rejected Melitius from Alexandria appear to have set up communities, as did the Manicheans, as early as the 320s. Pachomius, a pagan of peasant stock who was converted to Christianity while in the army, was a pioneer in the process. His background must have given him experience of communal living and he seems to have enforced harsh discipline on his followers but he was a charismatic organiser who had founded at least nine monasteries in the Egyptian desert before his death in 346. Pachomius saw his communities as waiting in perpetual readiness for the Second Coming. There were pragmatic reasons for sharing tasks but Pachomius also recognised that communal living in itself might have a transcendent quality. Service to others through providing for their needs was part of the ascetic journey; total withdrawal, in contrast, suggested self-indulgence. By 350, monasteries were springing up throughout the Egyptian desert, some housing hundreds of monks.

An early visitor to the burgeoning monastic communities of Egypt, Palestine and Syria, was Basil of Caesarea. Basil went on to found his own monastic community in Cappadocia but also thought deeply about the purposes of communal life. He realised how difficult it was to sustain stable communities of irascible eccentrics who competed with each other for ascetic stardom. It was enormously important to establish a structure or rule of conduct. Everyday conflict could be avoided if charity towards others was seen as central to community living. The despotism of abbots (the word comes from the Hebrew *Abba,* father, and was first used of Pachomius) could be alle-viated if humility was made a mark of office. 'He must be compassionate, showing long suffering to those who through inexperience fall short in their duty, not passing sins over in silence but meekly bearing with the restive, applying remedies to them all with kindness and delicate adjustment.'[4] The purpose of abstinence was not to take delight in self-torture; it was rather to remove the soul from pleasures that might destroy it. The monastic rule of Basil, full of good sense and moderation, was to prove very important as a model in western monasticism.

Jerome continued his task of translating the Hebrew and Greek scriptures in Bethlehem. He had his own library there and was also able to exploit that of Origen in Caesarea. It was a demanding task. Quite apart from the linguistic challenges of translating into Latin, there were variations between the copies of different texts. A hundred and fifty years earlier Origen had complained how negligence or, in some cases, deliberate additions or deletions to the originals of the scriptures had made his work harder. One of Celsus' complaints against the Christians was how they changed their texts when difficulties arose.[5] Scholars today identify at least four different types of Latin translations of the scriptures and many more, now lost, must have been circulating in Jerome's day. Jerome prefaces his own response to Damasus' request for a new Latin translation of the gospels with his fears that he will be ridiculed for choosing the wrong text from the many Latin variants scattered throughout the Mediterranean world.

Before he left Rome, Jerome had completed revisions of the gospel texts, even though he often chose those Latin versions that were closest to the Greek originals. He then completed the rest of the New Testament which had only reached its final form in Greek a few years earlier (see Chapter Nine.) He followed the new canon even though he recognised that the status of the Letter to the Hebrews and the Book of Revelation was still questioned by some. In some cases, he seems to have adopted translations from other sources rather than creating them himself. Now he tackled the Old Testament using the original Hebrew text as the basis for his own translation. His aim, he told correspondents, was to help Christians by giving them a more accurate version of the Hebrew with which they could refute the Jews!

Yet Jerome soon touched on raw nerves. The Septuagint, the third-century BC Greek translation of the Hebrew scriptures, had achieved a sacred status in the Christian world and when he claimed to be offering a better rendition of the original Hebrew there was outrage (not least from western conservatives such as Augustine). In the introduction to each new book, he hits back at his critics: 'Filthy swine who grunt as they trample on pearls' was one sally. There was only one text in which he would admit the superiority of the Septuagint over the Hebrew, that from Isaiah stressing that it was a virgin, and not merely 'the young woman' of the original Hebrew text, who would conceive Jesus. (Here he was at one with Justin Martyr who had made the same concession two hundred years earlier.)

Jerome persevered until in 406, fourteen years after he had begun, he could present a full version of the Bible in Latin. It was a remarkable achievement even though scholars note how some of his translations, especially the later ones, are paraphrases and that he often adjusted the texts to overemphasise those that could be used as prophecies of Christ. It remains unclear how much of the work is really his own and as his original text was copied and recopied more variants appeared (the fate of all manuscripts in the age before printing). Gradually, however, through the sixth to the ninth centuries, Jerome's name remained attached to the Latin version, the Vulgate, or 'popular edition', and was accepted in the west. It remains, with some revisions, the official Latin, and hence Roman Catholic, translation of the Hebrew and Greek originals.

Jerome could never resist becoming caught up in the doctrinal controversies of the period even though his tortuous personality often made things worse for himself. His old travelling companion, Epiphanius, had become obsessed with heresies and had compiled, the *Panarion* ('a medicine chest of remedies'), a detailed account of how the original purity of Christian living had been corrupted first by the sin of Adam, then pagans and Jews and finally by a mass of alternative Christianities. One of Epiphanius' targets was Origen whom he berated for subordinationism and his denial of the resurrection of the body. By now an elderly man, Epiphanius set off for the Holy Land determined to root out any supporter of Origen, accusing the bishop of Jerusalem, John, of being the most prominent. It was clear that he was deranged in his obsessions and John stayed well clear of any involvement with him. It was all the more extraordinary therefore that Jerome, who had relied so heavily on Origen's scholarship, capitulated almost immediately to Epiphanius' demands and agreed to abjure his mentor.

His surrender did him no good. One of his oldest friends, Rufinus, who was also living a monastic life in the Holy Land, refused to submit to Epiphanius. He set his dogs on his emissaries as soon as they arrived at his monastery. Rufinus went on to make a Latin translation of one of Origen's major works, *Peri archon*, 'On the First Principles'. Aware that in Rome as well as in the east Origen was now under suspicion, Rufinus included a preface that told how one of the great Latin scholars of the age (unnamed) had praised Origen as an inspiration. It was clearly Jerome he was referring to and, if he was representing Jerome's earlier views, the preface was fair. Jerome responded by calling Rufinus a heretical Arian; Rufinus retaliated by quoting passages of Jerome which had been lifted from Origen.

These outbursts of Jerome's were noted for their abusive language and exposed the underlying rigidity of his mindset. He squandered any chance of a reasoned debate by his contempt for his opponents. Yet Jerome's outbursts also illustrate the debates of the day. One, already raised by Helvidius, was over the place of sexuality in everyday life. In 393, Jerome received a tract by one Jovinian that criticised celibacy and extreme asceticism. Jerome launched another vituperative counter-attack. Typically it contained a sweeping assault on Jovinian for his way of life including mixed bathing and debauchery. His writings were no more than 'his own vomit'. Again Paul's writings were distorted to suit Jerome's cause and even Peter was said to have renounced marriage when he followed Jesus. One of Jerome's favourite ploys, used by other ascetics of the day, was to link food and sex: 'Eating meat, drinking wine, having a well-filled belly – there you have the seed-bed of lust.'

Another important debate of the day was over the place of relics and their powers of healing. Traditional education stressed the importance of reason and many Christians were still reluctant to endorse what appeared to be the growth of superstition in Christian worship. Another old acquaintance of Jerome, Vigilantius, had written a tract criticising the veneration of relics. He went on to link asceticism with superstition and argued that clergy were much better off if they were married. The core of Jerome's argument in response, that relics were only a medium through which worship was offered and that veneration was an acceptable form of piety, was unremarkable but Jerome ruined his case by his virulent abuse of Vigilantius.

Despite the reams of his surviving invective, the true Jerome, obsessed as he was with real or imagined enemies, eludes us. He was to endure a long old age. Paula died in 404, Eustochium, who had joined her mother, in 417 and Jerome in 420, probably by this time in his mid-seventies. To the end he was engaged in controversy. His last known letter is to the bishop of Rome asking him to cut the followers of Pelagius, an opponent of Augustine, 'to pieces with Christ's sword'.

In later Christian iconography Jerome is shown either in the desert or in a study. He provides the model of the monk who is also a scholar. Yet this model has to be viewed with caution. Jerome never showed any genuine intellectual creativity or had the self-confidence to develop his own theology. In his letter to Eustochium, Jerome told her of a dream that he, the classically educated Christian ascetic, had had in which he had been flogged for preferring the works of Cicero over those of Christ. He had vowed never again to neglect the scriptures. In the same letter he echoes Tertullian: 'What has Horace to do with the psalter, Virgil with the evangelists, Cicero with the Apostle [Paul]?' It was this attitude that became the norm in the Christian west. Jerome's dream provides a foretaste of the growing rejection of the world of classical scholarship in which he had been raised.[6] While his work as a translator can still be admired, his passionate invective did much to undermine Christianity as a home of reasoned exposition.

The End of Optimism

AUGUSTINE AND THE CONSEQUENCES OF SIN

THE THEOLOGY OF AUGUSTINE DOMINATES THE WESTERN TRADITION. For centuries Augustine's view of humankind, his attitudes to free will, the certainty of eternal punishment in hell for most, and his support for a hierarchical misogynist society were to become part of the European religious, and, to some extent, secular, heritage. Yet like his mentor the apostle Paul, he was a loner. His African diocese was remote from the major centres of Roman intellectual life in the west when even in cities such as Rome and Milan knowledge of Greek was fading. Despite being well educated, Augustine was unable to read the letters of Paul in the Greek original. He was so cut off from the east that there is no evidence that he even knew of the Council of Constantinople of 381 that had endorsed Theodosius' legislation on the Trinity. The breakdown of the western empire, in the very last years of his life, went hand in hand with a collapse in literacy so, although his major works were preserved in monastic libraries, few could appreciate them.

Augustine's contribution to theology was to become influential only when the church of the west became the most powerful in Europe after intellectual life re-emerged in the eleventh and twelfth centuries. It was never healthy for a single man, whose theology was deeply caught up within his own brilliant but tortured personality, to be given such prominence. The tragedy was that there were no alternative theologies to put alongside his own and one reason for this was that he himself had denied the possibility of free discussion and had even developed a rationale for persecution of rival Christianities. It was to take centuries before Augustine could be viewed objectively, free of the official role as 'the supreme *auctoritas* of the Christian tradition'.[1]

None of this is to deny the originality of Augustine. He had an extraordinarily acute mind, sweeping in its imagination, intuitive in teasing out the nuances of language, sensitive to the myriad ways in which individuals reflect on the unknown. As a young man he showed a lively philosophical instinct. As he became older and more embedded in the hierarchy of the church, the challenges of justifying orthodoxy meant that he had to probe with greater skill the nature of God, the means by which his purposes might be understood. So, for instance, his defence of the Nicene Trinity leads him to an exploration of the philosophy of mind. This means that many later philosophers have found something they can draw on from Augustine even if they find the overall tenor of his world view dispiriting. With some five million words of his work still surviving (they were copied and recopied relentlessly by medieval monks), there remains much to explore, especially in his sermons and letters.

Augustine was born in North Africa, in the city of Tagaste in 354. His mother Monica was a Christian; his father Patricius, a civil servant, remained pagan until near the end of his life. Monica was the stronger of the two and appears to have been overbearing at times. Their determination that Augustine should succeed led to a traditionally elite education in Carthage, where Augustine mastered rhetoric, and with it the possibility of social advancement as a teacher or civil servant like his father. He began as a teacher in Carthage, although he was upset by the unruliness of his pupils. He was not totally cut off from Christianity but his early reading of the scriptures had left him cold. He found the masters of Latin prose so much more sophisticated and a reading of Cicero's *Hortensius*, with its call to the joys of philosophy, more attractive. So was his (unnamed) consort, the mother of his son, Adeodatus (who died young). Augustine was more social, at ease with physical relationships than, say, Jerome or John Chrysostom. Although celibacy was later to be intrinsic to his Christian ministry, he could accept that there might be a place for sexual desire within marriage and he talks at one point of the love of truth as similar to the love of man for a woman's naked body.[2] He also acknowledges without prurience the eroticism of the Song of Songs. In general, however, he was suspicious of sexual desire.

In 383 Augustine made an important psychological break. Leaving behind his mother, who was distraught at the 'betrayal', he sought a new life in Rome. After he had settled as a teacher, a patron, the senator Symmachus, secured him a prestigious appointment as city orator in Milan. From here his future within the imperial hierarchy might have been assured, especially with the good marriage that his status made possible. His mother followed in the hope of arranging one.

Yet Augustine's conscience always gnawed at him as did his desire to understand the deepest nature of things. He had already become attracted to the Manicheans. In the eastern empire, Theodosius had decreed the death penalty for membership of certain Manichean sects in 382, partly because of their origins, through the third-century AD prophet Mani, in Rome's enemy the Persian empire, so Augustine was joining a marginal and unpopular group. The Manicheists believed in the overwhelmingly evil nature of the world, symbolised as darkness. The forces of light, found weakly in the human soul and, more completely, in the sun and the moon, had to be consolidated to fight back. Christ was one of the divine forces that would help reunite the sources of light and the Manicheists also revered Paul. (An apocryphal 'Acts of Paul' was among their sacred writings.) The sect was only a temporary resting place for Augustine. His acute philosophical mind saw the inadequacies of classifying the entire material world as evil and he became disillusioned with those Manicheists who failed to live up to their own standards. He knew enough of Greek science to realise that eclipses were predictable, not sudden manifestations of evil as the Manicheists claimed.

Augustine now became fascinated by Plato and notably his third-century AD Neoplatonist follower Plotinus. The latter was a man whose sophistication was truly absorbing even if Augustine had to make do with Latin translations of his works. At the same time he was beginning to explore Christianity. In Milan he listened to the sermons of Ambrose and became more convinced that the scriptures had something to offer when the bishop assured him that the cruder passages could be understood allegorically rather than literally. Ten years later, in the mid 390s, in his *Confessions*, Augustine was to detail his hesitant moves towards his conversion to Christianity. He was finally convinced by verses of Paul, Romans 13:13–14, ' . . . not in revelling and drunkenness, not in lust and wantonness, not in quarrels and rivalries. Rather arm yourself with the Lord Jesus Christ: spend no more thought on nature and nature's appetites.'

In the months following his conversion, Augustine did not envisage a career in the church, even though he committed himself to celibacy. Rather he seems to have been drawn to a mystical Christianity in which the influence of the pagan Plotinus, and behind Plotinus, Plato, was still dominant. He withdrew with a group of friends to the countryside near Milan and they recorded their own individual thoughts and discussions. Works such as the *Soliloquies* and the *Contra academicos* (Against the Sceptics) show a mind that is open to new ideas. Augustine would always favour Plato over Aristotle, not least because Plato wrote so much more engagingly (something which mattered to Augustine). He talks rather condescendingly of the empiricist and logician Aristotle as 'a man of outstanding intellect, no match for Plato in style but well above the common herd'. Augustine was never one for abstract logic or building up knowledge from empirical evidence. In his *Soliloquies*, in which he creates a dialogue between himself and Reason, Reason asks Augustine what he wants to know:

'I want to know God and the soul . . .

Nothing more?

Nothing at all.'

In these early works Augustine is aware of the difficulties in finding certainty. One might argue that it is the mark of a true philosopher that he understands the limits of reason and language and the immense difficulty in saying anything of certainty beyond this. (Wittgenstein is a fine example of this.) So if there is a consensus that the universe began with a Big Bang, one then uses every method possible to discover what might have existed before this without necessarily believing one will succeed. Plato and Aristotle are both within this tradition – Plato did not expect his trainee philosophers, his future 'Guardians', to grasp the full nature of the ultimate reality before the age of fifty. Augustine worries about what can be known, from reason and through the senses. He knows that there must be some greater truths but he has, so far, failed to discover the means to access them.

These happy days of comradely speculation in rural Italy were not to last. Augustine returned to North Africa in 388. The church desperately needed men with the skills his education had given him. In Africa in particular, the orthodox church, now committed to Nicaea, was still in schism with the Donatists while the majority of the population remained pagan. Augustine was induced to become a priest in 391 and then four years later bishop of the coastal town of Hippo. He remained there until his death in 430 and his immense learning ensured that he became the spokesman for the North African church. It was another turning point and in the mid 390s he reflected on the process by which he had come to the Christian faith in his famous *Confessions* – the word carrying here the sense of 'testament'. It is the first time in history that an autobiography is not simply a list of achievements or self-justifications but an examination of the interior of a mind as it searches for ultimate meaning. Augustine portrays God as always there, waiting as it were for recognition while he, a miserable sinner, persisted in refusing to acknowledge this. The point is a crucial one for Augustine. Through pride, the corruption of the soul, or a refusal to carry out the search at all, we fail to appreciate the reality of a loving God.

The apostle Paul had already provided Augustine with the verse that had led to his conversion. In the mid 390s Augustine became obsessed with Paul, above all the Letter to the Romans on which he wrote numerous studies. One statement of Paul from Romans 7:18–25 became especially influential. It includes: 'For I know that nothing good lodges in me – in my unspiritual nature, I mean – for though the will to do good is there, the deed is not. The good which I want to do, I fail to do; but what I do is the wrong which is against my will; and if what I do is against my will, clearly it is no longer I who am the agent, but sin that has its lodging in me.' Only God, through Jesus Christ, can save one from the slavery of sin.

Many would read this passage as a personal account by Paul of his own struggles and of no universal relevance but it echoed something in Augustine's own experience and he chose to use it as the basis for a theology of the human condition. While Plato recognised how sensual appetites hindered the search for ultimate truth, Augustine wished to find a more comprehensive explanation and he developed the idea of the 'original' sin, the disobedience of Adam and Eve in Eden. This had been passed down from generation to generation through the act of sexual intercourse, so that even babies were born with it. Augustine may have drawn on Tertullian, Cyprian and Ambrose, all men preoccupied with sin, for the idea but he was to develop it in a much more sophisticated way (for the first time in a letter to a priest, Simplicianus, who was to succeed Ambrose as bishop of Milan). Later he backed it with a verse from Romans (5:12) that he interpreted as confirming that sin entered the human race through Adam (although this may have been a misinterpretation of the original due to a misleading Latin translation). Augustine did believe that infant baptism might have some effect in securing the grace of God but it was by no means certain.

Perhaps a loving God, realising that no single individual had a chance to escape the guilt of Adam, would act to forgive and save the vast majority of the human race. Augustine agreed that this was indeed possible but so angered was God by the sin of Adam that he was justified in offering his 'grace' only to a few. There was no knowing who these lucky ones would be and there was no way individuals could better their chances. So, for Augustine, the church could never provide total security and he would have been aghast at Christians who claim to know for certain that they have been saved.

In his final major work, *The City of God*, Augustine seems almost to rejoice in the unforgiving nature of God: 'The whole of mankind is a "condemned lump"; for he who committed the first sin [Adam] was punished, and along with him all the stock which had its roots in him. The result is that there is no escape for anyone from this justly deserved punishment, except by merciful and undeserved [*sic*] grace; and mankind is divided between those in whom the power of merciful grace is demonstrated, and those in whom is shown the might of just retribution.'[3]

Augustine's personality warmed to the reality of hell fire. Week after week, he must have stood before his congregation, knowing, according to his beliefs, that even though they had been baptised, that many engaged in good works, and others were people he was personally attracted to, most of them would still end up burning for eternity. In the final chapters of *The City of God*, he relishes depriving them of any hope that good works, the intercession of the saints, or the sacraments will save them. He even cites the case of the salamander to show, apparently, that a creature can be enveloped in fire without being destroyed and he berates 'the rationalists' for their view that a body cannot burn without being consumed. So the burning of hell can be eternal, the body surviving to experience it.[4] These last pages, written when Augustine was an old man, can only be explained as the writings of someone who has severed emotional contact with those around him. He shows no compassion for the tragedy of human existence which his theology left exposed.

If human beings are embedded in sin, can they freely decide to do good? Augustine argued that the only act of true free will was Adam's decision to sin, and he violently opposed those who believed that human beings had the ability to save themselves. This not only aroused opposition to him within the church, it also confronted the entire tradition of Greek philosophical thought which was rooted in the belief that not only were human beings curious by nature but that they could achieve a greater understanding of any area of knowledge through the exercise of rational debate. One can see the narrowing of Augustine's thought in his use of the word *curiositas*, the desire to know. Already in the *Confessions* he refers to *curiositas* as 'a disease', in that it tempts one to search for truths of nature, which are beyond human understanding and which are of no intrinsic use. Later he implies that *curiositas* is an indication of sin, the lack of proper humility before God's creation.

This denigration of the search for understanding, and the ability of human beings to think effectively for themselves, was to have a crucial impact on Augustine's theory of knowledge. The possibility in his earlier philosophical reflections that he might find effective ways of expanding what can be known was thrown away by a different approach – that understanding could be grasped by a leap of faith. So he took a verse of Isaiah, 7:9: 'Unless you believe, you will not understand.' Here the mediating power of the reasoning mind was abandoned. No longer did Augustine believe, with Plato, that one might begin with reason and see how far one could get; starting with reason was, he argued, in itself irrational. So with the Nicene Trinity one did not need to explore the theology rationally, one just had to believe it and then in some miraculous way it would be understood.

One result was that articles of faith became non-negotiable. If one made the leap and still did not understand, that was doubtless due to the corruption of one's soul through original sin. Augustine was too astute not to recognise the problems this raised. Suppose a subordinationist came along, armed, perhaps, with a great deal more scriptural backing than Augustine could provide for the Nicene view, and announced that by believing in subordinationism he understood it to be the truth. How did one distinguish between his belief and that of Augustine? Augustine has little option but to fall back on the concept of authority. He acknowledges that there are different authorities, each of which would claim legitimacy for itself, but one can use reason to discriminate between authorities. However, hardly surprisingly he opts for his own church. Famously Augustine said that he would not have believed the gospels without the authority of the Catholic church. He also suggests that the survival of the church is in itself proof of the rightness of its existence as the favoured organisation of God.

Those individuals who wilfully refuse to believe are, to Augustine, victims of their own stubbornness. In one of his more positive statements, Augustine argues that one must orientate oneself towards belief. He uses the word *voluntas*, or assent, a will to know. This is not a superficial commitment to learning or mere acceptance of what is offered, it is something more powerful, a form of love of God. Augustine argues that if one develops that love, then, when the leap of faith takes place, the love will enable one to understand the reasons why a particular article of faith must be believed as true knowledge. The problem is that Augustine has already argued that there is no guarantee that God will love one back enough to save one from eternal punishment!

One of Augustine's most influential works, *De doctrina christiana*, was written as a handbook to the exploration of Christian study of the scriptures. His task was to explore the relationship between secular knowledge and the newly determined canon of Christian sacred writings. In doing so he overrode the traditional Roman programmes for approaching knowledge, of which the most famous was by Marcus Terentius Varro (died 27 BC), in favour of a scheme of knowledge based on the Christian texts with secular learning subordinate to them. *De doctrina christiana* has been described as the founding charter of a Christian culture and in so far as it uses classical culture primarily as a means to more fully understand the scriptures, the assessment seems justified. Although there is immense controversy over the long-term impact of the book on intellectual life in the west, there is no doubt that it conveyed the message that the main areas of traditional learning were of diminished value in comparison to the teachings of the scriptures. One had to wait until Petrarch in the fourteenth century before classical learning was again respected in its own right. (Petrarch made the point by coining the term 'Dark Ages' to describe the period between himself and these last years of the empire.) Augustine has to be seen as one of the architects of 'darkness' and it is a mark of his narrowing perspective that he forgets that his own beliefs had evolved through extensive reading of secular sources. He assumes all too readily that the 'truths' he has culled from them are incontrovertible.

It was inevitable that Augustine would be asked to defend the Nicene Trinity, especially the problem of there being three divine forces, Father, Son and Holy Spirit, but only one Godhead. In his *Confessions* he admits to his own difficulties: 'Who understands the omnipotent Trinity? Yet who among us does not speak of it, if it indeed be the Trinity that he speaks of? Rare is the soul that knows whereof it speaks, whatever it may say concerning the Trinity'. It was to take him some twenty years, from 400 to 420, before he had completed a work with which he was satisfied. *The Trinity* is certainly a massive achievement, above all in the determination Augustine shows in exploring every aspect of the question not only from scripture but from a philosophical and psychological perspective. Yet it is a mark of Augustine's isolation that it was written with no input from the eastern theologians – the only commentator Augustine mentions in the entire work is Hilary of Poitiers.

The initial premise of *The Trinity* was that the Trinity was a mystery that could only be grasped through faith. Furthermore the three members of the Trinity always acted in unison, however much some passages in scripture appeared to suggest that one, God the Father in the Old Testament, for instance, worked alone. Next, in the first four books of the work, Augustine had to take on those, the subordinationists, including the Eunomians, who provided scriptural support for their beliefs. He had some difficulties here and his reinterpretations of scripture do not always convince. Faced with the mass of texts, in John, for instance, where Christ clearly says that he is sent by the Father, and thus subordinate to the one who does the sending, Augustine has to argue that 'sent' does not have its normal meaning but refers only to God as the origin of Christ, as in 'God from God, Light from Light'. Is this any more than semantics? Again, when confronted with texts which cannot be interpreted other than to suggest that the Son is less than equal to the Father (for instance, John 14:28, 'The Father is greater than I'), Augustine has to argue that these refer to Christ speaking in his human capacity, while 'I and the Father are one' (John 10:30) is Christ speaking in his divine capacity. So Christ shifts between natures at will. One has to admire the agility with which Augustine wriggles his way through every complication, but one feels that a subordinationist would be able to argue back with as much success. (Augustine had a famous confrontation with an 'Arian' bishop, Maximinus, on the issue in the 420s, a confrontation that many felt Maximinus won.)

The 'philosophical' section of *The Trinity* (Books V to VII) has to deal with the difficulties of translating words such as 'substance', 'essence' and 'personality' from Greek to Latin. It is, of course, an interesting question whether such translations lose the essence of the argument in the process. In the Greek world, the terminology had become so precise and had so many connotations that a less philosophical language such as Latin could not embrace, that Augustine was certainly hampered in his task. One only has to realise how limited the English 'the Word' and the Latin *verbum* are compared to the richness of *logos* to appreciate the problem. Yet this section of the work was to contain one of the most explosive of Augustine's innovations. He had argued that the only way in which the three members of the Trinity could be distinguished from each other was through their relationship (one of equality for Nicenes, of course). The Father and the Son can be distinguished by their relationship as 'unbegotten' and 'begotten'. So where did the Holy Spirit fit in? In John 15:26 the Spirit is described as 'processing' from the Father. The Greek fathers had assumed that this meant processing from the Father alone and it is a further mark of Augustine's isolation that he does not seem to be aware of this. He argued instead that the Spirit must be assumed to process from the Son as well, in order to maintain an equal relationship between Father and Son. He therefore added the word *filioque*, 'and from the Son'. When the eastern theologians heard of the addition, they were outraged and the dispute became one of the issues that divided the two churches. (The fact that a single phrase of Augustine could divide the two churches is testimony to his immense influence.)

However much Augustine's arguments can frustrate, his imagination and the quality of his language often inspire. He was determined to elevate the Trinity as the supreme example of God's love and to prove that God had provided the human mind with the capacity to grasp the mystery. The prompt was provided by Genesis (1:26): 'Let us make man in our image and in our likeness.' Augustine claims that the mind, made in the image of God, is composed of three parts: the mind itself, its knowledge of itself and its love of itself. These are equal and of the same substance as each other, just as the Trinity is. Three faculties, memory, understanding and will, echo this and, Augustine argues, act together as a single force, as the Trinity does. In short, God has impressed a Trinitarian make-up on the human consciousness through which the essence of the Trinity can be understood. Of course, Augustine was acting arbitrarily by dividing the mind into three and naming attributes which fitted his argument but it is a good illustration of how he was able to go beyond mere theology, here into the psychology of human consciousness, to broaden his argument.

Augustine was living in a disintegrating empire. In contrast to the panic of others, Augustine took the news calmly that Rome had suffered a sack by the Goths under Alaric in 410. (It is worth remembering that the Goths were Christian, even if of the 'Arian' variety, and respected the churches of the capital.) He responded with his last major work, *The City of God*. He drew on the early chapters of Paul's Romans to suggest a world of the saved and the unsaved but he elaborated this to define two cities, one of the rejected, the 'city of the world . . . dominated by the very lust of domination'[5] and one of those who would be saved and finally find peace and fulfilment in the love of God.

The work provides a history of Rome in which it is shown that its addiction to paganism has led to its eventual doom. Augustine makes no reference to the view, which Eusebius and others had championed, that with the coming of Constantine one had entered a new era in which the church would triumph. This is still essentially a pagan world. After his depiction of the 'City of God' as the only true home of peace and justice, the most influential part of the work comes when Augustine describes the 'city of the world' as it exists on earth, with those to be saved, still unidentified living in its midst. This is as close as he ever gets to a work of political philosophy.

Augustine is, of course, constrained by his view that all are sinners and one cannot know who will be saved after death, so his government is one which has to be preoccupied with maintaining order among those who lead lives of sinful disorder. 'The peace of the whole universe is the tranquillity of order.

Order is the arrangement of things equal and unequal in a pattern which assigns to each its allotted position.' Authority becomes an end in itself. Augustine, citing Paul, stresses that one must obey the powers that be even if they act corruptly.

Augustine rejects two alternatives. The first is the tradition developed by all the pagan philosophers that the purpose of good government is to ensure the flourishing of the city. Whether philosophers favoured the autocracy of a ruling few (Plato) or some system of oligarchy or democracy, the end was the creation of a community in which virtue could be cultivated and the citizens would have the opportunity for personal fulfilment through participation as citizens. Augustine would have none of this. He shows that any hope that human beings can be good is a chimera. The most that could be hoped for is that the community would survive as an entity as a result of being kept in order and that Christians would maintain their freedom to worship. They are merely pilgrims, adrift and in exile until they reach the heavenly city that is unattainable on earth. Augustine upheld hierarchy, tolerated torture and executions and saw slavery as a punishment for sin. The second alternative he rejects is any form of society based on the gospels. They do not even appear to provide a model that Christian leaders might aspire to. Christians are expected to behave as harshly to the orders beneath them as the pagans do. So torture may be ordered even if the innocent suffer, and the church is justified in persecution. Augustine provides a model which justifies the linking of Christianity to authoritarian systems of government.

Augustine had to fight for his beliefs that humanity was hopelessly compromised by original sin against one group of his fellow Catholics, the followers of Pelagius. Pelagius was a monk, never as far as is known an ordained cleric, from Brittany. He moved to Rome in about 380 and was a highly respected ascetic in aristocratic circles at the same time as Jerome was there. He taught that renunciation was a choice that could easily be made as God had endowed human beings with free will. Their ability to use reason was a mark of their supremacy over the animals. Human beings were not totally dependent on the grace of God although God would provide support for those who committed themselves to him. Pelagius gave the example of a man in a boat who had set out under his own power to row in a defined direction (towards spiritual goodness). God would help him on his way just as the wind might. To Pelagius, Augustine's view that human beings were born so deeply corrupted by original sin that they could not act to save themselves simply did not make sense. What was the point of Jesus giving out commandments, as was recorded in the gospels, if human beings were so full of sin that they could not choose to follow them? One must trust on the essential goodness of God, not be cowed by his anger as one so easily thwarted by Adam.

Despite Augustine's growing influence in the west, these two theological approaches co-existed and in the east Pelagius actually achieved an endorsement of his own approach at a council in Jerusalem. This was after he had been denounced by Jerome who had tried unsuccessfully to persuade two bishops to accuse Pelagius of heresy. Augustine now weighed into the controversy and two councils of North African bishops condemned Pelagius, as well as his leading disciple, one Caelestius. The fight was then on to win over the bishop of Rome. Augustine gained the upper hand when he wrote to the incumbent, Innocent, suggesting that the exercise of free will by individual Christians would undermine the authority of the bishops. Innocent acquiesced in the condemnation but allowed Pelagius and Caelestius to appeal. Pelagius wrote out his own defence and sent it in; Caelestius went to Rome in person just as a new bishop, Zosimus, a Greek who had no relationship with Augustine, had taken office. Pelagius and Caelestius' personal submissions to Zosimus persuaded him that they were not heretics.

However, now the emperor Honorius intervened. Apparently worried by Pelagius' attacks on corruption, he condemned him from his court in Ravenna. There were rumours that Honorius had been swayed by bribery provided by one of Augustine's colleagues, the bishop of Tagaste. At yet another council, the North African bishops recorded their support of the emperor. Zosimus had to submit to Honorius' command, infuriating eighteen Italian bishops in his diocese who continued to support Pelagius.

One of the dissenting Italian bishops was Julian, bishop of Eclanum, and he now became the leader of the opposition to Augustine. The contrast between the two men was significant. Augustine was now an old man and it is not unfair to say that his mind often drifted into fantasy. However difficult it was to find reasoned, or even unambiguous, scriptural support for the idea, the doctrine of the resurrection of the body at the Last Judgement was now accepted as orthodoxy. Augustine could not resist telling readers of *The City of God* exactly how they would reappear in this imagined world. He is very precise. Everyone will keep their sex, including their genitals, although these will be relieved of desire. Everyone will appear as they were in their maturity – the old in a younger form, children in an older one, even if they died as babies. All bodies will be perfect, amputated limbs will be fixed back on. One warms to Augustine's confident promise that 'fat people and thin people need not fear that in that world they will be the kind of people that they would have preferred not to be while they are in this world'. He even describes how people who have been eaten by cannibals will be reconstituted. One of the central tenets of Greek philosophy, that one should know where the limits of knowledge lie, had been totally eclipsed by this feat of speculative fantasy.

Julian, on the other hand, was more rooted in the real world. The use of medical and legal analogies in his writings suggests that he was able to integrate secular knowledge into his theology much more readily than Augustine was prepared to. He was a forerunner of Thomas Aquinas in acknowledging the importance of rational thought. God would not have allowed his two major gifts to the human race, scripture and reason, to conflict with each other, so one could be sure that reason would always find the correct understanding of scripture. There was no need to accept something just as a matter of faith. Against Augustine, Julian argued that it would devalue God if he had allowed sinful souls to be brought into being and so he must have created each soul anew. It had no link with earlier generations as Augustine imagined. God even gave us sexual desire and it clearly had a good purpose; without it human beings would not procreate. Of course, human beings had to use their God-given free will to control their sexual instincts, but there was no reason why this should be especially difficult. Sexual desire did not rage for Julian in the way it did in the fevered mind of the likes of Jerome. Julian also stressed the humanity of Christ. It is because Christ is close to us in nature that he is an inspiration. If his divinity was elevated then he would not be nearly so impressive an exemplar.

While Pelagius appears to have lived his life on the defensive, Julian was determined to go on the attack. He was clearly a man of compassion – during a time of famine he is known to have distributed his possessions to the poor – and he was repelled by Augustine's obsession with the sinfulness of mankind and the way in which he seemed to accept the burning of unbaptised infants without emotion. He let Augustine know of the depth of his disgust, through highlighting Augustine's most bleak suggestions, among them the idea that deformity in a baby was a manifestation of its original sin. He forced Augustine into defensive responses.

The Pelagian debates have been seen as the first theological controversy to take place within the western church (a reminder of how far the west lagged behind the east in such debates). The exchange with Julian was still on-going when Augustine died but it was by now impossible to save Pelagius and Julian's views. The central issues related to whether human beings could control their fate and whether God was a force for goodness in the human world, on the side of humanity rather than against it. Pelagius could, of course, be criticised for his optimistic view of human perfection, as if being good was simply a matter of willing it. Augustine's vision of a church that contained the sinners as well as the saints and the self-righteous was attractive but the ultimate fate Augustine decreed for most of them, saints or sinners, at the hands of a God still smarting from his rejection by Adam and Eve, was not. Most serious of all, the controversy had been settled through power politics and, probably, bribery rather than through rational argument.

The episode marks a low point in the history of western theology. Human beings were for centuries defined predominantly in terms of their sinfulness (and as such, this marks the triumph of Paul's Letter to the Romans) and this filtered through into political philosophy in the sense that it made authoritarian societies easier to justify. It took centuries before secular forces and alternative ways of defining human values were able to reassert themselves – the achievement of the Enlightenment. The way that the dispute was settled did nothing to promote theology as a means of finding ultimate truth. As with the disputes over the Trinity, theologians had been reduced to the subservient role of finding arguments to support what the authorities had already decreed as doctrine.

Augustine died in 430 just as the Vandals, one of the Gothic tribes, had reached the gates of Hippo. Miraculously his library was saved and his pre-eminence as the theologian of Catholic Christianity ensured that it was copied. Over five hundred of his sermons survive in addition to most of his major works. He has to be acknowledged as one of the greatest minds of late antiquity, if not equal, say, to his mentor Plotinus. However, in an age where horizons were narrowing, his intellectual dominance became corrosive. By the time of Gregory the Great, at the end of the sixth century, the major figures of Latin Christianity were reading only Augustine. No tradition of learning can flourish on the adulation of a single individual, however brilliant. The combination of his authority as a teacher and his pessimism about the human condition was a major factor in stifling independent thought in the medieval era. All too often the works of Augustine would be brought out as a battering ram against those who began to speculate freely.

Equally, Augustine helped create a mood. Cardinal Lothario dei Segni, who came to the papal throne as Innocent III in 1198, wrote what was a best seller by medieval standards, *On the Contempt of the Worlds*. It was as if the thought of Jerome and Augustine had fused in his religious imagination: 'Man has been formed of dust, clay, ashes and, a thing far more vile, of the filthy sperm. Man has been conceived in the desire of the flesh, in the heat of the sensual lust, in the foul stench of wantonness . . . His evil doings offend God, offend his neighbours, offend himself . . . Accordingly, he is destined to become the fuel of the everlasting, eternally painful hellfire: the food of the voracious consuming worms.'

The European mind was too vital to be cowed by this but this ideology of pessimism, with all that implied for the sapping of intellectual vigour, was certainly prevalent in the centuries to come.

Divine but Human

WHILE AUGUSTINE WAS WRITING AND PREACHING IN NORTHERN Africa, events were moving fast in the eastern empire. On the death of Theodosius I in 395, the empire was split between his two young sons, Honorius in the west and Arcadius in the east. Power sharing between emperors had become common since the time of Diocletian but now the division into western and eastern empires became permanent. The fates of the two halves were to be very different. The western empire collapsed while, in one of the most remarkable survival stories in world history, the 'Romans', as the Greeks now called themselves, sustained the Byzantine empire until it was finally overthrown by the Ottoman Turks in 1453. They did this despite blow after blow from their surrounding enemies, including the Persians and the forces of Islam which overran much of the southern half of the empire in the seventh century. The Byzantine empire used to be seen as stagnant and exotic, introspective and consumed by court intrigues, but its capacity to adapt its administration and defence towards new threats was extraordinary.[1]

So far as the eastern church was concerned, however, Theodosius' coup of the 380s had left many issues unresolved. The boundaries between orthodoxy and heresy had only been tentatively defined and it was impossible to find a way of clarifying them. The 'Arians' survived in Constantinople and in one riot had even burned down the church of Santa Sophia. Paganism had been confronted in the 390s but could not easily be eradicated, especially in the rural areas where it showed a tenacity rooted in centuries of custom. Assaults on paganism also meant challenging the major philosophies and education system that between them had upheld and fostered rational debate and high-quality rhetoric for centuries. Within the Nicene church itself, the new supremacy of the bishop of Constantinople, second only to Rome, had caused enormous resentment in Alexandria. It was still uncertain whether the emperors were ready to use their power and influence to impose religious uniformity as Theodosius I had done.

However, Arcadius showed none of the resilience and political intelligence of his father. Nectarius had been a shrewd appointment as bishop of Constantinople in 381 and remained in his post until 397. His successor, John Chrysostom, the 'Golden-mouthed' preacher of Antioch, on the other hand, was the choice of the imperial eunuch Eutropius. John was prickly in temperament, hopelessly antisocial and reckless in asserting his authority. While he denounced the rich for their profligacy, he believed that a bishop should enjoy precedence, even in the imperial palace. At first Eudoxia, the pious wife of Arcadius, welcomed him for his asceticism, but she and the other members of the Constantinople elite were soon unsettled by his outspoken attacks on their finery. Only the poor, who relished John's vivid attacks on the extravagance of the rich, supported him but such a volatile group was to prove impossible to control.

As John's popularity waned, it was inevitable that Theophilus, bishop of Alexandria, a city still smarting from the elevation of Constantinople in 381, would watch for an opportunity to discredit him. At first things did not look hopeful for Theophilus. His destruction of the Serapeion in 391 had unsettled the emperors. He had now decided to join the campaign against Origen and he exiled a group of Origenist monks. These, led by four Tall or Long Brothers, as they became known, arrived in Constantinople to complain of their treatment. Eudoxia and Arcadius demanded that Theophilus come to Constantinople to explain himself and John was ordered by the court to preside at the interrogation. A confrontation between the bishops, one technically superior to the other who did not recognise his status, seemed inevitable.

Theophilus could hardly defy the imperial summons but he took the longest route possible to the capital, overland through Palestine, Syria and Asia Minor, canvassing for support among other bishops as he did so. His retinue arrived in Constantinople a year after the summons with a mass of hangers-on, including bishops from Asia whom John had deposed for corruption. Once they had settled outside the city, they began gathering grievances against John who did nothing to help himself by refusing to preside over the coming tribunal. In desperation the court abandoned him, and Theophilus, with the support of Eudoxia, arrogantly pronounced his deposition. In June 404 John left Constantinople. He returned briefly but died in exile in 407.[2]

John's unhappy experience shows that the relationship between church and the emperors was still undefined. It depended on the personalities involved and the degree to which they were prepared to manoeuvre, with or without scruples, to achieve their ends. In theory, the court held all the coercive power and could use it, as Theodosius had done, to impose its will on the church. In practice, the weakness of Arcadius, the impulsiveness of Eudoxia and John's self-created isolation, had allowed Theophilus to snatch a temporary victory from what appeared to be a hopelessly weak position. There were to be long-term repercussions. Theophilus included his nephew, Cyril in his retinue, and when Theophilus died in 412, Cyril, as has been seen, came triumphantly and violently into his own. He had no inhibitions about confronting a bishop of Constantinople as ruthlessly as his uncle had done.

Arcadius died in 408. His son, Theodosius II, who survived until 450, achieving the longest rule of any emperor, saw it as his duty to defend orthodoxy. This was not easy. The boundaries were never clear. One of Theodosius' laws, of 428, listed over twenty heretical sects, including Arians, 'Macedonians' and Manicheists. Furthermore, the wealth of the church was such that rival groups would taunt each other with accusations of heresy in the hope of dislodging their opponents. Heresy and orthodoxy became very flexible concepts. One unfortunate bishop of Synnada (in Phrygia) travelled to Constantinople to complain of 'heretics' in his diocese only for these to declare that they were now 'orthodox' and justified in seizing control of the diocese in his absence. They were never expelled.

Pagans continued to be targeted. In 435 orders were given for all pagan shrines still standing to be destroyed and three years later Theodosius commanded the praetorian prefect of the east to 'exercise watchfulness over the pagans and their heathen enormities' as 'despite a thousand terrors of the laws' they continued to sin 'with audacious madness'. In the same year, 438, a law deprived Jews of all 'honours and dignities' and banned them from any administrative role, even those involving the defence of a city.[3]

These laws were comparatively ineffective. Synagogues continued to be built and paganism was still strong in the countryside well into the sixth century. The most important reason for the lack of imperial success was a fresh debate which consumed the energies and ambitions of the leading bishops. One result of the elevation of Jesus into the Godhead was to leave it unclear how his humanity, as described in the gospels, could be related to his new divine status. The Nicene creed simply stated that 'he became a man' but provided no further enlightenment. How had he shown his continuing divinity while on earth? One might suggest his miracles, the special nature of his teachings, the inability to sin and the resurrection, yet what room did this leave for his humanity? Did he switch from being divine to human at will or did two natures co-exist at all times? Did Jesus have emotions or did he transcend them? Were they 'real' emotions or only designed to ensure effective contact with his followers? Could he suffer pain? If he could, then was he really a god? If not, what was the point of the crucifixion?

No two theologians were likely to agree on a single precise formula to describe the relationship between the two natures and so the issue became caught up in the existing rivalry between Constantinople and Alexandria. In

428 a new bishop of Constantinople, Nestorius, had taken office. Like John Chrysostom he was socially clumsy, offending Pulcheria, the emperor's pious elder sister, by refusing to allow her to come up to communion with the emperor and pointing out an apparent contradiction between her assertive presence in public life and her professed virginity. He annoyed others by vigorously asserting his authority over the eastern church. On the issue of Jesus' humanity, he followed the tradition of Antioch, which taught that as Mary was fully human, she could not have given birth to someone who was fully God. Jesus must be accorded a human nature of some sort although it was unclear how this related to his undoubted divinity.

This view was now threatened by the increasing veneration shown for the Virgin Mary. A new title for her had been proposed, perhaps as early as Origen, that of Mary as *Theotokos*, 'the bearer of God'. The title did not offend Nicaea but it assumed that the primary nature of Jesus was divine. Naturally, the supporters of *Theotokos* accepted that Jesus had some human elements but placed these somewhere within a single divine nature. This approach was more popular in Alexandria. When Nestorius unwisely preached his own views, which included the title of 'bearer of Christ', rather than 'bearer of God', for Mary, Cyril, now bishop of Alexandria, saw his chance to challenge him. Cyril accused Nestorius of asserting that Christ had two natures, and issued a list of 'Twelve Anathemas', his own version of Nestorius' apparent 'heresies', including the denial of Mary as *Theotokos*, which he called on Nestorius to renounce. He then sent a distorted version of Nestorius' views to the bishop of Rome, Celestine, who was only too happy to join in a campaign against a bishop of Constantinople.

The concept of a single or a divided nature of Christ was a purely artificial one. It could never be related to any text from the gospels although it could perhaps be argued that the synoptics favoured the Nestorian position and the gospel of John the Alexandrian. This, of course, helped no one as it was impossible to propose that one gospel contained more theological truth than another. It was an issue that could be recognised as insoluble or, if the debate became too fractious, as one to be settled by imperial decree. Theodosius failed to appreciate this. As a result the church was torn apart by bitter argument for the next twenty years and when Theodosius' successor Marcion did finally intervene to impose a solution it led to a major split within eastern Christianity.

The first attempt to settle the issue was a stage-managed council in Ephesus that Cyril persuaded Theodosius to endorse. It met in July 431. It was an astute choice of venue because of the legend that Mary had come here with the apostle John after the crucifixion and here as much as anywhere she was venerated as *Theotokos*. There was no easier way of isolating Nestorius and when he arrived from Constantinople, he was barred from the council where Cyril and his followers declared him a Judas. His supporters were outraged. Theodosius realised he had lost the initiative and vainly tried to excommunicate the major participants on both sides of the controversy.

Cyril knew how to respond. He scoured Egypt for gifts, and an impressive array of gold coins and exotic items including ostrich eggs was shipped from Alexandria to Constantinople for distribution around the court in the hope of winning the emperor's support. It had some effect. Theodosius understood that it would be impossible for Nestorius to remain as bishop of Constantinople and he was sent off to a monastery in Antioch. Before he went he announced that he would accept *Theotokos* so long as the term could be interpreted in a way he could support. Officially he had escaped the stigma of heresy. Cyril was allowed to retain his bishopric.

Cyril also showed that he was ready to compromise. Secure now that his rival in Constantinople had been deposed, he accepted a formula which retained *Theotokos* but which talked of two natures in union, Christ as both perfect god and perfect man with the latter 'one in substance' with the rest of humanity.[4] This satisfied no one. Many of Cyril's supporters felt that any talk of a two-nature Christ was a concession to Nestorius and a declaration by Theodosius in 435 that Nestorius was indeed a heretic was not enough to calm them. When Cyril died in 444, he was succeeded as bishop of Alexandria by Dioscorus, a hardliner who wanted to discard Cyril's compromise and return to a one (divine) nature formula. Dioscorus launched his own assault on the new bishop of Constantinople, Flavian, and once again Theodosius was induced to summon a council to Ephesus.

The triumphant Dioscorus called on Leo I, bishop of Rome, 440–61, to support him by coming to Ephesus. It was to his credit that Leo avoided getting drawn into the political and theological quagmire and he refused. Leo was not a creative theologian but he had a clear and vigorous mind and saw his chance to draw up a statement of what he understood was western belief on the matter of Christ's humanity. To the horror of Dioscorus, it was not far from that of Nestorius. Leo's Tome (the term for an official papal letter) set out a Christ in whom divine and human natures co-exist. Each has its own sphere of activity but these operate without becoming separate. 'He who is true God is also true man: and in this union there is no lie, since the humility of manhood and the loftiness of the Godhead both meet there. For as God is not changed by the showing of pity, so man is not swallowed up by the dignity. For each form does what is proper to it with the co-operation of the other; that is the Word performing what appertains to the Word, and the flesh carrying out what appertains to the flesh. One of them sparkles with miracles, the other succumbs to injuries.' This description – it can hardly be called more than that – of two natures had the virtue of clarity.

The Council of Ephesus of 449 was a nasty affair. Dioscorus set it up to achieve his own end, the condemnation of Flavian. He would not even allow

Leo's *Tome*, which Flavian was happy to support, to be read. He proposed the council endorse what appeared to be an uncontentious reaffirmation of Nicaea. Once this had been agreed he announced that Flavian had violated the creed and must be deposed. The doors of the church were flung open and a gang of heavyweights poured in. Dioscorus announced that all must sign the decree excommunicating Flavian, who had taken refuge in the sanctuary. Blank pieces of paper were provided for signatures. Flavian was so badly beaten that he died soon afterwards. In Rome, Leo denounced this 'robber council' to the emperor. Theodosius, once again outmanoeuvred, meekly told Leo that 'peace reigned and pure truth was supreme'. A new bishop of Constantinople, a protégé of Dioscorus, was eased into place. It was one of the last acts of Theodosius' life. Out hunting in July 450, he fell from his horse and died.

So here was a dispute that had been festering for twenty years but was still no closer to resolution. The impossibility of finding a coherent theological statement was now obvious. Even if a council had met in peace to discuss the matter, wrangling and rivalry would have disrupted it. The failure lay with Theodosius. The full range of his legislation on religion is preserved in a separate section in the famous Theodosian Law Code of 438 and it can be seen that many of his laws appear to be responses to crises rather than part of a defined strategy. He should either have left the church to sort the matter out and concentrated on his political duties or imposed a solution. While claiming that he wished to gain the goodwill of 'Our Lord and Saviour Jesus Christ' by maintaining orthodoxy, his inconsistency had simply allowed the bullyboys such as Cyril and Dioscorus to gain the upper hand.

There was then a remarkable development. Pulcheria emerged from the shadows and promptly took as her consort one Marcian, a soldier whom she elevated as emperor beside her. She was a supporter of Flavian and Leo and loathed Dioscorus. The remains of Flavian were welcomed back for burial in Constantinople. Pulcheria's niece, Galla Placidia, wife of the western emperor Valentinian III, wrote to her from Rome telling her to 'subvert the wretched Council of Ephesus' and to respect the primacy of Leo. Order was to be restored. A new council was to be summoned and this time it was to be within imperial reach, in Chalcedon, just across the Bosporus from the capital.[5]

No one could call the Council of Chalcedon of 451 harmonious. Sessions were often rowdy, rivals taunting each other with accusations of heresy. However, under the guidance of imperial commissioners whose names head the official accounts, some order was given to the proceedings. The Acts of the Council of 449 were read out and most of the bishops were ashamed at what they had consented to. Dioscorus blustered in his defence but he was eventually condemned and deprived of his see. His senior supporters were pardoned so long as they supported his condemnation and assented to the *Tome* of Leo which was now becoming the talisman of orthodoxy.

Then a new formula began to be put together. No one dared to mention Nestorius' name. Although he was alive, he was officially a heretic. Cyril's theology still had support and, while his Twelve Anathemas were rejected as too extreme, some of his earlier writings against Nestorius were more acceptable. It was decided that *Theotokos* would be part of any agreed formula. Leo's *Tome* was welcomed and a declaration that Flavian had made of his views to the emperor was included among favoured documents. The bishops did begin to put these together but this time they had to contend with highly trained members of the imperial staff. These rejected one formula as too close to the beliefs of the condemned Dioscorus and then set up a small committee of bishops that they could supervise. Marcian met protests at the imposition of his authority by threatening to close down the council and transfer it to Rome! On 25 October 451, the emperor, accompanied by Pulcheria, crossed the Bosporus. Acclaimed as 'the new Constantine', he presided over the session that affirmed a new Definition of Faith.

While much of the final wording of the Definition of Faith came from Cyril's works, it was the *Tome* of Leo that provided the most significant phrases. Christ was declared to be 'at once complete in Godhead and complete in manhood, truly God and truly man'. He was begotten of the Father 'as of his Godhead' but born of the Virgin Mary, who was given the title of *Theotokos*. Within this 'one person, Christ had two [*sic*] natures without confusion, without change, without division, without separation; the distinction of natures being in no way abolished because of the union, but rather the characteristic property of each nature being preserved and coming together to form one person and subsistence.' The extreme Alexandrian position that Jesus had only one incarnate nature was thus rejected. Ironically, the final definition was not, apart from the *Theotokos*, far from what Nestorius himself had preached! In fact, in his exile, he produced a text, only rediscovered in 1895, known as the *Bazaar of Heracleides*. Written before the Council of Chalcedon, it includes phrases such as 'the same one is twofold' that were very similar to those of Chalcedon.

Marcian had imposed his will on the church. He was not to miss his chance of improving church discipline and he now insisted that the bishops condemned abuses such as the sale of bishoprics. With the bishop of Alexandria deposed and the bishop of Rome not present, other than in the person of legates, the powers of the bishop of Constantinople, the emperor's 'own' bishop, could also be strengthened. Henceforth the bishop would be able to hear appeals against the decisions of the metropolitan bishops, including Antioch and Alexandria. He would be directly responsible for all the bishops of Thrace, the province of Asia and Pontus, as well as any bishop outside the borders of the eastern empire. While Constantinople remained second in place in honour to Rome, within the eastern empire it was to enjoy identical privileges to those of Rome in the west. The papal legates were furious but were easily overruled. Other canons dealt with the monks. As they were in effect self-appointed and not officially clerics or subject to bishops, their unruly behaviour had to be contained. Now all monks had to be subject to a bishop and were bound to celibacy. Marcian signed off the council. 'All therefore shall be bound to hold the decisions of the sacred Council of Chalcedon and indulge no further doubts. Take heed therefore to this edict of our Serenity: abstain from profane words and cease all further discussion of religion [sic]'. Marcian even ordered his soldiers to take an oath of allegiance to the Chalcedonian decisions.

The declaration of Chalcedon was in fact a ritualistic formula. It was a statement of what was to be believed and did not actually explain anything. While contemporaries talked of Christ's human nature being expressed when he wept over the body of Lazarus and his divine nature expressed when he raised him from the dead, one could not go back to the gospels and apply the formula in any coherent way to other events in his life. There is no mention of a 'union of natures' in the New Testament. While the word used for 'person', the Greek prosopon, is found in the New Testament it is not in the sense used at Chalcedon. It was completely unclear how these natures, in any of the ways they were expressed, actually related to the 'historical' Jesus of the gospels. This was not the issue. No formula would have satisfied everyone. The crucial point was that once again it had been shown that only an emperor, with all the coercive force he had at his command, could define doctrine. He had, however, to be determined to assert this role. Marcian had behaved resolutely where Theodosius had faltered.

The Closing of the Schools

DESPITE THE INTERVENTION OF MARCIAN, THE COUNCIL OF Chalcedon did not bring peace to the church. In Alexandria the mere mention of the phrase 'two natures' set off rioting by the monks and anger among traditionalists. The inclusion of extracts from Cyril's works in the Chalcedonian formula was not enough to calm them. They dug out phrases from the *Tome*, such as 'the Word performing what appertains to the Word, and the flesh carrying out what appertains to the flesh', which, they claimed, could only refer to two natures and thus to 'heretical' Nestorianism. They were so furious with the betrayal of Chalcedon that they consolidated their own belief in the single nature of the divine *logos*, made flesh in the person of Jesus, monophysitism as it became known. Monophysitism spread from Egypt to Armenia and even into Ethiopia. To this day, Dioscorus remains honoured in Coptic Christian churches in Egypt. Of Egyptian Christians, 95 per cent are members of the Coptic Church, which claims to have maintained the true teaching of the nature of Christ against the 'heresy' instituted by Chalcedon.

At the same time Nestorius was not forgotten. His followers remained strong in Syria and Nestorianism spread eastwards, across the border into Persia. The Nestorians' views were often expressed in Syriac, adding another dimension of complexity to the whole debate. Nestorian missionaries proved enormously energetic and spread the gospel as far as India and China. No other branch of Christianity covered as wide an expanse as that of the Nestorians until the sixteenth century when the Spanish and Portuguese created their 'Christian' empires in the Americas.

Despite Marcian's initiative and effective handling of his fractious Christian subjects, the result was a church which had become fragmented into three branches. Even so, the emperor had reasserted himself as the focal point for the Chalcedonian church. When Marcian died in 457 (Pulcheria had predeceased him in 453), the bishop of Constantinople, the patriarch as he was now known, presided for the first time over the coronation of an emperor. An acclamation from the congregation called on God to accept the new emperor Leo and linked his rule directly with that of Christ. It was a ritual which became inseparable from the rule of the Byzantine emperors and was even used by the Doges in Venice at their coronations in St Mark's.

Certainly, seventy years later (527), when one of the last great figures of antiquity, Justinian, took the imperial office he personified the role of emperor as the chosen of God. His determination to restore supremacy and unity to the church was paramount. His Law Codes, a triumph of consolidation of existing Roman law, were issued in the names of the emperor and the Lord Jesus Christ. He put in hand legislation to restrict citizenship to orthodox Christians alone. While the closing of Plato's Academy in Athens in 529 is the symbol of Justinian's shutting down of pagan philosophy, it was the laws that immediately followed that enforced the ban on pagan worship. One law, of about 531, exhorted all pagans to come forward for baptism, prohibited them from teaching and ordered that their children should be forcibly instructed in Christianity. *Parrhesia*, the freedom to teach others or be consulted on public matters without risk of condemnation, which pagan philosophers had traditionally enjoyed, was withdrawn. The last functioning Egyptian temple, that on the island of Philae dedicated to Isis, had been closed down in 526. Of course, one could not suppress paganism. It lingered as 'superstitions' in the countryside. As late as the Quinisext Council of 692, the church was attempting to ban public dances, invocations to Dionysus and the lighting of fires to the new moon. Yet this was the moment when Christianity became compulsory for all subjects of the eastern empire.

Nor was Justinian slow to enforce orthodoxy. It was now over fifty years since the last emperor of the west, Romulus Augustulus, had abdicated, but the eastern emperors had never abandoned their claim to rule the whole of the former empire. Justinian was particularly incensed that the 'barbarian' successor states in the west were 'Arian'. The 'barbarians' had faithfully retained their belief in a subordinationist Christ ever since their conversion by Ulfilas. In North Africa, Arian Christianity had been imposed on the population as early as 429 when a determined group of Goths, the Vandals, led by their inspiring leader Gaiseric, overran the African provinces. The relationship between 'orthodox' Catholics, the remaining Donatists and the ruling Arians had not been stable over the following century. Gaiseric was intent on eradicating Catholic Christianity from the Vandal heartland, the African province of Proconsularis of which Carthage was the capital, even if persecution, often intense, alternated with periods of tolerance. The fate of the Catholics haunted the conscience of Justinian and he claimed that a vision of a martyred bishop inspired him to re-conquer North Africa.

The campaign of 533 was cleverly planned. A revolt was provoked in another Vandal enclave, Sardinia. Vandal forces rushed to put it down, allowing

Justinian's general Belisarius to land in the bay of Tunis on the mainland of Africa and quickly defeat the remaining Vandal troops. The Vandal elite simply disintegrated. The Africans now found themselves under a Greek-speaking administration that represented the Christianity of Constantinople, not Rome. Archaeology shows that Justinian embarked on a major programme of church building but Byzantine rule only survived until the next wave of invaders, the Muslims, swept along the North African coast in the seventh century.

Buoyed up by his initial success, Justinian now turned to Italy. Following the collapse of the empire, the Ostrogothic leader Theodoric had established his own kingdom based at Ravenna in 493. The kingdom extended from Italy into southern France and over the Visigoths in Spain and, although Arian in belief, was tolerant to the mass of its Catholic subjects. The 'Arians' worshipped in Gothic but in many ways the two Christianities were hard to distinguish. While the Arians proclaimed, 'Glory be to the Father through the Son in the Holy Ghost', the Catholic version was 'Glory be to the Father and the Son and the Holy Ghost'. In the east such things mattered; there is not much evidence that they did in western Europe.

In Ravenna itself, it is virtually impossible to distinguish between Arian and Catholic churches. The palace church of Theodoric was Sant' Apollinare Nuovo, where the Ostrogothic leader commissioned the dazzling mosaics of Christ's miracles, his Passion and resurrection, the first-known cycle of these which survive. The sumptuous *Codex Argenteus*, a 'silver' bible – the lettering being in silver and gold – is a Gothic text of the gospels probably commissioned by Theodoric himself. When Theodoric visited Rome in 500, 'Pope Symmachus and all the senate and people of Rome came joyfully to meet him outside the city'. One can hardly imagine how Ambrose or Athanasius would have reacted to this welcome of a heretic. 'Although he himself was of the Arian sect', one chronicle records, Theodoric 'nevertheless attempted nothing against the Catholics, so that by the Romans he was hailed as another Trajan or Valentinian.'[1] There is evidence that he restored some of the decaying buildings of Rome.

So Justinian did not need to rescue oppressed Catholics from a harsh heretical elite. Nevertheless, the temptation of another easy victory, this time to recover the ancient core of the Roman empire, was too great. Justinian and Belisarius misjudged the campaign badly. The mountainous terrain of Italy has always been difficult to fight in, the Ostrogoths proved resilient and the local population was ambivalent about being 'rescued' by a Greek-speaking emperor. The war dragged on for twenty years and it saw the final collapse of the Roman administration, including the extinction of the last of the senatorial families and the cutting of the aqueducts that had served Rome so well for centuries. In the event, the 'Romans' of the east were among the most effective destroyers of the empire of the west. Victory, when it came in 554, was limited to control of the shell of Rome, Ravenna, a fragile corridor between them and a scattering of fortresses and cities. In Ravenna, the victorious Catholics obliterated evidence of Theodoric in the mosaics of Sant' Apollinare but otherwise preserved the church. In the astonishing church of San Vitale, begun by the Arian Ostrogoths but completed by the Byzantines, triumphant mosaics show Justinian and his empress, Theodora, whom he had raised from a dubious past as a circus artiste, first as his mistress, then his wife. The mosaics mask a hollow victory, made even emptier when the Lombards exploited the breakdown to invade Italy from the north and establish their own kingdom there.

The final design of San Vitale may echo Justinian's audience chamber in Constantinople. The emperor's supreme architectural achievement, the church of Santa Sophia, was closer to home. The original church of this name, founded by Constantine, had been destroyed in riots of 532 that had come close to overthrowing Justinian. (The resolute Theodora persuaded her husband to massacre the insurgents.) The new Santa Sophia, completed, after its first dome collapsed, in 563, is one of the finest buildings from antiquity, equalled only perhaps by the Parthenon in Athens and the Pantheon in Rome. Its centrepiece is a great dome rising from four massive piers with two huge semi-domes on the eastern and western sides. The whole was originally sumptuously decorated with mosaics and marble. The dome, wrote one contemporary, the historian Procopius, appears as if suspended from heaven. A thousand lamps lit the interior – its glow, wrote another contemporary, Paul the Silentiary, showed the returning seafarer not only his passage home but 'the way to the living God'.

Justinian was equally determined to restore Christian unity in his kingdom where the split between his own Christianity and the Nestorian and Monophysite alternatives remained. When a devastating plague swept through the empire in the 540s, even infecting Justinian, he took it as God's judgement for his failure to heal the wounds of division. More pragmatically, he desperately needed to regain the allegiance of the provinces of Egypt and Syria and he decided that the priority was to bring the Monophysites back into the church. His way of doing this was clumsy. He hoped to impress the Monophysites by condemning the apparent Nestorian sympathies of three earlier theologians, Theodore of Mopsuestia, Theodoret of Cyrrhus and Ibas of Edessa who had always been seen as orthodox. Their works were condemned under the name of 'The Three Chapters', specific writings of each of the three.

When Vigilius, the bishop of Rome, was summoned to Constantinople to give the condemnation an ecumenical dimension, it was in the face of immense opposition from the western bishops who deplored the posthumous excommunication of the three theologians. Vigilius managed to avoid attending the council that Justinian held in his capital in 553 and the Three Chapters were condemned in his absence. Vigilius put himself in a hopeless position by succumbing to pressure from Justinian and agreeing that he did support the condemnation! This damned him back in Rome and when he died in Sicily on his way home his body was refused burial in St Peter's.

Unity was no easier to achieve in the east. Over a hundred years after Chalcedon, it was by now far too late to win back the Monophysites. Their leaders had given up any hope of converting the empire back to their own 'one nature' formula and had established themselves as fully independent churches with boundaries that stretched beyond the empire. Yet there were some important consequences of the council of 553. It established the standards by which orthodoxy was to be judged. Allegiance was pledged to 'the things we have received from Holy Scripture and from the teachings of the Holy Fathers and from the definitions of one and the same faith by four sacred councils'.

This did not, of course provide any kind of stable basis for theology. How could one reconcile the very different contributions by these three sources of orthodoxy to establish any tenable theological conclusion? The best that could be hoped for was that any established dogma could be 'proved' by calling on one or the other source for support. It was the shift from scripture to 'the teachings of the Holy Fathers' that was most significant for the future of eastern theology. The scriptures were allocated a diminished place alongside the church fathers and the councils. It was now that Athanasius was enshrined as the beacon of orthodoxy and it was he who was credited with the declaration of Mary as *Theotokos.* At the same council of 553, Origen was condemned as a heretic, probably from a distorted version of his writings. Christian history was being rewritten to fit with the Nicene and Chalcedonian formulas and the words 'church father' now became synonymous with orthodoxy. 'The often fallible and brawling bishops of history had become the sainted and infallible authorities for a monolithic, unchanging Christian tradition' as one commentator puts it.[2]

What did this mean for pagan philosophy? The Athenian philosophers who had been banned in 529 made for exile in Persia where the atmosphere was more tolerant. One of them, Simplicius, wrote some of the most penetrating commentaries that exist on Aristotle while he was there but after the first burst of energy the exiles fade entirely from history. In the increasingly Christianised empire, the philosophical mind turned to criticising the more empirical of the classical philosophers such as Aristotle. In the hands of John Philoponus, 'the lover of toil', of Alexandria (*c.* 490–570), this was a sophisticated attack. Philoponus noted the contradictions in Aristotle's works and the weaknesses of his arguments for the eternity of the world (arguments which any orthodox Christian had to confront). He went further to challenge Aristotle's explanation of dynamic processes, putting forward his own theories of impetus. He used these to explain how God sent the heavenly bodies into their paths at the moment of creation.

Philoponus' works went into abeyance after he was declared a heretic a hundred years after his death for an analysis of the Trinity that implied that there were three gods within the Godhead. However, when Aristotle's philosophy had become entrenched orthodoxy in the Middle Ages, his critiques were rediscovered and provided ammunition for the Renaissance counterattack on Aristotelian scholasticism. Philoponus' critical thinking existed uneasily within Christian belief but he showed that even some scientific advance might be made so long as it did not challenge the authority of the church or any of the major articles of faith. These were regarded as unassailable and Philoponus' own condemnation makes the point.

The other trend in sixth-century Christian philosophy was towards mysticism, notably in the works of Pseudo-Dionysius (see p.321 below). Here, the surrender to contemplation meant that the heart had been taken out of the ancient tradition of reasoned empirical thought. There was a major decline in the copying of ancient authors. The rubbish dumps in Egypt have provided us with a reliable century-by-century record of what was being copied. The number of classical authors reproduced drops off after 300 and no more than twenty papyri which cite the Greek classics are known for the entire reign of Justinian.

While in the west in the thirteenth century the classicist Petrarch bemoaned the 'dark age' which had fallen on Europe, he is echoed by the twelfth-century Byzantine chronicler John Zonaras, who accused Justinian of being responsible for a new level of 'boorishness' as a result of his closing of 'the schools'. 'The sixth century' writes one modern scholar, 'is a period in which the philosophical glory that was Greece was wearing thin. Philosophers, and especially pagan ones, are rare birds indeed, flocking together for shelter and survival in various parts of the empire.'[3]

In 787, a seventh ecumenical council met at Nicaea. Its proceedings have been described as 'long and verbose, at an intellectual level far below preceding councils' with the primary business being the restoration of icons as worthy of reverence (after a campaign against the depiction of sacred images had led to the mass destruction of many of them).[4] It was at this council that the bishops of the east closed down their church to further change. They accepted the decrees of the six earlier ecumenical councils and then announced: 'To make our confessions short, we keep unchanged all the ecclesiastical traditions handed down to us, whether in writing or verbally'.

By now book learning, and certainly original composition, were rare. Nothing is known of any Christian schools in the Byzantine world in this period. It was left to a group of civil servants to copy out some of the great works of Greek literature that still survived in earlier manuscripts. The histories of Herodotus and Thucydides and a few plays of Aeschylus and Sophocles are known only because of the dedication of these secular scholars.[5] By the tenth century, it is estimated that there were no more than three hundred scholars receiving a higher education in Constantinople in any given year. The Orthodox churches of the east continued to provide mystery and a theological underpinning to the regime but the tradition of debate lay dead under the mantle of ritual and ceremony.

A Fragile Church

CHRISTIANITY AND THE COLLAPSE OF THE WESTERN EMPIRE

THE EAST SAW THE GREATEST DESTRUCTION OF PAGAN SHRINES, BUT their obliteration was also common in the west. Martin of Tours, one of the most popular bishop-saints of the late fourth century, was renowned for miracles which caused the collapse or burning of a shrine. There is a dramatic falling off of pagan activity in the archaeological record after the fourth century and the written sources of the time give us triumphant accounts of the breaking up of pagan statues. In the later *Ecclesiastical History of the English People*, the Venerable Bede describes with approval the massacre of a group of heretical Welsh priests 'because they had despised the offer of everlasting salvation' through their obstinacy.

Much of this was sheer vandalism or the exploits of a local holy man trying to improve his status as a committed Christian. It was Augustine who elaborated a more sophisticated ideology which condoned the persecution of pagans and heretics. His thinking developed slowly as a result of his experiences with the Donatists, the majority Christian church in North Africa and ardent rivals of Augustine's Catholicism.[1]

The Donatists had adopted the Nicene Trinity and so could hardly be called heretics. They regarded themselves as the true church in that they had kept the purity of their faith isolated from the Catholic church which, ever since the reign of Constantine, they had seen as rooted in compromise, too sympathetic to the lapsed and seduced by the wealth on offer from the emperors. Any confrontation by the state simply reinforced their identity as the church of the martyrs and they were happy to throw back Jesus' words from the Sermon on the Mount, 'Blessed are they who are persecuted for righteousness' sake', at their opponents.

In the early fifth century, the state authorities began to move against the Donatists. Quite apart from the challenge they presented to what was now a state church, their more fanatical members were engaging in violent campaigns in the countryside and had to be confronted for reasons of good order.

The emperor Honorius knew that they would not be eradicated easily and he approached the problem through a stage-managed council of some six hundred Catholic and Donatists bishops meeting in Carthage in 411. If there was a core theological issue, it was whether a Christian community should be essentially an assembly of saints, those who had remained pure, as the Donatists argued, or a more worldly body made up of saints and sinners alike. Augustine attended and his voice gradually became more dominant. He quoted Matthew on the gathering of fish, with the worthless being thrown away only at the end of time (13: 47–50). One could never distinguish who would be saved, even from among the faithful members of the church, argued Augustine, so it was impossible to select an elite on merit. Nor could the Donatists claim that the Catholics were so unworthy that any Catholic converting to Donatism had to be baptised anew. (Here the Donatists followed the teaching of Cyprian, the martyr-bishop of Carthage, whom they deeply revered.) It was decreed that the sacraments of the church existed as sacred vessels, independent of those who administered them, so that even a baptism by the most unworthy of priests had validity. It followed that rebaptism would always be superfluous. This view, also set out in Augustine's *De doctrina christiana*, is still official Catholic teaching.[2]

The presiding civil servant had been instructed by Honorius to make sure that the Donatists were condemned by the majority in the council. They duly were and in 412 the very act of being a Donatist was declared a criminal offence. In these years Augustine developed a sophisticated rationale for their persecution. He claimed, for instance, that many of the Donatist faithful had been bullied into acquiescence by their church and that the Catholics had a duty to 'liberate' them from their faith. He soon went further to argue that the church had the right to save the surviving Donatists from the perdition which would be their undoubted fate if they kept loyal to their church, and force was justified to this end. He gave examples of where God had used force in the scriptures, especially in achieving the conversion of Paul (by throwing him on the ground).

It is true that Augustine worried over how an individual could be sure that he was carrying out God's will when he persecuted others but he believed that sincere members of the church would always act in accordance with God's will. Here his view, that the church itself is made up of saints and sinners and so even committed Catholics might commit sin in their persecuting zeal, became submerged. His conclusion: 'What does brotherly love do? Does it, because it fears the short-lived fires of the furnaces for the few, abandon all to the eternal fires of hell?' is a chilling one, not least in ethical terms. Does the end really justify the means? Yet, it was this rationale that was developed by the medieval church to justify the burning of those defined as heretics.[3] The Donatists eventually vanished under the waves of invaders, Vandals, Byzantines and finally Muslims that swept through North Africa in the next three centuries.

The medieval church would never have come into being if a hierarchy had not been established under the primacy of the popes. There were many reasons why the bishops of Rome had found it difficult to assert their authority in the first centuries of Christianity. Rome itself was distant from the larger Greek-speaking Christian communities of the eastern Mediterranean. No bishop of Rome had attended any of the ecumenical councils, so Rome's status within the wider Christian world was limited. Within the city, congregations had been founded by immigrant leaders from many different parts of the empire and so drew on a number of different Christian traditions. It was hard for a single bishop to secure their common allegiance, one reason why the elections, such as that of Damasus in 366, were so violent. Moreover, the scattered Christian communities were grouped around the centre of a city whose temples were hallowed by centuries of traditional worship. The pagan senatorial aristocracy was strong and even an emperor as devoutly Christian as Theodosius I had acquiesced in their authority when he visited Rome in 389. It was only in the early fifth century that most of these families converted.[4] The Gothic sack of 410, in which Christian churches were spared, was perhaps crucial in suggesting that the pagan centre of the city was no longer protected by the gods of old. A church such as Santa Sabina, built on the Aventine Hill in the 420s, is symbolically important in that its columns come from an earlier pagan building.

The first bishop to take advantage of the possibilities of effective Christian leadership of the city was Leo I (ruled 440–61). Leo developed his authority on the basis that he was as much the legal as the spiritual heir of Peter and he exerted himself with total confidence through a series of decrees on church government and the status of bishops. He achieved a further condemnation of Pelagius by the Italian bishops. Faced with the high-handed conduct of Hilary, bishop of Arles, who behaved as if he had primacy in Gaul, Leo sought a decree from the emperor through which to reassert his own primacy. There is a legend that Leo, abetted by an apparition of Peter and Paul, forced Attila and the Huns to withdraw from northern Italy. (There were good strategic reasons for the withdrawal and one does not need to invoke the miraculous but the story is an indication of how Leo's reputation prospered.) When he needed to intervene in civilian affairs, he carefully did so as if he were the representative of the emperor. His sermons and writings were in simple direct Latin, a contrast with the more rhetorical and complex language that aristocrats tended to use, and he can be credited with ensuring that there were Latin rites that could be used in the church outside Rome.

Leo had been furious when he heard of the confirmation of Constantinople's elevated status after the Council of Chalcedon. It was an affront to the primacy of Rome. Christ had given authority to Peter, Peter had passed it to the apostles and every bishop, east, west or elsewhere, derived theirs from the apostles. Thus the new status of Constantinople, which had no

apostolic heritage, could not be accepted. It took some diplomatic manoeu-
vring before the emperor Marcian could persuade Leo to split the Definition
of Faith off from the subsequent canons and accept the former.

Yet it was Leo who benefited from the compromise. It was the very first
time that the bishop of Rome had played an important part in the making of
Christian theology. Leo could never hope to have much influence over the Greek-
speaking church, whose major bishoprics were well beyond the reach of the Latin
church in Rome, but this meant he could call the Chalcedonian formula his own
without much chance of rebuttal. The orthodoxy of Chalcedon now went hand
in hand with the rise of papal supremacy. So long as the authority of the pope
was paramount there was no need to provide any further theological justification
for the Definition and it has been accepted by the western churches to this day.

It is really from now that one can talk of popes and the papacy. (*Papa*,
'father', had been used widely in the church but was gradually to be used
exclusively of the bishop of Rome.) Yet no pope could exert effective authority
in an empire that was in the last stages of collapse. The formal end of the
western empire came in 476 when the young emperor Romulus Augustulus
was deposed, although some order was maintained by the Ostrogothic leader
Theodoric. Under Theodoric, for instance, intellectual life continued through
the works of 'Roman' civil servants such as Boethius and Cassiodorus.[5]

It was the campaign against the Ostrogoths by the Byzantine general Belisarius
that brought the greatest destruction to Italy. Looking back from the end of the
sixth century, Gregory the Great lamented the collapse of civilisation. 'Towns are
depopulated, fortified places destroyed, churches burnt, monasteries and
nunneries ravaged . . . Rome itself is disintegrating, the senate is gone, the people
perish, pain and fear grow daily for the few who are left . . .' In his *The Fall of
Rome and the End of Civilization*, Bryan Ward-Perkins details the archaeological
evidence for the total collapse of what had been a relatively prosperous economy.
In many areas living standards in the west now fell below those of pre-Roman
societies and Roman levels of industrial activity may not have been regained
before the sixteenth century. The survivors shrank back to defensible sites.

This is the background to Gregory's reign as pope (590–604). Gregory was
the son of a Roman senator but he had been drawn to monasticism and had
sold his extensive properties and diverted the proceeds to the poor. He was
sent to Constantinople to serve as the emissary of the pope in the eastern
capital but his heart always remained in Rome and he avoided the fate of the
unhappy Vigilius by refusing to get entangled in the disputes that gripped
the eastern church. Back in Rome, he was a natural, if reluctant candidate
for the papacy when it fell vacant in 590.

Gregory was haunted by the experience of living 'in the last times'. Even if the
Byzantines had eventually conquered parts of Italy, the Lombards had taken

advantage of the collapse of the Ostrogoths to assume control over most of northern Italy. The popes accused the Lombards of being Arians although it has proved very difficult to define their Christianity with any clarity. Catholic bishops certainly survived in northern Italy but they had a much lower status than their colleagues in France, as it was now becoming under the Franks, and the Iberian Peninsula. In all Gregory had very little effective power, even though he did manage to launch a mission to England, which resulted in the foundation of the English church at Canterbury, then the capital of the kingdom of Kent.

Despite his restricted influence, however, Gregory was the founder of a new Latin Christianity that was to provide the template for the medieval church. He formulated a basis for his authority. Reluctant to accept the legitimacy of the council of 553 he was nevertheless prepared to acknowledge that those of Nicaea (325), Constantinople (381), Ephesus (431) and Chalcedon (451) were the foundations of orthodoxy. 'In like manner,' wrote Gregory, 'all the four holy synods of the holy universal church we received as we do the four books of the Holy Gospels.' This did not mean that they were authoritative in themselves. 'Without the authority and consent of the apostolic see [Rome] none of the matters transacted by a council have any binding force.' Gregory had effectively positioned the western church apart from the east as well as strengthening the rationale for papal supremacy. Although it was to be another four hundred years before the papacy became a force in European politics, and then as leader of a Christianity which was officially split from the east (in 1054) and with much territory lost to Islam, Gregory deserves to be seen as the founder of the medieval papacy. His stature was enhanced by his writings on pastoral care and his insistence that his bishops enforce their own authority with moderation. Famously, he decreed that pagan shrines should be consecrated as churches, not destroyed, as more ardent Christians such as Martin of Tours had demanded.

Gregory was not an original thinker and he followed Augustine in being suspicious of secular learning, accusing the philosophers of diverting attention from God. He was a man of his times in that he accepted that history unfolded under the auspices of God. So, looking back a hundred years to the conversion of the Frankish king Clovis to Catholic Christianity, which was followed imme- diately by a victory over his Arian rivals, Gregory declared that it was Clovis' orthodoxy that had earned him success. This was a significant shift in the pres- entation of the past. The classical historians did not assume that history was moving in any particular direction but rather that it was the interplay of different forces. It had been Eusebius who had ushered in this new genre of history, one in which God drove events. Eusebius saw the Old Testament as a preliminary to the coming of Christ which led, after the centuries of persecu- tion, to the advent of Constantine and triumph of God in human affairs (which Eusebius could then interpret with reference to Old Testament prophecies). The end time, towards which all is tending, is the Last Judgement (and Gregory can be forgiven for believing that the last times had indeed arrived).

There is a clear moral dimension to Eusebius' approach that was endorsed by later Christian historians. The destruction of the Temple in AD 70, for instance, is a clear indication of God's rejection of the Jews. God intervened, according to Theodoret, to win the battle of Frigidus for Theodosius. If the will of a Christian God is destined to triumph, then the persecution of pagans is justified. So Bede approves of the massacre of heretical priests who assemble unarmed against King Aethilfrith – his English settlers have become God's instrument for the punishment of sinners. Events have to be defined within the parameters of what it is assumed God wills. So although it was perhaps inevitable that the tiny Arian minorities would become assimilated into the mass of Catholics, each 'conversion' of a ruler, whether in Spain or France, was announced as a triumph of God's will. It is hard to overestimate the importance of this ideology for the unfolding of medieval Christendom. It justified the authority of the church as the instrument of God's power and so provided an effective cloak for its territorial and political ambitions. It was not until the fifteenth century that the recovery of the Roman historians inspired the Renaissance humanists to write histories that were rooted once again in secular values.[6]

There were other forces that sustained Christianity in the west at a time when material life was so diminished. One heritage that bound the Christian elites together, whether they were bishops, monks or administrators, was the use of Latin. As literacy was low even in Christian circles and few records survive, it is difficult to delineate the ways in which Latin adapted itself to the new Europe. In Rome, of course, it remained the language of bureaucracy. The major texts, such as those of Augustine, were in Latin and so was the mass and the rest of the liturgy. The church could hardly communicate other than through Latin. In Ireland, which had never been Romanised, Latin was, of course, a foreign language but this gave it a sacred quality that was seen as appropriate for passing on the Word of God.

There were also the monasteries. The first in the west had appeared in the early fifth century and were as much places of refuge from the political turmoil as permanent homes of committed ascetics. The monastery of Lerins, on an island off the coast of southern Gaul, was a stepping stone from which aristocrats moved into bishoprics. Monasteries often grew up close to the shrines of holy men. By the beginning of the sixth century, monks were settling into more stable institutions. In general terms, those parts of Europe which had been most fully Romanised were ruled by bishops who embedded themselves in the ruins of Roman cities; those free of Roman influence, such as the Irish and the Anglo-Saxons, preferred monasteries. 'Rules', especially that of St Benedict (*c.*480–*c.*547), were enormously important in defining communities that had an austere but humane regime of work, study and prayer. Monasteries that chose to exploit their surrounding land could also have an important economic impact in an age when living standards had fallen so dramatically. Crucially each monastery was independent under its own abbot, reinforcing the pattern of a decentralised Christianity.

In recent years, however, the claim that monasteries were centres for the copying of classical texts has been challenged. The average monastic library in Anglo-Saxon England was small, perhaps fifty books in a box, and limited to the Christian staples. The library of Bede at Jarrow, with perhaps some two hundred books, was exceptional. Paradoxically the adoption of minuscule script in the ninth century (in both east and west) led to the loss of much of the classical heritage as enthusiastic copyists in the new script discarded those works they did not choose to reproduce. Across the whole of western Europe only the *Timaeus* among works of Plato, the pagan philosopher whose output was most closely attuned to Christianity, survived into the eleventh century.

There was a spiritual nexus based on a shared belief in miracles and the efficacy of holy men and their bones to effect them. Miracles, 'wondrous things', had always been part of both pagan and Christian societies but the crucial development in Christianity was a rejection of the Greek empirical tradition by the educated elites in favour of a surrender to the miraculous. One can see this transition in the works of Augustine. In about 390, in his *True Religion*, he argues that, while he does not reject the miracles of Jesus, 'miracles would not have been allowed to stretch into our time, or the soul would always be looking for sensations, and the human race would go jaded with their continual occurrence'. Miracles simply did not seem to be part of his everyday experience. Some twenty years on, in *The City of God*, on the other hand, he regales his congregations with a long list of local miracles, which includes the raising of the dead. He tells how earth and baptismal water brought to Hippo from Jerusalem have effected a mass of cures. Gregory follows Augustine in spreading stories of miraculous happenings. Here one can see, perhaps, a church which is institutionally weak being forced to compromise with local spiritual forces in order to survive. What was lost for centuries was any form of restraint on the exploitation of credulity. The exploitation of the miraculous by both religious and secular elites acted as a major brake on intellectual progress.

The emerging rulers of the new European nations were crucial in effecting the mass conversion of their subjects. The bishops were also important. Until the eleventh century, when the papacy began to exert its authority over the continent, one is talking of dioceses that were largely responsible for their own affairs. Often the bishops were capable men. Sidonius Apollinaris, a Gallic aristocrat, who had been prefect of Rome, was living out a relatively settled life as bishop of Clermont in the 470s. He saw his role as much that of maintaining civilised standards as of spreading Christianity but at least a structure of authority was being preserved. Bishops were often supported by the kings or, alternatively, in Anglo-Saxon England, for instance, kings founded and supported bishoprics.[7] What this actually meant in terms of belief and behaviour is obscure but it suggests a continual process of compromise between a variety of spiritual forces, some probably still rooted in pagan belief, and authorities, both church and secular. Christianity in this period jumped 'from one cultural and political context to another, repeatedly mutating and reconstituting itself in ways that preserved its core features'.[8]

The early medieval centuries in western Europe represent a period between two Romes – the Rome of the empire and the Rome of the papacy. It was only slowly that the economy revived sufficiently to sustain urban life and the possibilities of administrative recovery. As the papacy once more defined itself as an institution that demanded obedience (Gregory VII (1073–85) was the key figure), many of the patterns of authority defined by Leo and Gregory the Great were revived. The idea that heretics, however disparate, formed a network which not only stretched territorially across Europe but back in time to the days of the empire became part of the medieval consciousness. Jewish communities faced widespread persecution, mass conversion or even annihilation. When Pope Urban II proclaimed the first crusade to regain the Holy Land from Islam in 1095, he used the language of Christian soldiers led by Christ, which echoed that of Ambrose seven hundred years before. This was the new world of medieval Christianity. Yet, even if it exercised its authority in different ways, effectively exploiting relics and the miraculous, for instance, it was the undisputed heir of the imperial Christianity of the ancient world.

On the other hand, recent scholarship has tended to see the church as much less influential and homogenous that was once thought. Much of church wealth was diverted towards prestigious, magnificent but ultimately unproductive ends. It was the Islamic economies that first stimulated the revival of western economies. The secular elites of the Italian city states exploited the expanding economies with ruthless opportunism. It was they who produced the most highly educated communities in Europe and were as influential in founding universities, primarily for their own administrative needs, as the church. It would be wrong, therefore, to end this book with a picture of a Christianity that stifled all initiative. The medieval church simply did not have the power to destroy inventiveness and curiosity. Even though the return of reasoned thought was to be challenged by Catholic traditionalists, Thomas Aquinas' championship of Aristotle was eventually accepted within Catholicism. It was the interaction of religious and secular patterns of thinking that was crucial in allowing further progress.

CHAPTER THIRTY-TWO

Faith, Certainty and the Unknown God

BYZANTINE CHRISTIANITY TENDED TO REMOVE GOD AS FAR AS possible from the believer. An important Syrian writer of the early sixth century, known as Pseudo-Dionysius, as his works were once believed to be the genuine thoughts of the Dionysius converted by Paul, expressed his belief that 'the saved and hidden truth about the celestial intelligences should be concealed through the inexpressible and the sacred and be inaccessible to the common masses . . . We have no knowledge at all of God's incomprehensible and ineffable transcendence and invisibility.' Here is the complete contrast to Eunomius' belief that the nature of God could be grasped through reason. In Pseudo-Dionysius' theology human beings can make no contribution to the understanding of God. This, however, leaves any theological statements, other than apophatic ones, those which define God only by saying what he is not, without foundation. If God is unknowable, how can one proclaim, with any meaning, that he is one in substance with his Son or even that Jesus was his incarnated Son?

Pseudo-Dionysius' theology is the end result of many of the processes that we have followed in this book. It has been one of its main arguments that theological certainty is impossible to achieve. Once the emerging church had decided to integrate the Hebrew scriptures with the gospel memories of Jesus Christ and the distinctive, if complex, letters of Paul and proclaim them as equally the Word of God, one was left with the challenge of finding any kind of coherent message from them. This did not matter in the early days of Christianity because Christians were free to form their own communities and there was no means by which an orthodoxy could be declared, let alone enforced. The New Testament did not, as such, exist. So different communities had their own sacred texts, their own methods of worship and made their own relationships with Judaism or pagan rituals. It is possible that some form of united church was evolving in the third century but the turning point was the adoption of Christianity by Constantine in 312. Constantine probably had no appreciation of the diversity of Christian belief but his patronage of the church forced him, and Theodosius I after him, to define the nature of a Christianity acceptable to the state. Church and state moved towards a symbiotic relationship and as the state became more authoritarian so it expected the church to be the same.

The consequence was the silencing of debate not only within the church but across the whole spectrum of intellectual activity. The imposition of the Nicene Trinity, with Jesus Christ elevated into the Godhead, was followed by legislation banning the alternatives, and including the harassment of heretics and the burning of their books. Pagan worship was largely suppressed in the following two centuries and Jews were pushed to the margins of society even if their religion did manage to survive.

This legislative programme was not always easy to enforce but there were important shifts in intellectual life that reinforced the challenge to learning and free debate. The traditions of reason and free enquiry which had characterised Greek thought from the sixth century BC onwards may only have reached a tiny elite but it only needs the effective use of reason by a few for major progress to be made. Only one Pythagoras, or a follower of him, was needed to produce a mathematical proof which then acted as a template for many others and so defined an academic discipline still vibrant today. Euclid (c.300 BC) consolidated it in a series of interlocking mathematical proofs which have never been disproved.

The Greeks gave priority to the exploration of the natural world and the explanation of the forces that underpinned it. They placed human beings at the centre of all things so that their thoughts on politics, history or ethics concentrated on relationships that were not subject to supernatural forces. 'Man is the measure of all things', as the philosopher Protagoras put it in the fifth century BC. The progress they made is apparent even today: every modern academic discipline, including mathematics and the sciences, is rooted in the approaches defined for it by the Greeks.

All this was already under threat with the decline of the empire. Intellectual life needs cities, schools, including those for young adults taught by philosophers, and a hunger for knowledge. Above all it needs optimism and a confidence in the possibility of progress. An empire succumbing to attack can hardly provide these but there were specific ways in which imperial Christianity created an ethos in which free discussion was next to impossible. The subjugation of philosophical thought went hand in hand with a denigration of the natural world.

The roots of this denigration may lie in Paul's rejection of 'the wisdom of the wise' but Paul was echoed by almost every church father. Lactantius questions the point of worldly knowledge. What will the enquirer gain, for instance, from knowing where the Nile rises or the other subjects which the scientists rave about? It is not in the interests of the church, opines Basil of Caesarea, for believers to turn from the simplicity of their faith to the study of 'the essence of things'. John Chrysostom pleads with God to clear his mind of secular learning and reasoning itself, so that he is open to 'the reception of divine words'. Augustine too denies the need for any form of *curiositas* and subjects secular learning to sacred ends. While biblical texts continued to be cited and there was much talk of reliance on the scriptures, it was the abdication of any form of reasoned thought that predominated. This was an age where even the elite succumbed to credulity and the reassertion of reason in the later Middle Ages was to be a tortuous and contested process.

Any incentive for independent thought was also crushed by the threat of punishment in the afterlife. No empirical evidence for a world beyond this one could be provided; it was conceived purely in the imagination. It involved a number of quite sophisticated, if unprovable, concepts: that a 'soul' encapsulates the essence of a human being, that the soul survives in some form after the physical death of the body and can feel pain or pleasure in the supernatural world, that God is willing to inflict eternal pain on those who offend. Jesus did talk of a judgement in which believers in him would be saved and the rest cast out. The gospel of Matthew suggests that salvation depends on one's behaviour, in helping the poor, for instance, implying that any committed Christian will be saved. (Those who reject Christ have invariably been denied salvation.) By the fourth century this no longer held. Augustine elaborated on eternal suffering in hell but now even sincere Christians could be sent there if God did not extend them his grace or they held the wrong beliefs about his nature. One can think of few more committed Christians than Origen or Ulfilas, the missionary to the Goths, but the subordinationist beliefs of both now made it likely they would go to hell. In short, the nature of the afterlife recorded in the gospels, disturbing enough even in this context, was distorted by the political needs of the imperial church.

Augustine worried over how belief in orthodox doctrine could be justified and thought deeply about the concept of faith. It is, however, a difficult concept to use, largely because it has a variety of shifting meanings. The word has connotations of trust and loyalty that give it a positive tone. The ability to have faith is thus seen as a virtue and, in Christian terms, 'the faithful' are to be applauded. However, this can often lead to 'believing' in the unknown because one is told to, so that faith becomes a medium through which conformity is enforced. 'Faith in God has no merit, if human reason provides proof for it', argued Bernard of Clairvaux, the enormously influential twelfth-century Cistercian monk.

Then there is the very different use of the word as in 'articles of faith', specific items of belief that are declared impossible to prove through reason. From the historian's point of view, there is much that is arbitrary about what becomes accepted as an article and what does not. The Nicene Trinity only became an undisputed article of faith when it was imposed by Theodosius in 381. The perpetual virginity of Mary has no scriptural backing (in fact, it seems to contradict scripture) and appears to have evolved in the fourth century, notably in the works of Jerome, as the result of the increasing veneration of the Virgin as *Theotokos*, 'the bearer of God'. It is hard to find any unambiguous scriptural support or theological rationale for the resurrection of the body as a physical rather than spiritual entity at the Last Judgement, although this did not prevent Augustine and the other church fathers from fantasising on the subject.

When one reads studies of 'faith and reason' critically, one can often spot how the word 'faith' shifts between different meanings (whether the writer intends this or not) and the arguments in defence of faith lose coherence. The positive connotations of the term all too often cloak the unresolved philosophical problems inherent in the concept. This is particularly worrying when 'faith' is used as a justification of authority. Even in the twelfth century, intelligent Christians could see the intellectual stagnation that was the result. Abelard (1079–1142), the most brilliant mind of his generation, explored the issue in his *Collationes*, a dialogue between a Christian, a philosopher and a Jew. 'Human understanding increases as the years pass and one age succeeds another . . . yet in faith – the area in which threat of error is most dangerous – there is no progress . . . This is the sure result of the fact that one is never allowed to investigate what should be believed about what is said among one's own people, or to escape punishment for raising doubts about what is said by everyone . . . People profess themselves to believe what they admit they cannot understand, as if faith consisted in uttering words rather than in mental understanding.' The problem could not be expressed more clearly.

This book began with what was an intense emotional experience undergone by a small group of Jews in Jerusalem after their spiritual leader had been crucified by the Roman authorities in collaboration with the Jewish priesthood. That experience is irrecoverable but very soon Jesus was being conceived in formulas that used Jewish terminology, all that they had to hand, but which also transcended these formulas so as to give him a divine status. It came to be believed that God required his son to suffer so horribly so as to lift the weight of sinfulness that was perceived to be the predominant feature of humanity. The movement became sustainable, its teachings and beliefs passing from one generation to another and transferring into the spiritually complex world of the Greeks and then still further afield, surviving and adapting to different cultural contexts.

It was when attempts were made to bring order to Christianity that problems arose. First, it was impossible to find secure foundations on which to build an enduring institutional framework for a 'church'. In the end the doctrine of apostolic succession, the passing on of an original 'deposit of faith' from generation to generation of the priesthood, proved the most effective rationale for stability. This did not, of course, mean that the 'deposit of faith' was in itself a coherent body of belief. Neither scripture, nor philosophy nor tradition provided a stable base for theology. To say, with Pseudo-Dionysius, that 'we have no knowledge at all of God's incomprehensible and ineffable transcendence and invisibility' is a recognition of this fact.

Second, boundaries could only be drawn around orthodoxy by excluding those defined as heretics. Orthodoxy and heresy were inseparable, although where the boundary between them was drawn was always arbitrary. It was a particular and unhappy feature of Christianity that the punishments decreed for those who found themselves on the wrong side of the fence were so dire. They leave a contradiction at the heart of the Christian ethical tradition. What does it mean to talk of a loving God whose forgiveness appears so limited?

None of this invalidates the experiences of Christians who found comfort in their own communities, the pattern of rituals and the sense that they at least would be saved if they conformed to the demands of their faith. One has to try and balance the achievements of Christian communities in providing security for their members through ritual and mutual care with the loss of the lively tradition of intellectual thought which had been preserved in the Greek world over many centuries. In the short term, for many Christians, this may have been of no concern, but in the long term societies have never prospered without the rational underpinning that allows progress. This appreciation of reason went into abeyance for some centuries as the rule of faith was enforced.

This is too bleak as a conclusion. The churches have fulfilled many needs. The belief that the divine has reached out to humanity through becoming human has provided spiritual inspiration and comfort for many. Christian communities did integrate principles of mutual support into their everyday life and this provided security for many in a wider society that was often unforgiving. *Pace* Augustine, most Christians have trusted that their commitment to Christ will offer them salvation in an immaterial world beyond this one.

Every society develops rituals in which the most profound moments of human existence, including birth and death, are commemorated and Christianity has evolved sophisticated ways of doing this by linking these inevitable events to the wider Christian story. While the institution of the church seems to have gone far beyond anything envisaged by Jesus, there have been times of breakdown, at the end of the Roman empire in the west, for instance, when the church has provided a framework of administration and cohesion which has helped community life survive. Again, while it is hard to find a coherent Christian ethics from the various scriptural traditions – the Old Testament, the gospels and the letters of Paul offer very different perspectives – a commitment to ethical standards has been an essential part of Christian life. In today's world, Christianity has often provided an effective medium for challenging the corruption and oppression of elites.

The adoption of the scriptures may have been far more of a protracted process than modern Christians are led to believe but they have remained at the core of western culture ever since the fourth century. Vast amounts of resources have been transferred into the glorification of God in the arts and architecture. One has only to reflect on Dante's *Divine Comedy*, Milton's *Paradise Lost*, the works of Dostoyevsky, as well as art or music, to recognise this. Again none of this might have been imagined from the teachings of Jesus, but it is the legacy of the Christianisation of the west.

Yet while in some ways Christianity broadened human perspectives, in others it has narrowed them. One phrase has haunted me as I have been writing this book. It comes from Themistius, the pagan orator, who pleaded with the emperor Jovian for religious tolerance. He talks of how God rejoices in the diversity of human society and how he actually responds to being worshipped in a variety of ways. Such an approach became inconceivable within Christianity. Even today one senses a fear that pervades Christian worship that God will be offended if things are not done the right way. Yet it is hard to see on what grounds one could ever build a consensus on what is this 'right way'. This is surely the most important lesson any study of theological debate teaches us. While it makes sense to accept that we are naturally religious, imaginative about the spiritual possibilities of a life beyond materialism, anxious to find deeper ethical truths which will enable us to live in harmony with each other and the over-exploited planet we live on, we appear to be without the means to define the supernatural in any coherent way. One of the most enduring legacies of the Christianisation of the west is the tension between institutionalised formulations of 'God' and the deeper, more free-ranging, spiritual impulses of the human mind.

Notes

I have used notes sparingly, to explore particular issues that might not be easy to find in the Further Reading or to provide extra information that could not be incorporated into the main text. My intention is that the books listed in the Further Reading will between them offer more than enough material for those who wish to continue further research.

Preface

1. See the excellent chapter by Segal, 'The Resurrection: Faith or History?' in Robert Stewart (ed.), *The Resurrection of Jesus, John Dominic Crossan and N. T. Wright in Dialogue*, Minneapolis, MN, 2008.

Part One: Beginnings

Chapter One: A Trial

1. Ann Wroe, *Pilate: The Biography of an Invented Man*, London, 2000, is an imaginatively written study.
2. The alternative account in Matthew, Mark and Luke that the crucifixion took place during the Passover is therefore unlikely to be accurate. Geza Vermes' *The Passion*, London and New York, 2005, sets out the details.
3. See Christopher Rowland, *Christian Origins*, second edition, London, 2002, p. 91, for a good summary of Jewish belief on the Messiah.
4. Paula Fredriksen, *Jesus of Nazareth, King of the Jews*, London, 2000, explores this idea, pp. 233–4.

Chapter Two: The Seedbed: Judaism in the First Century AD

1. Ernest Renan, *Vie de Jesus*, Paris, 1863; English translation, London, 1864.
2. See Rowland, *Christian Origins* and Martin Goodman, *Rome and Jerusalem: The Clash of Ancient Civilizations*, London and New York, 2007, for recent accounts of Judaism in this century.

Chapter Three: Jesus before the Gospels

1. See Richard Horsley, *Bandits, Prophets and Messiahs: Popular Movements in the Time of Jesus*, new edition, Harrisburg, PA, 1999 and Sean Freyne, 'Galilee and Judaea in the First Century' in Margaret Mitchell and Frances Young (eds), *The Cambridge History of Christianity*, volume 1, Cambridge, 2006, for the background.

2. John Meier's summing up that 'it is a second century pastiche of traditions from the canonical Gospels, recycled through the memories and lively imagination of Christians who have heard the Gospels read and preached many a time' is a fair assessment but fails to acknowledge that some of the material is not found in the canonical gospels and may come from independent early sources. John Meier, *A Marginal Jew: Rethinking the Historical Jesus*, New York, 1991, pp. 117–18.

3. This quotation is often attributed to Albert Schweitzer but the original source is the Jesuit theologian George Tyrrell (1861–1909).

4. See Meier, *A Marginal Jew*, volume 1, p. 265.

5. Excavations by the University of Nebraska show that although Bethsaida had been an important city a thousand years earlier, there was very little building in the first century AD. There are the remains of fishing equipment from the period.

6. Richard Bauckham, *Jesus and the Eyewitnesses: The Gospels as Eyewitness Testimony*, Grand Rapids, MI and Cambridge, 2006.

7. When the diaries kept daily by a selected group of British observers during the Second World War were compared to their own memories thirty years later, there was virtually no correspondence at all. 'Any relationship between the incident they had described in the diary and the story they told in 1975 was almost entirely coincidental. They got everything wrong: date, places, the sequence of events.' From the Foreword by Philip Zeigler to *Our Longest Days: A People's History of the Second World War*, London, 2008.

8. From Rudolf Bultmann, *Jesus and the Word*, English translation, 1926, New York, p. 8.

9. E.P. Sanders, *The Historical Figure of Jesus*, London, 1993.

10. Luke talks of an empire-wide decree that required Joseph and Mary to go to Bethlehem. There is no record of such a decree. Roman taxation worked on a provincial basis and Quirinius did carry out a survey of Judaea in AD 6 when it became a province. However, Jesus would have been about ten by then. The survey would not have reached Nazareth as that was not part of a Roman province. Even if it had been, subjects were taxed on the land in their villages and listed for a poll tax. It would have made no administrative sense to have summoned Mary and Joseph and other descendants of David to Bethlehem. Whatever may have taken them to Bethlehem at the time of Jesus' birth, it would not have been a census by the Romans. This has not prevented biblical scholars from attempting highly imaginative but usually unconvincing explanations in order to defend Luke's text.

11. Philip Davies, 'Qumran Studies' in J. Rogerson and Judith Lieu (eds), *The Oxford Handbook of Biblical Studies*, Oxford, 2006.

12. G. Vermes, *Jesus the Jew*, London, 1973; see also, among other studies, his *The Changing Faces of Jesus*, London and New York, 2000.

13. Some studies which follow this path are Paula Fredriksen, *From Jesus to Christ*, second edition, New Haven and London, 2000; Bart Ehrman, *Jesus: Apocalyptic Prophet of the New Millennium*, Oxford, 1999; Geza Vermes, *The Authentic Gospel of Jesus*, London and New York, 2003.

14. Vermes, *Authentic Gospel of Jesus*, p. 416. See also Rowland, *Christian Origins*, p. 147.

Chapter Four: Breaking Away: the First Christianities

1. Note the unhealthy preoccupation with suffering in Mel Gibson's *The Passion* which seemed to want to coerce converts into the church on the grounds of this suffering alone. Before the last ghastly twenty-four hours, Jesus' life appears to have been of higher quality than that of the mass of his fellow Jews with, in contrast to Paul, no record of any physical disability.

2. The gospel of Peter is reproduced in full in Bart Ehrman, *Lost Scriptures: Books that Did Not Make It into the New Testament*, Oxford and New York, 2003, p. 31.

3. The work of Jon Levenson, e.g. (with Kevin Madigan), *Resurrection: The Power of God for Christians and Jews*, New Haven and London, 2008, is especially important here. A resurrection was not expected, even though stories that Jesus would rise again after

three days were later inserted into the gospels (e.g. in Mark 8:31, 9:9, 10:33–4: if these were authentic sayings of Jesus they had been ignored by the disciples).

4. Justin Martyr, *First Apology*, Chapter Twenty-one, gives a list of gods and emperors who are believed to have ascended into heaven. Depictions of emperors being welcomed into heaven, sometimes as spirits, sometimes in chariots, are common in Roman art.

5. Alan Segal, *Life after Death: A History of the Afterlife in Western Religion*, New York and London, 2004, p. 430. See also Jon Levenson, *Resurrection and the Restoration of Israel*, New Haven, CN, and London, 2006, p. 189, where he notes the Jewish belief, echoed by Paul in 1 Corinthians 15:44, that 'resurrection was thought to yield a transformed and perfected form of bodily existence and thus a state of being both like and unlike anything we can know in the flesh'.

6. See a concise summary of the issue of the addition of Mark's ending in P. Achtemeier, J. Green and M.M. Thompson, *Introducing the New Testament: Its Literature and Theology*, Grand Rapids, MI and Cambridge, 2001, p. 143.

7. I am not arguing that the disciples consciously made up a story but any study of 'the third day' must begin with assessing the enormous stress that the disciples were under. The concentration of reports of the physical appearances of Jesus within a short period just after the crucifixion deserves noting. See, as a general survey, Geza Vermes, *The Resurrection*, New York and London, 2008.

8. Minneapolis, 2003, p. 781. As the quotation suggests, Tom Wright seems to assume that there is a 'right' interpretation that has to be disproved. Historians would work from the opposite direction.

9. M. Borg and N.T. Wright, *The Meaning of Jesus: Two Visions*, London, 1999, p. 118.

10. Vermes, *The Resurrection*, Chapter 14, makes these points.

11. See Larry Hurtado, *Lord Jesus Christ: Devotion to Jesus in Earliest Christianity*, Grand Rapids, MI and Cambridge, 2003, especially the early chapters.

12. Ibid., pp.98–101.

13. Note, in a pagan context, the rooms set aside for ritual banquets at the important healing shrine of Aesclepius at Epidaurus in Peloponnesian Greece.

14. 'The Messianic Rule', translated by Vermes in *The Complete Dead Sea Scrolls*, London, 1997, pp. 159–60.

Chapter Five: What Did Paul Achieve?

1. The areas of disagreement over Paul's life, work and theology are so extensive that any short account must be inadequate. A model has been provided by Jerome Murphy-O'Connor who in his *Paul: A Critical Life*, Oxford, 1996, sets out all the issues, outlining his own stand on them. In his subsequent shorter *Paul: His Story*, Oxford 2004, he simply gives the life and assessment based on his conclusions. Murphy-O'Connor deals with Paul's Roman citizenship in *Paul: A Critical Life*, pp. 39–41.

2. The sequence of letters is disputed and many scholars place 1 Thessalonians first, although the emotional immaturity of Galatians in comparison to, say, Thessalonians, suggests that it is one of Paul's first attempts at writing to a recalcitrant community.

3. The Vatican has recently settled on AD 8 and commemorated the two thousandth anniversary of Paul's birth in 2008.

4. Murphy-O'Connor is particularly good at outlining the demands of the journeys.

5. Stephen Mitchell, *Anatolia: Land, Men and Gods in Asia Minor*, volume 2, Oxford, 1994, Chapter Fifteen.

6. See ibid., Chapter Sixteen, Part Four, pp. 37–42 for a detailed analysis.

7. See Murphy-O'Connor, *Paul: A Critical Life*, p. 269, for the argument.

8. Jerome Murphy-O'Connor, *Paul the Letter-Writer*, Collegeville, MN, 1995, for details.

Chapter Six: The Letter to the Hebrews

1. See, for instance, Raymond Brown, *An Introduction to the New Testament*, New York and London, 1997, for a reliable introduction to the issues.

2. Kenneth Schenck, *A Brief Guide to Philo*, Louisville, KY, 2005.
3. Ibid.; see here the discussion 'Philo and Hebrews', which has references to some recent studies of the relationship.

Chapter Seven: Fifty Years On: the Gospel Writers Reflect on Jesus

1. See R.A. Horsley, J.A. Draper and J.M. Foley (eds), *Performing the Gospel: Orality, Memory and Mark*, Minneapolis, MN, 2006.
2. Some scholars have suggested a setting in Rome itself. This view originates from the belief that Papias' Mark is Irenaeus' Mark and that Peter passed on his information in Rome before he died there. The evidence for Rome has recently been gathered in Brian Incigneri's *The Gospel to the Romans: The Setting and Rhetoric of Mark's Gospel*, Leiden, 2003, but it remains circumstantial.
3. See Chapter Three, note 10, above.
4. The genealogies are contrasted in Geza Vermes' *The Nativity*, London and New York, 2006, p. 36. They cannot be reconciled.

Chapter Eight: John and the Jerusalem Christians

1. Brown, *Introduction to the New Testament*, is good for the main issues.

Chapter Nine: Creating a New Testament

1. On formation of the canon, see Jaroslav Pelikan, *Whose Bible is It?: A History of the Scriptures through the Ages*, London and New York, 2005, and Karen Armstrong, *The Bible: The Biography*, London, 2007, for introductory surveys. Scholarly analysis is to be found in Rogerson and Lieu, *Oxford Handbook of Biblical Studies*.
2. See David Taylor, 'Christian Regional Diversity' in P. Esler (ed.), *The Early Christian World*, volume 1, London and New York, 2000, pp. 330–43.
3. E.g. Edgar Goodspeed in his *An Introduction to the New Testament*, Chicago, 1937.
4. Frances Young, *The Theology of the Pastoral Letters*, Cambridge, 1994, p. 65.
5. See Bart Ehrman, *Misquoting Jesus: The Story behind Who Changed the Bible and Why*, New York, 2005.
6. Letter to General Alexander Smyth, 17 January 1825.
7. Bauckham's introduction to the Book of Revelation in John Barton and John Muddiman (eds), *The Oxford Bible Commentary*, Oxford, 2001.

Chapter Ten: No Second Coming: the Search for Stability

1. James Ault, *Spirit and Flesh*, New York, 2004. See especially Chapter Thirteen, 'Fundamentalism and Tradition'.
2. A short introduction to the *Didache* is to be found in Henry Chadwick, *The Church in Ancient Society*, Oxford, 2001, Chapter Ten.
3. The most exhaustive study of the early church in Rome is Peter Lampe's, *From Paul to Valentinus: Christians at Rome in the First Two Centuries*, translated from the German by Michael Steinhauser, Minneapolis, MN, 2003. A late fourth-century sarcophagus which, it is claimed, contains the bones of Paul has been discovered under the basilica of St Paul's outside Rome.

Part Two: Becoming Christian

Chapter Eleven: Toeholds in a Wider Empire

1. F. Braudel, *The Mediterranean and the Mediterranean World at the Time of Philip II*, second edition, London, 1972.
2. J. North, M. Beard and S. Price, *Religions of Rome*, Cambridge, 1998, p. 267. This book is useful for discussing the range of religious life in the empire.

3. Ramsay MacMullen cites this example in his *Christianizing the Empire (AD 100–400)*, New Haven and London, 1984.
4. Mitchell, *Anatolia*, volume 2, p. 48.
5. The two texts are Tertullian 'On Baptism' and the 'Apostolic Tradition' of Hippolytus, both of which are dated to the early third century.

Chapter Twelve: Open Borders: the Overlapping Worlds of Christians and Jews

1. Skari Hakkinen, 'Ebionites' in Antti Marjanen and Petri Luomanen, *A Companion to Second-century Christian 'Heretics'*, Leiden and Boston, 2005.
2. Quoted in Heiki Raisanen, 'Marcion' in ibid. For Marcion's views on the canon, see Harry Gamble, 'Marcion and the canon' in Mitchell and Young, *Cambridge History of Christianity*, volume one, Cambridge, 2006.
3. The list includes the seven letters scholars still accept as genuine, see p. 47, plus 2 Thessalonians, Ephesians and Colossians.
4. This extract comes from Justin's *Second Apology*, 13.4.
5. Daniel Boyarin, author of one of the most perceptive studies of the issue, *Border Lines, The Partition of Judaeo-Christianity*, Philadelphia, PA, 2004, is surely right to say that even if there is a boundary equipped with customs officers, there will always be individuals who fail to recognise it as a boundary at all or choose to ignore it.

Chapter Thirteen: Was There a Gnostic Challenge?

1. From the Book of Thomas the Contender 2.138, 14–18. Quoted in Bart Ehrman, *Lost Christianities: The Battles for Scripture and the Faiths We Never Knew*, Oxford and New York, 2003, p. 124.
2. Strictly speaking this is the 'Gospel of Judas' but, in order to avoid confusion with Judas Iscariot, the writer had added 'twin', Didymus in Greek, Thomas in Hebrew, which reflects the legend that Judas Thomas was indeed a twin brother of Jesus, at least on a spiritual level.
3. From Von Harnack's *History of Dogma*, originally published in German for the first time in 1885. Quoted in Karen King, *What is Gnosticism?*, Cambridge, MA and London, 2003, p. 55, at the beginning of an extensive discussion of Von Harnack's views.
4. See E. Pagels and K. King, *Reading Judas and the Shaping of Christianity*, New York and London, 2005, especially Part One, Chapter One, 'Judas: Betrayer or Favoured Disciple?'
5. See, for instance, A. DeConick, *The Thirteenth Apostle: What the Gospel of Judas Really Says*, London and New York, 2007.

Chapter Fourteen: The Idea of a Church

1. Stuart Hall, 'The Early Idea of the Church' in G.R. Evans (ed.), *The First Christian Theologians: An Introduction to Theology in the Early Church*, Oxford, 2004, p. 49.
2. Ehrman, *Lost Christianities*, covers these issues well.

Chapter Fifteen: To Compromise or Reject: Confronting the Material World

1. Many examples from this chapter draw on the excellent overview by Carolyn Osiek, 'The self-defining praxis of the developing *ecclesia*', Chapter Fourteen, in Mitchell and Young, *Cambridge History of Christianity*.
2. See Jan Bremmer, *The Rise and Fall of the Afterlife*, London and New York, 2002, especially Chapter Five.
3. See, for instance, Justin, *First Apology*, Chapter Twenty-nine; *The Octavius* by Minucius, Chapter Thirty.
4. This is normally seen as an early version of the so-called Apostles' Creed, which runs as follows: 'I believe in God, the Father almighty, creator of heaven and earth, and in Jesus Christ, his only Son, our Lord, who was conceived by the power of the Holy Spirit, born of the Virgin Mary, suffered under Pontius Pilate, was crucified, died,

and was buried. He descended into hell. On the third day he rose again from the dead. He ascended into heaven and is seated at the right hand of God the Father Almighty. From thence he shall come again to judge the living and the dead. I believe in the Holy Spirit, the holy catholic Church, the communion of saints, the forgiveness of sins, the resurrection of the body, and the life everlasting. Amen.' This final form is only first recorded in *c*.700 but the tradition remained that the creed went back to the apostles themselves, each one of the twelve contributing a verse.

5. There is an excellent summary of developments by Daniel Sheerin, 'Eucharistic Liturgy', Chapter Thirty-five in Susan Ashbrook Harvey and David Hunter (eds), *The Oxford Handbook of Early Christian Studies*, Oxford, 2008.

Chapter Sixteen: Celsus Confronts the Christians

1. This survives in Origen's answer to it, *Contra Celsum*. The extracts Origen uses have been brought together as a single text: *Celsus – On the True Doctrine: A Discourse against the Christians*, Introduction and translation by R. Joseph Hoffmann, New York and Oxford, 1987 and this is used here. Origen's response is considered in Chapter Eighteen.
2. Many of the *Meditations* of the Stoic philosopher-emperor Marcus Aurelius stress the way in which all things are bound together. When the Christians followed Genesis in saying that human beings were made in the image of God and so superior to the rest of creation, they broke this link and later theologians claimed that Christians were free to exploit the earth and its creations as they willed.

Chapter Seventeen: The Challenge of Greek Philosophy

1. The Greek approach to creationism is now covered in David Sedley, *Creationism and its Critics in Antiquity*, Berkeley, CA, and London, 2007.
2. Eric Osborn, *Clement of Alexandria*, Cambridge, 2005.

Chapter Eighteen: Origen and Early Christian Scholarship

1. Well covered in Anthony Grafton and Megan Williams, *Christianity and the Transformation of the Book*, Cambridge, MA and London, 2006.
2. This idea comes from Caroline Walker Bynum in *The Resurrection of the Body*, New York, 1995, p. 66.

Chapter Nineteen: New Beginnings: the Emergence of a Latin Christianity

1. David Wright, 'Tertullian', in Esler, *The Early Christian World*, volume 2, pp. 1,027–47, p. 1,031.
2. These issues are discussed in Peter Brown's important study, *The Body and Society*, London and New York, 1988.
3. The title of a study of Tertullian by Eric Osborn, Cambridge, 1997.

Chapter Twenty: Victims or Volunteers: Christian Martyrs

1. *The Passion of The Holy Martyrs Felicity and Perpetua*, available online at www.newadvent.org.
2. 4 Maccabees is a martyrdom narrative. 2 Maccabees, which is part of the canonical scriptures, has an account of the martyrdom within the wider context of the persecution.
3. The account of the martyrdoms at Lyons is to be found in Eusebius, *History of the Church*, 5.1.41.
4. Robin Lane Fox, *Pagans and Christians*, London, 1986, p. 446.

Chapter Twenty-one: The Spread of Christian Communities

1. See W.V. Harris (ed.), *The Spread of Christianity in the First Four Centuries*, Leiden and Boston, 2005.

2. Full text in John Behr, 'Gaul' in Mitchell and Young, *Cambridge History of Christianity*, volume 1, p. 378.
3. See Taylor, 'Christian Regional Diversity', p. 332.
4. Rodney Stark in his *The Rise of Christianity*, Princeton, NJ, 1995, suggests a decade on decade growth rate of 40 per cent. He does not tackle the diversity of Christianities, the very uneven spread of the movement or the decades of persecution where the institutional church must have faltered, all of which make any consistent growth over the empire as a whole unlikely. In fact, he provides very little historical evidence to back his calculations.
5. Mitchell, *Anatolia*, volume 2, p. 63.

Part Three: The Imperial Church

Chapter Twenty-two: The Motives of Constantine

1. An allusion to Psalm 98, 'Sing to the Lord a new song'.
2. Quoted in Beard, North and Price, *Religions of Rome*, volume 1, p. 367.
3. See Caroline Humfress' essay on Constantine's laws in N. Lenski (ed.), *The Cambridge Companion to the Age of Constantine*, Cambridge, 2006.
4. See H.A. Drake, *Constantine and the Bishops: The Politics of Intolerance*, Baltimore, MD, and London, 2000, pp. 292–305, for a full discussion of the Oration.
5. Quoted in Theodoret's fifth-century *History of the Church*, reproduced in the Appendix of Rowan Williams, *Arius*, second edition, London, 2001.
6. Socrates, *Ecclesiastical History*, Book One, Chapter Six.
7. The number in Abraham's household was 318, which seems to have been transferred for use here.
8. In his *Oration before Constantine* of 336, Eusebius states: 'This only begotten Word of God [i.e. Christ] reigns, from ages which had no beginning, to infinite and endless ages, the partner of his Father's kingdom.' Nothing is said of any moment of creation and 'partner' is an imprecise way of expressing the relationship.
9. M. Edwards, 'The First Council of Nicaea' in Mitchell and Young, *Cambridge History of Christianity*, volume 1, p. 564.
10. Richard Hanson, *The Search for the Christian Doctrine of God*, Edinburgh, 1988, p. 168.
11. See Mark Johnson, 'Architecture of Empire' in Lenski, *Cambridge Companion to the Age of Constantine*, and Johannes Deckers, 'Constantine the Great and Early Christian Art' in Jeffrey Spier (ed.), *Picturing the Bible: The Earliest Christian Art*, New Haven, CN, and London, 2007.

Chapter Twenty-three: Debating the Nature of God

1. Lewis Ayres, *Nicaea and its Legacy: An Approach to Fourth-century Trinitarian Theology*, Oxford, 2004, p. 70.
2. *An Address to Young Men on the Right Use of Greek Literature*, available online at www.ccel.org.
3. Quoted in M. Wiles, *Archetypal Heresy: Arianism Through the Centuries*, Oxford, 1996, p. 28.

Chapter Twenty-four: The Stifling of Christian Diversity

1. The events of this chapter are covered in detail in my AD 381: *Heretics, Pagans and the Christian State*, London, 2008.
2. Epistle 130, quoted in Rosemary Radford Ruether, *Gregory of Nazianzus: Rhetor, and Philosopher*, Oxford, 1969, p. 48.

Chapter Twenty-five: The Assault on Paganism

1. Neil McLynn, *Ambrose of Milan: Church and Court in a Christian Capital*, Berkeley, CA, and London, 1994, pp. 44–53, has full details of the manoeuvrings by which Ambrose had become bishop.

2. E. Sauer, *The Archaeology of Religious Hatred*, Stroud, 2003, has the details.
3. It is reproduced in Bart Ehrman and Andrew Jacobs (eds), *Christianity in Late Antiquity, 300–450 CE: A Reader*, New York and Oxford, 2004, p. 57.
4. Richard Hanson, 'The Doctrine of the Trinity Achieved in 381' in *Studies in Christian Antiquity*, Edinburgh, 1985, pp. 243–4.

Chapter Twenty-six: 'No one is honoured before him': the Rise of the Bishop

1. For Paulinus on art see Jeffrey Spier, 'The Earliest Christian Art: From Personal Salvation to Imperial Power' in Spier, *Picturing the Bible*, pp. 18–20. Claudia Rapp, *Holy Bishops in Late Antiquity*, Berkeley, CA, and London, 2005, Chapter Four for a discussion of bishops and the ascetic way of life.
2. In his *Voting about God in Early Church Councils*, New Haven, CN, and London, 2006, Ramsay MacMullen notes how accounts of the church in this period tend to ignore the evidence of violence.
3. By Mark the Deacon, accessible through search engines.
4. See Rapp, *Holy Bishops*, p. 242 for a survey.
5. Peter Chrysologos, quoted in P. Brown, *Poverty and Leadership in the Later Roman Empire*, Hanover and London, 2001, p. 46.
6. D. Janes, *God and Gold in Late Antiquity*, Cambridge, 1998, p. 57.

Chapter Twenty-seven: An Obsession with the Flesh

1. The quotation comes from Jerome's Letter to Eustochium, No. 22 in collections of his letters.
2. Doctors of the Church: an accolade awarded to major intellectual figures in the church, originally just four. The three others from this period honoured in the west are Ambrose, Augustine and Gregory the Great.
3. The fullest cycle in the western church based on the *Protoevangelium* is Giotto's frescoes in the Scrovegni Chapel in Padua.
4. Quoted in M. Dunn, *The Emergence of Monasticism: From the Desert Fathers to the Early Middle Ages*, Oxford, 2000, p. 39.
5. Ehrman, *Misquoting Jesus*, especially Chapter Two, 'The Copyists of the early Christian Writings'.
6. Megan Hale Williams, *The Monk and the Book: Jerome and the Making of Christian Scholarship*, Chicago and London, 2006, p. 105.

Chapter Twenty-eight: The End of Optimism: Augustine and the Consequences of Sin

1. M.W.F. Stone, 'Augustine and Medieval Philosophy' in Eleonore Stump and Norman Kretzmann (eds), *The Cambridge Companion to Augustine*, Cambridge, 2001, p. 263.
2. In his *Soliloquies* 1.13.22.
3. The City of God. Book XXI, Chapter 12.
4. Ibid., Book XXI, Chapters 4 and 5.
5. Ibid. From the Preface.

Chapter Twenty-nine: Divine but Human

1. 'Byzantine' derives from the original Greek name of Constantinople, Byzantium. Many date the birth of the Byzantine empire to 330, the foundation of Constantinople; others delay it to the reign of Justinian two hundred years later.
2. It was another thirty years before the emperor Theodosius II allowed his body to be returned to Constantinople where it came to be deeply venerated. John was later to be revered alongside Basil of Caesarea and Gregory of Nazianzus as one of the three Holy Hierarchs of the Orthodox Church. His body was looted from the Church of the Holy Apostles by the Venetians during the Fourth Crusade of 1204 and presented to the pope. The head was returned to the east in 2004 and is now in a monastery on Mount Athos. It is credited with many miracles.

3. The legislation is detailed in Fergus Millar, *A Greek Roman Empire, Power and Belief under Theodosius II, 408–450*, Berkeley, CA, and London, 2007.
4. Full text in Leo Donald Davis, *The First Seven Ecumenical Councils, 325–787: Their History and Theology*, Collegeville, MN, 1990, pp. 161–2.
5. The council is now fully covered in Richard Price and Michael Gaddis, *The Acts of the Council of Chalcedon*, Liverpool, 2007.

Chapter Thirty: The Closing of the Schools

1. Quoted in Julia Smith, *Europe after Rome*, Oxford, 2005, pp. 259–60.
2. Patrick Gray, 'The Legacy of Chalcedon' in Michael Maas (ed.), *The Cambridge Companion to the Age of Justinian*, Cambridge, 2005, p. 235.
3. Christian Wildberg, 'Philosophy in the Age of Justinian' in ibid., p. 316.
4. Davis, *The First Seven Ecumenical Councils*, pp. 308–11, 'The Council of Nicaea II'.
5. See Cyril Mango, 'The Revival of Learning', Chapter Eight in Cyril Mango (ed.), *The Oxford History of Byzantium*, Oxford and New York, 2002.

Chapter Thirty-one: A Fragile Church: Christianity and the Collapse of the Western Empire

1. The word Catholic derives from the Greek for 'universal'. Strictly speaking, historians use it of both eastern and western churches before the formal split between them in 1054, from when it was used only of the western church, but it seems the best term to define the church of the papacy as it was now emerging.
2. There is a good summary of the issues in Carol Harrison, *Augustine: Christian Truth and Fractured Humanity*, Oxford, 2000, pp. 154–7.
3. A philosophical survey is provided by John Rist, *Augustine: Ancient Thought Baptised*, Cambridge, 1994, pp. 239–45, 'Towards a Theory of Persecution'. See also Augustine's letter to a military tribune, Bonifatius, in 417 on the right of the secular powers to inflict punishment, quoted in Serge Lancel, *St Augustine*, translated by Antonia Nevill, London, 2002, p. 303.
4. See Michele Renée Salzman, *The Making of a Christian Aristocracy: Social and Religious Change in the Western Roman Empire*, Cambridge, MA and London, 2002.
5. Both were Christians but they were among the last generation to have access to a full range of classical texts. Boethius was an aristocrat with a deep interest in philosophy. He translated all Aristotle's works on logic into Latin and thus preserved them for the west when Greek was being forgotten. He had hoped to add the works of Plato and even combine the two great philosophers into a coherent text but, for reasons that are unclear, he was imprisoned by the normally tolerant Theodoric and eventually executed in 524. Before he died he composed a slight but attractive work, *The Consolations of Philosophy*, which counsels a concentration on 'the Good', the only constant in a world of constantly changing fortunes. It became one of the most popular texts of the Middle Ages.

    Cassiodorus (490–*c.*585), another aristocrat, argued for an education based on the seven liberal arts – grammar, logic, rhetoric, music, geometry, arithmetic and astronomy. In his retirement on his estates at Vivarium in southern Italy, Cassiodorus collected both pagan and Christian manuscripts and set a band of monks to work copying them. They included some Greek texts such as Eusebius' *History of the Church* and the medical works of Galen and Hippocrates. This was a rare initiative. In the centuries that followed, the number of classical texts recopied became fewer so that one of the larger libraries of the early eighth century, that of the Venerable Bede (672–735), had virtually no classical works, not even, it appears, the *Aeneid* of Virgil.
6. The issues are well covered in John Burrow, *A History of Histories: Epics, Chronicles, Romances and Inquiries from Herodotus and Thucydides to the Twentieth Century*, London, 2007, which has chapters on both the 'Christian' histories and the revival of secular history.
7. Matthew Innes, *Introduction to Early Medieval Western Europe, 300–900: The Sword, the Plough and the Book*, London, 2007, pp. 362–3.
8. Smith, *Europe after Rome*, p. 223.

Glossary

A reference book such as *The Oxford Dictionary of the Christian Church* provides much fuller definitions for most of these entries. I have not included references to specific texts here.

AD: Anno Domini, 'in the year of the Lord'. Dating system first elaborated in the sixth century which started with the birth of Jesus – although this is now generally believed to have taken place in 4 BC ('Before Christ').

Adoptionism: The belief that Jesus was adopted by God as his Son only at his baptism or at the resurrection.

Adversus Judaeos **texts**: Christian texts first appearing in the second century which focus on the denigration of the Jews and their religion.

Alexandria: The major city of the eastern Mediterranean, capital of the Roman province of Egypt and an important centre of early Christianity. Its bishops played a major part in the doctrinal controversies of the fourth and fifth centuries.

Allegory: An ancient form of literary interpretation, adapted to biblical studies, which explores deeper meanings behind the literal words of a text.

Anathema: Words of condemnation used especially to denounce heretical views or expel heretics.

Antioch: Capital of the Roman province of Syria, the first city in which the word Christian was used and an important centre of Christian scholarship.

Apocalyptic: Concerning the revelation of what is hidden, often in the form of a prophecy of future events.

Apocrypha: Texts accepted as authoritative by Christians but which were not originally accepted as such within Judaism; **apocryphal** also refers to texts falsely attributed to an early Christian, e.g. the apocryphal gospel of Peter.

Apologists: Early Christian writers who wrote defences of Christian belief for pagans and the imperial authorities.

Apophatism: The belief that God can only be defined in terms of what he is not. Essentially the rejection of any attempt to provide a reasoned understanding of God.

Apostasy: The act of rejecting or lapsing from Christianity, often believed to be unpardonable.

Apostle: A missionary leader of the early church, especially one chosen for this role by Jesus himself. Traditionally there are twelve apostles, including Paul who had never known Jesus.

Apostles' creed: Early and simple creed of the western church, believed to originate in the responses required of baptismal candidates.

Apostolic succession: The belief that the truth of Christian doctrine was passed by Christ to the apostles and through them to each successive generation of bishops.

Apotheosis: The reception of an individual into heaven, a possibility recognised by both pagans and Christians.

Aramaic: A Semitic language widely spoken across the eastern Mediterranean; the language which Jesus himself used.

Arianism: In its correct form, the teachings of Arius, notably that Christ was an early creation of the Father, i.e. did not exist from eternity. Used loosely and abusively from the mid-fourth century to describe all **subordinationists**.

Asceticism: A complex term used to describe practices and beliefs which involved disciplining the body and mind for spiritual purposes.

Atonement: The belief that God had willed the crucifixion of Jesus so that, through the sacrifice, sinful humanity might be reconciled to Him.

Baptism: The rite of initiation into a Christian community inspired by the baptism of Jesus Christ by John the Baptist.

Basilica: Originally, in Greek and Roman cities, an all-purpose meeting hall. Adapted from the time of Constantine as a model for the larger Christian churches.

Bible: From the Greek *biblia*, 'the books', used to describe the unified body of canonical scriptures.

Bishop: Originally 'the overseer' of a Christian community, the bishop's authority grew to make him a political as well as religious leader in the Christian city.

Byzantine empire: From Byzantium, the name of Constantinople before its rebuilding by Constantine. The eastern Roman empire as it survived after the fall of the western Roman empire, until 1453.

Caesarea: There were two important cities of this name – the capitals of the Roman provinces of Judaea and Cappadocia. The first was famous for the library created there by Origen, the second as the diocese of Basil of Caesarea who built a major complex of charitable buildings, the *Basileia*.

Canon: Used in a Christian context to describe those texts that have authority as sacred scripture.

Cappadocian Fathers: Basil of Caesarea, Gregory of Nazianzus and Gregory of Nyssa, three later fourth-century theologians who made important conceptual contributions to the doctrine of the Trinity.

Carthage: Important centre of North African Christianity from the third century onwards. The **Council of Carthage** (411) attempted to resolve the schism between Donatists and Catholics by condemning Donatism.

Catacombs: Subterranean burial chambers and passages traditionally associated with the burials of Christians in the soft tufa rock around Rome.

Catechumen: One who is committed to membership of a Christian congregation but who has not yet been baptised.

Catholic, Catholicism: The original meaning of the word is 'universal' and so of the emerging church as it defined itself in terms of the wider Christian world. Increasingly it was used of the western church alone as it developed under growing papal power, hence **Roman Catholicism**.

Celibacy: The practice of sexual abstinence, especially as a requirement for the clergy. It was gradually enforced more rigorously in the eastern and western churches and is still compulsory for bishops of the eastern churches and all clergy in the Catholic Church.

Chalcedon, Council of, 451: Important council in which a definition of the two natures of Christ was imposed upon the church, largely through the offices of the emperor Marcian.

Christianity: The word derives from the Greek *Christos*, 'the anointed one', a title used of Jesus from the time of his earliest followers.

Christology: The process of defining the nature of Christ, especially, in these early centuries, his relationship to God the Father and to the human race.

Church: The community of Christian believers as it came to define itself in the early Christian centuries, through the definition of orthodox belief and the rejection of heresies and the consolidation of an institutional framework.

Church fathers: A select group of early theologians whose works were considered authoritative by the later church.

Codex, plural **codices:** A manuscript bound in book form, which gradually supplanted the traditional papyrus roll, especially for the recording of Christian texts.

Constantinople: Inaugurated in 330 as his eastern capital by the emperor Constantine on the site of the ancient city of Byzantium. Elevated by the emperors, after the councils of 381 and 451, as the second Christian city to Rome. The **councils of Constantinople of 381** and **553** were important moments in the definition of orthodoxy.

Consubstantial: See *homoousios*.

Coptic, Coptic Church: Coptic is the native Egyptian language written in Greek and many early Christian texts survive in it. The **Coptic Church** emerged in the fifth century from the Nestorian dispute over the two natures of Christ as an independent church believing that Christ had only one nature (**monophysitism**).

Corinth: Important Roman colony on the Isthmus between the Peloponnese and mainland Greece whose fractured Christian community was the recipient of important letters from Paul and later (AD 90s) from Clement of Rome.

Covenant: A bond of trust, used originally to describe the relationship between the God of Israel and his people. The sacrificial death of Christ was seen as marking a '**New Covenant**'.

Creation: While the Old Testament God was accepted as Creator, there was dispute in the early Christian world over whether he brought order to existing chaos, as a reading of Genesis might suggest, or created *ex nihilo*, out of nothing. The latter eventually became orthodox Christian belief.

Creed: A statement of Christian belief. Early creeds took different forms as Christian doctrine evolved, but the Nicene creed as finalised at Constantinople in 381 became the standard of Christian orthodoxy.

Crucifixion: The standard form of execution for rebels in the Roman empire, possibly adopted from Carthaginian precedents.

Dead Sea Scrolls: A collection of papyrus rolls, 750 documents in all, discovered in caves by the Dead Sea between 1947 and 1960. Of immense importance for understanding first-century Judaism and the development of biblical texts.

Demiurge: From the Greek *demiourgos*, a craftsman, the term used by Plato to describe the force that had created the world.

Diaspora: The 'scattering' of Jews across the Mediterranean and ancient Near East from the sixth century BC onwards which led to substantial Greek-speaking Jewish communities in most major cities of the Roman empire.

Diatessaron: The combination of the four gospels into a single narrative by the Syrian Christian Tatian in the second half of the second century. The standard text for Syriac Christians for many centuries.

Docetism: From the Greek *dokeo*, 'I appear'. The belief that Jesus only 'appeared' as human, rather than having an actual physical body.

Doctors of the Church: A title given to theologians whose contribution to the making of Christian doctrine is considered outstanding. The original four Doctors were Ambrose, Jerome, Augustine and Gregory the Great.

Doctrine: A body of teachings, normally used of beliefs which are considered central to the Christian faith.

Dogma: An item of belief which is enforced by a religious institution and considered impossible to refute. Dogmas are therefore inseparable from the authority of the institution concerned.

Donatists: From Donatus, the bishop of a hardline community of North African Christians who refused to compromise with the state when Constantine offered toleration to the church.

Dura-Europus: City on the banks of the Euphrates and thus the border between the Roman and Persian empires, famous for the earliest known (230s–40s) example of a Christian house church, with decorated baptistery.

Easter: Feast marking the celebration of the resurrection of Christ, the most important day in the Christian calendar.

Ebionites: A Jewish Christian sect who worshipped Jesus but did not accord him any divinity or believe in his virgin birth.

Ecumenical council: 'Of the whole inhabited world'. The term used to describe councils which were later seen as especially authoritative. In the first six centuries these were Nicaea (325), Constantinople (381), Ephesus (431), Chalcedon (451) and Constantinople (553).

Edessa: Capital of Armenia. Important centre of early Syriac Christianity.

Edict: An announcement, by a Roman magistrate or emperor, of a proposed course of action. Not valid as a law until implemented as such.

Edict of Toleration: Edict issued by the emperors Constantine and Licinius in 313 in Milan extending toleration to Christians and all other sects.

Elvira, Council of: Early fourth-century Spanish council important for its definition of codes of correct Christian behaviour.

Ephesus: Major city of Asia Minor, famous for Paul's preaching and the legend that the Virgin Mary lived her remaining life there with the apostle John. The two **councils of Ephesus, 431 and 449**, were unsatisfactory and rowdy attempts to define the human and divine natures of Christ.

Epicureans: From the philosopher Epicurus (341–270 BC). They taught that the purpose of life was to find personal fulfilment and that the gods, while they might exist, had no effect on the world.

Epistle: From the Greek *episotolē*, a formal letter. The term is often used of the letters of Paul and other Christian authors.

Eschatology: The study of 'the last things' – what will happen to the individual and the world at the end of time.

Essenes: A highly organised ascetic community, with an estimated four thousand members at the time of Christ, who lived in Palestine between the second century BC and second century AD. Possibly the community described in the Dead Sea Scrolls, they are enormously important in providing material for the understanding of first-century Judaism and the Christianity that emerged from it.

Eucharist: 'Thanksgiving' through the sharing of 'the body and blood of Jesus' in the form of consecrated bread and water. The most important rite of Christian worship for those who have been baptised.

Evangelist: One who proclaims a message, used specifically of the four writers of the canonical gospels.

Exegesis: The process of interpreting a text, especially in this context, the canonical texts of Christianity.

Faith: The act of trust, in the goodness of God or the saving work of Christ, for instance. Also used to describe acceptance of those articles of Christian belief which are said to be the direct revelation of God or beyond human reason. In general terms, 'the Christian faith'.

Filioque: 'And the Son'. Phrase added, first by Augustine, to the Nicene Creed so that the Holy Spirit is said to process from both the Father and the Son, rather than the Son alone. A major cause of dispute between western and eastern churches which has never been resolved.

Freedman: A slave who has been freed by his master, a common practice in the Roman world and one which gave direct access to Roman citizenship (as, possibly, in the case of Paul's family).

Galilee: A region of northern Israel, the site of Jesus' ministry. Ruled by a Roman client king, Herod Antipas, during Jesus' life.

Gentiles: 'The other nations', those who were not Jews.

Gnosticism: From the Greek *gnosis*, 'knowledge'. In a second-century Christian context, a complex set of religious beliefs which taught secret knowledge restricted to 'those who know'.

Good Shepherd: One of the titles of Christ which has inspired the representation of Christ in much early Christian art.

Gospel: 'The good news', primarily as expressed in the four gospels of the New Testament.

Grace: The bestowal of the favour of God, without which, according to Augustine, no sinner can be saved.

Greek: The culturally dominant and sophisticated language of the eastern Mediterranean in which most early Christian texts were written and theological debate conducted.

Hagiography: Literally 'writing the lives of the saints'. In practice such accounts became dominated by the miraculous exploits and unsullied goodness of the subject.

Heaven: Conceived as the home of God. The nature of heaven and who occupied or came to occupy it alongside God was always the subject of debate.

Hebrew: A Semitic language in which most of the Old Testament was originally written. Few Christians mastered the language and so read the scriptures in the not always accurate Greek translation from the Hebrew, the **Septuagint**.

Hell: Place of eternal punishment. By Augustine's day, the destination of all, Christians or pagans, who had not been saved by the grace of God from the **original sin** which had condemned them to sojourn there.

Heresy: Originally a choice to follow a specific philosophical school. In a Christian context, it came to mean a deviant belief outside the boundaries of what was defined as orthodoxy.

Hexapla: An edition of six versions of early Greek and Hebrew texts of the scriptures made by the scholar Origen so that inconsistencies between them could be spotted and resolved. Seen as one of the major feats of early Christian scholarship.

High priest: The head of the Jewish priesthood, also responsible under the Roman empire to the Romans for the good order of the province of Judaea. Title used of Christ himself in the Letter to the Hebrews.

Holy Spirit: The third member of the Trinity. The form, nature and function of the Spirit in the church remained confused until at least the late fourth century.

Homoousios: 'Of the same substance'. A term first used at the Council of Nicaea (AD 325) to describe the relationship between God the Father and Jesus the Son, eventually becoming the orthodox terminology. To be distinguished from the terms *homoios*, Greek 'like', and *homoiousios*, Greek 'like in substance', alternative descriptions that were declared heretical.

Hypostasis: 'Personality', the Greek word used to differentiate each member of the Trinity within the single Godhead.

Incarnation: The doctrine that a pre-existent Jesus come into the world through the motherhood of the Virgin Mary without losing his divinity.

Israel: The Hebrew nation, used especially in the sense of the chosen people of God.

Jerusalem: Ancient religious capital of Israel, the focus of Jewish worship in the Temple and the place of Jesus' crucifixion (*c*.AD 30).

Jesus Seminar: A group of scholars, set up in 1985, who attempted to find the 'real' Jesus through an analysis of his recorded sayings.

Judaea: Roman province established in AD 6, centred on what had been the ancient kingdom of Judah. Its capital was Caesarea, not, as might be imagined, Jerusalem.

Justification (by faith): The process by which an individual is accepted as righteous in the eyes of God. The early Christian texts on the subject, notably those of Paul, are notoriously difficult to interpret.

Kerygma: From the Greek, 'preaching'. The proclamation of the Christian message.

Kingdom of God: The imminent 'coming of the kingdom' was the central focus of Jesus' teaching, even though the details of the kingdom were left unclear.

Last Supper: Jesus' last meal with his disciples before the crucifixion, normally seen as instituting the Eucharist.

Latin: Dominant language of the western Roman empire. No Christian text in Latin is known from before AD 180 and significant Christian works only from the third and fourth centuries. Later the language of western Christianity.

Law, or Torah: The 'Will of God' as defined by the Jewish priesthood and enshrined in written precepts. The degree to which Jesus had superseded the Law was a major issue in the early Christian communities.

Liturgy: The ceremonies and texts surrounding the rituals of the church, especially that of the Eucharist.

Logos: In Greek philosophy, a reasoned account (as in a historical or scientific narrative). Later the term became associated with 'reason' as an intermediary between God and man, and then through the gospel of John with the person of Christ.

Maccabees: Jewish family who successfully led the revolt against the ruling Seleucid dynasty in Judaea in 168 BC to independence for Judaea in 161 BC. Later accounts of their martyrdoms may well have inspired Christian martyrs.

Manicheism: Important religious movement, based on the teachings of the third-century Persian prophet Mani, that saw the world as an evil place which 'the forces of light' had to re-conquer.

Martyr: In Greek 'witness', in the sense of a witness who suffers or dies as a result of their allegiance to Christ.

Messiah: The 'anointed one'. A person seen, in Jewish tradition, as especially favoured of God, usually by being associated with kingship and success in war. Christians used the term in relation to Jesus being the one and only Messiah, so that the Greek *Christos* became and remains his normal title.

Metropolitan bishop: A bishop, normally of the capital of a Roman province, e.g. Alexandria, who is given responsibility for all dioceses in his province.

Middle Platonism: An important second- and third-century AD development of the philosophy of Plato that stressed the hierarchy of the immaterial world and the existence of a Supreme Good. Provided the medium for some reconciliation between Christianity and traditional Greek philosophy.

Miracle: A wondrous happening; in Christian terms an event that transcends normal physical laws or expectations.

Mithraism: Followers of the cult of Mithras, a Persian deity. Often seen as direct competitor to Christianity.

Monasticism: Ascetic movement that first became prominent in the fourth century in Egypt and Syria by which communities of individuals separated themselves from society and focused on the search for God.

Monophysite: One who believes that Christ has one predominantly divine nature in which human elements are subsumed.

Monotheism: The belief that there is only one God. Much early Christian theology was concerned with defining the divinity of Christ without offending this belief.

Montanists: Followers of Montanus, a second-century prophet from Phrygia who claimed to be speaking through the Holy Spirit.

Muratorian fragment: Named after the historian Father Ludovico Antonio Muratori, (1672–1750). It is the oldest known list of the books of the New Testament, possibly dating from c.AD 200.

Nag Hammadi texts: An important collection of fourth-century codices containing earlier, mostly second-century, texts, discovered in 1945. Their contents have invigorated the debate over **gnosticism**.

Neoplatonism: The most developed form of Platonism as seen especially in the work of the great (pagan) religious philosopher Plotinus (c.205–70) whose terminology may have been adapted by the **Cappadocian Fathers** in their definition of the Trinity.

Nestorianism: The belief, originating with Nestorius, bishop of Constantinople, that Christ had two natures, human and divine, which co-existed without mingling with each other (cf. **monophysitism**).

New Testament: The collection of twenty-seven canonical texts, including the gospels and letters of Paul, recognised by the church as orthodox by the fourth century.

Nicaea: Site of the first ecumenical council, presided over by the emperor Constantine, 325. See **Nicene creed**.

Nicene creed, Nicene-Constantinopolitan creed: The creed passed at the Council of Nicaea (AD 325) as amended at the Council of Constantinople (AD 381). Later became the authoritative creed of the orthodox churches.

Novatianists: Followers of Novatian, a third-century Roman priest, who argued that those who had lapsed under the pressure of persecution should not be readmitted to the church.

Old Testament: The books of the Hebrew scriptures as adopted by the Christian church, normally in their Greek versions, the **Septuagint**.

Original sin: The sin of Adam believed to be passed on from generation to generation so as to infuse all humanity. Elaborated by Augustine in the late fourth century.

Orthodox: Christian doctrine accepted by the mainstream Christian churches as representing correct and authoritative belief. The eastern Orthodox churches are the heirs of the Christianity of the Byzantine empire.

Ousios: Greek 'substance'. Philosophical term of some complexity which was eventually accepted as describing the shared being of the three members of the Trinity.

Pagan: Literally 'country dweller', but increasingly used by Christians as a derogatory term for all those who remained unconverted to Christianity.

Paideia: A state of cultural and educational excellence, the goal of the traditional Greek education of the elite.

Palestine: The Roman name given to the region between the Mediterranean and the River Jordan by the second-century AD emperor Hadrian so as to obliterate the name of Israel after his defeat of a Jewish revolt.

Papacy: The designation of the bishop of Rome as the senior bishop of the Christian church as assumed successor of Peter in that role.

Parrhesia: The right to speak openly. An accepted convention in Greek society which was abolished by the emperor Justinian in the 530s.

Passion: From the Latin 'suffering'. The last week of Jesus' life up to and including the crucifixion.

Passover: The pre-eminent Jewish festival that commemorates the Exodus from Egypt. The Eucharistic meal may well have developed from the Passover feast. The three synoptic gospels link Jesus' death to the Passover.

Patriarch: 'Father of the nation'. Originally used of Abraham and other Old Testament figures. In a Christian context used of senior bishops, those of Alexandria, Antioch, Constantinople and, after 451, Jerusalem.

Patristics: The study of the theology of the period of the church fathers, especially between AD 100 and 600.

Pelagian controversy: Important controversy over the place of free will in human nature, named after the champion of free will, Pelagius. Resolved against Pelagius in favour of Augustine.

Pentecost: The Jewish festival held on the fiftieth day after Passover, the moment in Christian history when the Holy Spirit was said to have descended on the apostles.

Pharisees: Small religious Jewish party, pervasive in Galilee during Jesus' ministry, who challenged many of his teachings on the grounds that they disregarded the letter of the Law.

Pilgrimage: A journey undertaken to a holy place, e.g. Jerusalem or Rome, in the hope of spiritual enhancement or reward.

Predestination: In its extreme form, the idea that human beings are totally dependent on the grace of God for salvation which cannot be predicted or necessarily achieved with good works. Leaves the status of free will unresolved and contested, e.g. by Pelagius, for this reason.

Pre-existence: The belief that Jesus had an existence in heaven alongside God before he was incarnated, an essential feature of orthodox Christian belief.

Presbyter: Originally a Jewish elder, a title adopted by the early Christian communities and later synonymous with priest.

Prophecy: The proclamation of supernatural knowledge. The difficulty in distinguishing between true and false prophets was a major challenge in the early church.

Q: A selection of Jesus' early sayings believed to have been drawn from a common source by Matthew and Luke.

Qumran: A small and reclusive Jewish community of the first century AD whose beliefs and activities are represented in the Dead Sea Scrolls.

Ravenna, Italy: Capital of the late Roman emperor Honorius and later the Ostrogoth Theodoric; recaptured by the Byzantines in 540. Famous for its splendid church mosaics.

Relics: Conventionally used of the bones of martyrs and holy men but also of sacred objects such as 'the True Cross' which are venerated for themselves and their power to effect miracles.

Resurrection: The belief that Jesus rose from his grave three days after the crucifixion, in either a physical or spiritual form.

Resurrection of the body: The belief, contested in the early church, that at the Last Judgement all would regain their physical bodies (or, in Paul, a 'spiritual' form of them).

Revelation: The truths about God which Christians believe that God himself has revealed.

Rome: Capital of the Roman empire and centre for many early Christian communities. By tradition its first bishop was Peter although it was not until the fifth century (e.g. under Leo I) that the bishops were effectively asserting their authority over the western Latin-speaking church.

Rule: A code of conduct developed for the good order of a monastic community. The most famous Rule in the western church is that of St Benedict.

Sabellianism: After a third-century Roman priest, Sabellius. The belief that Jesus was a temporary manifestation of God and never had a personality distinct from him.

Sacrament: Literally 'a mystery', but commonly applied to a sacred rite such as baptism or the Eucharist instituted by Christ himself.

Sacrifice: The most common ritual in pagan and Jewish worship, usually involving the slaughter of an animal. Christ's sacrifice on the cross was seen as superseding all other forms of sacrifice and the Christian emperors banned any other form of the ritual.

Sadducees: A grouping of aristocratic priests in first-century Judaism who were sympathetic to Roman rule and antagonistic to Jesus and his teachings.

Sanhedrin: The Jewish council of seventy elders, presided over by the high priest, which had the pre-eminent role in defining Jewish belief and its implementation through the Law.

Santa Sophia: 'The Holy Wisdom'. Magnificent church in Constantinople, constructed in its first form by Constantine but rebuilt in its present splendour by Justinian.

Sarcophagus: A stone coffin, often with a carved façade and sides. Christian sarcophagi provide excellent evidence of the development of Christian art and iconography.

Schism: A split within the church, usually arising from irreconcilable differences over its institutional form.

Second Sophistic: A revival of Greek learning notably in the second and third centuries AD which created the philosophical background to which Christian theology related.

Septuagint: A Greek translation of the Hebrew scriptures made in the third century BC (traditionally by seventy-two scholars) to meet the needs of the Jews of the diaspora. Used by Paul and other early Christians as an authoritative text despite its differences from the original Hebrew.

Sethianism: From Seth, the son of Adam and Eve, a second-century 'gnostic' school which privileges Seth as one who has received the 'pure spirit' from above.

Soul: The immaterial part of a human being conceived by Plato as the seat of the rational intellect and superior to the physical body. Absorbed into the Christian tradition in that the soul survives after death and responds to pleasure or pain in heaven or hell.

Stoicism: An important philosophical system which taught the unity of all creation, its relentless move through cycles and the need for perseverance in the unfolding of fate. Many Stoic beliefs were attractive to educated Christians.

Subordinationism: The belief, widely held in the first centuries of Christianity, and supported by gospel evidence, that Jesus was a subordinate figure to his Father.

Synagogue: Building used by Jews for prayer and the reading of scriptures, also used by early Christians for the same purposes. Later the focus of hostility and even destruction by Christian groups.

Synod: A small or localised meeting of bishops.

Synoptic: 'Seeing with a single eye', the traditional description of the gospels of Mark, Matthew and Luke which share many of the same sources and perspectives.

Syriac: A branch of the Aramaic language in which many early Christian texts were written or translated from the Greek. Syriac Christian literature is celebrated for its poetical renderings of liturgy.

Theocracy: 'Government by God', usually through the medium of a favoured king or emperor who is declared to be the chosen of God.

Theotokos: 'Bearer of God', the title used to define the status of the Virgin Mary from the fifth century onwards.

Torah: See **Law**.

Trinity: The three central figures of Christian belief, Father, Son and Holy Spirit and the relationship between them. While many early Christians saw them as a hierarchy, Son subordinate to Father and Holy Spirit subordinate to both, the orthodox definition, held since 381, is that they are three distinct personalities within a single Godhead.

Tritheism: The belief, heretical to orthodox Christians, that there are three distinct gods, rather than one single Godhead, within the Trinity.

Virgin Birth: The belief that Jesus was conceived by Mary through the power of the Holy Spirit and thus without a human father (and in some traditions that she remained a virgin even during the act of birth). First recorded about AD 85 in the gospels of Luke and Matthew.

Vulgate: The Latin translation of the scriptures from the original Greek and Hebrew, largely the work of Jerome, which became the authorised version for the Roman Catholic church.

People

The major figures of the Old Testament and Jewish history have not been covered here but can be found in any standard dictionary of the Bible.

The following figures receive extensive treatment within individual chapters and the reader is referred to these:

Augustine, bishop of Hippo: Chapter Twenty-eight.

Constantine: Chapter Twenty-two.

Cyprian, bishop of Carthage: Chapter Nineteen.

Jerome: Chapter Twenty-seven.

Jesus Christ: Chapters One and Two.

John, evangelist: Chapter Eight.

Luke, evangelist: Chapter Seven.

Mark, evangelist: Chapter Seven.

Matthew, evangelist: Chapter Seven.

Origen: Chapter Eighteen.

Paul, apostle: Chapter Five.

Tertullian, theologian in Carthage: Chapter Seventeen.

Alexander: Bishop of Alexandria, 312–28, and believer in a Christ who had existed eternally, rather than as a separate creation. He attempted to enforce his authority on the priest **Arius** and saw his cause triumph at the Council of Nicaea.

Ambrose (*c.*339–397): Formidable bishop of Milan and ardent supporter of the Nicene faith. Attempted to enforce the authority of the church over that of the emperors.

Ammianus Marcellinus (*c.*330–after 391): Important historian of his times, the best source for the fourth-century empire even if his references to Christianity are few and dismissive.

Anthony (?251–356): Hermit who was the subject of a famous hagiographical Life by Athanasius which presented him as unlettered but orthodox. In reality he seems to have been a more sophisticated thinker than Athanasius allowed.

Aristotle (384–322 BC): Outstanding philosopher known for his work on logic and the empirical sciences. His rigorous analysis and focus on the material world made him an object of suspicion to early Christians.

Arius (died 336): Presbyter in Alexandria, vocal in his belief that Jesus was a later creation of the Father. His name was used by his enemies to condemn all forms of subordinationism as 'Arianism' and hence heretical.

Athanasius (*c.*296–373): Tempestuous bishop of Alexandria, champion of the Nicene creed and scourge of his subordinationist rivals.

Barnabas: Early apostle and companion of Paul who appears to have travelled widely in the service of the early church.

Basil (*c.*330–379): Bishop of Caesarea (Cappadocia). Major intellectual, one of the 'Cappadocian Fathers' responsible for defining the terminology of the Trinity, but also an impressive administrator, organiser of charity and founder of eastern monasticism.

Bede (*c.*673–735): The foremost scholar of Anglo-Saxon England, although limited in his perspectives by the constraints of his times. His *Ecclesiastical History of the English People* is heavily biased towards the triumph of the Anglo-Saxons against the natives of the island.

Benedict (*c.*480–550): Revered as the founder of western monasticism and the Benedictine order. His Rule, of conduct for his monks, is respected for its moderation and good sense.

Bultmann, Rudolf (1884–1976): German New Testament scholar famous for his declaration that Jesus can never be known as a historical figure, other than as one who was crucified for the salvation of humanity.

Caiaphas: High priest between *c.*18 and 37, increasingly recognised as a supreme political operator who successfully held his own in Jerusalem against his Roman overlords.

Cassian, John (*c.*360–after 430): Having experienced life as a monk in Bethlehem, Cassian moved to the west *c.*415 where he passed on his experience of monastic living in his *Institutes* and *Conferences*, enormously influential guidelines for the early western monasteries.

Celsus: Author of a detailed and wide-ranging attack on Christianity of *c.*180. Important for showing the attitudes of educated Greeks to the emerging religion.

Clement of Alexandria (*c.*150–*c.*215): Philosopher and Christian theologian who recognised the contribution Greek philosophy could make to Christian doctrine.

Clement of Rome: Author of a famous letter to the Corinthians, *c.*96, influential for its rationale of church order and mention of a possible martyrdom of Peter and Paul in Rome.

Constantius: Son of Constantine, sole ruler of the empire 351–61. Imposed a subordinationist creed on the church at Constantinople in 360.

Cyril (died 444): Bishop of Alexandria and able theologian of monophysitism, notorious for his aggressive behaviour to his pagan and theological opponents.

Diocletian: Roman emperor, 284–305. Brilliant reorganiser of the Roman empire who reluctantly acceded to demands that he persecute Christians in the final campaign against Christianity before Constantine's toleration.

Dioscorus: Bishop of Alexandria, 444–51, and outspoken supporter of monophysitism, deposed after his aggressive behaviour at the Council of Ephesus, 449.

Epiphanius (*c.*315–403): Intemperate bishop of Salamis in Cyprus known for his obsession with heresies which he detailed in his *Panarion*.

Eunomius (died 394): Important theologian who preserved the use of reason notably to argue that Jesus the Son was distinctly different from and subordinate to God the Father. Condemned as heretical by the supporters of Nicaea in 381.

Eusebius (*c.*260–*c.*340): Bishop of Caesarea and important Christian intellectual of his period. Ardent supporter of Constantine and author of the first full history of Christianity.

Eusebius (died *c.*342): Bishop of Nicomedia who offered support to Arius and spoke on his behalf at Nicaea in 325.

Evragius of Pontus (died 399): Important eastern ascetic who defined a path through which self-discipline could lead to reconciliation with God.

Gregory (*c.*330–*c.*395): Bishop of Nyssa and brilliant theologian, one of the Cappadocian Fathers, the first-known Christian advocate of the abolition of slavery.

Gregory the Great: Impressive pope, 590–604, who maintained the prestige and vigour of the papacy at a time of economic and social breakdown in Europe.

Gregory of Nazianzus (*c.*329–*c.*390): A fine theologian, one of the Cappadocian Fathers, known for his sophisticated defence of the Nicene Trinity but less successful in his short term as bishop of Constantinople.

Gregory the Wonderworker (*c.*213–*c.*270): Pupil of Origen, and whom tradition (uncorroborated) credits with many miracles and the conversion of the pagan population of Neocaesarea in Pontus.

Hadrian: Roman emperor, 117–38, who maintained the stability of the empire and inspired the confidence of the Greeks in their own culture. Brutally suppressed a Jewish revolt in AD 135 but was reluctant to persecute Christians.

Harnack, Adolf von (1851–1930): Controversial German theologian who argued that Christian theology had been unduly influenced by Greek philosophy and that the moral claims of Christianity outweighed its doctrinal beliefs.

Helena: Mother of the emperor Constantine, who was credited with finding the True Cross on her pilgrimage to Palestine in the 320s.

Herod Antipas: Ruler of Galilee, 4 BC–AD 39, as a client king of the Romans, during the time of Jesus' ministry in the region.

Herod the Great: Ruled an extensive kingdom based on Judaea, on behalf of the Romans between 37 and 4 BC. An Idumaean and hence an outsider to the majority Jewish population; brutal but effective. Rebuilt the Temple in Jerusalem.

Hilary (c.315–c.367): Bishop of Poitiers and the first western theologian to mount a defence of the Nicene Trinity against subordinationism.

Hypatia (c.375–415): Respected pagan philosopher in Alexandria, put to death by a Christian mob in 415.

Ignatius (c.35–c.107): Bishop of Antioch, martyred in Rome. His letters to seven Christian communities are important in defining the role of the bishop.

Irenaeus (c.130–c.200): Bishop of Lyons, important for defining the church as an institution based on apostolic succession which must defend itself against heretics. The first advocate of four, and only four, canonical gospels.

James: Reputed brother of Jesus, who assumed leadership of the Christian community in Jerusalem after Peter left the city until his martyrdom in 62.

John the Baptist: A missionary preacher, responsible for the baptism of Christ. Executed by Herod Antipas.

John Chrysostom, 'the golden mouthed' (c.347–407): Brilliant if often vituperative speaker. Bishop of Constantinople, 397–404, his intransigent personality led to his deposition and exile.

John Philoponus (c.490–c.570): Philosopher working in Alexandria whose attempt to use Aristotelian logic to define the Trinity led to him being declared heretical in the seventh century. His thoughtful critques of Aristotle were revived during the Renaissance.

Josephus (c.37–c.100): Important Jewish historian who provided extensive background evidence for the history and culture of the Jews in the first century AD.

Julian: Emperor, 361–3. A lapsed Christian, the last of the pagan emperors, responsible for the critique 'Against the Galileans' and a failed attempt to restore the diversity of pagan worship.

Julian (c.386–454): Bishop of Eclanum (Italy). Important and broad-minded opponent of Augustine on the question of free will whose views were eventually condemned.

Justin Martyr (c.100–165): Christian apologist, well known for his *Dialogue with Trypho* which explores the differences between Christian and Jewish belief. Martyred in Rome in the reign of Marcus Aurelius.

Justinian: Byzantine emperor, 527–65, and the last great figure of antiquity. Determined to create a united Christian state based on the reconquest of the western empire and the resolution of doctrinal controversy with the monophysites. Worked hard to eradicate paganism. Achieved only limited success in these aims.

Lactantius (c.250–c.325): Apologist for Christianity who advocated toleration for all faiths. Responsible for a lurid account of the punishments inflicted by God on those who persecuted Christians. Appointed by Constantine as tutor for his son.

Leo I, 'the Great': Pope, 440–61. Impressive bishop of Rome whose forceful personality did much to increase papal authority. His Tome (letter) on the natures of Christ helped define doctrine on the issue in both eastern and western churches.

Macrina (died 380): Saintly sister of Basil of Caesarea and Gregory of Nyssa and the subject of an influential Life by the latter which did much to publicise the virtues of ascetic life for women.

Marcian: Byzantine emperor (450–57) who played a major part in defining and enforcing the Chalcedonian formula on the human nature of Christ.

Marcion (died 160): Champion of Paul who challenged the status of the Old Testament God and wished to disown the Hebrew scriptures for this reason. Declared heretical but retained immense influence.

Marcus Aurelius: Emperor, 161–80. Doughty defender of the empire's borders and traditional values, which involved sporadic persecution of Christians. Famous for his Stoic *Meditations*.

Martin (died 397): Bishop of Tours. Former soldier, then monk who retained his ascetic lifestyle when he became bishop. Celebrated for his miracles and, later, for those effected by his bones.

Mary, mother of God (i.e. Jesus the Son as God): Although little is said of Mary in the gospels, her status rose steadily in the early Christian centuries (see *Theotokos*). She was said to be perpetually virgin and her life is recounted in many legends.

Mary Magdalene: An early follower of Jesus who witnessed his death and a resurrection appearance. She is given a major role in some gnostic writings.

Melania the Elder and Younger: Early fifth century, the latter granddaughter of the former. Noted ascetics who freely spread their wealth among churches and monasteries.

Melito (died c.190): Bishop of Sardis and author of a polemic against the Jews in the form of a Paschal hymn.

Nectarius (died 397): A senator consecrated bishop of Constantinople in 381 in the hope of calming unrest over the imposition of the Nicene creed.

Nestorius (died c.451): Bishop of Constantinople who taught that Christ had two separate natures, human and divine. Condemned as heretical but his views were close to those later declared orthodox at the Council of Chalcedon in 451.

Ossius (or Hosius) (c.256–357): Bishop of Cordoba, ecclesiastical adviser to Constantine before and during the Council of Nicaea.

Pachomius (c.290–346): Founder and effective organiser of a number of early monasteries in the Egyptian desert.

Paulinus of Nola (c.354–431): Aristocratic bishop who renounced his wealth and devoted his later life to the shrine of St Felix at Nola.

Pelagius (late fourth/early fifth centuries): Important defender of free will and the essential goodness of God against Augustine's more forbidding teachings. Eventually declared heretical.

Perpetua: The first Christian woman whose voice survives in her account of the events leading to her martyrdom at Carthage in 203.

Peter: Leader of the apostles and recognised as such by Jesus. Traditionally said to have been the first bishop of Rome.

Philo (c.20 BC–c.AD 50): Important Jewish philosopher who integrated Greek philosophical concepts into Jewish belief and was a major influence on Christian theology.

Plato (427–347 BC): Greek philosopher whose concentration on the understanding of the 'realities' of the immaterial world and enduring influence into the early Christian centuries were of immense importance in the formation of Christian theology.

Plotinus (*c.*205–70): Religious philosopher (pagan) whose work displays an understanding of mysticism without sacrificing reason. Arguably the finest spiritual thinker of these centuries.

Polycarp (died 155 or possibly later): Staunch member of the early Asian Christian community whose early life may have overlapped with the longer-living apostles and revered by Irenaeus as such. Martyred in extreme old age.

Pontius Pilate: Roman prefect of Judaea, AD 26–36, responsible for ordering the crucifixion of Jesus.

Pseudo-Dionysius (*c.*500): The name given to the author of a series of enormously influential works of Christian mysticism which talk of the impossibility of expressing knowledge of God.

Simon Magus: First-century spiritual leader from Samaria condemned by Peter and later regarded as 'the father of all heresies'.

Socrates (*c.*469–399 BC): Important Greek philosopher whose search for the ultimate meaning of things is recorded or developed by his admirer Plato.

Socrates (*c.*380–450): Native of Constantinople, writer of a clear and well-organised church history of the fourth and early fifth centuries.

Sozomen: Early fifth-century historian of the church, often used as supplementary to Socrates.

Stephen: The first Christian martyr, *c.*35. Reputedly stoned after he had given eloquent expression to his Christian belief before the Sanhedrin.

Themistius (*c.*317–*c.*387): Important pagan court orator whose experience of warring Christian factions impelled him to speak in favour of religious toleration.

Theodoret (*c.*393–460): A native of Antioch and supporter of Nestorius, remembered for his church history which recasts events as the unfolding of the will of God in history.

Theodoric (*c.*453–526): King of the Ostrogoths. An 'Arian' whose sympathy for classical civilisation and tolerance of the Catholic majority in his kingdom earned him respect.

Theodosius I: Emperor, 379–95. One of the most important Christian emperors. Used the law to enforce the Nicene Trinity as the only acceptable form of the Trinity and initiated a sweeping campaign against paganism.

Theodosius II: Emperor, 408–50. A pious ruler who, however, failed to resolve the doctrinal disputes over the nature of Christ which consumed the church in these years.

Tiberius: Emperor, AD 14–37. Maintained the stability of the empire established by his predecessor, Augustus.

Timothy: Intimate friend and right-hand man of the apostle Paul. By tradition the first bishop of Ephesus.

Titus (39–81): Emperor, 79–81. Brought the Jewish revolt of 66–70 to a bloody end with the destruction of the Temple.

Trajan: Emperor, 98–117. One of the finest Roman emperors, known in a Christian context for his letters to Pliny, the governor of Bithynia, concerning the appropriate treatment of Christians.

Ulfilas (*c.*311–83): Important Christian missionary to the Goths and the translator of the Bible into Gothic. Condemned as heretical for his subordinationism but his conversions proved enduring.

Valentinus (second century): Intellectual Egyptian Christian who moved to Rome, *c.*140, where he established a popular following. His individual teachings were seen by his opponents, probably unfairly, as 'gnostic'.

Vermes, Geza (born 1924): Hungarian-born scholar, later at Oxford University, who is known for his work on Jesus' Judaism and the Dead Sea Scrolls.

Vigilius: (Pope, 537–53). A weak pope who allowed himself to be manipulated by the emperor Justinian in the controversy over monophysitism, to the fury of his fellow bishops in the west.

Further Reading

This is a selective list designed to help the reader on to the next stage of study.

Original Sources

The Bible is, of course, available in many translations. Almost every early Christian text mentioned in this book will be found in the Christian Classics Ethereal Library, ccel.org, or the new Advent collection, newadvent.com.

Bart Ehrman, *Lost Scriptures: Books That Did Not Make It into the New Testament*, Oxford and New York, 2003 includes the texts of many of the apocryphal Acts of Apostles and gospels.

Eusebius' *History of the Church* is available in a translation by G.A. Williamson in Penguin Classics.

Eusebius' *Life of Constantine*, translation and commentary by Averil Cameron and Stuart Hall, Oxford, 1999

Works by Augustine, *The Confessions*, *The City of God*, etc., are also available in Penguin Classics.

The following readers provide a great deal of original source material:

Bart Ehrman and Andrew Jacobs (eds) *Christianity in Late Antiquity, 300–450 CE: A Reader*, New York and Oxford, 2004

A.D. Lee, *Pagans and Christians in Late Antiquity: A Sourcebook*, London and New York, 2000

Michael Maas, *Readings in Late Antiquity: A Sourcebook*, London and New York, 2000

General Histories

Henry Chadwick, *The Early Church*, London and New York, 1967, has held its own for forty years. Still an excellent introduction. I particularly like Philip Esler (ed.), *The Early Christian World*, London and New York, 2000, two volumes of essays on themes and personalities in early Christian history. It is very good for introductions to the early church fathers. There are interesting essays in *A People's History of Christianity*, volume 1, *Christian Origins* (ed. Richard Horsley) and volume 2, *Late Ancient Christianity* (ed. Virginia Burrus), both Minneapolis, MN, 2005.

Peter Brown's survey, *The Rise of Western Christendom*, second edition, Oxford, 2003, takes the story only from AD 200 but is a beautifully written survey. Judith Herrin, *The Formation of Christendom*, London, 1987, another acclaimed history, concentrates more on the east from the fifth to sixth centuries onwards.

For the **Bible** in general: Karen Armstrong, *The Bible: The Biography*, London, 2007; Jaroslav Pelikan, *Whose Bible Is It?: A History of the Scriptures through the Ages*, London and

New York, 2005. Bart Ehrman, *Misquoting Jesus: The Story Behind Who Changed the Bible and Why*, New York, 2005 is interesting, although less provocative than the title suggests. More detailed work and references to the individual books of the Bible and the key figures of the Old Testament can be found in Bruce Metzger and Michael Coogan (eds), *The Oxford Companion to the Bible*, Oxford and New York, 1993.

Jesus. There is a vast range of studies. As a historical introduction, E.P. Sanders, *The Historical Figure of Jesus*, London, 1993 is reliable. Geza Vermes has explored the Jewishness of Jesus in a number of important studies including *Jesus the Jew*, London, 1973, *The Changing Faces of Jesus*, London and New York, 2000 and *The Authentic Gospel of Jesus*, London and New York, 2003. See also his *The Nativity*, London and New York, 2006, *The Passion*, London and New York, 2005 and *The Resurrection*, London and New York, 2008, all of which approach the issue from a historical point of view. Also recommended: Paula Fredriksen, *From Jesus to Christ*, second edition, New Haven, CN, and London, 2000, her *Jesus of Nazareth, King of the Jews*, London, 2000 and Bart Ehrman, *Jesus: Apocalyptic Prophet of the New Millennium*, Oxford 1999.

James Dunn, *Jesus Remembered*, Grand Rapids, MI and Cambridge, 2003 is a large volume (one of a proposed three) which contains an in-depth study of the problems of finding the historical Jesus. Leslie Houlden (ed.), *Jesus in History, Thought and Culture*, Oxford and Santa Barbara, CA, 2003 and D. Ford and M. Higton (eds), *Jesus* in the Oxford Readers series, Oxford, 2002, provide good material on the changing ways Jesus has been seen over the centuries.

Larry Hurtado, *Lord Jesus Christ: Devotion to Jesus in Earliest Christianity*, Grand Rapids, MI and Cambridge, 2003, is outstanding in showing how Jesus evolved into Christ. His views are expressed in shorter introductions: *How on Earth Did Jesus Become God?*, Grand Rapids, MI and Cambridge, 2002 and *At the Origins of Christian Worship*, Grand Rapids, MI and Cambridge, 2000.

Judaism is well covered in a general history by Martin Goodman, *Rome and Jerusalem: The Clash of Ancient Civilizations*, London and New York, 2007 and Christopher Rowland, *Christian Origins*, second edition, London, 2002. Philip Davies, George Brooke and Phillip Callaway, *The Complete World of the Dead Sea Scrolls*, London, 2002, is a useful introduction.

New Testament. An excellent starting point is Raymond Brown, *An Introduction to the New Testament*, New York and London, 1997. It covers each work in a detailed and readable commentary.

Paul has a strong psychological hold on his adherents and many Lives and studies are personal and even idiosyncratic. Jerome Murphy-O'Connor, *Paul: A Critical Life*, Oxford, 1996, or the more concise *Paul: His Story*, Oxford, 2004, are an acknowledged authority's survey of the known facts. E.P. Sanders, *Paul* in the Past Masters series, Oxford, 1991, is a good introduction to the theology. For a good selection of recent scholarship on Paul and his theology, see James Dunn (ed.), *The Cambridge Companion to St Paul*, Cambridge, 2003.

Philo. Kenneth Schenck, *A Brief Guide to Philo*, Louisville, KY, 2005

Second and Third Centuries

The sources are very scattered and it is difficult to make much coherent sense of them but the following deal with the main themes of Part Two of this book:

Mary Beard, John North and Simon Price, *Religions of Rome*, Cambridge, 1998, provides
    essential background.

Geoffrey Bowersock, *Martyrdom and Rome*, Cambridge, 1995. Bowersock's argument that Christian martyrdom owed nothing to Jewish precedents is disputed but this is a good introduction.

Daniel Boyarin, *Border Lines: The Partition of Judaeo-Christianity*, Philadelphia, PA, 2004. Brilliant challenge to the thesis that Christianity and Judaism had separated by the second century.

Peter Brown, *The Body and Society: Men, Women and Sexual Renunciation in Early Christianity*, London and New York, 1988. Part One deals with the second and third centuries. A classic study of ascetic texts from this period.

Henry Chadwick, *Early Christian Thought and the Classical Tradition: Studies in Justin, Clement, and Origen*, New York and Oxford, 1966

H. Crouzel, *Origen: The Life and Thought of the First Great Theologian*, translation by A.S. Worrall, Edinburgh, 1989

Bart Ehrman, *Lost Christianities: The Battles for Scripture and the Faiths We Never Knew*, Oxford and New York, 2003. Good study of the emergence of an orthodox church from among the alternatives.

Anthony Grafton and Megan Williams, *Christianity and the Transformation of the Book*, Cambridge, MA and London, 2006. Deals with Origen and Eusebius in the context of the library at Caesarea.

Peter Hinchcliff, *Cyprian of Carthage and the Unity of the Christian Church*, London, 1974

Keith Hopkins, *A World Full of Gods: Pagans, Jews and Christians in the Roman Empire*, London, 1999. Lively and imaginative study of these centuries.

Karen King, *What is Gnosticism?*, Cambridge, MA and London, 2003

Peter Lampe, *From Paul to Valentinus: Christians at Rome in the First Two Centuries*, Minneapolis, MN, 2003. Absorbing study of what is known about early Christian Rome.

Robin Lane Fox, *Pagans and Christians*, London, 1986. A famous study which still contains a vast amount of material not available elsewhere.

Judith Lieu, *Neither Jew Nor Greek*, Edinburgh, 2005. Essays on the problems of understanding the relationship between Christians and Jews in these centuries.

Ramsay MacMullen, *Christianizing the Roman Empire (AD 100–400)*, New Haven, CN, and London, 1984

Marvin Meyer, *The Gnostic Discoveries*, San Francisco, 2005

Eric Osborn has provided a series of biographies of theologians from these centuries: *Tertullian, First Theologian of the West*, Cambridge, 1997; *Irenaeus of Lyons*, Cambridge, 2001; *Clement of Alexandria*, Cambridge, 2005.

James Rives, *Religion and Authority in Roman Carthage*, Oxford and New York, 1995, deals with Cyprian.

M.A. Williams, *Rethinking 'Gnosticism': An Argument for Dismantling a Dubious Category*, Princeton, NJ, 2006

AD 313–600

There is a wealth of material dealing with Part Three of this book and the following is only a selection.

General Background

G.W. Bowersock, Peter Brown and Oleg Grabar, *Late Antiquity: A Guide to the Postclassical World*, Cambridge, MA and London, 1999

Peter Brown, *The World of Late Antiquity*, London, 1971. Brilliant study which excited considerable interest in this period.

Averil Cameron, *The Later Roman Empire, AD 284–430*, London, 1993 and *The Mediterranean World in Late Antiquity*, London and New York, 1993. Standard introductions to the period.

Peter Garnsey and Caroline Humfress, *The Evolution of the Late Antique World*, Cambridge, 2001. Perceptive essays.

Peter Heather, *The Fall of the Roman Empire: A New History*, London, 2005. Lively narrative history of the period.

Cyril Mango (ed.), *The Oxford History of Byzantium*, Oxford and New York, 2002. Good introduction to the emergence of the empire.

Bryan Ward-Perkins, *The Fall of Rome and the End of Civilization*, Oxford, 2005. Excellent on the archaeological evidence for the collapse of Rome in the west.

General Books Dealing with Christian Issues in these Centuries

Peter Brown, *Poverty and Leadership in the Later Roman Empire*, Hanover and London, 2001. Good on Roman and Christian attitudes to poverty.

Averil Cameron, *Christianity and the Rhetoric of Empire*, Berkeley, CA, and London, 1991. Excellent study of how Christians transformed the way in which their world was described.

Henry Chadwick, *East and West: The Making of a Rift in the Church*, Oxford and New York, 2003. Discusses the important theme of how the churches divided from the earliest times.

Pierre Chuvin, *A Chronicle of the Last Pagans*, translated by B.A. Archer, Cambridge, MA and London, 1990

Gillian Clark, *Christianity and Roman Society*, Cambridge, 2004

Charles Freeman, *The Closing of the Western Mind: The Rise of Faith and the Fall of Reason*, London, 2002; New York, 2004

Ramsay MacMullen, *Christianity and Paganism in the Fourth to Eighth Centuries*, New Haven, CN and London, 1997

Ramsay MacMullen, *Voting about God in Early Church Councils*, New Haven, CN, and London, 2006

R.A. Markus, *The End of Ancient Christianity*, Cambridge, 1990. Discusses the changes in Christianity between the fourth and sixth centuries.

Michele Renée Salzman, *The Making of a Christian Aristocracy: Social and Religious Change in the Western Roman Empire*, Cambridge, MA and London, 2002. Looks at the conversion of the western aristocracy to Christianity.

Eberhard Sauer, *The Archaeology of Religious Hatred*, Stroud, 2003. Reviews the archaeological evidence for Christian destruction of pagan art and architecture.

Asceticism and Monasticism

Marilyn Dunn, *The Emergence of Monasticism: From the Desert Fathers to the Early Middle Ages*, Oxford, 2000

Philip Rousseau, *Ascetics, Authority and the Church in the Age of Jerome and Cassian*, Oxford, 1978

Philip Rousseau, *Pachomius: The Making of a Community in Fourth-century Egypt*, Berkeley, CA, and London, 1985

V. Wimbush and R. Valantasis (eds), *Asceticism*, Oxford and New York, 2002

Bishops

Peter Brown, *Power and Persuasion in Late Antiquity*, Madison, WI, 1992

Claudia Rapp, *Holy Bishops in Late Antiquity*, Berkeley, CA, and London, 2005

Christian Art

Dominic Janes, *God and Gold in Late Antiquity*, Cambridge, 1998. Important study of how the church became reconciled with opulence in art.

Robin Margaret Jensen, *Understanding Early Christian Art*, London and New York, 2000

Jeffrey Spier (ed.), *Picturing the Bible: The Earliest Christian Art*, New Haven, CN, and London, 2007

Christian Emperors

Sabine MacCormack, *Art and Ceremony in Late Antiquity*, Berkeley, CA, and London, 1981, is an excellent introduction to the way that emperors displayed themselves in this period.

Constantine. H.A. Drake, *Constantine and the Bishops: The Politics of Intolerance*, Baltimore, MD, and London, 2000
Noel Lenski (ed.), *The Cambridge Companion to the Age of Constantine*, Cambridge, 2006
Hans Pohlsander, *The Emperor Constantine*, London and New York, 1996

Theodosius I. Charles Freeman, *AD 381: Heretics, Pagans and the Coming of the Christian State*, London, 2008. Deals with the imposition of the Nicene Trinity by Theodosius.
Gerard Friell and Stephen Williams, *Theodosius: The Empire at Bay*, New Haven, CN, and London, 1994
N. King, *The Emperor Theodosius and the Establishment of Christianity*, London, 1961

Theodosius II. Fergus Millar, *A Greek Roman Empire: Power and Belief under Theodosius II, 408–450*, Berkeley, CA, and London, 2007

Justinian. M. Maas (ed.), *The Cambridge Companion to the Age of Justinian*, Cambridge, 2005
John Moorhead, *Justinian*, London, 1994

Philosophy and Theology

P. Athanassiadi and M. Frede (eds), *Pagan Monotheism in Late Antiquity*, Oxford and New York, 1999. Shows how pagans as well as Christians were developing monotheistic religions.
Jan Bremmer, *The Rise and Fall of the Afterlife*, London and New York, 2002
Caroline Walker Bynum, *The Resurrection of the Body*, New York, 1995
Leo Davis, *The First Seven Ecumenical Councils, 325–787: Their History and Theology*, Collegeville, MN, 1990
Richard Hanson, *The Search for the Christian Doctrine of God*, Edinburgh, 1988, is essential for the Nicene debates.
Jaroslav Pelikan, *The Emergence of the Catholic Tradition: 100–600*, Chicago, 1977. Classic study.
Jaroslav Pelikan, *Credo*, New Haven, CN, and London, 2003. Thorough introduction to the creeds across the centuries.
H. Gregory Snyder, *Teachers and Texts in the Ancient World: Philosophers, Jews and Christians*, London and New York, 2000. Excellent study of how Christian teachers existed alongside pagan philosophical traditions.
Christopher Stead, *Philosophy in Christian Antiquity*, Cambridge, 1994. Looks at the development of Christian theology from a philosophical perspective.
Frances Young, *From Nicaea to Chalcedon*, London, 1983. Good survey of theological developments between 325 and 451.

Religious Leaders

Ambrose. Neil McLynn, *Ambrose of Milan: Church and Court in a Christian Capital*, Berkeley, CA, and London, 1994
Arius. Rowan Williams, *Arius*, second edition, London, 2001
Augustine. The famous biography is by Peter Brown, updated edition, Berkeley, CA, and London, 2002, but Serge Lancel, *St Augustine*, English translation by Antonia Nevill, London, 2002, is also good. Studies in Augustine's theology are Carol Harrison, *Augustine: Christian Truth and Fractured Humanity*, Oxford and New York, 2000, and John Rist, *Augustine: Ancient Thought Baptized*, Cambridge, 1994
Basil of Caesarea. Philip Rousseau, *Basil of Caesarea*, Berkeley, CA, and London, 1998

Eunomius. Richard Vaggione, *Eunomius of Cyzicus and the Nicene Revolution*, Oxford, 2000
Gregory the Great. Robert Markus, *Gregory the Great and his World*, Cambridge, 1997
Gregory of Nazianzus. John McGuckin, *St Gregory of Nazianzus: An Intellectual Biography*, New York, 2001; Rosemary Radford Ruether, *Gregory of Nazianzus: Rhetor and Philosopher*, Oxford, 1969
Jerome. J.N.D. Kelly, *Jerome*, London, 1975
John Chrysostom. J.N.D. Kelly, *Golden Mouth: The Story of John Chrysostom*, London, 1995
Paulinus of Nola. Dennis Trout, *Paulinus of Nola*, Berkeley, CA, and London, 1999

Advanced Reading with extensive booklists

J.W. Rogerson and Judith Lieu (eds), *The Oxford Handbook to Biblical Studies*, Oxford, 2006
S.A. Harvey and D. Hunter (eds), *The Oxford Handbook to Early Christian Studies*, Oxford, 2008
M. Mitchell and Frances Young (eds), *The Cambridge History of Christianity*, volume 1, Cambridge, 2006
A. Casiday and F.W. Norris (eds), *The Cambridge History of Christianity*, volume 2, Constantine to *c.* 600, Cambridge, 2007

Timeline

All dates BC unless otherwise specified.

1200: First mention of Israelites in a written text.

C.1000: Possible date of King David.

C.924: Division of Israel into two kingdoms, Israel (ten tribes) and Judah (two tribes). Hope remains of the eventual reunion of twelve tribes.

605–562: Sacking of Jerusalem by the Babylonians. The Babylonian exile leads to the first consolidation of the Hebrew scriptures. The earliest diaspora ('scattering') of Jews into the Mediterranean world.

539: The Jews return from exile after the destruction of Babylonia by Cyrus of Persia. The Temple is rebuilt initiating the Second Temple Period (which lasts until AD 70).

332: Alexander destroys the Persian empire. Judaea eventually passes under the rule of the Greek Seleucid dynasty.

167: The beginning of the Maccabean revolt against the Seleucids. The Maccabean martyrs. The independent Hasmonaean kingdom emerges in 161.

63: The Roman general Pompey the Great enters Jerusalem and destroys Jewish independence. Following an attack from Parthia (the successor state to the Persian empire), Herod 'the Great' is appointed as an independent ruler under Roman hegemony (37). Herod dies in 4 BC.

C.4 BC: Birth of Jesus.

AD 6: Judaea made an official Roman province with its capital at Caesarea on the coast. Day to day administration delegated to the high priest (Caiaphas, AD 18–37) in Jerusalem. Galilee, to the north, remains under the rule of Herod Antipas, a son of Herod.

AD 26: Pontius Pilate appointed prefect of Judaea.

C.AD 30: Crucifixion of Jesus in Jerusalem.

AD 66–70: Major Jewish revolt against Roman rule ends with the destruction of the Temple in AD 70.

AD 135: Jewish revolt by Simon Bar Kokhba decisively defeated by the Romans. Jerusalem reconstituted as a Roman colony, Aelia Capitolina.

THE EMERGENCE OF CHRISTIANITY

All dates AD.

30s:
: Emergence of Christian communities in Jerusalem and their spread to Antioch and other cities along the Syrian and Judaean coasts as a result of the first persecutions after the martyrdom of Stephen.

c.34:
: Conversion of Paul.

c.37–8:
: Paul visits the Jerusalem Christians, still under the leadership of Peter.

?48:
: Paul's second visit to Jerusalem. Agreement that Paul should preach to the Gentiles. His missionary journeys begin, first to Cyprus and the Galatians.

?49:
: Paul's Letter to the Galatians.

50s:
: Paul's missionary journey to Philippi, Thessalonika, Athens and Corinth. Followed by third visit to Jerusalem.
: Paul's stay in Ephesus. He writes his First Letter to the Corinthians after he hears of tensions within their congregation.

56:
: Paul returns to Corinth.

?57:
: Paul's Letter to the Romans. Evidence that a Christian community has already established itself in Rome.
: Final visit to Jerusalem where James, the brother of Jesus, is now leading the Jerusalem Christians.

c.61:
: Paul sent to Rome on appeal to the emperor.

62:
: James martyred in Jerusalem.

61–2:
: Paul's Letter to the Philippians.

?64:
: Martyrdom of Paul in Rome. Tradition suggests that Peter has also migrated to Rome and may have been martyred at the same time in the persecution by Nero, described by the historian Tacitus.

?65:
: Writing of the Letter to the Hebrews by an unknown author, showing that serious theological thought about the nature of Jesus is progressing.

70–5:
: Mark's gospel, the first of the 'canonical' gospels to survive.

c.85:
: Gospels of Matthew and Luke. The 'Pauline' letters to Colossians, Thessalonians and Ephesians were probably written in this same period.

c.90–100:
: Gospel of John.

90s:
: Some evidence of the persecution of Christians by the emperor Domitian.

96:
: Letter of Clement from Rome to the Corinthians. First mention of a martyrdom of Peter and Paul, possibly in Rome itself.

100:
: Evidence of stable Christian communities in Syria, Asia Minor, parts of Greece and Rome. Trajan's letters to Pliny (after 111) show that Christianity has spread as far north in Asia Minor as Bithynia. Tradition also suggests a Christian community in Alexandria.

c.107:
: The letters of Ignatius, bishop of Antioch, to Christian communities, including Ephesus, stress the growing importance of the bishop and the need for Christian communities to distance themselves from Judaism.

c.135:
: Apocryphal Epistle of Barnabas suggests growing antagonism between Jews and Christians.

135:            Record of Christian bishop allowed into Aelia Capitolina, formerly Jerusalem, by Roman authorities.

LATER 130S: Arrival of Marcion in Rome. Excommunicated by the Christian community for his refusal to accept the Hebrew scriptures.

140S: Justin Martyr arrives in Rome. Writes his *Apology* (*c*.150–55) and *Dialogue with Trypho* (set in Ephesus in *c*.135). Martyred in the reign of Marcus Aurelius. Evidence of several Christian teachers in Rome with some rivalry between them. The most prominent is Valentinus from Alexandria.

155:            Martyrdom of Polycarp in Smyrna.

160S: Montanist movement begins in Phrygia, prophesying through the Holy Spirit. Spreads widely in the Roman world.

177:            Persecution of the Christian community in Lyons (detailed in Eusebius' *Church History*).

C.180:   Arrival of Christianity in Carthage and first evidence of Christian texts in Latin. Tertullian, 'the father of western theology', writes his first tract in the city *c*.195. Celsus writes his attack on the Christians.

185:            Irenaeus, the new bishop of Lyons, launches a sweeping attack on gnosticism, especially in the works of Valentinus in his *Adversus haereses*. Irenaeus is the first known Christian to talk of four canonical gospels and gives the name of an author to each. He also argues for apostolic succession as a symbol of orthodoxy. Tatian responds to Irenaeus by producing a single narrative gospel, the *Diatessaron*, compiled from all four for the Syriac-speaking community. Irenaeus specifically mentions Christian communities in Germany, Spain, among the Celts, and in Egypt and Libya.

190S: Clement of Alexandria, leader of a school in the city, defends Greek philosophy as a foundation for Christianity.

203:            Martyrdom of Perpetua and her companions in Carthage. Tertullian defends martyrdom but himself drifts towards the Montanists and leaves the institutional church in the city.

215:            Apostolic tradition by Hippolytus in Rome gives details of baptismal requirements for Roman Christians.

220S: Origen, the finest Christian mind of the early third century, teaching in Alexandria. Moves to Caesarea *c*.231 and dies there after persecution in 254.

230S: The Christian community at Dura-Europus on the Persian border construct their own church building and baptistery, the earliest to have been discovered.

248–9:   Cyprian becomes bishop of Carthage.

250:            Beginning of empire-wide policy of restoring the traditional gods by the emperor Decius, leading to persecution of Christians who refuse to sacrifice. In Carthage, Cyprian goes into hiding. Reasserts his authority through *De unitate*, 'On the Unity of the Church'.

253:            Dispute breaks out between Cyprian, who believes in rebaptism of lapsed Christians, and Stephen, the new bishop of Rome, who does not. Cyprian calls local church councils to reassert his authority. Dispute still unresolved on the death of Stephen and new persecution by the emperor Valerian which leads to the martyrdom of Cyprian in 258.

261:            New emperor Gallienus restores toleration to Christians. They are largely unmolested for the next forty years. In his church history, Eusebius talks of a long period of growth.

303: The emperor Diocletian accedes to the pressure of his co-emperor Galerius to launch a comprehensive wave of persecutions, although its impact varies across the empire.

EARLY 300S: Council of bishops at Elvira in Spain lays down a wide-ranging code of conduct for Christian behaviour.

312: Battle of the Milvian Bridge. Constantine's victory over Maxentius is followed by a declaration of toleration for all Christians.

EVENTS OF THE ROMAN EMPIRE

31 BC–AD 312

31 BC: Victory of Octavian, nephew of Julius Caesar, over Mark Antony and Cleopatra brings Rome's civil wars to an end. Egypt is added to the empire by Octavian and order is restored across the Mediterranean.

27 BC: Octavian is granted the title Augustus by the Roman senate and stays in power until his death in AD 14. The transition from a republic to an empire.

AD 14–37: Tiberius, Augustus' successor, maintains comparative peace in the empire during the years of Jesus' life, ministry and crucifixion.

64: The emperor Nero launches a vindictive persecution of Christians following a great fire in Rome.

66: Outbreak of revolt in Judaea.

68: Nero's suicide results in a vacuum exploited by the commander of the legions in Judaea, Vespasian, who becomes emperor in 69. His son Titus, later emperor 79–81, cleans up the Jewish revolt and destroys the Temple. Comparative stability in the empire under Vespasian's Flavian dynasty which ends, however, with the assassination in 97 of the emperor Domitian as a result of his dictatorial behaviour.

98–117: New emperor Trajan rules the empire with efficiency and moderation. Restrains persecution of Christians. Trajan is the last expansionist emperor, adding Dacia to the empire.

117–138: Emperor Hadrian accepts that expansion must stop and that the empire needs consolidation. Hadrian encourages a revival of Greek culture and refuses to support persecution of Christians, although he brutally represses the revolt of Simon Bar Kokhba in Jerusalem.

138–161: Reign of Antoninus Pius. The empire is at peace. Sporadic local persecutions of Christians.

161–180: Reign of Marcus Aurelius, philosopher emperor. Beginnings of trouble on the Danube border. Marcus Aurelius reasserts importance of traditional gods and there is some persecution of Christians who refuse to recant. His son, Commodus (assassinated 192) is unsatisfactory in many ways, but does not persecute Christians.

192–3: Septimius Severus seizes power and restores order to the empire. Some persecution of Christians recorded in early 200s.

237: The end of the Severan dynasty coincides with the revival of the Persian empire under the Sassanids and renewed pressures from German tribes. Initiates a period of crisis with a high turnover of emperors. Persecutions of Christians under Decius (249–51) and Valerian (253–60) relate to fears that the traditional gods have abandoned Rome.

284: Accession of the emperor Diocletian. Widespread reform of the empire and its consolidation under four co-emperors with reorganised provinces and improved use of resources. An astonishing achievement. Final but extensive persecution of Christians.

306: Constantine acclaimed emperor on the death of his father Constantius in York for the region covering Britain, Spain and Gaul.

312: Constantine defeats Maxentius and gains control of the rest of the western empire, including Italy and North Africa.

313–395

313: Edict of Toleration, or Milan, issued by Constantine and Licinius, emperor in the east, provides toleration to all cults and restoration of property to Christians. Constantine backs the moderate Caecilians in North Africa against the rigorist Donatists, initiating a schism which lasts until 411.

324: Constantine defeats Licinius and becomes emperor over both east and west. He begins the building of Constantinople and the first Christian basilicas in Rome and the Holy Land.

325: Constantine presides over the Council of Nicaea in an attempt to resolve the dispute between Arius and Alexander, bishop of Alexandria. *Homoousios* formula brings temporary victory for Alexander against Arius.

330: Dedication of Constantinople.

337: Constantine baptised. Dies at Constantinople. Buried in the Church of the Apostles as the 'Thirteenth Apostle'. By now he has reconciled himself to the Arians condemned at Nicaea.

351: Battle of Mursa sees Constantine's son, Constantius, emerge as sole emperor. Constantius determines to impose an 'Arian' creed on the empire and, following councils at Ariminum and Seleucia, this is done at Constantinople in 360.
In Alexandria, Athanasius emerges as the champion of the Nicene creed.

361–3: Reign of the emperor Julian, who attempts to restore pagan cults but without success. Christian clergy forbidden to preach outside their churches.

364–75: Reign of Valentinian I, probably the last of the effective emperors.

374: Appointment of Ambrose as bishop of Milan. He becomes the champion of the Nicene creed in the west, linking it to the success of the empire in war. In the east, the Cappadocian Fathers are developing the theological terminology that can support a Nicene Trinity.

378: Valens, emperor of the east, brother of Valentinian, is killed by the Goths at the battle of Adrianople. Gratian, Valentinian's successor in the west, appoints a tough Spanish general, Theodosius, to restore order in the east.

380: Theodosius announces in an edict that a Trinity based on the Nicene formula, Father, Son and Holy Spirit 'of equal majesty', will now be the new orthodoxy. Arriving in Constantinople in 381, he dismisses the city's bishop and appoints the Nicene Gregory of Nazianzus before calling a council of eastern bishops to endorse his position. The Council of Constantinople (381) is disordered but is associated with a revised Nicene creed which is still used today. Constantinople is declared second to Rome within the church hierarchy, to the anger of Antioch and Alexandria.

383: After widespread unrest among the 'Arians', Constantine calls a smaller council of church leaders in an attempt to bring unity to the church. The council ends with a renewed imposition of the Nicene Trinity.

380s: Jerome begins his Latin translation of the New and Old Testaments. He is
           forced to leave Rome for a monastery in Bethlehem where he completes his
           translation over the next twenty years.

385:       Augustine appointed city orator in Milan. He meets Ambrose and eventually
           converts to Christianity. He returns to his native Africa in 388 and becomes
           bishop of Hippo in 395.

388:       Theodosius moves to Milan after the defeat of a usurper, Maximus. He is now
           effectively ruler of the entire empire and begins planning to hand it on to his
           two sons, Arcadius and Honorius. He has a confrontation with Ambrose over
           the destruction by Christians of a synagogue at Callinicum which Ambrose
           persuades him not to restore. Another confrontation over a massacre at
           Thessalonika leads to Theodosius coming to offer penance at the cathedral in
           Milan to the satisfaction of Ambrose. The event is used to justify the
           supremacy of the church over the secular powers.

390s: Theodosius launches a campaign against paganism, probably at the behest of
           his more ruthless Christian ministers.

394:       Theodosius defeats a usurper, Eugenius, at the battle of Frigidus. Christian
           historians proclaim it as the triumph of Christianity over paganism.

395:       Death of Theodosius. Ambrose presides at the funeral and his oration claims
           the Theodosian dynasty for God. The empire is split between Theodosius'
           two sons. Ambrose dies in 397, leaving Milan ringed by the basilicas he has
           built.

           The Eastern Empire, 395–565

395–408:   Arcadius is emperor. John Chrysostom becomes bishop of Constantinople in
           397 but falls to the machinations of Theophilus of Alexandria and is sent into
           exile in 404. He dies in 407.

408–450:   Reign of Arcadius' son, Theodosius II. A pious emperor, Theodosius fails to keep
           order in the church. The Nestorian controversy over the human nature of Christ
           is allowed to split the eastern empire. A large number of laws are passed against
           heretics, Jews and pagans, but it proves difficult to enforce them comprehensively.

412:       Cyril succeeds Theophilus as bishop of Alexandria. He is responsible for wide-
           spread disorder and is associated with the lynching of the distinguished pagan
           philosopher Hypatia.

431:       Council of Ephesus proclaims Mary to be *Theotokos*, 'bearer of God', but is
           notable for the hijacking of events by Cyril. He succeeds in having his rival,
           Nestorius, bishop of Constantinople, dismissed by Theodosius after distrib-
           uting bribes extensively throughout the imperial court.

449:       A second council at Ephesus under Dioscorus, Cyril's successor at
           Constantinople, succeeds in imposing a 'one nature' of Christ formula on the
           attending bishops.

450:       Death of Theodosius.

451:       Theodosius' successor as emperor, Marcian, summons a council of bishops to
           meet at Chalcedon. By keeping the proceedings under tight control, he
           succeeds in imposing the Chalcedonian formula which accepts the two
           natures of Christ, human and divine. The Tome, a formal statement, by Leo,
           bishop of Rome, makes up part of the formula, the first instance of a bishop
           of Rome contributing to the making of doctrine. Leo, however, is outraged by
           the granting of greater authority to the bishop of Constantinople. At the same

time, there are important factions, the Monophysites and the Nestorians, who feel excluded by the formula and refuse to accept it.

457: Death of Marcian. A period of instability follows in the eastern empire until good order is achieved under the emperor Anastasius, 491–518.

518–27: Reign of Justin, formerly commander of the palace guard.

527–565: Reign of Justinian, one of the great figures of late antiquity. Justinian is famous for his Law Codes that bring Roman law together in a coherent form. He reconquers North Africa for the empire and, with much greater difficulty, parts of central Italy. He closes down the schools of philosophy in Athens and orders the conversion of all to Christianity. The council he calls to Constantinople in 553 to resolve the problem of church unity is, however, a failure and Nestorian and Monophysite churches, including the Coptic Church in Egypt, become permanent.

The rebuilding of Santa Sophia in Constantinople is perhaps the greatest architectural achievement of the late empire.

The Byzantine empire survives until the conquest of Constantinople by the Ottoman Turks in 1453.

The Western Empire, 395–600

395–423: Honorius moves his capital from the exposed Milan to the secluded Ravenna on the east coast of Italy, an admission of weakness. The empire is increasingly in the hands of strong military men.

406–7: Major invasion of Vandals, Sueves and Alamanni leads to the collapse of Roman rule in Britain and Spain. The western empire is now beginning to crumble.

410: Alaric and the Goths sack Rome, a terrible psychological blow. One response is Augustine's *The City of God*, which differentiates between the earthly city such as Rome and the true 'city of God' in heaven.

411: Council of Donatists and Catholics in Carthage sees condemnation of Donatism.

416–430: Pelagian controversy over the relative status of free will and the dependence on the grace of God for salvation. Augustine wins imperial support against Pelagius.

429: The Vandals under Gaiseric move into North Africa. They reach Hippo as Augustine lies dying there in 430.

Increasingly, barbarian tribes are settling in the empire and being given 'federate' status, ostensibly requiring them to fight with the empire, but it becomes ever more difficult for any central government to control them.

Leo, bishop of Rome, 440–51, exploits the chaos to assert his own authority as the successor of Peter.

458: Sicily, the oldest of the Roman provinces, is captured by the Vandals.

Over the next twenty years the empire disintegrates. The deposition of Romulus Augustulus in 476 marks the formal end of the empire. In practice, the barbarians, most of whom are already Christians (though 'Arians') and some of whom are partly Romanised, are already well established in the empire but the years of fighting and unrest have led to a dramatic collapse of the economy.

c.480–550: Life of Benedict, whose Rule for monastic living becomes the most influential of those adopted in the west.

493–526: The Ostrogoth (and 'Arian') Theodoric establishes a state in Italy, with its capital at Ravenna, which expands to include Provence and Visigothic Spain.

Ravenna is graced with his palace church of San Apollinare Nuovo, whose mosaics of the life of Christ survive in their magnificence. Theodoric rules the Catholic majority of his subjects with tolerance.

498 OR 499: The conversion of the Frankish king Clovis to orthodox Christianity, and his subsequent victories over his rivals, lay the foundation of a large Frankish kingdom.

520s: Building of San Vitale in Ravenna. One of the finest churches of the period.

524: Boethius' *The Consolation of Philosophy*. Boethius is the last Latin speaker to have a good command of Greek.

530s: Building of San Apollinare in Classe, Ravenna.

533: Justinian successfully regains North Africa from the Vandals.

535: Invasion of Italy by Justinian but campaign stalls and it is twenty years before control of Rome, Ravenna and some cities is achieved. Final breakdown of order in Italy; Lombards invade the north.

540: Cassiodorus organises the collection and copying of classical and early Christian manuscripts.

586–601: Reccared, king of Spain, announces that he has converted to Catholic Christianity.

590–604: Pope Gregory develops the concept of papal authority in the west, laying the foundations of the medieval papacy. His mission to England succeeds in the conversion of the kingdom of Kent.

With most rulers now 'Catholic' and a loose network of bishops surviving through western Europe, a decentralised Christianity spreads through Europe. Despite the continuing prestige of Rome, there is no effective authority until the re-emergence of papal power in the eleventh century.

Index

Texts are under the names of their assumed writers, e.g. 'Luke, gospel of'. See also the Glossary (pp. 337–52) for additional definitions of selected themes, places and people.